To Kath

Enjoy the Memories

Harley + June Flathers

2-21-04

BACK IN A MOMENT

BY HARLEY FLATHERS

AND JUNE FLATHERS

WITH ANNE BEISER ALLEN

Photography Credits — *Rochester Post Bulletin, Abbot-Northwestern Hospitals, Mayo Clinic Archives, Olmsted County Historical Society, Phil Revoir Studios-Red Wing, American Dairy Association, American Farm Bureau Federation, C-D-C Washington, Roger Byrne–Hale Threshing and Farm Family Photos, and Clint Kueker's "Remember When" & cover illustrations.*

ISBN 0-9747424-0-6

First Printing – December 2003

Printed by Davies Printing, Rochester, Minnesota

Table of Contents

FOREWORD

In the New Testament, there is a passage you can carry with you daily, as I have: "I can do all things through Christ which strengthens me." (Philippians 4:13) The late Norman Vincent Peale said that this verse is an antidote for every "defeat-feeling." When you feel downed by situations, and the going is hard, this statement will remind you that you do not need to depend upon your own strength entirely, because Christ is with you and is now giving you all the help you need. You will find yourself meeting problems with new mental force. You will carry your burdens with ease. Your new "lifting power" will amaze you.

The Prayer of St. Francis

Lord, make me an instrument of thy peace;
Where there is hatred, let me sow love;
Where there is injury, pardon;
Where there is doubt, faith;
Where there is despair, hope;
Where there is darkness, light;
And where there is sadness, joy;
O Divine Master,
Grant that I may not so much seek
To be consoled as to console;
To be understood as to understand;
To be loved, as to love;
For it is in giving that we receive,
It is in pardoning that we are pardoned,
And it is in dying that we are born to Eternal Life.

13th Century Guidelines for Today.

Through a half-century of collecting "special things," I have saved this poem that I would like to share at the beginning of this story. I wish we had the author's name.

Don't Quit

When things go wrong as they sometimes will,
When the road you're trudging seems all up hill,
When the funds are low and the debts are high,
And you want to smile, but you have to sigh,
When care is pressing you down a bit,
Rest if you must, but don't you quit.
Life is queer with its twists and turns,
As everyone of us sometimes learns,
And many a failure turns about,
When he might have won had he stuck it out;
Don't give up though the pace seems slow —
You may succeed with another blow.
Success is failure turned inside-out —
The silver tint of the clouds of doubt,
And you never can tell just how close you are,
It may be near when it seems so far;
It's when things seem worst,
That you must not quit.

Author unknown.

Acknowledgments

This story started out with just a few memories in mind, but it soon got "out of control." And I'm glad it did. Suddenly, at 72-plus and in my 52nd year of broadcasting, I wanted to share some "fun times." This is not a "tell-all" book, but rather some segments of my life, which have involved many others, from play-time to various boards and committees, from musical concerts to parade broadcasts. We'll go from horsepower to tractor power and through marriage and family. You may recognize a few names from this southeastern part of Minnesota, especially in Red Wing and Rochester. I've tried to maintain a high level of accuracy, checking my memory against newspaper clippings and the memories of others whose lives have intersected with mine at various points. Since this book covers many events, you'll find quite a few actual dates, times and quotes listed, including the birth and death dates of many other people in these stories. If your name isn't in the book, don't fret....just keep reading, and tell your friends and neighbors that you saw theirs.

****

I thank June, my dear wife for 44 years...my sister, Elaine, who "pushed" me out to country school...my dear parents, who kept loving me in spite of all the times I "goofed up" as an exuberant young lad on the farm...all those teachers at all levels, who made sure I got a proper education...no end of nurses, physicians and physical therapists, who have kept my body in working order over the years...and the Lord, who has truly provided for my needs. Special thanks also to the late Harold Cooke, Director of Rochester Civic Music Bands and Symphony Orchestra, and to Anne Marie Plunkett for encouraging me to go forward in the Rochester Arts Council and Southeastern Minnesota Regional Arts Council in 1973. Also my writing assistant, Anne Allen, whose goal has been to create order out of chaos in the stories and events I've told her.

Moment 1

F.D.R. and Me: Life After Polio

As I was looking at the weekly Stewartville Star newspaper in April of 2001, I saw a cartoon by my old friend Clinton Kueker, a retired police officer from the Rochester Police Department. Clint is a fine cartoonist. He actually grew up across the fields from me when we were young boys in the 1940s. Clint was about five years younger than I. Bill Kueker and his wife and their two kids, Clint and his older sister Gloria, came down from Lake Crystal, Minnesota, and bought that 240-acre farm. I remember sometimes seeing the family drive by on their way to the movie on Saturday night in Chatfield or to Stewartville on Friday, or vice versa. They didn't stay there very many years, but they were good neighbors.

I met Clint again in 1957, when I was working in Rochester. I had finished my evening shift at KROC radio and closed up, and I went to the Capitol Eat Shop and there was Clint, a young police officer. So we got reacquainted. He had a strong interest in the past, and he and I later did a lot of nostalgic interviews on radio — people like Clayton Moore (The Lone Ranger) and Jim Jordan (Fibber McGee).

For several years now, Clint has put out a cartoon every week in the Stewartville Star under the title "Remember When." His cartoons are filled with memorabilia, recalling some event during the past years. April 12 was the anniversary of the death of President Franklin Delano Roosevelt, and so Clint's cartoon that week was entitled, "Remember When Franklin Delano Roosevelt died, April 12, 1945."

In his drawing, a nine-year-old Clint is sitting in the middle of a spare tire, in the yard in front of his house. His dad has their 1937 Ford jacked up and is changing the tire on the rear wheel while talking to Rob Hudson. Rob Hudson's farm bordered ours on the west, right along what is now county road 2, between Stewartville and Chatfield. Rob was a good old hard-driving, corncob-pipe smoking neighbor who liked to have a pretty good time with spirits, but he was always there to help you out with the threshing and such. Clint's mother is standing at the front door, and she calls out, "I just heard the news on the radio — President Roosevelt is dead!" Clint drew it exactly as I remember it. That cartoon had such detail that I thought, what a wonderful place to start this story.

Franklin Delano Roosevelt was elected president in 1932, when I was a year old, and when he died in 1945, I was in the eighth grade. I recall how the whole nation mourned him. Hollywood stars came on the radio, saying, "We're sorry to lose President F.D.R."

It impressed me so vividly because we were Republicans, and F.D.R. was a Democrat. I remember going with my mother and father in November 1936 to our little Sumner Township Town Hall, where they went to vote. The town hall was underneath the school, about three and a half miles from our farm in Sumner Township, Fillmore County, some twenty miles southeast of Rochester, Minnesota. I rode down with my dad and mother, and we went in to vote. It was all new to me, and it was exciting. They went in these little cubicles with curtains in front and voted. (I suppose today there are still curtains in some places, but most of the time we just get into a three-sided cubicle to vote.) At that time, Roosevelt's opponent was Alfred Landon, who was from Kansas. I would hear the folks say, "Landon or Roosevelt, Landon or Roosevelt," and of course, Landon being Republican, I said to my parents, "Well, I would vote for Landon and just be done with it." That's what I was saying at age five!

In 1971, when I was working at KROC, Clarence Fischer, an auto dealer here in Rochester, told me a great story about F.D.R. It seems that in late 1933, he and Greg Gentling, who was then working for the Rochester Post newspaper, had an idea. Clare and Greg were members of the American

Legion, and they knew that Franklin Roosevelt was also an American Legion member. They wanted to bring F.D.R. to Rochester, Minnesota, to honor Dr. Will and Dr. Charlie Mayo, and to speak at the Soldiers' Memorial Field, which the local American Legion had created in 1926 as a memorial to the fallen soldiers of the Rochester area from all the country's wars up until the present.

Clare and Greg worked and worked. They wrote letters, they made phone calls. They even went to Washington on the train, where they spent a lot of time talking with Harry Hopkins, F.D.R.'s friend and political adviser, who was then administrator of the WPA (Works Progress Administration, one of F.D.R.'s New Deal programs). They pleaded and begged. They said, "We want to get Franklin Roosevelt to come to Rochester to speak at Soldiers' Memorial Field, and to honor Dr. Will Mayo and Dr. Charles Mayo for all they have done." The only answer they got was, "We'll get in touch with you."

So they came back home and waited and waited, and in the spring of 1934 they received word from Washington that Franklin Roosevelt would come to Rochester on August 8, 1934, to speak at Soldiers' Field. It was a terribly hot day. Around 75,000 people were there. There are pictures of it on the Rochester Post-Bulletin's front page from that date. Roosevelt spoke, and his speech went out by microphone to a radio station somewhere else — probably St. Paul — for transmission. (There was no local radio at that time — Greg Gentling would not start KROC until September 30, 1935.)

After it was over, Roosevelt went on back to Washington to do his business as president. Then in September 1938, Jimmy Roosevelt — one of Franklin and Eleanor Roosevelt's four sons — came to St. Mary's Hospital in Rochester for surgery on a duodenal ulcer. During the course of his stay here, Franklin and Eleanor came to see him. They arrived in their own private train car.

And the first thing F.D.R. said when he got here was, "I want the same driver as we had in 1934." That was Clare Fischer. Clare was a dealer in Buicks and Packards, a very nice person, a real patriot who loved his country and had been a soldier in the first World War. So Clare drove the president and his party around during the course of their visit.

On September 13, President Franklin Roosevelt said, "I want to see the countryside. I want to see what this southern Minnesota looks like." So they took off heading south on highway 63 towards Stewartville, an eleven mile drive. The plan was to cut easterly on highway 30 and go on to Chatfield, but for some reason they missed the turn — right in the heart of town — and kept proceeding southerly for another mile and a half. There they found a road, and turned easterly.

Well, from where they turned off highway 63 to our Flathers farm would have been exactly 6½ miles on that road. About halfway — three miles or so down — they pulled over to the south and went up to see old Fred Sandte. They didn't know Fred Sandte, but they saw a set of buildings on the right about half a mile away, and they pulled into the yard. They asked Fred for directions to Chatfield, and talked with him. They asked him, "How are the crops?" and things like that.

I remember Fred Sandte very well. He had lost his left thumb, and had a habit of talking out of the side of his mouth. Farmers are always complaining, you know. The old joke is that when you put two or more farmers together, there'll be an argument. And Fred always had a lot of opinions on a lot of things. So he visited with the president.

Then the president and his entourage went back to the east-west road and headed easterly again.

This is where my own memory of that day kicks in. Now, it's getting to be about 3:45 in the afternoon, and here I am walking home from our little country district 118 school. We're proceeding to our farm, my sister and I — my sister Elaine is five years older than I am, and a good student. I'm about seven years old, and in second grade. I'm just kind of trudging along, heading home on a sunny afternoon, and I look up to the west for about a mile and I see this long line of vehicles coming at us. Goodness! All those cars! And when we get closer, I see motorcycles!

So here they come, moving along at a pace of maybe 25 miles an hour. First there was a pair of motorcycles — they were highway patrolmen, though I didn't know that at the time. Then came a convertible, with people inside waving at us. Then a second pair of motorcycles. After that came a big black enclosed car — and it was big! Then two more motorcycles, and another convertible with laughing young ladies. The convertible tops are down and everybody waves at us.

After they went by us, my sister said, "Why, that's the president!"

And I, I am sure, replied, "Oh?" When you're seven years old, you're not into world events yet. Things don't impress you. You're not awe-stricken.

We never told a soul in school the next day, because nobody would have believed it. In fact, I don't know if we told anybody other than my mother and father. Today, there probably would have been cameras along there, with reporters interviewing the kiddies as the car went by: "How did it feel to have the president wave to you?"

In that 1971 interview, Clare Fischer, F.D.R.'s driver, told me, "Yes, there was a time that day we actually were lost. Only God knew where the President of the United States was!"

Well, only God and I!

I recently shared this story with my neighbor, Dr. Fred Helmholz, 92, a retired physician who was on staff at Mayo Clinic for many years. His memories of Dr. Will and Dr. Charlie Mayo are vivid. I said, "Fred, I've wondered since if Will and Charlie might have been riding with the president that day as they went from Stewartville to Chatfield."

Fred replied emphatically, "No, the Mayos knew all the back roads. They would not have been lost."

In 1988, on the 40th anniversary of Franklin Roosevelt's visit here to Rochester to see his son Jimmy, Clint Kueker again had a cartoon in his "Remember When" in the Stewartville Star: "Remember When F.D.R. came and visited Rochester and drove through the Stewartville area in September 1938?" When I saw it, I wrote a letter to the editor, telling my story about our "association" with F.D.R.

By then, I knew that F.D.R. was a polio survivor, but it wasn't until 1998, when my wife and I visited our daughter Jane in Auburn, Alabama, that I really came to know what an amazing man he was. During that visit, Jane told us that not very far away was Warm Springs, Georgia, where President Franklin Roosevelt spent a lot of time during the years that he was recuperating from polio. Franklin D. Roosevelt was born in 1882, and in 1921, when he was 39 years old, he was hit by polio, and hit very hard. But despite that, he went on to become president through some of the nation's hardest times, fighting his own paralysis for 25 years. He never shared his struggle with the people, though. He asked photographers to take pictures of him only from the waist up, so you couldn't see the braces on his legs. When he was standing and speaking, you usually saw his son John or one of his aides helping him to walk over to the podium, although sometimes he actually walked on his own.

Years before he became president, he'd heard about this place in Georgia that had naturally hot springs, and he went down there. The warm springs made his legs feel better. He visited it quite a few times over the years. When he was president, he built a house there that he called "The Little White House," and he would often conduct official business there.

June and I drove to Warm Springs to see Roosevelt's home. Although it was only about 65 miles from Jane's home in Auburn, Alabama, it was quite a lengthy drive, because it is up in a mountain area, on beautiful Pine Mountain, Georgia. When we got up there, we toured the "Little White House" and all its grounds. He bought the grounds, and built the "Little White House" and everything around it — sentry huts and quarters for his staff to live in.

We learned more about Roosevelt when we saw some of the films at the "Little White House" during our visit. He loved to drive, and we saw two of his cars that were on display, with the hand controls that he personally designed. He put a lever down for the brake, and a lever down for the clutch (these were the days before automatic transmissions). It was amazing. He also designed his own bathtub, with a ridge around it so that he could get hold of the edges better to get in and out. To keep the soap from getting away, he made a place where it could slide down along the rail. He designed his own wheelchair out of a kitchen chair — a solid wooden kitchen chair. He asked his people to put wheels on this kitchen chair so he could get around, before the early custom-made wheelchairs were available. It was a moving experience for me, to see all those things he had invented. F.D.R. was quite a person.

He loved his neighbors, too. He would get in that car and go out to farms nearby and talk with the neighbors. At Thanksgiving and Christmas, he would put on wonderful dinners for the children, and they would all eat together at the "Little White House."

There was a portrait of him that was being made at the time of his death in 1945, and it was left there in the house, so you can see F.D.R. as he looked shortly before he died. You can also see the room in which he died of a cerebral hemorrhage on April 12, 1945, right there in the "Little White House" at Warm Springs, Georgia.

I was so moved by that visit in 1998 that we went back again in the year 2000, and spent equally as much time refreshing our memories. Having had polio myself, and knowing firsthand what a battle it can be, I was amazed at how well he managed — not just physically, but dealing with the Depression and World War II — doing all of that together. What a person!

F.D.R and The March of Dimes

I began to develop a deeper understanding of F.D.R. during the years 1966 through 1981, when I was deeply involved in fund raising and education for the Rochester chapter of the March of Dimes. Dr. David Welte (now a retired optometrist in Rochester) called me one day when I was at work at KROC, playing music, and said, "Harley, we'd like to have you become our March of Dimes chapter's fund-raising chairman."

My first response was, "Hey, we got polio licked!"

He laughed and said, "Well, we know that, but you know, the March of Dimes has turned to battling birth defects now."

I said, "Oh, yeah, I heard about that." So we hemmed and hawed around and talked a bit and finally I agreed. From that day in late 1966 all the way through the autumn of 1981, I was very closely associated with the

March of Dimes here — the first ten years strictly as a volunteer, fund raiser and you-name-it, and the last five years as its part-time, paid executive director. Then I really put a lot of time into fund raising and education.

The March of Dimes began back in 1938. I can still recall the late Eddie Cantor, a great entertainer on radio, talking about the March of Dimes on his Sunday night program. The nation was just starting to realize the seriousness of polio. We'd heard the story of Sister Elizabeth Kenny, the Australian nurse who went to the Outback in 1911 and tried her darnedest to get hot packs on people whose limbs would suddenly start shriveling up and people suffering pain from polio. In 1942 she established the Elizabeth Kenny Institute in Minneapolis for the treatment of polio victims. I saw the movie about her life, "The Sister Kenny Story," starring Rosalind Russell, at the Capitol Theatre in Chatfield with my parents in 1947.

Not much was known then about polio. At that time it was called infantile paralysis. Later we got to know it a little better as poliomyelitis, called polio for short. It was a disease caused by a virus in the nervous system. Nobody knew how it came or when it would come. There were nationwide epidemics in 1940, 1946, 1947, 1948, 1949, 1951, 1952, up to 1955. It was a horrendous threat to public health. Heart disease and cancer were the number one and two killers, but polio at that time was the number one crippler. (We don't use the word crippled any more — we said handicapped for a while, now we say physically challenged. We try to keep things politically correct.)

Well, Eddie Cantor was talking one Sunday night back in 1938 on his radio program about the seriousness of infantile paralysis, and as he was closing his program, he said, "If we could only do something to help this. If we could only fund it, like if everyone could just send one dime" — and I can still hear Eddie Cantor saying that — "just send one dime, we could call it the March of Dimes." And so the name came about, and it worked.

Franklin Roosevelt and his law partner Basil O'Connor did a lot during those years for the polio drive. They established a foundation for research into the causes and treatment of polio. And through the efforts of F.D.R.

and many others — especially a figurehead like the president, who had survived the disease and fought through it — awareness of the disease was increased. It gave people an impetus to give and to learn more about polio.

Finally, in 1952, fourteen years after the effort started, Dr. Jonas Salk developed the Salk vaccine. I recall in 1954, when I was in Red Wing broadcasting, the word went out that everybody needed to get their polio vaccine. (This was before the official announcement on April 10, 1955, that tests had proven the Salk vaccine to be effective.) So we all gathered at a little school west of town called the Vasa Elementary School. We lined up and were given our little paper cups of white milky fluid — that was the polio vaccine. And people said, "Wow! What a relief!"

I said, "Yeah, what a relief — only for me it's five years too late!"

Polio Strikes Me

Polio hit me in the summer of 1949. I had just graduated from Chatfield High School on Friday, June 3, and I was going to farm, nothing else. I lived with my parents, Homer and Vivian Flathers, on the old farm in rural Stewartville that had been in our family since 1861, when Abraham Lincoln took his first oath of office as president. My sister Elaine, who by then was teaching school in Waseca, also lived with us on the farm during the summers.

I took sick no more than five weeks after graduation, on July 12, 1949, while I was cultivating our corn and beans. I didn't feel well that day, but I kept on working. The back was hurting and the legs were hurting, but I wanted to get that field done. That night, my dad said, "Well, we better take you to see Dr. Risser."

Dr. Alden Risser was our Stewartville family doctor, a man who had been doing much good in our community for many years. (He died December 5, 1999, at age 87.) Dr. Risser looked me over and said, "I'll try to get a spinal tap." That was the key. The first thing a doctor needed to do to diagnose polio was to tap the spinal fluid. But I was a little muscular in those days, and he couldn't get the needle into the spine to do the spinal tap.

Dr. Risser said, "I don't know. Tell you what: go home, go to bed. I'll come out to see you at noon tomorrow, and if you aren't any better, we'll send you to Sister Kenny Institute in Minneapolis." He opted to do that rather than Rochester, where they also had a polio ward.

The next day, July 13, 1949, we got in our old 1936 Chevrolet and drove for three hours up through unknown areas and through the traffic there in the Twin Cities. We got to the Sister Kenny Institute at four o'clock. I was able to walk in on my own power, but my knees were buckling. I remember so distinctly climbing those steps in front of the Sister Kenny Hospital at 1800 Chicago Avenue South, Minneapolis, not knowing when I walked in there that it would be a whole ten months before I came out.

I went in, and Dr. Solgeskog took the spinal tap. I said to the nurse, "Well, nurse, what's the word?"

She said, "Well, I can't say, but we have a bed for you." And that was it.

I was there. And it hit me hard. When I awakened in the morning, I was in total paralysis from the waist down. Very little movement has come back in the succeeding fifty-four years. But I had good arms. The Good Lord gave me strong arms and the will to go forward. I was thankful for that, and I've never forgotten it.

When I went into the hospital in July 1949, I spent the first twenty-eight days in what they called Contagion, or the Contagious Ward. Nobody could come in and visit you other than the doctors and staff who were taking care of you. There were two wards: Ward 1 for men and Ward 28 for women. They each had about seven patients in them. I could look around and see others who were much worse off than I. All my life I've been able to recognize that. Most of the young men there were my age or a little older — I was 17 going on 18, and I guess we were aged from 17 to 33 in that first ward. There was Russ Youngburg, from Hoffman, Minnesota, and Gordie Anderson from St. Peter. I used to correspond with them in the earlier years, after I left the hospital. Others whom I remember so well were Ray Hanson, from Eau Claire, Wisconsin, Bill Burnet, from Bloomington, Minnesota, Oscar Anderson from Albert Lea, and Leonard Anderson from Otisco, just south of Waseca, Minnesota.

Some of those men in the Contagion Ward didn't live long after they got out, because they had been so hard hit with polio in their lungs. When polio paralyzes your lungs, you can die from lack of oxygen. I remember one night an 18-year-old boy named Roger, over in the other corner of the room, died. He had been in an iron lung earlier, but he was out of it, and then he took a turn for the worse. I can hear the cries of his mother yet. It was late at night; everything was quiet. The doctor was there, and the family pastor, and you just knew. Finally they wheeled him out. I never knew any more than that. But he had a severe case.

With polio, you had two varieties, spinal or bulbar. With spinal, you had a better chance perhaps of overcoming the illness. With bulbar, you had two results: you either got over it quite rapidly, totally, or you died. It just depended how severe it was. I've seen it both ways. Sometimes it was nip and tuck for several days in the iron lung and they pulled out of it. Sometimes they didn't.

One of the long time patients here at St. Mary's Hospital in Rochester, whom I didn't know personally, was Dave Madden from Eyota. He had bulbar polio. He was in the iron lung at St. Mary's for many, many years, and put up such a long fight. And finally, he died. A lot of them died in those polio epidemic years, from 1940 into the early 1950s.

One of the survivors was a neighbor of ours out on the farm, who had been my school teacher in my sophomore year of high school. Leslie King, who was born on February 1, 1921, was my biology teacher in Chatfield in 1946-47. And I looked up one day to see him walking into that ward at Sister Kenny's with polio. His arms were hanging down like two ropes. It was a sad thing. He could not feed himself, he could not scratch his nose. I'd grown up with him as a neighbor who lived four miles south of our farm, I had him as a school teacher, and now I was two beds away from him in the hospital. But he had a great brain and a loving wife and family, and he got out of there eventually. His arms were still useless, but he had good legs, and mechanics fixed his car with a floor-rotating steel plate for a steering wheel, so that he could actually drive with his feet. He went on to the University of Minnesota and earned a master's degree in educational administration and a doctorate in counseling psychology. He held a high position at the university, because he had such a brilliant mind. What a man! Dr. King died on August 18, 1997, at age 76. Leslie King — what a fighter!

When we got out of Contagion, we were moved into a huge ward for men. Now it was big, about fifty feet by eighty feet. It was like a barracks. There were forty-two beds, with men and boys aged five through fifty-four. The beds lined both walls, and there were two more rows of beds down the middle of the room. We were on the second floor of the west wing. Our windows overlooked the street, and we could hear the street cars going by at all hours of the day and night.

We managed to have some fun, though, at Sister Kenny. There was an old joke that when you came back from working with the physical therapist, someone would ask, "Well, did you get any new muscles today?"

And you'd answer, "No, I'd just like to have some of my old muscles back!"

We passed the days having physical therapy, resting, doing leatherwork (making belts and billfolds) or talking. We watched sports on a newly-introduced contraption called television, especially the Minneapolis Lakers basketball team with Mikan, Mikkelsen, Pollard, Schaefer and Martin — and occasionally the "jumping kangaroo kid," Tony Jaros, who hailed from Faribault, Minnesota. There were movies on Friday nights, and church services on Sunday. On Sunday evenings, groups would come from local churches and the like to entertain us, singing, playing accordions and other instruments.

We had quite a few youngsters in the ward, and often we would wake up in the morning to the noise of little boys playing on the floor with their toy cars, back and forth. Maybe one of them had a bad leg, one of them a bad arm — children just accept it in a hurry. Little kids probably took polio better than anybody else when they were just partially crippled. These little guys would get up there, and we'd holler, "Hey! Quiet down now!" It didn't do any good, you know. Five thirty, six in the morning, you're still trying to sleep, and there they were playing.

Every day, we would go to physical therapy. The therapist I remember best was a man called Higgins. I think he may have been British, although

I'm not sure. He had some sort of accent. He would ask me, "Now, Harley, if I buy two sheep, will they keep the grass down on 250 acres?"

I told him, "Well, you might need a few more sheep than that."

In physical therapy, the first thing they did was to put hot packs on your legs. These were steam packs, wrung out dry and wrapped around your thigh, calf and foot, with a plastic wrap over it to keep the heat in. The hot packs were Sister Kenny's invention. Then, when they removed the hot packs, the therapist would lift your leg, and then he would say, "Okay, now you do it." And of course, I couldn't.

They told me after my initial exam that I might have French polio — Guillain-Barre, I think they called it. They told me that most people did better with that type in the long run, whatever that meant. I know now that Guillain-Barre Syndrome isn't the same thing as polio, although it's also caused by a virus. From the symptoms I had, I think I probably had genuine spinal polio.

I had treatment for paralysis from the waist down, and although I started out with my legs totally paralyzed, within thirty days my toes were starting to wiggle. Now, more than a half century later, they still do little more than that.

Approximately three months after my arrival at the Elizabeth Kenny Institute, I actually met the famous Sister Kenny herself.

It was mid-morning on that October day — enema time for many of us patients, since polio had a way of shutting down the body's systems. One of our fine young male attendants (orderlies, as they were called) was administering this every-other-day procedure to me. There I sat, on my "throne," as the bedpans were affectionately called. A curtain on wheels had been pulled around my bed to give me some privacy. My orderly was called Bay Trelawney, an English-sounding name that made me think of the characters in Robert Louis Stevenson's "Treasure Island."

I can still see Bay, standing at the foot of the bed, just inside the curtain, holding up a small container of warm soap suds and letting them run down a rubber tube into my body. It was about 10:30 am when Bay said, "Oh my gosh, here comes Sister Kenny!"

Still holding the warm soapy water above his head, to maintain a proper flow of gravity into the tube, he reached into his white shirt pocket with his free hand, pulled out a black comb, and quickly ran it through the hair covering his forehead. He wanted to be sure that he was "patiently correct" when Sister Kenny arrived.

She paused long enough to look over the curtain and say to me, "Good morning, and how are you, young man?"

I replied, "Just fine, thank you."

And she moved on, visiting many of the other forty-two patients in that big ward full of men and boys.

Oh, if I'd only had the vision at that moment to whip out a microphone and cassette machine and ask her some questions, as I would do today! But at that moment, that particular 18-year-old lad was just interested in getting off his "throne" and staying off — and in getting back home again. I had no inkling then of the new broadcasting career I would be starting three years later, with its continuous joys and successes.

There were so many brave men and women whom I met there in the Elizabeth Kenny Institute. In the big ward, I met Herb Krippner, a 33-year-old farmer from Owatonna, and his 5-year-old son Stan; his 2-year-old daughter Virginia was in the women and children's ward down the hall. Then there was Lloyd Nelson from Luck, Wisconsin, a city famous for its yo-yos. There was Louis Hoiser, from Tomahawk, Wisconsin, and Dr. Dick Burke, from Lincoln, Nebraska. Bill Fabian was a sugar beet farmer from the Red River area of northwestern Minnesota, the oldest man there at age 54. Bill Frawley, aged 11, was from Faribault. We had Elmer Kuhl, from Goodhue, Dave Eilenfeldt, from Mankato, Dale Edberg, from Belle Plaine, Les Walker, from Oklee, Johnny Moline and Ronnie Gustafson, from Minneapolis. In the bed next to mine was Alger Dahlien, from Richfield. I remember Marvin Wolf, Delmar Anderson and Luther Steen. We were teenagers, little kids, older adults. Charles Hale transferred early to St. Mary's Hospital in Rochester. There was a married couple, John and Muriel Hustoft, turkey farmers from Willmar, Minnesota. And there were others whose names I've forgotten. Polio was no respector of gender or age.

I stayed in the Sister Kenny hospital over Christmas in 1949, because I wasn't in any shape yet to go home. My parents visited me as often as they could. Another couple who visited several times were Paul and Ida Gunderson, friends of ours from church, whose sons both had polio. Dick and Dennis Gunderson, aged ten and twelve respectively, were hit with polio in the summer of 1949, shortly after I was. Dick was hospitalized for several weeks with me at Sister Kenny. As I recall, his case was bulbar, which usually damages the throat and weakens the lungs. Patients often require a tracheotomy on the throat just to be able to breathe. Little Dick recovered after just a few weeks there. At first, I remember his consuming a lot of popsicles when other foods were impossible for him to swallow. Dennis was not hospitalized, and Dick came home in a few weeks, in recuperation.

I remember that Paul Gunderson had a 1948 Chrysler, with fluid drive transmission. When it was time for me to come home, Paul Gunderson came up to Minneapolis in that Chrysler and brought me home.

Treatment at the Sister Kenny Institute cost $10 a day — $300 a month. To my parents, this was a shocking amount. They just didn't know how they were going to be able to come up with that amount of money. And yet, what choice did they have? That was where the Fillmore County March of Dimes came in. My dad went down to their office in Preston, and they said to him, "Can you afford five dollars a week?" Well, yes, he thought he could manage that. And the March of Dimes paid the rest, out of the money they were collecting every year in their fund drives. In 1949, you could buy a fancy new car or 80 acres of good farmland for the $3000 it cost for my ten months' stay at the Sister Kenny Institute.

On May 10, 1950, after learning how to walk again in a limited fashion with crutches, I went home to the farm and slowly got started doing farm work again. I drove the tractor in July, cultivating corn. You couldn't keep me off that John Deere B tractor — I had to be there! For three summers, with my dad, I did everything I could, tractor-work wise. It was awfully difficult to hook and unhook a plow or a disk, but once you got that hooked up, I could go ahead and do a full day's work. I didn't spare myself. I guess I was young. I just didn't want to stop.

But when winter came, with the snow and ice, that's when I realized I had to stop. There was nothing I could do in the winter. Most days it was impossible for me to walk across the yard. I would have to find something else.

And what I found, of course, was radio broadcasting.

Clint Kueker illustration "FDR DIES" April 12, 1945.

Clint Kueker illustration "FDR GOES THRU STEWARTVILLE . . . TO THE Fred Sandte farm and minutes later pass Harley & sister Elaine on Olmsted Co. #2 walking home from school. Every body in President's entourage waves at us . . . Sept. 13, 1938.

Sister Kenny Hospital 1800 Chicago Ave. South, Minneapolis. Harley spent 10 months there, 1949-1950. Photo from archives of Sister Kenny Hospital and Abbot Northwestern Hospital. Photo taken in 1942.

Iron Lung, a life-saving machine for thousands during polio epidemic years. Photo courtesy Mayo Clinic Archives.

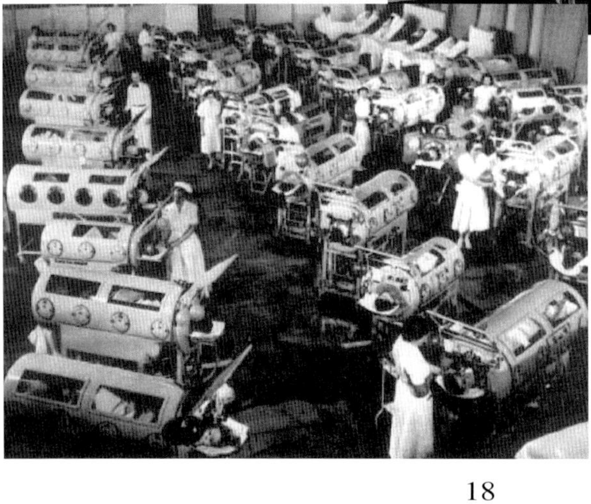

Room filled with Iron lungs. Los Angeles Co. Hospital during polio epidemic 1952. Photo from CDC Washington.

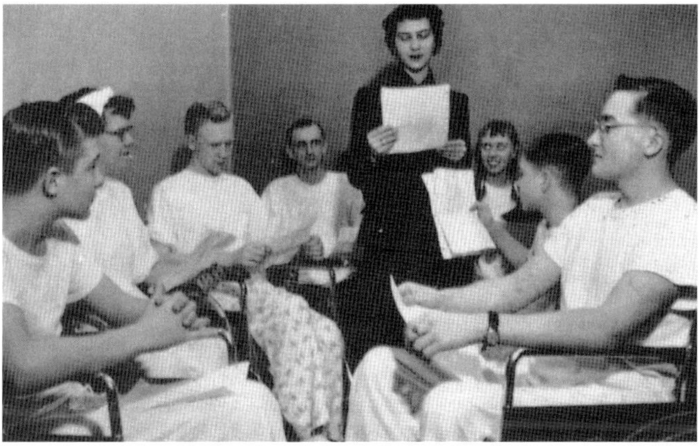

Polio Patients forget Cares in Drama Class. Terry LeClaire coaches patients into Shakespeares best that Kenny Institute could produce. Some names L-R . . . Marvin Wolf, Martha, Johnny Moline, Louis Hoiser, Tomahawk, Wis. & Terry LeClaire, instructor. At right Harley Flathers, 18 and still slender.

Fellow patient Ray Hanson and Nurse Hylda Rhylick. Ray from Eau Claire, Wis. Hilda each night would rub our lower spines and tail-bones with CITROX to help prevent bed sores. We nick-named her the "FANNY RUBBER." Both have since died. Christmas photo 1981 from Lorraine Hanson, Ray's wife.

Dismissal Day, May 10, 1950. Harley is now medically discharged from Elizabeth Kenny Institute in Minneapolis following 10 months of Kenny treatment. At left is Vivian Hannen, a top Physical Therapist at the Institute. (Photo: Stewartville Star)

Harley Home on the farm with his "Kenny Sticks" and dog "CHUM", Winter 1951. Photo by my Mom.

Moment 2

Not Everyone Can Be A Flathers
Edward Flathers & His Descendants

Recently while recuperating from surgery on my right arm, I read John Hildebrand's book, *Mapping the Farm.* John is a professor at the University of Wisconsin at Eau Claire, and he acquired first hand information on the O'Neill family. He wrote this book in the early 1990s about a family that had come to the United States from Ireland after the potato famine in the late 1840s and 1850s. Eventually they settled in Marion Township, about seven to eight miles southeast of Rochester. In the upper 1970s or early 1980s, John Hildebrand married Sharon O'Neill, a daughter of one of the sons who owned that farm in the last half of the 1900s. I found the book interesting, because it parallels our Flathers family history, which dates back to England in the mid-1700s.

The facts we have are based on a lot of research that was finally put into a book in 1988 by a man named Jennings Flathers, a distant cousin of mine. He wrote two books on the family, and the second, hard-cover book is titled *Edward Flathers and His Descendants: Ten Generations in America.* To follow the story from that first Flathers to where we are today in this community fascinates me.

I once told Jennings Flathers, "Anyone could end up a Smith, a Jones or a Johnson, there are so many of them, but it takes guts to be a Flathers." Although it's a typically Anglo-Saxon name, there aren't a lot of us around who use it.

This does have one advantage. If you're looking through historical records for people named Flathers, you're pretty sure that the ones you find are our relatives.

In reconstructing the story of how the first Flathers came to America, I have combined my memories of the stories my father told me repeatedly during my early years with notes from Jennings Flathers' book on the Flathers family.

Edward Flathers was born in England in 1755. He grew up at a time when England was changing from a mainly agricultural country to a semi-industrial one. Young people from the countryside were crowding into the cities, where they hoped to find employment. Those with a sense of adventure flocked to ports like Bristol, Liverpool and London, where they had the possibility of travel to the New World. It was common in those days for young men to be "impressed" by roving gangs of thugs who virtually kidnapped them off the streets and sold them to sea captains, who took them to the colonies and sold them to landowners as indentured men. They then had to work for the landowner for a period of time, usually seven years, to "pay off the cost of their passage."

The story my father told me, which he had heard from his father and his grandfather, was that young Edward and his brother Benjamin had been standing on the bank of the River Thames in London, when a captain approached them and asked if they would like to come aboard and "view the craft." Once on board, they were not allowed to leave, and they were taken to the New World. Around 1774, when this took place, a captain could get twenty pounds for an able-bodied man.

The real truth is buried in time, but in 1992 we found a reference to Edward and Benjamin Flathers in Coldham's book, "English Convicts in Colonial America" (Polyanthos 1974). According to this source, the two arrived in America separately. Edward, who was identified as a stowaway, arrived in Virginia in 1774. Benjamin, whose address is listed as St. Paul, Covent Garden SW, arrived in June of 1775. The book doesn't say whether he "stowed away" or not, but it says that he eventually went to the West Indies. However it was that he came to America, we do know that Edward

Flathers was an indentured man who worked for several years in Fauquier County, Virginia, until he paid off his passage.

Edward served in the Virginia militia during the American Revolution, probably as a paid substitute for other men — a common practice at that time. Family tradition places him with Washington's army when it crossed the Delaware River in December 1776 to attack a Hessian brigade at Trenton, New Jersey, and at the Valley Forge encampment during the terrible winter of 1777-78. In 1781, he worked to build a road through the Virginia forest for Washington to use during the siege of Yorktown. Edward Flathers was present on October 19, 1781, when General Cornwallis's British Army surrendered at Yorktown. As a member of the Virginia militia guard, he helped to march the 7,000 British and Hessian prisoners of war 250 miles north to a prison camp near Winchester, Virginia.

In 1988, my wife and I visited Jennings and Elizabeth Flathers at their Virginia home and toured Yorktown's battle site, where the British General Cornwallis had surrendered to General Washington. All the old cannons were in battle positions high above the town. Visiting this historic site makes you appreciate what those new "Americans" accomplished when they "stepped up to the plate" to start the preservation of freedom. Jennings had just completed his book on the Flathers family when we visited him. He died the following year, in March 1989.

When the war was over, young Edward Flathers acquired some land, probably as payment for his service in the Virginia militia during the war. He also had three slaves, probably given to him as payment by those men for whom he substituted in the army. He may have sold the slaves for more land. In 1797, when he was 42 years old, he again appears in official records, married to a woman named Clarissa Legg.

After the birth of three children, Edward and Clarissa decided to sell their property in Fauquier County and move west, hoping to find more fertile land upon which to settle permanently. They reached Greenbrier County, in what is now West Virginia, in 1785. By the time they left West Virginia about eleven years later, they had six children. They traveled through the Cumberland Gap to Kentucky, on the trail made by Daniel

Boone. It seemed that every time they got to new land that seemed to have fertile soil, someone else had already staked a claim to it. This is the sad part of moving west. You know land is there, and you want to know, how can we get it? How can we stake the claim?

They stayed in Kentucky until 1829, and then finally they moved to Hendricks County, Indiana. By this time, their sons had grown up, and they moved to Indiana, too. Edward died there in 1847, at the age of 92. His wife, Clara, died two years later, at the age of 94. They are buried in the Gentry family cemetery, which is just a little cemetery, outside of Danville in Hendricks County. June and I visited Danville, and found the cemetery. We could see it at a distance, but it's up in a cow pasture, so we didn't go up to the graves. We were told that a man was taking care of it, keeping it mowed, at least during the 1970s and 1980s. We don't know what condition it is in today.

Edward and Clara had six children, four sons and two daughters. As I grew up, I learned that I was the sixth generation to bear the Flathers name after Edward's arrival in America. In our particular line, Edward had a son named Isaac, and he had a son, Lindsey, who was my great-grandfather. Lindsey had several sons and daughters, but two in particular that I want to mention in conjunction with this story are William and John Wesley. William's son was my father Homer. Then you have myself, Homer's son, and then my sons, Edward John and Jeffrey Alan, making seven generations in our family that are named Flathers.

Lindsey Flathers and his family decided to leave Danville, Indiana, in 1854. Lindsey's brother-in-law John Pace had moved to Minnesota in 1852, and his descriptions of the place evidently convinced Lindsey that he should come, too. They took the train to Dunleath, Illinois, just across the Mississippi from Dubuque. There they got on a steamboat and worked their way up to Winona. John Wesley and Will were still young boys. Will was born in 1848, and John Wesley was born in 1845. When they walked out behind the covered wagon, driving their few head of cattle from Winona to Pleasant Grove in 1854, they were 8 to 10 years old. Their sister Nancy was 6, and there was a baby brother, Milton, who would die a year later in Pleasant Grove. Three more children were born after they got to Minnesota.

The family acquired a farm about three miles northeast of Pleasant Grove, where Lindsey Flathers raised his boys to manhood and managed a good piece of land. He started out, I believe, with a quarter section, located just a mile west of highway 19 on county 139. Eventually they built a large brick house and a stone barn, both of which are still standing. The farm is owned now by Janet Lowrie. When Lindsey and Mary Flathers sold the farm, it was sold to a Lowrie family, and it's belonged to the Lowries ever since.

Lindsey helped his two sons, John Wesley and Will, acquire land in the early 1860s. John Wesley's farm was about a mile and a half from the original farm, and Will's farm — my home, where I grew up — was about four miles away from it, and three miles southwest of John Wesley's. Those men had to break the land and clear the trees, using oxen. Our home farm had originally been 160 acres, but all the years when I grew up there, it was 120 acres. My father often said he was so proud that our home farm had been officially put in the Flathers name — homesteaded — by his grandfather in 1861, the same year that President Abraham Lincoln took the oath of office.

John Wesley Flathers

John Wesley Flathers's story is an interesting one. He finished Chatfield High School, and then got involved in some positions in Olmsted County and on the soil conservation board. He ran for state office in 1888, and was a state representative in the Minnesota legislature until 1892. After that, he came back and was a businessman here in Rochester, acquiring property. He was on the welfare board, and was a county commissioner in Olmsted County from 1904 till 1920.

In downtown Rochester, John Wesley lived on the land which is now a parking lot directly north of the Franklin heating station. On the east is the former Martin Hotel, now the Colonial Inn, directly across 2nd Street

Southwest from the Plummer Building. When John Wesley Flathers lived there in the early 1900s, before the Plummer Building was built, the Mayos were just getting started with their clinic work. They hadn't really built a clinic yet. Where today's Siebens Building is located on 1st Street Southwest, a block north of the Plummer Building, is the site of the original red brick Mayo Clinic Building, built in 1914. At the turn of the century, on that site, was the home occupied by Dr. William Worrall Mayo, father of Dr. Will and Dr. Charles Mayo. That home was razed in 1912, and the red brick 1914 Building, the first Mayo Clinic, was put up in its place. It remained there until 1986, when the Siebens Building was constructed. In 1928, the Plummer Building was built, and that really was the beacon to Rochester — twenty-eight stories high, complete with a carillon.

So John Wesley Flathers lived just a block away from Dr. William Worrall Mayo. I have a feeling there might have been a little competition between them for who was doing the most things in the community, because shortly after John Wesley returned from the Minnesota legislature, Dr. William Worrall Mayo became a state senator.

Around 1904, a group of Lutherans came to John Wesley Flathers and said, "Mr. Flathers, we'd like to buy this piece of property where you live here downtown." (That would be the corner lot at 2nd Street and 2nd Avenue Southwest.) And so, for a sum of $2500, they bought the property and built the Evangelical Lutheran Synod Church of Rochester. (Second Street Southwest was called Zumbro Street at that time, so the church in 1926 changed its name to Zumbro Evangelical Lutheran Church. It remained on the 2nd Street corner from 1909 to 1927.)

After he sold his house on 2nd Street, John Wesley Flathers moved west to what is now 14th Avenue. The new St. Marys Hospital was just starting then, on 2nd Street Southwest just east of his property. He owned a lot of acreage that he developed into Flathers Addition, with homes along 14th Avenue Southwest from 2nd Street Southwest for many blocks south. In the early 1900s, 14th Avenue Southwest was called Flathers Avenue.

John Wesley was a county commissioner then — in fact, he'd been a county commissioner for the past sixteen years. He'd built several houses, including four big block homes where the Blondell Motel is now located, at the corner of 14th Avenue and 2nd Street Southwest. I can remember when they were torn down in the late 1960s and 1970s, when the motel was being planned.

He'd married Olive Collins of Pleasant Grove back in 1873, and she died in 1913. A few years later (we don't know how many), he married Myra Agnes Sloan of Belchester, Massachusetts and moved to Southgate, California. From there, in 1920, he resigned as county commissioner. He had to make an important vote on property that he owned, and he resigned because he didn't want a conflict of interest. His term was nearly over anyway.

John Wesley Flathers served his county very well, as county commissioner and on the welfare board. He and a Mr. Russell had owned the Stewartville Elevator at one time. They also owned lumber yards, and he had an interest in a grocery store. I suspect that, when he was on the welfare board, the vouchers that were issued to those on welfare may have been redeemable only at John Wesley Flathers's grocery store.

John Wesley Flathers died in California in 1928 at the age of 83, survived by his third wife, Ida Elliot Flathers who is buried with her parent in the Elliot lot at Oakwood Cemetery, Rochester. He is buried at Pleasant Grove's Union Cemetery, near his.parents, Lindsey and Mary Pace Flathers.

I tell this story because I am proud of what the Flathers family has done in Rochester before me.

William Murry Flathers

Will Flathers, my father's father, and his wife Rachel spent their married life on our home farm, on what is now county road 2. Today all the buildings are gone, with the exception of one, a hog barn that our neighbor Claude Bernard and his father helped my dad build in 1938. Only the memories remain.

My dad told us how his father used to carry water forty rods uphill to the house from a spring when the family lived northeast of Pleasant Grove.

Once when Grandpa Will went out there, he found a big buck deer standing in the water, and it wouldn't let him near the spring.

Grandpa Will also told my dad about a trip that he took to Winona, fifty miles away. He took that trip many times. Driving a team of horses, it took five days, Monday through Friday, to get a load of wheat to market there and return home. Once, while he was there, he bought two hand corn planters and brought them back to show his sons. "Boys," he said, "see what they have invented. Something to plant corn with! What will they think of next?" At that time, it took two men with hoes to plant twenty acres, with two boys following behind to drop the seed corn in the ground. The new gadget was called a "chuck-planter." June and I donated the last one to the Olmsted County History Center after my dad died in 1977.

Will used to raise turkeys. Now, turkeys would sleep in the trees at night, and it seems that there was a lot of theft going on in those days as well. One time the family was away from the farm, and when they came back, they found that the turkeys, most of them, had been stolen. Grandpa Will Flathers said, "Don't say a word to anyone. Don't say a word, don't breathe a word."

Years later, in some particular gathering, a man came up to him and said, "Mr. Flathers, did you ever find out who stole your turkeys?"

And Grandpa Will said, "Nope! Not until now!"

Will Flathers married Rachel Eichhorn on December 2, 1874. Rachel was born in Germany on July 18, 1857. She came to America with her family when she was ten years old. The ocean crossing on the steamship Schmidt was a stormy one, and it made a deep impression on Rachel. Years later, she wrote a song about her experiences, which was published in 1885 by the Occidental Music Company in Chatfield, and we have a copy of that song today. The voyage, which should have taken twelve days, lasted four weeks, and when they arrived in New York, they found that they had been given up for lost. From New York, the Eichhorns went by rail to Winona and then by oxcart to Racine, Minnesota, where her uncle lived.

Although she had loved school in Germany, Rachel's first day at school in America was so miserable that she never went back. The children laughed at her because she couldn't speak English. Over the next few years, she taught herself to speak, read and write in English. As a hired girl, she would make a point of placing the newspapers she used to line the shelves with right side up, so that she could pick out familiar words that someone had spelled out for her and memorize them. Later in life, she became a dynamic public speaker, visiting local meetings of the Women's Christian Temperance Union (WCTU) and giving impassioned talks without the use of notes.

She was also a talented musician. When the officials at the Church of Christ in Pleasant Grove told her that they would buy an organ if she would learn to play it, she agreed and became the church's first organist. She also gave piano lessons.

Will Flathers, my grandfather, died on June 10, 1915, at the age of 67. He suffered a lot during his life, because a tree limb had fallen on him when he was eight years old, crushing his collar bone and chest. They didn't expect him to live. For the rest of his life he had a sunken spot in his chest and he had a difficult time breathing. A lump on his shoulder turned out to be a loose piece of bone that his wife removed nearly sixty years later. But when he died, he died of appendicitis. He had been recovering from surgery performed fifteen days earlier at St. Mary's Hospital in Rochester, when he suddenly grew worse and died. Those were the days before penicillin, and even the best surgeons couldn't always prevent infection, especially with abdominal surgery.

My grandmother, Rachel Flathers, died in Mankato on October 26, 1943, at the age of 86. She had lived forty-three years in each century. She was a large woman, and I remember her funeral well. While the minister said a prayer, the coffin was held in place over the grave by ropes extended across a tubular metal frame. It was to be lowered when the prayers ended. Suddenly one of the ropes slipped and the coffin tilted sharply. I can still hear my Aunt Ila crying out to the pall bearers (my cousins Dale and Lyle Turner among them), "Don't let her fall, boys! Don't let her fall!" And they didn't. I was twelve years old then, and it made quite an impression on me.

My great-grandfather Lindsey and his wife, my grandparents, my parents and some other Flathers are all buried at Pleasant Grove, fifteen miles southeast of Rochester. When I die, my grave will be in the same lot, next to my great-grandfather, Lindsey.

Homer William Flathers
1898-1977

My father was 16 years old when his father died. Homer Flathers was born on August 22, 1898, and was the youngest of Will and Rachel's five children. He attended the same little country school (built in 1866) that I did, and in his 8th grade year, his sister Ethel was his teacher. He once told Elaine that he never worked so hard at schoolwork in his life as he did that year. Ethel would continue to "teach" him at home in the evenings at the kitchen table, to prepare him for high school.

Dad was a close man with a dollar. Of course, most of those people who lived through the Great Depression were tight-fisted — they had to be, to survive. But my Dad learned the value of money early. Belva Dumez Bernard, who grew up on a farm a mile and a half west of ours, was just a bit younger than my father. Dad was born in 1898, and I think Belva might have been two, maybe three years younger. As children, they became friends, because their parents were friends. In the late 1950s, Belva compiled a history of Pleasant Grove and Stewartville, and she told me tales of when she and my father were growing up in the early part of the century.

One of the things they did, my Dad told me as I was growing up, was to go to the fair, the Olmsted County Fair in Rochester, together with his parents, Rachel and Will Flathers. The fair was then held on land across from the present canning factory in Rochester.

Belva described their adventure that day, when she became Dad's first financial secretary, in a letter she wrote to me in September 1984: "As to Homer and Belva's adventure at the fair," she wrote, "as I recall we each had nickels. Likely a total of 25 cents each. But we were not to buy food. Believe me, we fingered those nickels, and Homer purchased a tiny shell case pocketbook for Belva to carry the money. Likely took one or two of our nickels. In recent years, I donated that purse to the Olmsted Historical Museum."

Through that day at the county fair, my Dad told me years later, Homer and Belva went on some rides. I don't know whether they adhered to their instruction to buy no food or not, but when the day was done, they still had some change left from their original fifty cents. And they were tired. They curled up together in the back seat of my grandfather's buggy as they rode home. It took three hours and fifteen minutes to travel from the Olmsted County fair in Rochester to the home farm. Dad used to tell me, it took three hours with a real fast team of horses, or if you let them lag a little, and take their time, it was 3 hours and 15 minutes. The road they took was the Poor Farm Road, also called the Dubuque Trail (today county road 1), that goes through Pleasant Grove and Simpson to Rochester.

"Another event I recall," Belva wrote in her letter, "when we were older and going to a community picnic at Tunnel Mill, Homer drove the team. His cousin Lesley Kinsley rode in the front of the surrey, while Ila Flathers [that's Dad's older sister] sat between Myrtle Kinsley and Belva as chaperone in the back seat, much to the lads' disgust. Anyway, we were always friendly neighbors of the various Flathers families."

When Dad went to Pleasant Grove on a Saturday morning in the spring of 1913 to take the state examinations for entry into high school, his father drove him the four miles to the school, but he couldn't wait around until Dad's examinations were over, because it was planting time and he needed to get the horses back to the farm to use in the fields. Dad had $1 that his mother had given him to buy a new pair of shoes, so that he would look respectable when he took the test. The shoes cost 80 cents, and he was to use the rest to buy some bologna and crackers for lunch. Well, he did that, and passed the test, and then he walked home. In the fall, he went to the high school in Stewartville.

After his father died, Dad and Grandma Rachel continued to farm for several years. Then they rented the land out and Rachel, Aunt Ila (my dad's sister), and my father all moved to Mankato, so that Ila could attend college. Dad took a year of business college in Mankato, but then found he wanted to get back to farming.

He met my mother, Vivian Raabe, of Spring Valley, and she being the musician she was and he loving music as he did, they fit together well. They were married on November 28, 1922. They spent a couple of years in California, to see if they wanted to live out there. It took them seventeen days to drive from Minnesota to California, and there were only about forty miles of paved road along the way. Dad worked as a carpenter, and Mother gave piano lessons, but by 1924 they had decided to come back to Minnesota and the farm. They went through the Depression, had us two children (Elaine on May 12, 1926, and Harley on August 27, 1931), and spent the rest of their lives there on the farm, until my Dad's death on October 6, 1977. My mother lived to be almost 90. She died on January 6, 1983.

The Flathers farm then was sold. My father had bought a second farm, just east of Sumner Church, and we continued to operate it for a number of years, renting it out. We finally parted with it in the early 1990s.

I loved the farm. I love the memories of the farm, from the time I was a small lad. I remember my sister, my Dad and I, all out there cultivating corn with three pairs of horses pulling three single-row corn cultivators across those fields. It was a wonderful experience. I never saw my dad start planting a crop in the spring, but what he would stop and offer a prayer first. He knew the soil, and he knew what it meant to be close to God.

I can still see my Dad plowing with those six horses on a two-bottom gang plow. I remember myself walking behind four or five horses and two sections of digger, digging the field, or five sections of drag, twenty-five feet wide, walking for hours. These are things that a young lad remembers, growing up. And then, of course, finally getting to the place where we could order that Model B John Deere tractor to make life a little easier. We waited three years for that tractor during the war, from 1943 till 1946. When it finally arrived, it came to the Olmsted County Implement store, the John Deere headquarters, on 4th Street Southeast in Rochester, a site now occupied by the Dos Amigos II restaurant in the restored train depot. The original depot had been built there years earlier, in the mid-1800s, and other businesses later occupied the site. But in 1946 it was the John Deere place. In the spring of 1949, we would buy our John Deere combine there. It was a Model 12-A pull-type combine, with a six-foot cutting bar and a 20-horsepower Wisconsin motor, and it sold for $1950.

Vivian Raabe Flathers
1893-1983

I need to give my mother's family equal time. Vivian Jenny Raabe, my mother, was born February 16, 1893, at her home near Spring Valley. She was the fifth daughter, followed by three brothers, for a total of eight children born to Theodore Raabe and Carrie Rathbun. Theodore Raabe's parents had come from Germany, and settled first in Dodge County, Wisconsin, where Grandpa Theodore was born in 1858. After a few years in Wisconsin, the Raabes decided to come to Spring Valley, Minnesota.

Theodore Raabe's father, Ludwig Raabe, had saved his money. He was a very frugal person. They had to be back at that time. They tell me that in 1867, when someone else was looking at this very fine quarter section of land near Spring Valley, and the real estate person was trying to sell it to him, there stood old Ludwig Raabe nearby, with his hands in his pockets, and in the end, he pulled out the cash and paid for the land himself. He bought it right out from under that other fellow's nose.

They had very little, but they worked hard. Theodore Raabe eventually amassed up to half a section of land, farming all of it with horses. Theodore Raabe and Carrie lived together 32 years before she died in 1915, at the age of 52. Then in 1919, Theodore married Myrta Tebay, and lived with her for 32 years before he died at age 92, on September 1, 1950. Theodore and Myrta had one daughter, Ione, born in 1921.

I have fond memories of Grandpa Raabe. He was a craftsman who could make furniture and build houses and barns. He was not only a farmer, but he also sold insurance, and he loved story-telling.

Theodore Raabe built a huge home, called Pinehurst, on that farm, which was located about three miles southeast of Spring Valley. They built the house in 1899, when my mother was six years old. It was a 17-room home, three stories high, and it was the first home around with a bathroom upstairs, with a cistern and a pump that could pump water up to a tank on the third floor, so that they could have running water in the bathroom in their home. The house is now owned by the Harvey Merkel family, who have lived there for about the last forty years. It is still in beautiful condition. It's cared for very well during the years, and it is a fine sight to behold.

Mother grew up on the farm and went to school in Spring Valley. She loved music, and after graduating from Spring Valley High School in 1913, she went to Minneapolis, where she studied piano and music theory at Northwestern Conservatory and then at MacPhail School of Music. She studied under Theodore Bergman, an organist. After she graduated, she went on and taught piano at MacPhail, until she married my dad on November 28, 1922. With her schooling, she began a music career which stayed with her throughout her life. She was the church organist and pianist at our Sumner Center Church for over forty years, and also gave private piano lessons.

My sister Elaine and I had the opportunity to learn piano from our mother. Elaine did a very good job of learning to play the piano early on. I may have had free lessons at home, but not enough spanking was done on my rear side for it to sink in, because I could always find something else to do.

"Practice your lesson, Harley," mother would say.

And I'd say, "I got work to do. I got chores to do."

Actually, when I was in the 8th grade, about 13 years old, I was playing hymns and doing very well. But that skill dropped away. I was like many other kids — unless they stay with it, it drops. But I developed a love for music, nonetheless.

Elaine Flathers

My sister Elaine has meant a lot to me as a sister. She not only learned to play the piano, but later put in a full life of teaching school. She graduated from Mankato High School in the spring of 1944 and went on to Mankato State Teachers College, graduating in 1948. Then she started teaching at Waseca, Minnesota, where she remained for thirty-six years.

During that time, she made trips to Minneapolis and other cities, taking continuing education classes, until she earned her master's degree in English in 1958.

The newspaper in Waseca published a story one year on some of the teachers who had been named teachers of the year. Elaine Flathers was one of those who were honored. The paper said that Elaine, "who taught 7th through 9th grade English and served as declamation coach for 17 years, spent all of her 36 years teaching in Waseca. The rural Stewartville native began in 1948 at a salary of $2475 per year." I remember we thought at the time, when she told us about her contract, that the $2400 was for teaching and the $75 was for her work in declamation, or "declam," as they called it. Elaine did a super job of teaching for all those years in Waseca.

She also is a writer. She wrote stories about the life of my mother. She's a real historian, who contributed to the Flathers family genealogy, and helped to draw up the Raabe and Rathbun sides of my mother's family for our own family tree.

I have a copy of a letter that Elaine once wrote to the editor of the newspaper about her first teacher at district 118. She called it "A Tribute to My First Teacher." Elaine wrote, "Dear editor, This month as a special recognition for teachers, I would like to pay tribute to Mrs. Harold King, Minerva Ellis, my very first teacher and lifelong friend. In the days before kindergarten for rural students, she took a very shy little girl onto her lap and taught her to love to read in district 118 in Fillmore County. Last June, I retired from teaching after 36 years in the Waseca Public Schools. I've always been grateful for that good first year that started me down the road to education. Signed, Elaine V. Flathers, Waseca, Minnesota."

Elaine told me she was very angry as a little girl when this man, Harold King, came and took her teacher away to be married, and she could no longer have her as a teacher. Those were still days when most school districts wouldn't hire married women as teachers. Many people knew and loved Harold and Minerva King over the years. They were great friends of our family and members of our church for more than 60 years. I knew them growing up. They both died in the 1990s.

My Home Farm . . . in Flathers family for 122 years . . . 1861-1983. 8 miles S.E. of Stewartville . . . 8 1/2 miles west of Chatfield on County #2. All buildings from this 1955 photo are gone but one.

Pleasant Grove Cemetery . . . Sometimes referred to as "Evergreen" Cemetery in earlier years. Also called Union Cemetery. At least 16 Flathers family members are buried here.

Christian Church in Pleasant Grove. Built in 1860s. . . Burned down in 1948. Bricks in church came from Pleasant Grove Brick yard. Several homes in the area were built from Pleasant Grove bricks including ours.

My grandparents William & Rachel seated. Back row L-R: daughters Ila & Ethel, and sons Clarence & Homer. 1910 photo which means my father is 12.

Theodore Raabe & wife, Carrie (Rathbun). 5 daughters . . . my mother, Vivian at right in back row. Others L-R, Laura, Flossie, Louise and Lillian. Sons L-R, Ralph, Ted and Clifton. Photo, Aug. 11, 1911. Seven years later Ted would die in battle WW I.

Pinehurst 17 room home built in 1899 by Theodore Raabe for about $4,000. He stands at right. Wife Carrie at right of porch on ground. My mother, Vivian is 7 years old, top of steps, holding a doll. Home is still a "showplace" today owned by the Merkel family.

Elaine V. Flathers, my sister, just before retiring at Waseca Public Schools, where she taught English for 36 years.

Moment 3

When I Grow Up, I'm Gonna Be A Farmer

In those early years, I loved so much being with my Dad on the farm. We didn't have a tractor. We had horses, cows, pigs and laying hens. And we carried lanterns instead of electric lights. We did oat threshing, silo filling and shredding of corn.

I had fun during those years, growing up with him. I would look forward to Friday nights, because then I didn't have to go to bed early to get up for school the next morning. He taught me how to box. We didn't have boxing gloves. We used big old padded mittens. Of course, as a little fellow, I would hit as hard as I could, and he had to be careful that he didn't hit back as hard as he could.

I loved working out in the barn with him. I'd say, "Dad, am I helping?" And I'd pick up a fork, and we'd start cleaning the barn.

He'd say, "Yeah. Am I helping?"

And I'd say, "Yeah!" One time, I remember saying, "Dad, am I getting paid for this?"

He said, "Yup!"

I said, "Oh, goodie! How much?"

And he said, "The same pay I get. If we all work hard and pull together, we'll have a roof over our heads, we'll have food to eat, we'll have a place to sleep, and we'll have fun together." And you know, it worked!

I learned how to do farm work, and I wanted to work. I wanted to be there when calves were born. When we sold calves and cows. When we carried straw in during a windy night to bed the cows. When we got up in the middle of the night to check on whether the lambs were born yet.

When I was in high school, we had a flock of sheep, and sheep have a tendency to want to deliver baby lambs in the middle of the night, on the coldest night, and so we had a plan. We would take turns. Every two hours, one of us would go out — at 9, 11, 1, 3 and 5, and then by 7 we were all up anyway. Everybody took a turn to check on the lambs, or baby pigs, or calves. Many a time, we would go out, and there was a baby lamb, or a litter of pigs, and one was very cold, or maybe it was a runt. We would bring that little animal into the house and put it in a box behind the kitchen stove, where it could be warm. It would come in barely breathing, and in the morning that little lamb would be going, "Baaa!" Or if it was pigs, they'd be squealing. Then you would take them back to be with their mother.

You just haven't experienced life till you can see it like that on the farm, looking after the animals. It was the same way with horses. We lived with the horses, saw baby colts being born and being created. If young folk haven't had a chance to see these things first hand, they can't possibly understand them. When you live with them, you aren't surprised by these things.

These farm memories stay with me, and I treasure them. The reason why I've become so involved in our Rochester Agriculture Committee since 1980 is to try to encourage young folks to go into agriculture, and if they're in 4H or whatever, to stay with it. They don't all have to go out and farm, but if they love it, there are so many facets to agriculture that they can pursue today. A lot of good things can come of it.

Those Old-Time Threshing Days

One of the events that I have vivid memories of, that always pleased me, took place in late July or August — threshing time on the farm. It was exciting, because this big machine would come in to finalize what we'd been doing, harvesting those fields of grain.

First we would put the oats into bundles with a grain binder, and then get them shocked so they could dry. You set up about six or eight bundles together on their butts, standing up like a little wigwam, and then you laid one bundle across the top to be the cap of the shock. When you tucked it down, it became a protection for the other bundles. It was a wonderful sight, to see the field full of shocks, but let me tell you, it was even more wonderful when the field was cleared of shocks, and what was left was a big golden straw pile.

Threshing played a big role in our lives. When I first was old enough to really appreciate this process, the threshing machines were run by gasoline-powered tractors. The era of the steam engine, which was an exciting thing in itself, was over by then. But the process was the same. There were still bundle teams. The farmers would get together and form a threshing ring, as they called it. Maybe there were seven or eight farmers in a two or three mile radius, and one of them owned a separator, a threshing machine. (There were many names for it. You could call it either a threshing machine or a grain separator.)

They'd have a threshers' meeting first, to decide where they'd begin. They'd say, "We're going to go ahead and try to take care of each one, and we hope there's no rain, so that we can get this done without going on forever." You might have a sunny half day of threshing, and then the rains would come for two or three days, and you'd lose the rest of the week. Or you might go through a whole session, get six of the seven farmers done, and then the rains would come and the last one just wouldn't be done till later. It was just one of those things. In farming, a lot depends on the weather.

There was so much preparation, especially for the women. Every mother just had a momentous job. Usually she had a neighbor or two in to help, and a daughter, and maybe the neighbor's daughter, depending on the size of the threshing ring. When you have up to twenty men to feed, you've got to have help in the kitchen. It takes a lot of help, a lot of planning. If you could always get the job done in one day, it might be fine. If you can get noon dinner done, and then supper, you've done a big day, because there are dishes to wash, too, and then you no more than get done and there's the next meal to prepare. In later years, the threshers began to want an extra lunch at 4 o'clock, so somebody would bring out a gallon pail full of sandwiches. The threshers loved that, because they didn't have to stop the threshing machine. Those fellows that were running bundle teams, they took a couple of sandwiches and went back to work, eating on the way to the field. Nobody has an appetite like men who are threshing or filling silos. It just takes a lot out of them, and they're always ready to eat. So the women are kept busy in the kitchen, preparing meals.

Outside, I can see this big threshing machine now, coming down the road, pulled by an F-20 Farmall tractor, about a 1937 or 1938 model, driven by my uncle Henry Turner. Uncle Henry was married to my Dad's sister, Ethel. They lived about three miles south of us, so we were on the very north edge of their threshing ring, which was mostly down around Sumner Center. There were some others involved in it, the Leibolds and Earl Ellenberg and others. When Dad went threshing down there, he had the farthest to go. He had to travel about three miles with his bundle team before he pitched his first bundle. But that's the way it went. They got it done. Then they all had to come up and help us. Henry's teenage sons, Lyle and Dale, helped out. Lyle could do a lot of work. Dale was a little younger, but he could do some work, and he always looked forward to mealtime very much. We all looked forward to mealtime, especially if there were hot dogs!

So that big threshing machine would come in, and they'd get it set up, and the men would come and load those bundles of oats. After a while, I got old enough so that I could tend the blower. My Dad would be up on the straw pile, gently stacking it, trying to make a nice firm base that you could build a pile of straw on, because that was very important. The straw pile supplied the straw that we would use for bedding the cows in the winter. If you had a good straw pile, you knew that you were going to have good bedding for your livestock in the winter. So we would work to build that straw pile, and it was dusty! I mean, this was a dusty job, threshing, and it was always hot. But it was so much fun to see that big straw pile forming. And when it was done, there was just a kind of quiet atmosphere in the barnyard.

We had to keep the cattle away from that straw pile for a while, because they would run and play in it, and suddenly it would start looking like a toadstool, thin in the bottom and fat on top. Then you had the danger of the straw pile capsizing, turning over on you. So we were very careful to keep them away until it actually settled. Once the straw pile has settled, and the winds have come and driven it, and winter comes, your straw pile is safer, and the cattle are safer.

So we would work on building the straw pile, and then at noon we would stop. The men would tie up their horses, get them watered, maybe unhitch them from the wagons. They would come in and eat, and oh, how they would eat! Afterwards they would leave the house and sit in the shade to rest a while, and I can still hear some of the stories being told. Finally, someone would say, "We've got to get back at it," and they'd go back to the fields. It probably wasn't more than an hour and a quarter at the most that the machines were stopped. And then the next day, when we were done, they would go to another farm. It was always good when the job was done.

A farmer would say, "Okay, I've helped you thresh two days, and I only threshed one, so you owe me three or four dollars. Or I'll come and help you out sometime." Very little money changed hands. Farmers had a way of helping each other with a kind of barter — "Hey, I'm going to need you for the weekend," or "You can come back and help me when we're shelling corn, or when we're shredding. You owe me a half day." Nobody really got hung up on it. Only the man who had the threshing machine would be paid in cash. That was the agreement. And the same went for silo filling.

Henry Turner did our threshing for a number of years, with Lyle and Dale helping out, and then Rob Hudson came into the scene for a few years in the early 1940s. Rob had a threshing machine on his farm just immediately to the west of us, so that was a little closer home. I think we only had about four people in that threshing ring, but it worked out well.

Then in the later years, from 1945 to 1948, we did our threshing with Bill Baker, who had the farm adjoining us on the north. Bill had a 1936 Allis Chalmers U tractor. It was a powerful thing, and I can remember when Bill got it new. I was just a little fellow, less than half a dozen years old then. I remember that he loved to go out and plow late at night. His tractor did not have lights on it, but his eyes got used to the darkness, especially if the moon was out. I could hear him late in the evening, that tractor humming, half a mile to a mile away. Bill Baker and his wife Rose were our neighbors. Their children, Harlan Baker, my dear friend all those years in school, and his sister Marjorie, and I all went to school together at district 118, and their sister Eileen was one of our teachers for two years, 1942-43 and 1943-44.

We had some wonderful neighbors during those years. Neighbors would always help neighbors out, too! Some of them had tractors, some of us just had horses.

Finally, when we got into the late 1940s, I said to my Dad, "I think we've threshed enough, dad. Let's get a combine."

I remember the first time I saw a combine. In 1935, Dad had decided to break up one of our fields that we had used as pasture. We had someone break it up with a tractor and plow, and then he planted flax. And it produced very well. When it came time to be harvested, he called on good old neighbor Ed Hale.

Ed, Robert and John Hale were three brothers who grew up on a farm just about two miles straight west of Sumner Center Church, toward Racine. They were big farmers, as was their father before them. To show you how big their farm was, I'll tell you that their barn was 50 feet wide and 202 feet long. Those who remember the Hale Barn know what I'm speaking of. They had hired men by the dozen. Day laborers would say to themselves, "Hey, I think maybe I can find a job at Hale's." They were always taking on men. They needed a lot of men, because they had well over a section of land. (A section would be 640 acres.)

Well, Ed Hale came to our farm with his new Allis Chalmers combine. I was then four years old. I can see myself yet, this little fellow standing along the roadside watching, saying in awed tones, "Ed Hale and his combine!"

Ed Hale was so kind. All the years I was a kid, Robert and Ed Hale were just two of the finest people we knew. They were leaders in their community, in so many things — farm organizations, Farm Bureau and 4-H. I've gone to their home often for summer Farm Bureau meetings on the lawn. When you went to Hale's, it was an experience.

Everybody knew the Hale brothers. Ed and John Hale died in recent years. The last brother, Robert, died on February 25,2002, at the age of 94.

In the 1970s, the Hale brothers hosted an old fashioned threshing bee on their farm. A fellow named Roger Byrne, from Racine, who loved old tractors and engines, organized it. John Hale, who was a railroad engineer for a great share of his life, owned the steam engine, so naturally they had the event there on the Hale farm, and it was a memorable day. The ladies from Racine Methodist Church served pie, coffee, Mexi-burgers and all that good stuff that we remember.

They held that threshing bee at Hales' for a few years in the early 1970s, and then they carried on a few years more with Threshing Days in Racine, at the Clarence Klenke farm. Eventually the whole thing moved into the Root River Antique Power Association at the 5-Js campground north of Spring Valley on Highway 63, and it continues there annually.

It's the love of these things from the past that makes these old threshing bees continue today in farm states like Iowa, Nebraska, Minnesota and the Dakotas. They use steam engines and tractors, both. They hold one here at the Olmsted County History Center every year during their mechanical history days in late July or early August, when actual threshing would have been going on. They have some old fashioned threshers, and the men who run them are men who had grown up with the steam engine and know how it was done. It's good to know that a certain group of people care enough about history to preserve it for those who would otherwise never have the opportunity to experience it first hand. I've been fortunate, being able to see things like this in my own life on a working farm.

I Love Those Tractors!

I was always intrigued by farm tractors. They had all that power, while we were farming with horses. I got to know everybody's tractor in the neighborhood. Fred Baker bought a new Massey Harris with huge rubber tires in 1937. This was an eye-opener, since so many tractors then were still on steel wheels with those dangerous protruding lugs.

Bill Baker had a 1936 Allis Chalmers U. Walter Engel had an F-20 Farmall, and Harry Carothers a DC Case. Theodore and Otto Baker had two tractors, a 10-20 and a 15-30 McCormick-Deering, both of them with wide steel wheels with lugs.

In 1940, Art and Loretta Finn and their son Roy moved into the neighborhood from Byron, and soon afterward they bought a John Deere B. Dad liked that one, so we ordered one in 1943, but we had to wait until after the war for it to be delivered.

Earlier, between 1938 and 1940, I'd seen Lyle Buchholtz driving a John Deere D tractor when they lived across the field from us. (That was before Lyle came down with polio in 1941.)

In the late 1940s, the Pat Horan family moved onto the farm adjoining ours on the east. Soon they bought a Massey Harris 44-4 Cylinder, then a Massey-Harris 44-6. There was a lot of power in those tractors, and I remember how their son Lyle Horan's eyes really lit up when he talked tractors.

Today I have a few miniature tractors, John Deere, Case and Farmall, on a shelf in my den. Oh, the happy memories they bring back of those days when we went from horsepower to tractor power!

Early Farm Auction Sales

Farm auction sales probably haven't changed a lot from when I was a lad. The main difference today is that there are more electronic approaches to this whole thing. You have cell phones and calculators and things like that. But there's still an auctioneer. There still needs to be a crowd. There still needs to be a farm.

Sadly, many farms have been sold during the years just to pay off a debt, sometimes going back to the Depression years. Back in the 1930s, they had what they called the Sheriff's Sale. Farmers would band together, and they would bid maybe a penny or two, just enough to satisfy the law that said the farm had to be sold. The auctioneer knew, and he wouldn't push too hard. When the auction was over, a little money, very little, was given to the farmer, but the regulation was fulfilled, the auction sale would happen. Then the farmer could buy his farm back again for what was paid for it. Those things happened before I was old enough to get into the auction sales.

But I remember in the mid- to upper-1930s, when I was starting to go to auction sales with my Dad, oftentimes you went just because it was a neighbor, and you were curious. You wanted to see how something sold. Sometimes you bought something when you didn't expect to. My Dad was always coming home with buckets full of junk which he'd paid maybe a quarter for.

The auctioneer would start the auction with all the little stuff, the small tools. They always had buckets of junk spread out on the hayrack. There's a half-used roll of barbed wire. Here's three fence posts. Here's a pretty good jack for your car. Here's a plane, a saw, a hammer, nails.

I can hear the auctioneer say, "A quarter! 50 cents! Homer, give me 50 cents!" Finally Dad would nod, and he'd have bought two buckets full of junk.

Usually, when he got home, he found out that he had some pretty good, valuable things, along with the junk. There'd be tools, nails, bolts.

At these sales, you could buy the kind of things that pile up, that farmers use — window panes maybe. Sometimes you might even buy a cow. I can recall one time, when I was a little fellow back in the mid-1930s, my folks coming up to the Thurber farm auction near Rochester, out about where Willow Creek Golf Course is now, and buying four fine dairy cows.

One other thing you could buy at an auction was farm machinery, whether it was tractors, or old junk machinery, or good machinery. During the early 1940s, when tractors were not being made because of the war effort, the sale of new tractors came to a standstill. As I said earlier, we had to wait three years for our new tractor. So when farmers had a tractor to sell at auction, the government, the local commodity control office, would put a sealed bid price on it. This was a maximum price that could be bid on this particular item. Of course, the newer the item, the more expensive it could be. Mainly it was tractors back then. We hadn't gotten into combines yet, or corn pickers, in the late 1930s or early 1940s. They were just not being made yet in big numbers. Tractors were the big thing, and anything to do with the war effort, like tires.

I recall in 1942 Dad and I went to an auction sale in the heart of little Eyota, Minnesota, and looked at a little John Deere B tractor. It was just what we wanted. So we put our name in the hat. All the people who wanted that tractor put their names in the hat. That meant you were willing to pay $540 — that was the sealed auction bid price on that little tractor. After that, you were on the luck of the draw. Everybody was hoping his name would be drawn from the hat, and that he was the one that would be the buyer. The story always went around, that so-and-so had a lot of friends, and they stuffed his name in there 25 times, "and you know he bought them a beer afterwards." Well, we put our name in and we hoped, but we didn't get it. Somebody else did. After that phase of a farm auction, during the war, as my Dad said, "Only one person laughs — the winner."

Going to an auction sale was always interesting. You saw a lot of neighbors, you saw a lot of strangers. There was always a certain sadness to a farm auction, because it usually meant that something bad had happened. The announcement might read that, "Due to an accidental death, Mrs. So-and-so is selling all her property at such-and-such a time and such-and-such a date, clerking by such-and-such a bank, auctioneer is...."

The church ladies aid always sold a meal there. They had Mexi-burgers, or some type of hamburgers, hot dogs, pie, ice cream and coffee. Those were the standard things at farm auctions then, and still are today. Wherever there's an auction, there's got to be food, because when people are standing around, especially if they're out in the cold, they will buy food when they won't buy anything else.

The auctioneers themselves are a story. Many of those old-time auctioneers, I'm sure, were self-trained. I recall Rochester auctioneers L.A. and M.E. Fellows — Leonard Fellows and his son, Marty. They were good auctioneers. There was another auctioneer named Fred Hilmer, out here at Golden Hill. In Stewartville, we had Roger Griffin. And there were many others during the years. You got to know them, and they knew you.

I can remember the Ed Hunt auction, early on. Ed and Louise Hunt lived about a mile or so east of us. The auctioneer would ask the farmer to go ahead and describe the cow. "Well, how about this cow? What can she do?"

And Ed said, "This cow is a good cow. She's right in all four quarters. She milks in all four quarters. Anybody could milk her. Even my wife could milk her."

The auctioneer replied, "You mean your wife has always milked her," and there was a great burst of laughter around the sales ring.

Those were the kind of things that the farmers and auctioneers would say.

I heard my dad tell that story many times. The auctioneers had many stories. They were always telling stories. They wanted to keep the crowd laughing, keep them happy, because then the people were more ready to buy. The buyers answered the auctioneer with as little as a nod or a wink. Some buyers did not want it to be known that they were bidding. They would maybe raise a hand or say, "Yup!" Usually, there was a person in the ring, working the auction, spotting, and when somebody looks at him and they wink, he will say, "Yep!" and the auctioneer will know that a bid's been made. This goes on while the auctioneer's still chanting, keeping the price going.

It is an art indeed. My cousin Dale Turner, of whom I've spoken before, changed professions from farming and went into auctioneering in 1952. He went to the auctioneering school in Mason City, Iowa, and became a fine auctioneer. He later developed a career in hotel management at the Kahler Hotel in Rochester.

Most auctioneers have to start out by doing the church basket social, doing the rummage sale — doing things that are free. Auctioneers, all their lives, will do some things free. I've seen our 1st District Representative, Gil Gutknecht, doing the Salvation Army Auction, free. There are various others that do auctions free, going in a series for a fall festival at St. Francis

Church Parish, or St. Pius Church. Wherever a church is having a fall festival, and there is also an auction, they'll be there, and usually they don't charge for it. John Kruesel, a well-known Rochester auctioneer, has for years given his time for the Rochester Arts Center's Whole Earth Auction. These people have done so much, and they continue helping the community.

The Egg and Milk Men

Growing up on the farm, I recall sometimes getting rides home from school with the egg man, Red Christianson, from Lanesboro. Often he would have a sandwich left over at 3:30 or 4 in the afternoon, and maybe he had a cookie or a banana, and he would share it with me when he gave me a ride. He would pick me up on the way home, because he was going to stop and pick up a case of eggs at our farm. I was always cleaning eggs, because this was part of our income. We would sell Red a case of eggs, and he would put them in the truck and take them back to Lanesboro Produce Company. We sold a case or two of eggs every week (that's 36 dozen, or 432 eggs to the case.)

When the folks started paying me for cleaning eggs, they would give me any change they got when Red paid them. He always paid in cash. They would give me the change. One time, I remember, I got 4 cents. Next time it might be a nickel, or a quarter, whatever. One time I came in with the money, and I said to the folks, disappointedly, "Oh, just dollars!" Just dollar bills, I meant, no change, no money for me. Years later, Red opened the Feed and Egg Produce store in Stewartville, and he was there for many years.

My parents in those early years had several hundred laying hens, because eggs provided cash income. Cream or milk was also sold, and those items supplied the cash-flow for day-to-day living. Occasionally there would be veal calves or boars or gilts for sale. Hogs were valuable both on the market and for breeding purposes. All of these facets of farming were vital to our financial survival.

One of our faithful milk men from 1941 to 1944 was Byron Lowrie. He would come by regularly to collect the milk from our dairy cows. He later became a farm implement dealer, and we bought our Ferguson 30 tractor from him in late 1952. I loved that little tractor. It could snake along three 14-inch plows. It was a little tractor, but it had a lot of power.

Another milk man in the 1930s was Francis Haney, from Simpson, Minnesota. We didn't sell milk directly to Rochester Dairy. We sold our cream to Simpson Creamery, which in turn brought it up to Rochester Dairy. Elaine and I would sometimes ride to school with Francis Haney in his little cream truck.

How and why did we sell cream instead of milk? We had a small herd of milk cows, and dad felt it best to separate the whole milk that came from the cow into cream, which we would sell, and skim milk, that we would feed to baby calves and hogs. Our livestock diversity of cows, hogs and horses was important. It all helped to pay off the farm debt and to buy new machinery.

I love the memory of turning the crank on that DeLaval Cream Separator, that was made in Holland. Dad bought it brand-new for $100 in 1935. It had a big bright red seven to eight gallon open bowl-type tank with a white enamel interior, mounted on top of a heavy base stand to hold the fresh milk from the cows. When the last cow was milked, I would start slowly turning the handle, which set up a rotating action of high-speed metal discs that separated the milk from the cream. A bell rang to keep us from turning the crank too rapidly while separating. There were two spigots, one for cream and one for skim milk, sending it out into other five-gallon cooler cans. There's just nothing nicer than drinking fresh, newly-separated milk.

But, oh, the work for Mother each morning, to completely wash all the milking pails, cans, discs and the tank, after we carried it to the well-house when we finished the morning milking!

In the early 1940s, we quit separating milk ourselves and started selling whole milk, as farmers do today, through pipelines and bulk tanks and bulk trucks.

hives, with 1800 colonies, producing over 400 fifty-gallon barrels of honey a year. During those years, the price of honey rose from 14 cents to 50 cents a pound. At this writing, Harold and Mrs. Smith have been married 65 years, and still live in Spring Valley.

There were other great hired men. Marvin Behrens of Eyota was always such a polite person. I don't remember where Floyd Van Wert came from, but I do recall how well-dressed he was when he went to town on Saturday night, complete with suit and tie. Then there was Bill Bramble of Pleasant Grove. I remember Bill Bramble shocking grain in hot weather and telling me, "the hotter the weather, the better." I was a little lad, carrying cold water out to Bill in a two-quart crock-jug, and my, how he could drink that cold water! He really set up a lot of grain shocks, which was so vital after the grain binder went through before threshing started.

Stanley Livingston, also from Pleasant Grove, helped Dad put a new channel iron roof on the barn in the summer of 1940. We had purchased that iron roof from Frank Cermak at Chatfield Lumber Yard for $150. There were two lengths of iron for that hip roof, eleven feet on the lower part and nine feet on the upper part. It was all done using only ladders, no staging. I was nine years old that summer, and my job was on the ground, cutting two 23-inch boards to close in the cupola which was always a haven for pigeons. When you had pigeons, you always had unwanted hunters shooting at them, putting holes in the roof and the old weathervane horse atop the cupola. There were three lightning rods on the forty-four foot ridge of the roof. That iron roof really dressed up the old barn, originally built in 1902. The barn is gone now, as are all the other buildings on the farm, with the exception of the hog house that was rebuilt in 1938.

In early 2001, I read the obituary in the Rochester Post-Bulletin of Boyd Baker, age 80, of Chatfield. Boyd had been a good hired man working for Dad the summer of 1936, when he was just 16. Boyd was a very likeable young man, and I'm sure I drove him crazy that summer. I was four, going on five, and I always tagged along, hanging on to the hammer-loop on his overalls' right hip. Wherever he went, I'd be hanging on. He never told me to stop, but I'm sure he must have felt nervous with me always beside him while he was trying to work. One day he cut off that hammer loop, and I really felt lost. Boyd's brothers Gordon and Norbert also worked for Dad at various times. The Baker family lived next to the stone church three and a half miles southeast of our farm. Later I'd attend Chatfield High with Maurice and Jon Baker and their sister Margie.

They Rolled Their Own

Cigarettes today sell over the counter for $3 to $5 a pack. I wonder how many laborers remember how to roll their own smokes.

This was the procedure used by the hired men on our farm during the 1930s and 1940s. A man would carry in the breast pocket of his shirt a small cloth bag filled with finely-chopped leaf tobacco. He also had a roll of flat cigarette papers. He would hold the paper between the forefinger and long finger of his left hand (if he was right-handed). Then, slowly and gently, he would pour the tobacco into the oval-shaped "weed." When it was full enough, he rolled it into a cylindrical cigarette and licked the edge of the paper with his tongue, supplying enough moisture to make it stick.

Then he would put it in his mouth and strike a match. If he had a match book, he'd strike the match on its cover, but if he was using wooden matches, he would lift his right knee, so that the cloth of his britches was pulled tight against the back side of his thigh. Then he would strike the match on the smooth surface of his trousers, and there was flame.

There was always the danger of sparks out-of-doors, with the straw stacks and all. The safest place to smoke was in an open field. My family did not smoke, so if a hired man was smoking in the house, Mother would put out an old dish for him to use as an ash tray. If there was no ash tray handy, the smoker would often flake the tobacco ash into the cuff of his overalls pants leg.

I must have seen these men making their cigarettes hundreds of times in those years. I can't recall any of them ever smoking a pipe, although Rob Hudson, our next-door neighbor to the west, always smoked a corncob pipe.

Harley, age 10, and "Jack" the St. Bernard Dog.

My Dad, Homer W. Flathers, in 1951, surrounded by several steers and spotted Poland China boars.

Hale's Barn — 202 feet long . . . a Clint Kueker illustration.

Auctioneers illustration by Clint Kueker

This is the last major building on the farm, the 20 by 20 hog house, rebuilt in 1938-39. Harley cared for 8 sows with new litters when he was 8 years old each morning before school. That meant cleaning, bedding and feeding. He wanted those pens to be a "show place." Photo by Leonard L. Smith, Sept. 2003

Hale farm with 202 foot long barn 5 miles northeast of Racine, Minnesota. Many great 4-H & Fillmore County Farm Bureau meetings were held in this beautiful home . . . built in the early 1900s.

The three Hale brothers at Steam Threshing Day at their farm August 1971. L-R Edward, John, a licensed Steam-Locomotive railroad engineer, and Robert, standing beside John's steam engine.

Steam threshing in early 1970s. Robert Hale pitches grain bundle into the slat-belt feeder of the 36 inch Minneapolis grain separator. Machine is belt driven by steam engine 60-75 feet away, thus the long drive belt.

Steam thresher in action. Standing on ground next to wheel is Stewartville black smith Stan Lecy, with a love for steam engines. On the platform is John Hale, owner and engineer.

Stan Lecy & John Hale—We watched them driving this "giant" steam engine thru Stewartville's July 4, 1949 Celebration Street Parade. It's the height of the polio epidemic and 8 days later Harley's life changes with this mysterious virus.

Moment 4

What Depression? Christmas on the Farm

If Homer and Vivian Flathers, and their children Harley and Elaine, were poor during those Depression years, we kids didn't know it. We always had ample to eat and a roof over our heads, just like my Dad had promised that we would, if we all worked together. So what did it take to put together a wonderful Christmas for a family of four during the Depression when there was very little money?

We didn't have money to buy a Christmas tree from the store, where they cost $1 to $2. I recall my mother going out to the pine trees on the lawn or in the woods near the house, and cutting off a limb or two, and making them into a nice Christmas tree. She had a knack for doing that, as a number of mothers did. On the morning of the 24th, the day before Christmas, she would put that tree up in the living room, and decorate it with those very special little ornaments, and it was beautiful.

Then in the afternoon, she'd say to us kids, "Okay, I'm going to go upstairs now, and I'm going to help Santa." Well, that turned us kids on. We knew what she was doing. She was going up there to wrap packages while Dad was out doing the chores, feeding the cows, milking whatever cows there were to milk in the winter, feeding the horses and pigs. And while she was upstairs, my sister and I would get over next to the stove in the living room. There was a grate above it, where the stovepipe went up through the floor to heat the rooms upstairs. And we listened very quietly together. We tried not to let Mother know that we knew what she and Santa were up to. Once we heard a little doll cry, and of course, my sister let out a scream.

In the evening, when Dad came in and supper was done, Elaine and I would put on a program for the folks. We'd put three or four chairs together in the living room, and one of us would get up and speak a piece while the other sat in the chair and listened. I suppose we applauded each other. Then we would have old Pooch, the black dog, speak a piece. The way we did that was my sister would gently step on his tail, and he'd go, "Arrrh!"

Everybody had a part in Christmas Eve. My Dad would come in, carrying a big sack, a big grocery bag full of stuff which we kids had not known anything about. There were some good things in there, maybe some toys, definitely some things for the home — clothes, maybe a shirt and sweater — things that Mother and Dad had picked out before and hidden someplace. I remember one year I got a new comb. Well, I suppose a boy who is 8 or 9 years old had better start appreciating a comb. There were many other things, too. He came in with the bouncing sack on his shoulder, saying, "I want my Christmas now! I want my Christmas now!" Of course, we kids were just filled with excitement.

After supper, Mother would read a little Christmas story from the Bible, and we'd sing some Christmas carols, and then we'd open our gifts.

We weren't a big family, but it was a good family. Mother and Dad showed us a lot of love, and we're thankful for that.

Sunday Night Music at Home

Another thing we enjoyed in those years was Sunday night music. We loved Sunday night programming on the radio. Dad and I would hurry up to get our chores done, and at 5 o'clock we'd be back in the house to listen to Gene Autry, "Our Miss Brooks," and other programs. But many times on a Sunday evening there would be homemade music. Our homemade music was pretty good. My mother played the piano beautifully. She played at our church for over 40 years, first the piano, then later something called the organo, and then later the organ, as the church budget allowed the congregation to move up to a better musical instrument. She played at a lot of weddings, a lot of funerals, and taught kids, too.

She and my Dad would often write songs for someone who was going to have a wedding shower or a wedding reception, usually some gosh-awful humorous poetry that went along with a well-known tune. My Dad had a knack for poetry. He would think up poetry as he sat milking cows by hand. During the 1930s, he was a very prolific poet. He wrote some beautiful poems about children, the out-of-doors, nature. And Mother could put music together, so they would collaborate nicely. Often it was humorous. So and so would be getting married, and Homer and Vivian would write a song for them! Weddings, showers, funerals, anniversaries, you name it, they were there, singing, telling stories.

At home on Sunday nights, Mother would sit down and play a number of songs on the piano, and Dad would chime in with the violin. He was pretty good for a self-taught violinist. I don't know where he learned to play the violin, but he was okay. I can remember as a little fellow of three or four or five, sitting back on the davenport, enjoying that music, not realizing at the time how it was rubbing off on me.

Home-Made Ice Cream

Another thing we always enjoyed during the winter was making ice cream. There's nothing like homemade ice cream. We didn't often buy ice cream in the store. Goodness sakes, that was expensive! Why, in 1940, it was 15 cents for a pint, and 31 cents for a quart! Once in a while, on a hot summer day, Dad would come home with store-bought ice cream, and boy! No matter what time it was, we were all there. We had to eat it quickly before it melted, but that was no problem.

In the winter, we made our own ice cream. We did not have electricity. We did not have an ice box. We had a one gallon canister-type ice cream freezer, with a crank that turned in a wooden pail and a hole in the bottom for the ice to melt and run out. Dad would bring in a washtub full of snow. If you didn't have ice, didn't happen to have a pond there with ice you could cut up, snow worked very well. It took just a little longer.

Mother would make the custard, mix the milk and eggs and everything together. Then she would put it in the freezer, and guess who was ready to crank that freezer? It was I. And guess who was ready to lick the paddle, as soon as it was done? It was I.

And then I'd say, "Mom, I think I've got that paddle clean. Can I just sample a little more before you put it away?"

She'd say, "No. It's 4 o'clock. We're going to save some for supper."

It was always vanilla. You mixed the milk and the eggs and the vanilla, and added the snow and then the elbow grease. And you had homemade ice cream.

That was on a Saturday evening, and if we worked it right, maybe there would be some ice cream yet by Monday morning. The reason why I liked this was that not only did we have ice cream for Sunday noon and Sunday night, but on Monday morning, when Mother packed my lunch, she would take a 4-ounce cold cream jar — I can see it yet, an empty Pond's Cold Cream jar — and fill it with ice cream. I would take it to school with me in my lunch pail, and when I got to school, I'd put it in a little snow bank down beside the steps. Nobody else knew that ice cream was there. Then just at noon, when the bell rang for lunch, and the teacher was about ready to get the hot lunches out, I would go and bring in my ice cream and set it on my desk with my lunch.

The kids would say, "Look, Harley's got ice cream!"

And I'd just smile. I only had one spoon, so I couldn't share. That was fun.

The Be-Good Club

Looking back on my childhood, when I was about three to six years old, I remember how I was constantly "bugging" my sister Elaine. She was five years older, and really quite good to me, but I suppose I felt that I wasn't getting enough attention from my mother. And we quarreled, Elaine and I. Nothing she did was ever right.

Finally my mother started something she called the "Be-Good Club." She made two columns on a sheet of paper and put it up in the kitchen. My name was on the left side, and Elaine's was on the right. It seemed that my side always had a long list of infractions on it. Whenever I said a bad word about her, Elaine would quickly write it down on the list: "Harley said 'Phooey'...Harley said 'Pig'....Harley said 'Cow'," and so on. I'm sure that I said all those things to her when I got mad.

It seemed like Elaine was so perfect, because there were no infractions on her side of the list. Finally Mother kindly intervened and wrote down a couple of things under Elaine's name. That made me feel better. Of course, the main problem was that Elaine could write, and I couldn't!

Lightning

On a Thursday afternoon, May 29, 1941, my father came home from his weekly visit to Stewartville to pick up supplies, and he was crying. He told us, "Lightning has just killed Dickie Rogers."

Dick Rogers' death really hit the whole community. He was just 13 years old. Dick's parents, Arthur and Ruth Rogers, had been our neighbors for some time. They were married about the same time as my parents, and two of their five children were the same age as my sister and I. The Rogers family farm was a mile and a half straight west of ours, right across from the district 119 school house, where their children went to school. (It was the same farm where Belva Dumez Bernard had lived when she and my father were growing up.) Our family and the Rogers' went through all those Depression years together. The families were close. We children played together, and the parents went back and forth. Dickie's death was a great shock to us all.

Dick had been out on his bicycle with a friend, Leonard Smith, age 14, who lived in Pleasant Grove. They had been checking their gopher traps in the middle afternoon. When the storm came up, they started for home. They were riding easterly on highway 30 about four miles from Stewartville, and were about two miles from Dick's home. At the crossroads, Dick turned south towards his home, and Leonard Smith turned north.

Dick never made it home. We never quite knew whether he was walking, pushing his bike, or if he was trying to ride through the wind — the wind and rain were heavy that day. He was about 500 feet or so from home when the lightning struck him and he was snuffed out, just like that.

Through their tears, the neighbors rallied to help Arthur and Ruth Rogers. We all thought Dickie was a super boy. He was number two in the family of five children. His older brother Donald was about 16. Then there was Robert, who was 12, and Marjorie, who would be 10 only a few days after her brother's death. She was just three months older than I. And then there was little Ardith, who was about three.

Dickie Rogers could do everything. He could fix things, and his mother depended on him. At 13, he could even drive the car, although his legs were barely long enough to reach the pedals. He would back the car out and take her places, maybe all the way into Stewartville. He was always there, running errands for his mother when no one else was handy. His death was a terrible blow.

When it came time to plan the funeral, my father and some others said, "We're going to go door to door to collect funds to help with this funeral." My Dad went to several places. People would put in a dollar or two, one gave $5, and suddenly he had $30. Then another neighbor up to the west, a man named Cliff McGrand, said, "I'm going to go get a hundred dollars," and he came back with $99. Through the course of the next couple of days, the neighbors collected over $500, and they put it in my father's hands.

We got through Friday and Saturday. Little Dick's funeral was going to be Sunday at 2 pm. I can remember the pall bearers. Harry Geerdes, Dale Turner and Gilbert Doten were all neighbors close by. Howard Sackett and two brothers, Leo and Claude Bernard, were the others. Because we were friends, I was one of four young boys who were asked to be honorary pall bearers. The others were Harlan Baker, Dick Engel and Gilbert Doten's brother Edward. (A decade later Edward Doten would die at age 19 in a Navy plane training accident off the coast of Florida.)

The funeral began on Sunday afternoon, right there in the home. I can still see the hearse, owned by Patrick Griffin of the P.H. Griffin Funeral Home in Stewartville, backing up to the front porch, the men rolling the casket out, and the pall bearers putting it in the hearse. Then we all headed for Pleasant Grove to the Church of Christ, a beautiful old brick building.

A funeral is a scary thing for a little boy of ten. Here we were, the honorary pall bearers, and they told us, "Okay, you walk behind the casket, as we're rolling it in, and then you can sit right over here in the front seat." It seemed to me a long service. We were all confused. Our friend was gone.

After the funeral, we went to the cemetery at Pleasant Grove, just a quarter mile away. I can remember all of this so clearly. When it was all over, we went home. Nowadays we would all go to a luncheon at a church hall to have some refreshments after the funeral, but at that time, we all just went home. It was a sorrowful time. It was June first when he was buried, and Monday, June second, was his sister Marjorie's tenth birthday.

The next day, my father and I took a load of hogs to market in Spring Valley. They were barrows and gilts, well finished hogs, probably 240 to 260 pounds each. We called my cousin Ken Raabe at Spring Valley to bring his truck, load the hogs and take them to the Spring Valley stock yard. There was a buyer who might have been from Hormel's.

As they weighed the hogs, my Dad and I were trying to guess what we were going to get for them. He had a better idea than I, because he could look at them and estimate so much per hundred, and I just guessed by the whole lot. He said, "I think we're going to get $575 for these hogs." I don't know how many there were, probably 20 to 25 hogs.

I said, "Dad, I think we're going to get $525."

When the man had weighed them, he said, "Awright! $522 and a dime!" It made me feel good that I was closer, although it would have been nicer if Dad had been closer — we'd have taken home more money.

On the way back, we stopped at the Rogers family's farm. Dad went in and saw Ruth Rogers, who was still in great mourning, and he presented her with something over $500, probably more than enough to pay for the funeral. It was the money that was given by the friends and neighbors.

Our family was very close to the Rogers family in those years. I remember that we kids played together a lot. As a little fellow, I was always one that wasn't watching out for myself very well. I always had to be right there, with my nose in what was going on. One time, in the winter, we were at the Rogers home. I was maybe 7 or 8 years old, and Bob Rogers was 9 or 10. He had some balloons all blown up and tied to a piece of cardboard. Then he decided he wanted to cut one off, so he got out his jackknife. He was holding the cardboard right up in front of his face, cutting it, and I was right on the other side, peering around the cardboard to see what was happening, my nose right up close. And the knife slipped. It went right across the bridge of my nose, and boy, did the blood flow! And did I cry! Fortunately, the knife didn't go into an eye.

They patched up my nose right away, but that was me. I just had to have my nose right in there where things were going on. My Dad told me, "Son, you've got to start looking out for yourself. I will not always be there to look out for you."

We used to play with the Rogers kids in their barn. The old barn had a driveway in it, so they could drive a wagonload of hay in and mow the hay back on both sides. We kids loved playing up in the hay loft. We would run and jump across that eight to ten foot opening, trying to land in the hay on the other side. Well, one time, Bob Rogers didn't make it. He fell and broke both legs on the concrete floor. Boy, that was a setback! I can see Bob yet, lying in bed for weeks with double casts on his legs.

We helped out Art and Ruth Rogers when their last child, little Ardith Gail, was born in the winter of 1938. Our car at the time was working a little better than theirs, so they asked Dad if he could take Ruth to St. Mary's Hospital when it was time for her to have the baby. So he did, and she was there for a few days, and then he went up again and brought mother and baby home. Little Ardith was very sickly early on, quite frail, and she had to go back to the hospital again a few days later. Again dad took her up and brought her back. He said later that he brought that baby home from the hospital three times after she was born.

After a while, the Rogers family moved to another farm in the neighborhood. Their kids grew up and left home. Marjorie, my friend, married Jack Campion and had a large family. She eventually died of cancer some years ago. Friends keep coming and going in our lives.

Today that farm where the Rogers family lived is owned and operated by Jan Sackett. But shortly after the Rogers family left, Leonard and Helen Welch moved in with their six children. They were a fine family. Leonard's brother Howard lived just half a mile away to the north, and the brothers worked together. Their Uncle Walter Welch lived about a mile away to the west, so there were Welches all around there. They were great folks, good friends of our family.

Well, on July 17, 1951, a decade after little Dickie Rogers was killed by lightning, a tragic baler accident on that same farm took the life of Leonard Welch at age 38. He and his brother Howard were working together, and there was a problem with the baler. Leonard reached in to fix it, got caught in the machinery, and died instantly. It was a tragic thing. Helen Welch, bless her heart, went on and raised those six children just miraculously, all by herself.

After Dickie Rogers was killed on May 29, 1941, I recall reading in a newspaper article that "Others in the area who have been hit by lightning include Homer Flathers, struck on May 29, 1926." That was my Dad.

He was a young farmer then, with a young wife — they'd been married four years, and had a brand new little baby, my sister Elaine. I don't know whether he had a hired man at that time or not. But being quite young, just starting out, chances are he was doing everything alone.

There was a storm brewing overhead that morning, and he'd gone out to the pasture to bring in the cows. The cows had come and passed by him on up the lane to the barn, and he was waiting for one more horse. It was an old horse, and it might have been blind — blind horses could go by the sound of a person's voice. Anyway, the horse was coming. Dad put his hand on the wheel rim of an old abandoned seeder standing in the corner of the pasture. (Farmers are notorious for leaving a machine, when its usefulness is over, in the corner of the pasture, or in the corner by the willows, or wherever it was when they last used it.) He looked up and said to himself, "I wonder if I can get home before that storm?" And suddenly, boom! He was hit by lightning.

He lay there in the mud for a long time, he never knew how long. When finally he came to, he began to work his way home. He couldn't hold his head up. He used to tell us, "My head was down, my chin was on my chest. I couldn't figure out what had happened to me. I just stumbled on home."

My mother was tending to a baby, and he heard the baby crying. He said, "Whose baby is that?"

She said, "It's ours. Little Elaine. She's 17 days old." He didn't know that they had a baby. He was really hit hard.

Somehow they managed to contact Dr. Baird in Stewartville, who came out, examined him, and said, "You have been struck by lightning."

My father had been wearing a wool hat and rubber boots. When he put his hand on the wheel, that made an iron contact, a conductor. He was hit on the top of the head, and had severe burns on the back of his neck and in the middle of his back. Then the electricity went down his leg and burned a hole in the bottom of his foot. The doctor said, "Well, having the wool hat and the rubber boots, that's probably what saved your life." Then he said, "There's not much we can do but give you a lot of rest. Try to take it very easy." I think they went back to see that doctor several times. He told my Dad, "You're probably going to be able to live a pretty normal life. You're going to have a heart murmur, but you can live with a heart murmur. But you've got to have a lot of rest."

All those early years, I never knew why Dad had to have so much rest between every job. He would just be exhausted. I realize now that it's like having a hole in your heart. Something there isn't working right. He could never really get a good, big, deep breath of air. And yet he was very robust. He had a good physique, he was strong, and he did a lot of work. But he suffered from electrical storms for the rest of his life. After his death in 1977, I realized what a struggle he put up all those years, just to keep his strength.

Whenever an electrical storm would be coming, he would tell us 24 hours in advance. He'd say, "There's an electrical storm coming." He'd tell the boys in the threshing ring, when they were threshing, that a storm was coming, and they'd laugh. "Ha, ha, ha, there isn't either!" He'd say, "Yup. Be here in 24 hours." Well, the next day it would be raining and lightning, right about that same time of day.

He could feel it. He was charged up electrically. He would be so charged, he'd have to come into the house and lie down on that old cot in the kitchen. My mother would get a cold, wet cloth to put on his forehead. Then my sister and I, or Mother and I, would each take one of his hands and hold it, and draw the electricity out of him. It just came right out; we could feel the tingle. We did that for a lot of years.

Later in his life, it got a little easier. I think as time went by it subsided somewhat, because he didn't talk about it as much. But in those early years, it was always a problem.

He could never go near an electric welding shop. He would be in Stan Lecy's blacksmith shop in Stewartville — if you're a farmer, you're always going to a blacksmith shop — and when Stan would use the acetylene torch, there was no problem, because it was powered by gas. But when he used the arc welder, Dad had to get up and out. He not only had to get out of the blacksmith shop, he had to get about a block away, to escape the effects of that electric welder.

In 1947, when we finally put in the electric lines from the REA, he wondered, "What's this going to do?" But it wasn't as bad as he thought it was going to be. He could feel a little tingle when the radio went on, or when the electric motor on the washing machine started, various things like that. He could feel the electricity from the transformer on the yard pole, or the yard light.

I remember the paper said that in addition to Homer Flathers being hit by lightning, another man named Claude Bentley of Stewartville had been killed by lightning years earlier. These things happened. Yet after my Dad was hit in 1926, he lived another 51 years, till he was a bit over 79 years old. He lived a full, productive life, even though I know it was a very difficult one, because of the aftereffects of that lightning strike.

The Adventure of the Three Bull Calves

Sometimes, when I was a small lad, the grass in the pastures would get short in mid-summer. It didn't take long, if the cows had been out early, because cows eat pastures rapidly, and suddenly you realize, we need more grass. When that happened, Dad would say to his two children, Harley and Elaine, "Hey, herd the cows." That meant that after milking in the morning, we would take the cows out alongside the road, where there was always lush grass all the way up and down, a quarter mile or more in each direction.

For many summers my sister and I had the duty of keeping an eye on the cows grazing along the roadside. It really was a joy, as I look back on it, although it might not have seemed like a joy at the time. We generally tried to keep the cows on the side of the road next to the farm. We didn't want them crossing the road, because sometimes it could be a busy highway. And you always found one or two cows that wanted to cross the road, so we had to keep a close eye on them.

We kept the cows out there for a couple of hours at least, until they were satisfied. Then, after they'd had a good fill of fresh grass, we brought them back and put them in the pasture. That was part of our modus operandi during those early years.

There was a row of wild willow trees, or willow bushes, growing on the south side of the road in a kind of wet ditch. Along the bank, before the roadsides were mowed, there would be wild roses and strawberries or raspberries, growing wild. I can recall picking wild raspberries. We would wait for them to come out, and then Elaine picked the berries and took them home, where Mother made them into a pie. That was one of the pleasant things about herding the cows along the roadside.

When the cows finished grazing, we might take out some calves and tie them outside between the road and the fence. In the summer of 1940, we had three little bull calves, a red one, a black one, and one that was a sort of spotted maroon, what they call roan. They all had definite names. The roan was called Guppie, because he gulped his milk so greedily, as calves will do. The red one was named Hanky, because his mother had been named Sneeze, and his grandmother had been named Pepper. Old Pepper looked like pepper, and her daughter was named Sneeze, because when you have pepper you sneeze, and when a sneeze comes, then you grab a red hanky, so that's how the red calf became Hanky. That was my mother's way of naming calves. And the black one was named A.B. Trenton, because his mother was a Jersey, and the capital of New Jersey is Trenton, while A.B. stood for "almost black."

So there they were, Hanky, Guppie and A.B. Trenton — three bull calves. I suppose they were a month to six weeks old when we put them out there to graze by the roadside. We would carry water to them, and milk, and we tied them on a rope so they wouldn't stray. It wasn't a very long leash, because we didn't want them getting up in the road. We would go back and change their positions every once in a while, so they had fresh room to walk around in.

One morning when we awakened and went out to check on the calves, there were no calves. My, oh, my! The calves are missing! What has happened? Well, we soon figured out that they had been stolen. And what do you do then?

It was August, threshing time. My father was busy with the threshing. He was threshing with Uncle Henry Turner's ring, and as they threshed, he told the people what had happened. The other farmers that were with him probably made all kinds of suggestions and funny remarks and so on. The first chance he had, he went to the neighbors' house, where they had a phone, and called the sheriff, Knute Inglebrit. The sheriff's office was in Preston, the county seat of Fillmore county, twenty-five miles away from our farm.

This happened on a Friday. When my Dad called him, the sheriff said, "Well, I'm gonna keep thinking about this and we'll call you in the morning, or I'll just come out in the morning, and we'll make plans to see if we can take off." He added, "Maybe they have been stolen and taken to St. Paul." It was State Fair time, and there were always buyers looking for livestock at the State Fair.

About 9 or 10 in the morning, the sheriff came driving up to our farm, and he picked up Dad. They left and headed one hundred miles north to St. Paul, not knowing what was going to happen. They went to the South St. Paul stockyards, because the sheriff told my dad, "We've called the stockyards, and three calves are there. They're in a pen, they've been sealed in." It seems the buyers in South St. Paul were a bit suspicious of the two men that were selling these calves, just out of nowhere. They bought them for $40, but when the sheriff talked with the men, they weren't surprised to learn that the calves might have been stolen. That sheriff was pretty smart. He figured the men that stole those calves probably lived in the area of our farm, and they had gone to the Twin Cities to have a good time.

The men at the South St. Paul stockyards had a description of the truck that the calves came in, and they had written down the license plate on the truck. So the sheriff said, "Well, we'll wait a while. They've probably been over to the Fair spending some money and enjoying themselves. They're probably gonna start home soon."

It was almost like it was written for a TV script. Dad and the sheriff started back, driving down highway 52, and when they got about to Cannon Falls, they overtook this little pickup truck, moseying along, and there was the license plate that the men at the stockyards had told them about. They followed the truck quite a while.

Dad said, "Shall we take him?"

And the sheriff said, "Well, we're not in any big rush yet. We'll just follow a while, see what happens."

So they stayed back a ways, and they kept following. Finally, they overtook them, and pulled them over. Dad jumped out of his side of the sheriff's car, and the sheriff got out on his side, and they both went right back to stand by the truck.

Dad used to tell us, "I stood big and tall and burly on the other side, and the sheriff was on the driver's side, and those fellows were asking, 'What's happened? What's wrong? Why are you stopping us?'

"And the sheriff said, 'Well, I brought this man along because he needs to get his calves back.'"

There wasn't any struggle. They just surrendered right there, no problem. Because there were two vehicles, my Dad got in the thieves' pickup and sat in the passenger's side, while one of the culprits drove, and the sheriff took the other fellow with him. I don't know whether he put handcuffs on him or not — I would have, if I were a sheriff.

So there was my Dad in the truck. He told us, "I rode all the way back. I sat sort of sideways in the seat, looking right at him, with my arms right up here close by, and no funny business." If that man had started to pull anything, Dad would have had him under control.

They followed the sheriff all the way to Preston, to the county jail, and they took the men in and locked them up. It was late now, about 6 o'clock in the evening, and my dad was exhausted. Ever since he'd been struck by lightning back in 1926, he had tired easily. So he went out and lay down on the grassy lawn of the jail. Mrs. Inglebrit brought him out a nice meal, and he ate sitting in the shade, and drank cool lemonade. After that the sheriff brought Dad back home.

It was quite a day. My Dad told that story, and retold it — he'd get started, and somebody'd come along, and he'd tell it again. He was just reveling in it, because it happened the way it did.

The following day, we had a family reunion for Grandpa Theodore Raabe's 82nd birthday in Spring Valley, and I heard him telling it there. Then he went to the phone to call my cousin Kenneth Raabe, my mother's nephew. Ken was a resident of Spring Valley who had a truck he used to haul cattle and sweet corn back and forth. At that time, he was in St. Paul. Dad managed to locate him, and asked him to go over to South St. Paul on Monday and pick up these three calves and bring them back to our farm. He brought them back and unloaded them.

Dad said, "What do I owe you?"

And Kenneth said, "$7."

Now that isn't very much, and Dad paid it, but he just thought that was an awful price to pay — $7 to get those calves back!

Well, the calves were in fine shape, and they all lived happily for a couple of years, until eventually they were sent to market. But that's not the end of the story.

It wasn't long till those two men were tried and convicted. They were going to be sent, I think, to the St. Cloud Reformatory for several years. And somehow, before they were sent to prison, they broke out of the Fillmore County jail. A little later that year, the following article appeared in the Rochester Post-Bulletin, with a dateline from Rock Springs, Wyoming. The headline said, "Waitress Helps Trap Minnesota Fugitives." And the story went on to say, "A sharp-eyed waitress brought about the capture here of two men wanted by Minnesota authorities. The waitress, Nellie McIntosh, taking meals to prisoners at the city jail, noted pictures of two Minnesota fugitives on a bulletin board. She told police chief A.R. Hamilton she was certain she had seen the men in Rock Springs. Yesterday he apprehended the two, who he said admitted they broke jail at Preston, Minn., Sept. 1, while awaiting transfer to the Minnesota reformatory."

They were local boys, as the sheriff had suspected. And so then they did go on and spend their time in prison.

Mom Always Named the Calves

When my Dad purchased a cow or two at a farm auction sale, they didn't come with names attached (unless they were registered animals, and we weren't into owning a registered herd in the 1930s). Among our ten milking cows in a row of ten stanchions in the barn, we likely had six to seven different breeds. That was okay; the milk was all white. I remember when Dad bought those four Holstein cows in 1936 at the Thurber farm auction near Rochester, none of them had names.

But names were important for our farm animals, whether they were cows, horses, dogs or cats. There was one cow called Buttercup, who might almost have been termed the Franchise Player. She was a bit older, very gentle and an easy keeper. (An easy keeper is one who doesn't eat too much and really puts out the milk.) In those summer days when green pastures created milk, this cow was a real milk factory. I remember Dad, milking that cow by hand with the 13-quart galvanized milk pail held between his knees, telling me, "Son, I've got to dump this bucket and come back for more."

Going down the row from east to west, fresh straw beneath them and a squeaky-clean gutter behind them, those ten cows were called Betty, Lucy, Pansy, Roanie, Rosie, Buttercup, Lizzie, Topsy, Silver and Tillie. We had five other cows who shuffled in and out of that line-up, according to their annual "dry spells." They were Chewer, Sneeze, Pet, Pride and Pepper.

I've already told you about Pepper and her offspring, Sneeze and Hanky. Pride was the daughter of Pet. Mom thought that little heifer would bring a lot of pride to her mother, so she named her Pet's Pride, but we just called her Pride for short. Our Holstein bull was called Wimpy. He had a ring in his nose, was always a kind and gentle young man, and never caused us any problems.

There was one bull, whose name I've forgotten, who was a real trouble-maker. Even though he was tied up by his nose-ring and fenced in a stall, he went out through the back wall of the barn one day when he caught a whiff of a female outside. It looked like a straight-line wind had gone through that barn. He was really "out the door" after that episode, and Dad used A.I. (artificial insemination) on his cows thereafter.

Polly the Sheep

Merwin and Beth Leibold, from our church, had given my sister Elaine an orphan lamb. It was a little ewe lamb, and we named her Polly. Of course we all loved this lamb, and took care of her with plenty of T.L.C., or tender loving care.

And Polly the Sheep grew to full size and became ready for motherhood, and she was great with lamb. This was, I believe, in the winter of 1940. It was cold. And one night, unbeknownst to us, a dog or dogs attacked and killed Polly the Sheep.

This was heartbreaking, because she was a beautiful, big ewe, and she would have given birth to a lamb or maybe two lambs very shortly. We were, naturally, devastated. My sister was away at high school in Mankato, but she took it very hard, as we all did.

My Dad said, "Well, as I've been watching dogs go up and down the road past our farm, I've noticed that in the winter, dogs have a tendency to run. They get restless, and they will run for miles. They'll run down the middle of a highway, with their heads down, and they'll run singly, or they'll run together in packs." Apparently he had seen one particular dog, a big black dog, on various occasions running by our farm. He suspected that dog might have been the one that killed Polly the Sheep.

Dad bought a 16-gauge shotgun from Wilbur Bratrud, owner of Stewartville Hardware, and a box of shells. He kept them hanging up over the basement door in the kitchen, ready and waiting, knowing that dog would probably come back another night to get at the sheep's carcass, which was out behind the barn. We did not have electricity yet, so he was waiting for a moonlit night. He had it all figured out. Those folks back then knew how things worked, what would happen next. They could have mysteries solved in a short time.

One night, our dog Jack, a Saint Bernard who stayed in the kitchen, let out an old "Rrrr!" in the middle of the night. Dogs can sense when other dogs are nearby.

Dad got up. He went downstairs, put a shell in the gun, and opened the back door just slightly. In the moonlight, he could see this black dog running across the yard. I don't know whether the dog had been out tasting the sheep carcass again, or just what. I think that he had been there and was coming back toward the road.

I can hear Dad say yet, "I took a bead on him, and I opened fire, and the dog let out an awful yelp. He yelped and kept on running." And he added, "Of course, I didn't know what happened after that."

There were some of our neighbors who had been working with us, a father and two sons, haying during the summer. Dad ran into them again a few days after this, and somehow they got to talking, as farmers will — they'll share their news — and it came out that our sheep had been killed. The neighbor said, "Well, you know, our dog came home a few nights ago all wounded, terribly wounded. We didn't know what it was. He just came home bleeding and lay there for day after day." And they figured out that it was that dog who had killed our sheep.

There wasn't any fight put up about it. The son of the man just took the dog out and shot him. You can't keep a dog on a farm when it's started to kill livestock.

The Muskrat

In the winter, we always had a short watering tank inside the barn, because outside, if you didn't have a heater of some sort, the water would be all frozen over. It would be my job to hand-pump water to fill that tank. We had a well in a little 10' by 14' building addition right beside the barn, and a pipe leading out of it. I would pump water, and it would go through a hole in the barn wall and into the tank. Then when we were choring in the evening, we could let the cows loose, and they would drink.

Well, one time, as winter came, a muskrat came in the barn. Muskrats love water, but when it gets cold, all the water freezes, and they can't get at it. One evening, as my Dad and I were sitting there milking those ten cows by hand, we looked over and saw this little muskrat come in, shinny up the side of the water tank, get in and start swimming.

He became sort of a friend. When we would finish our milking, we would put the milk in 10-gallon milk cans, which had a kind of bell-shaped cover — farmers will know what that bell-top cover was like — and when we closed the wooden cover on the water tank, there was a little space left at the top, because the milk cans were a little taller than the tank. So the cover was up probably four inches, enough so that the muskrat could come in and out. If the water was up high enough, he could get out easily. And we always tried to keep the water up. We'd put the milk in there to cool at night, and we'd put in more milk the next morning, and then the milkman would come and take it away. In the winter, he came every other day.

One night, somehow, we let the water level get low. And it got cold. The water was low enough that the muskrat could not get out of the tank. The water froze, and in the morning, the little muskrat was dead — frozen stiff.

It made us sad. He had become a friend. We saw him often down there, swimming back and forth in the tank. He got to trust us. But it was too late. Now he was gone.

Going to Stewartville

I loved going to town with Dad, whether it was to Stewartville, Chatfield, Spring Valley or Wykoff. I remember going with him a few times to the old Cussons Mill next to Lake Florence in Stewartville. My calendar for March 2001 featured that Cussons Roller Mill at Stewartville. Under the picture, it says that the mill was built in April 1898, and it was purchased by the Cussons brothers, who earlier had a mill in Chatfield, from Charles N. Stewart, the man the town was named after.

I vividly recall meeting one of the brothers, Jack Cussons, a man with a youthful face and totally white hair. When we arrived, he was caring for the belts and pulleys that turned the machinery. I think Dad purchased four or five sacks of ground feed from him, or maybe we had brought in grain from our farm to be ground.

Dad said, "Meet my son, Harley, Jack." I felt very important, shaking hands with him.

Then Jack quickly left us and climbed a couple of flights of stairs, where he disappeared into the very top of the mill, what they called the head house.

Dad took me outside and showed me the old water wheel, which had been replaced and was lying on the ground. They had put a new wheel in the mill race, through which the water flowed to turn the grinding machinery.

Lake Florence was formed by damming up a docile branch of the Root River, making a beautiful recreation area at Lake Florence Park. It was named after Charles Stewart's daughter-in-law, Florence. The mill stood beside the dam, and the water was diverted through the mill race before flowing on downstream.

The life of the roller mills was doomed to change when electricity came in. The old water-powered mills were replaced by the Farmer's Elevator (today the All-American Co-Op), where the grain was processed. Cussons' Mill is now history, along with Fugle's Mill, which was located south of Simpson, and Tunnel Mill, which was six miles north of Spring Valley, both of them on Fillmore/Olmsted County Road 1.

Another thing I remember from those early days in Stewartville was the new-car showrooms. Oh, the excitement I felt as a boy when I saw the new Chevrolets in the showroom of E.F. House Chevrolet in Stewartville! Ed and Oscar House were always there to serve you. Dad bought a 1936 Chevrolet Town Sedan from them in early 1938 for about $800. It was a dandy, but it wouldn't start in the extreme sub-zero temperatures of those severe winters. Now, the old '28 Chevy which was my first car memory always started with the turn of a crank, or a short pull by a team of horses.

But I loved that '36 model Chevy. I learned to drive it, at the age of 12, out in the cow pasture. Naturally Dad was along, and only a streaked gopher and the pasture fences were at risk. The pocket gophers, who lived underground, were safe from me that day. I was setting no traps — just using a clutch, a starter, a brake, a foot-feed (as we called the accelerator) and a great big steering wheel. The gear shift lever was on the floor — no automatic transmission in those days. We had to use our brains to operate those cars!

Cousin Les Kinsley

Older Stewartville area folks remember Les Kinsley and his years of trucking ten-gallon milk cans and livestock, and later driving the school bus. We knew him well, because Les and my Dad were first cousins who grew up (almost) together, played as kids at the old family reunions and swapped stories. As young lads of 10 and 12, they once went into the pasture on a real frosty morning, grabbed the tails of young calves and braced their feet like a water-skier holding onto a tow rope. It was fun, Dad told me. His feet slid ahead of him at "calf speed." Les's calf ran across a wide open dry spot, without any frosty grass whatever, and Les did an unplanned somersault. Of course, Dad laughed. He didn't tell me whether they ever tried that trick again.

The two buddies were close because their mothers, my grandmother Rachel and Les's mother Winnie, were sisters who had come from Germany together in 1868 on that leaking steamer, the Schmidt. When the girls grew up, they both married local men. Dad and Les spent time together at Stewartville High School.

Later years found Les hauling cans of milk from area farms to the Stewartville Creamery. He also developed quite a livestock hauling business, and often came to our farm to haul market hogs and cattle to the Stewartville Stockyards, which was a buying station for Hormel's meatpacking plant in Austin. Cartoonist Clint Kueker recalls the big dent in Les's truck's front bumper, which just never would "disappear."

One day, Dad ran into Les on the street in Stewartville, and Les told him, "Homer, there'll be no more livestock hauling in my truck. I've bought a school bus."

Dad was shocked. "What?" he exclaimed.

"Yeah," Les replied. "This is easier. They load and unload themselves, now."

Sister Elaine, age 6 . . . Harley 8 1/2 months old.

1934 . . . Homer & Vivian Flathers, Elaine 8, Harley 3 (on stump).

Homer, Vivian & growing kids. Harley is now always wearing Big-Mac high bib overalls.

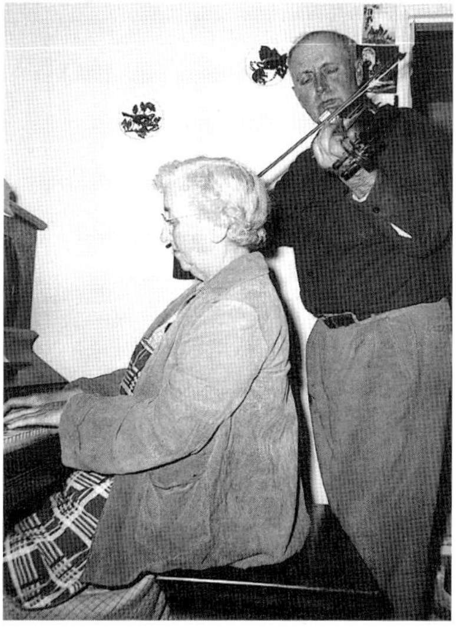

Sunday Night Music we grew up with. Mom at the piano and Dad with violin. I took this picture at home in 1955.

Kueker Illustration . . . Cousin Les Kinsley's truck, complete with "less-than-perfect" front right bumper. It never improved with age.

Kueker Illustration . . . Every farmer's friend . . . Stan Lecy, the Village blacksmith in Stewartville for many years.

Moment 5

The School At Dogtown Corner

One afternoon in the spring of 1937, I was playing at home on the lawn and saw my older sister Elaine walking home from the country school, a half-mile to the east, with Phyllis Gardner, the teacher. I continued to play with the sand and toys. They went into the house, and after a while my mother came out.

She said, "Harley, how would you like to go to school for four weeks this spring?"

I suppose I replied, "Well, gee, do I have to?"

But I did, and that was the start. That was kindergarten. The idea was to get started, to get the child there, so that when September comes, he's ready.

It was the perfect thing, because I had my sister, five years older than I, with me, and she was a mover. I went to school for a total of five weeks that spring. Then when summer was over, I started first grade in the fall of 1937.

To make sure I'd get going in the morning, Elaine would push me out of the house a little early. She'd say, "Get out. Get started. Walk that first forty rods, up to Fred Baker's corner post, and wait for me." Fred Baker's corner post was just at the corner of his pasture, along the edge of the road, and still a half mile to go. So I'd go that far and sit down in the grassy ditch and wait for her. She'd come along shortly, and then she'd kind of push me along to school. Elaine liked school. She always said, "I love the first day of school best of all — and the last day!"

This was a country school, and if we had ten to fifteen kids, that was the whole student body. If you had fifteen or sixteen, you had a full group. You might have two or three in a grade, or up to four, or down to one. We had to bring our own tablets, pencils, erasers and crayons — in grade school, crayons are very important. And we brought our own lunch, sometimes in a sack or an empty Karo syrup pail (those Karo syrup pails made good lunch boxes), but more often in a metal lunch box with pictures on the outside. We really preferred those metal lunch boxes with the pictures of a boy and his dog, or a pony. For girls, there was maybe a nurse or a nature scene. They were the best.

Sometimes, especially in winter, you would have a hot lunch. That was interesting, how they made those hot lunches. You didn't buy lunch on the spot. The teacher would say, "You kids bring a hot lunch from home if you want it." And kids would bring a half pint Mason jar of something — corn, or peas, or mashed potatoes and gravy, or scalloped potatoes — something that would heat up. In one of the cloakrooms, the teacher had a kerosene three-burner stove, and she would put a 16-quart kettle on it, with about three inches of water in the bottom, and a board to hold the Mason jars up, so they wouldn't burn. You would turn in your hot lunch when you came to school, and she would stop her teaching at 11:30 and go turn on the stove. Then she would put all the hot lunches in the kettle, and at noon she would take the tongs and pick out each individual hot lunch. The kids would pick them up and take them to their desks to eat, with whatever else they had brought from home. So you could have a hot lunch if you wanted. If you didn't, you had your own cold lunch — cheese or peanut butter and jelly sandwiches, an orange or an apple, with cookies or a donut or a piece of cake for dessert.

When it came to making those school lunches, my mother gave me a great variety in that little lunch bucket. Once in a while she put in potato salad, which I loved then as I do today. I also loved the bread she baked, but it was always a treat if dad brought home a couple of loaves of "store" bread from town. Put that together with a slice of ring bologna in sandwiches, coupled with potato salad, and I felt like I was on a picnic.

One day at lunch, James Yetter said, "Let's have a picnic."

There was no picnic table in the school yard, but the boys' toilet door happened to be lying on the ground, apart from its hinges. We carried that door about fifty feet from the old back house, set it on the ground, and it made a picnic table without legs or benches. There were four of us at that "picnic:" James Yetter, Dick Engel, Harlan Baker and myself.

James said, "Come on, Harley, share your potato salad, share your baloney sandwiches!"

I didn't want to share my potato salad and bologna sandwiches with anyone. Since I had only one spoon, the potato salad was mine. But I said, "All right, I'll give you one sandwich." In return, I got somebody's weak little jelly sandwich.

James grabbed my sandwich, stuffed the four slices of bologna into his mouth, and threw the four pieces of good "store bread" over his shoulder. It bothers me to this day, that throwing away of good food!

We had two cloakrooms, one on either side of the front entry's inner door. One was for coats, and it had two short iron pipes across the top of the open doorway that we used to exercise, or "chin" ourselves. The other room was the one the teacher used for the hot lunches. It also contained our water fountain. It wasn't really a fountain. It was a crock jar on a stand that had been filled with water pumped from the well outside. We carried it inside in a pail and poured it into the fountain so that we could have something to drink during the day from a bubbling spigot.

That school, district 118, Dogtown School, was first built in 1866. The original building burned down in 1929, and then this new brick building was put up for $7000. It was the finest country school in all of Fillmore County. We heard that from Irene Warren, the county superintendent of schools for many years. She told us, "This is one of the finest school buildings you'll ever see." It was built not smart but well. The ceilings were too high, so that there was too much room to heat. It had five big windows on the east side, more than they would allow today. The basement would flood. There was no electricity until 1947, after I had left for high school, and the only water was at the pump outside. The two outhouses — one each for boys and girls — were out back along the fence line.

The basement was finished, with a cement floor, and on rainy days we would go down there to play at recess. We loved the way the sound echoed in that basement room. I'm not sure exactly where the furnace was, but I believe it was next to the coal bin, which was under the east side of the front porch entry. I remember watching the coal truck from Stewartville Farmers' Elevator drive up and deliver coal into the bin.

The teachers were also the janitors, and it was their job to fire up the furnace. Sometimes they would come in on Sunday afternoon to start the furnace, so that the school would be warm when we arrived on Monday morning. At the end of each day, when we were leaving, the teacher would sprinkle a red dust, some kind of cleaning compound, on the hardwood floors, and sweep them carefully before she left for the day.

We had the old wooden desks with the inkwell in one corner, and a top that lifted up, with space to keep your books inside. There were several blackboards — blackboards were very important! There were four class periods each day. In the morning, we went from 9 to 10:30 and 10:45 to 12, with a 15 minute recess in between. Then we'd have either an hour or half an hour for lunch, depending on the weather — if the weather was good, we'd have an hour. In the afternoon we'd go from 12:30 or 1 to 2:15 and from 2:30 to 4. We studied arithmetic, English (including spelling and grammar), history, geography, health and hygiene, and science. Maybe there was also some social studies, I don't know. In the autumn of 1939, the teacher — Phyllis Anderson — started getting Life magazine, and once a week, on Monday morning, she would display the pictures as she read the captions to us, holding up the open pages for all to see. Those were the days when World War II was heating up. When she had finished, she would put the magazine on the library table in the rear corner of the room, next to the globe, under the picture of George Washington. The library had quite a few books. There was also a piano that had been given to the school in 1939 by Rob Hudson and his wife Zella, our farm neighbors to the west. That was when Phyllis Anderson came to teach. She played many songs on that piano, and boy, did we sing!

In a one-room school, you have some special advantages. The younger children learn things by listening to the questions the older ones are asked. Then when it's their turn, in a year or so, they are more ready to learn that subject. And you really liked to listen, especially when you knew the answers and the older ones didn't. If an older kid can't pronounce a word the way the teacher is saying it, and you can, you feel so good about it!

My sister Elaine took me to school every morning through grades 1, 2 and 3. By that time, I was pretty comfortable there. There were four of us in my grade after the autumn of 1940: Roy Finn, Jo Mae Engel, Harlan Baker and me. We were all pretty good friends. Jo Mae Engel is now Mrs. Warren Hess, and she has been manager of the Stewartville Senior Center for the past fifteen years. Her mother, Doris Engel, helped out quite a bit at the school. She often drove us on field trips. Doris Engel celebrated her 100th birthday before dying early in 2001.

Now, why did they call our school the Dogtown School? Well, immediately across the intersection to the southeast of the school, down about 1000 feet to the driveway, was a farm. All the years I was there, it was occupied by Theodore and Otto Baker and their sisters Julia and Ida. They were fine farmers. They did a lot of work with horses and they had a couple of McCormick-Deering 10-20 and 15-30 tractors to do their plowing. They had all of the equipment they needed, and they knew how to fix things. They were money makers, the Baker brothers.

But before the Bakers, somewhere around the turn of the century, the farm had belonged to a man who raised dogs for their pelts. So they called the area Dogtown. And the school on the corner became the Dogtown School — district 118 at Dogtown Corner. There was a move on in later years to change the name to something prettier. They said, "We can call it the school at Pleasant Corners." But that didn't last too long.

Those Dedicated Country School Teachers

My first grade teacher was named Phyllis Gardner. She was 23 years old, and a lovely teacher. I think she'd been there a couple of years, but I had her only one year. She's 88 now. Recently I've written to her, and she wrote back. It was so good to hear from her. She married Joyce Aronson, an auto dealer in Ellendale, Minnesota, in 1947, and they had six children. She was just a wonderful person.

The second year, I had Virginia Kammer of Chatfield. She was also a good teacher.

My third teacher, whom I had for grades 3, 4 and 5, was a dear neighbor who had grown up a mile and a half from our farm. Her name was Phyllis Anderson. She had taken piano lessons from my mother as a young girl. The Andersons were members of our church, and we loved the family. She was another fine teacher.

In grades 6 and 7, I had another neighbor as a teacher. Her name was Eileen Baker. She had a younger brother and sister, Harlan and Marjorie, in the school. Harlan, as I've said, was in my class.

For grade 8, we had Betty Rogers from Chatfield. She was only eighteen, and she had three eighth grade boys who were thirteen — Harlan Baker, Roy Finn and me. She was cute, she was pretty, and it was just very difficult to get much studying done that year. Betty Rogers was a lovely person. To this day, I run into her regularly. She is now Mrs. Ray Holtegaard of rural Rochester. Her birthday is January 24, one month after Christmas Eve. I used to wish her a happy birthday on the radio for many years.

Those teachers were all so very kind. They wanted us to learn, and they didn't watch the clock. In winter, they would help us get suited up, and I've often thought that when the teacher had finished helping the last child of the day into his or her coat, hat, scarf, mittens and boots, she must have heaved a great sigh of relief.

If we got sick at school, we had to go home. There was no telephone at the school, so the teacher couldn't call our parents to have them come and get us. So we would walk home. I remember one time going home, and I felt so sick. I think it was probably the 24-hour flu. My mother looked out the window and saw me coming, and she came out to meet me. I was so glad to see her!

For several years, my dad was school clerk of district 118. The school board meeting always took place in the month of June, and because Dad was clerk, by law he had to post a notice of the meeting in three places. He put one on the schoolhouse door, one on the telephone pole right next to the school, and another one someplace else in the district on a telephone pole about a mile away.

During the years that my father was school clerk, all the checks made out by the school board needed three signatures. He'd make out the check, and sign it. Then he would give it to me, and I would take it to school, stopping on the way at the Fred Baker farm, where Fred, who was the school board treasurer, would sign it. Then I'd give it to the teacher, who usually boarded at the home of Emma Engel, Mrs. John Engel, who was the school board secretary. She was the third one to sign the check. All of the teachers except Phyllis Anderson and Eileen Baker boarded with the Engels. Phyllis and Eileen managed to get Mrs. Engel to sign the check some other way. So I played an important role in delivering my teachers' paychecks.

Fun and Games On the Playground

Country school was sometimes very wonderful, and sometimes very frustrating, especially when some of the big kids would get a little rough with you. As a little kid, I was always the one getting picked on. But oh, how we loved playing out on the playground.— games like softball, running races, Pump-Pump-Pullaway and Anty-I-Over (where you throw the ball over the school — I don't think we ever broke a window). In the winter, we played Fox and Goose in the snow, and King of the Hill on those big snowpiles that the snowplows piled up along the road in front of the school.

In May, when it warmed up, the older boys would sometimes see a streaked gopher going into a hole in the middle of the schoolyard. Who did they call to pump a pail of water? "Harley! Go pump a pail of water! We're going to drown this gopher out." So Harley would go into the school, get the pail, come out there to the old pump — it had good water

— fill the pail, and carry it over to them. They'd pour the water down the hole, and the gopher would stick his head up out of the hole, water pouring off his little striped body, and then they'd kill him with a baseball bat!

We used to play softball in the school yard. I remember in the spring of 1943, when I was in sixth grade, I wanted a catcher's mitt. Every boy likes to have four things of his own — a bat, a ball, a mitt and a bike. My Dad had bought me a ball and bat from the Stewartville Hardware store, but I wanted a glove. I really didn't care if it was a catcher's mitt or not, just so I had my own glove. So I looked in the Montgomery Ward's catalog. I had no idea how to tell the quality of the gloves, but they all had big league players' names on them, and I picked out one that had Joe Gordon's name on it. I can't remember now what team he played for. It cost $2.95, plus ten cents for postage and handling. I had some money saved from doing lawns and catching gophers, and I gave it to my parents to send in with their order — they were always sending away for something or other.

I thought that glove would never come! One day, as I was playing ball with my friends in the schoolyard, I saw the mailman, Ed Sullivan of Stewartville, go by. I hollered out, "Hey, Mr. Mailman, have you got anything for me?" He just smiled and waved. I guess kids were always calling out something like that to him. But when I got home, there was my glove. It was a fielder's glove, and I still have it. I used to sleep with it under my head on my pillow. I took it to school with me. I was so fond of that glove! Today it's in my corner memorabilia case in my den.

We had a lot of fun there at the school on the corner. On special days, the teachers would have treats for us, candy or cookies. On Valentine's Day, we would draw names and exchange Valentines, and then there would be suckers. I remember when I was seven, I had a crush on Harlan Baker's sister Marjorie, who was nine. I don't think she ever knew that. It was a hopeless situation. I knew I would never be as old as she was, and she wouldn't be interested in a little kid like me. We had cookies for Halloween, too, but no drinks — nothing but the water from the crock in the cloakroom. It was all fun.

As I look back, I can see the school programs, all the kids together performing their pieces, their skits. I can see the plank stage which had been carried up from the lower level and put up on three long sawhorses at the front of the room to make a 10' x 12' platform, 18 inches high. We'd have a Christmas program every year, with a Christmas tree. The room was filled with families and neighbors. And we sang — how we sang! At the end, we sang "Jingle Bells," and that was the cue for Santa to come in. You know who Santa Claus was? He was my dad! Of course, I knew who it was, and the neighbors knew, but the little kids didn't. And it was exciting. The teacher had a gift for every child, and the kids exchanged names to get a gift. Christmas was something!

And then we were out for two weeks. We loved Christmas vacation. It was hard to go back to school again afterwards.

One early morning in the autumn of 1941, on a clear crisp day in early October, I was walking to school around 8:30 to 8:45 am, when a big long funeral car came up behind me and stopped. The driver rolled down the window and asked, "Want a ride?"

Since I never turned down a ride, I crawled into the front seat. There were two men in the car, and they were very kind. I looked over my shoulder and saw a big, empty space covered with maroon velvet fabric. There was nobody back there. No casket. I suppose they had taken a body somewhere else and were returning to Chatfield.

When I got out at school, I thanked the men for the ride. Some of the kids in the playground hollered out, "Wow! Harley got a ride to school in an ambulance."

"No," I yelled back. "It was a hearse!"

As they drove away, I could see the name of the funeral business on the side window: Boetzer Funeral Home. Don Boetzer, a hard-working business man, owned that funeral home for many years. He was the driver that morning. Later the business became the Boetzer-Aakeson Funeral Home, and for over thirty years now it has been the Riley Funeral Home of Chatfield.

Peggy Ellis, A Real-Life Angel

Peggy Ellis was one of the mothers who volunteered their time to help out at good old Dogtown School, district 118. She was truly an angel to the many people whose lives she touched.

Peggy and Jake Ellis lived across the road from the district boundary line, but no one complained when they started bringing their three little ones to our school in 1941 and 1942. Peggy's maiden name was Margaret Yungen. She was born in Pine Island in 1903, of Swiss descent. Peggy hauled children and adults in our neighborhood to school and church for many years. I recall riding with her to Sumner Church in a car full of kids in the early 1940s. She also took my mother and others to the church's ladies' circle, which at that time was called the Women's Society of World Service, or WSWS.

Peggy was a special person. She knew a lot of people, cared for many, and was loved by all. In 1978, Peggy cared for our four children when June and I hosted a tour to England and Scotland. By that time, her five children — Patsy, Joanne, David, Robert and Stephen — had left the nest. Our children still needed supervision, so Peggy just moved into our house for those two weeks.

On December 5, 1979, Peggy died while still performing her mission of service. She often took the Baker sisters — Julia and Ida — to town for their shopping. The Baker sisters had lived with their brothers, Theodore and Otto, on the farm near the school all their lives. After the brothers died, the sisters remained on the farm. Peggy Ellis and the Baker sisters had finished their shopping that day and were returning home from Rochester on county road 1, about a half mile south of Pleasant Grove, when Peggy's car left the roadway, traveled through the ditch, and rolled over in a field. All three women were killed instantly. Peggy Ellis was 75 years old at the time; Julia Baker was 77 and Ida Baker was 71.

The Baker sisters and their brothers, Ted and Otto, had amassed a considerable fortune over the years. They loved children, but had never married. I remember they usually bought Christmas Seals from us kids at

Christmas time in the late 1930s and early 1940s. In their wills, they left a large sum of money to the Boy and Girl Scouts.

Peggy Ellis was greatly missed by her many friends and neighbors, whom she had helped so often over the years.

Township Day

Annually on the first Friday in May, the six area schools in Sumner Township would join together for one day. All the teachers and kids and a few mothers were there, but not many fathers, because most of the fathers were out in the field planting at that time of year. Altogether, there were about seventy-five kids from six schools involved. This event was held for a number of years at the Sumner Center schoolhouse, district 122. That school was located in the Sumner Center Church complex. The town hall was in the lower level of the school. There was a big yard around both buildings. We didn't use the church as I recall, just the school room and the lower level town hall.

All the schools in Sumner Township, which was on the north edge of Fillmore county, got together on Township Day. The purpose: to display kids' talents. The kids could get out and enjoy themselves, do things together, display their art work, speak a piece on a stage before an audience, or participate in a short skit. Judges would select those who did the best job, giving out blue ribbons for first, red for second and so on. There were spelling bees. There was a quiz on current events and another one on Minnesota history. I loved that, because I took second one year in the Minnesota history quiz. We would also sing in groups, songs that had been selected as being appropriate on the county chorus level. The whole group of kids sang, directed by Miss Anna Seem.

At noon, we always had a pot-luck picnic on a big long table. And boy, could we eat! Kids that have been playing just have appetites. After lunch, there was usually a softball game, right there in that big schoolyard. There were three-legged races and more. I think some of the awards for three-legged races were candy bars — Snickers or Butterfingers. Baby Ruth was always a big favorite.

The schools that took part included our own school on the east side of the township, district 118, that we called Dogtown School. Two miles west of us was district 119, and still a little further two miles west, district 120, called Waterloo. Two miles south of Waterloo school district was district 123, called Kedron, after a river in the Bible. It was just a quarter-mile south of that famous long barn that belonged to the Hale family. Then two miles directly east of that was the host school location, Sumner, district 122, and east two more miles was Union School, district 121. Those were the six school districts involved. Occasionally, there was another one to the south called Washington, district 124. We didn't see them every year, just occasionally. That school was exactly four miles south of my school.

Each school district measured two miles on each side, about four square miles in area. The school was usually built in the middle of that square, so the students all had less than two miles to walk to get to school. Each district had a number, and you could tell where the schools were located by the numbers.

The winning art entries from Township Day would appear at the Fillmore County fair in August. I remember my sister had won first place in some artistic work twice, when she was in the sixth and eighth grades. We all looked forward to going down to Preston at county fair time and seeing our family member's work displayed. Likewise some speakers moved on to another level of poetry, declamation, reciting such works as "In Flanders Field," by John McCrae, or "O Captain, My Captain," by Walt Whitman. One year I did "Old Ironsides," by Oliver Wendell Holmes. I also recall winning second in the spelling bee once, as well as taking second in that Minnesota history quiz.

In 1943 Paul Dunneman, at that time a handsome eighth grade lad from district 124, won the spelling bee with the word "recommend." He took his time. "Recommend! Recommend!" He said it a couple or three times. Then he started to spell. "R-e-c-o-m," and he paused a bit, "m-e-n-d. Recommend." Well, that was correct, and Paul won that spelling bee. He came from little Washington School, down there around old highway 74 at Spring Valley. He graduated from Spring Valley High School in 1947.

Now he's a retired pastor, still living in Spring Valley, Minnesota.

My Fillmore County eighth grade graduation exercises were held Friday, June 15, 1945, at 1:30 pm in Harmony High School Auditorium. There were 162 eighth grade graduates, from ungraded and semi-graded elementary schools across the county. Again Miss Anna Seem directed the "County Chorus." I was proud to be one of the singers. We all recited the Pledge of Allegiance with the audience. Following the commencement address by Mr. Dean M. Schweickhard, State Commissioner of Education, we were presented with our diplomas by Miss Irene Warren, long-time Fillmore County Superintendent of Schools. Seventeen of us who gladly received our beautiful 8th grade diplomas that day would meet the following September as freshmen at Chatfield High.

Chatfield High School

Once I finished eighth grade, I was all set to go to high school. When it came time to decide which high school I would attend, I saw that there was a bus from Stewartville High that stopped about a mile away from our farm, and a bus from Chatfield High that stopped only a half mile away. So I decided I would go to Chatfield High.

In September 1945, we country kids caught the big orange school bus owned by Don Nagel that came toward our old brick school from the south and drove easterly to Chatfield, picking up kids along the way. Gerald Halloran, who owned the Co-op Oil Station across from the school, drove the route many times.

I felt lost that first week at Chatfield High. I told my folks I wanted to quit right then. I didn't think I needed a high school education to run a farm. Mom and Dad humored me, saying, "Well, Harley, keep at it this week." Dad added, with a touch of tongue-in-cheek humor, "You'd better go back at least one more day so you can bring home your books!"

Now I look back at my four high school years as a great time in my life. In the autumn of 1945, the Chatfield High "Gophers" football team played eight games and were undefeated, untied, and un-scored-upon. I remember well riding the fan bus to St. Charles to watch them play the "Saints" on their home field on November 11, 1945, for the Armistice Day Game, the traditional final game of the season. A lot of bragging rights always went to the winner. That very cold but sunny day found both teams scoreless until near the end of the third quarter, when senior Gopher running back John Ferguson scored on a 19-yard run to win the game, 6-0. It was a great year for Chatfield, and for team member Bob Glover, who was later named to the All-State High School Football Team.

I liked singing, and I was a member of both the boys' chorus and the mixed chorus. Then in my junior and senior years, I was in the class plays. The junior class play, which took place November 21, 1947, was called "Almost Summer," by Christopher Sergel. On May 20, 1949, we performed the senior class play, "Mollie O'Shaughnessey," by Dorothy Rood Stewart. I played the crusty old sheriff who was the father of a beautiful little Irish girl, Mollie O'Shaughnessey — played by Lucille Manahan. (Lucille today is Mrs. Robert Kuhl of rural Rochester.) Lucille was delightful as Mollie.

In the play, I suffer a heart attack. I have a no-good son (played by Gene Harwood), and he gets involved in a hold-up. A shot rings out and I die of a heart attack — while sitting in a wheelchair. Six weeks later, I was in a wheelchair myself with polio. My mother often said, "Wasn't that a bit of irony, seeing that happen within six weeks." Only a mother can say a thing like that!

After the senior play was over, I had noticed that some kids in previous years had written their names on the backdrop, behind the curtain. So I brought some gold paint and a paintbrush from home, and I climbed up a big stepladder and painted my name there on the backdrop. And it seeped through to the front of the canvas. The superintendent, Oliver P. Bakken, took me aside and said, "Harley, that's not good. That's permanent. We'll have to replace the whole backdrop." I felt so bad — worse than if he'd punished me.

We held the play in Potter Auditorium. It had been built in 1930-31, and named for George H. Potter, the superintendent of schools. For a few years, they called it "Potter's Folly," because it was huge. There were over 800 seats, including a balcony, and a stage so big it was used as a basketball court and gym. It is still used by the community today, and has seen three decades of Chatfield Western Days annual musicals.

So high school was good. I graduated then on June 3, 1949, and that finished my schooling. I had no intention of going on to college. I was going to farm. I didn't realize then that five weeks after graduation polio would change both my life and my career. You can't always prepare for the unknown.

The only other schooling I have had was the radio school I attended after I recovered from polio, in 1952-53, and a Dale Carnegie course I took in Rochester in 1968. I would recommend any and all to take the Dale Carnegie course in human relations and effective speaking. It's a fourteen-week course, and very valuable. It helps in so many ways, especially in improving your memory system for names and faces.

Although I never went to college, I have learned how important a college degree really is. In October 1980, when I was let go from KROC, I thought I could get a job at IBM or in the school system or the Olmsted county government. The first thing they always wanted to see was my college diploma. And I'd say, "Well, no, I don't have one of those." Then they'd ask to see my high school grades, and I'd say, "Well...we can get those..."

But I was very fortunate, getting a fine job a few weeks later at KWEB. I started out in radio in 1952, and here it is 2003 and I'm still in radio, fifty years later, and loving every minute of it. But I still regret not having that college diploma.

Dist. 118 Dogtown School. (Clint Kueker illustration. Kids & snow)

Another picture . . . 1943 of the school . . . Front Row L-R: David Ellis (pre-school), Joanne Ellis, Betty Engel, Patsy Ellis, Connie Quackenbush. Second Row L-R: Harley Flathers, Roy Finn, Harlan Baker, Joe Mae Engel, Beverly Oldenberg, Marjorie Baker. Standing 3rd row is teacher Eileen Baker (older sister of Harlan & Marjorie) Photo from Joe Mae Engel (Hess).

Santa Claus at the school house . . . (Clint's illustration).

UNDEFEATED UNTIED UNSCORED UPON

Chatfield		Opponents
40	Harmony	0
24	Lanesboro	0
45	Spring Grove	0
38	Mabel	0
40	Preston	0
18	Rushford	0
43	Stewartville	0
6	St. Charles	0

Bob Glover from the Chatfield 1945 champions.

An all-state running back, Glover is retired and a resident of St. Charles, MN

Harley's High School Graduation picture . . . for June 3, 1949 . . . Age 17.

Moment 6

Those Challenging 1940s
Armistice Day Blizzard

Many people in southeastern Minnesota recall the Armistice Day blizzard of November 11, 1940. That storm dropped in on everybody suddenly, with high winds, a lot of snow, and dropping temperatures. In 1940 we might have been listening to the radio, but I don't recall hearing about the weather. We didn't have a sophisticated weather warning system back at that time, and people were unprepared.

It was a time of year when we were used to sudden changes of weather on the farm. Armistice Day was on a Monday that year. That particular weekend had been warm, balmy, with temperatures in the 40s and 50s. If there was any snow yet, it had melted. It was drizzly, kind of cloudy and foggy, as I walked to school that morning. I had just turned nine years old that year, and was in the fourth grade. I wasn't thinking anything about a storm.

My father and neighbor Lyle Buchholtz were going to butcher a hog. Lyle, who would come down with polio two months later, was then a strapping young man of about eighteen. I think they were planning to butcher a hog at our farm in the morning, and another one across the field at Lyle's parents' farm in the afternoon.

Suddenly, at 2:00 pm, my Dad came driving up to the Dogtown school. He said to the teacher, "You've got to get these kids all home. There's a terrible blizzard on."

We kids hadn't been too excited until then. We may have seen snow coming, and we might have even played in it at noon outdoors, I don't recall that for sure. But I can recall my father coming in and saying, "We've got to get home. Harley, get in the car. I'm going to take you home right now." And I guess all the other kids probably started out immediately for home, too.

Dad took me home and said, "Well, now, I'm going to go on over and help Lyle finish with the butchering." He had told Lyle to go up to the district 119 school and get his younger brother Leonard, who was a friend of mine. Leonard was four years older than I, and went to a different school, but we played together in the summer. Leonard had started walking home across the fields before Lyle got there, and he managed to get home safely.

Dad went over to Lyle's, but I don't know whether they finished the butchering, because he came back home almost immediately. He told my mother and me, "This is bad." By now it was late afternoon, probably 4:30 or 5 o'clock. He told us, "You've got to start getting the chickens in out of the trees."

We had bought laying hens, as dad did each autumn, from Will Stellmaker, a neighbor who lived about four miles southeast of us. They had a lot of chickens. Sometimes farmers would buy another farmer's year-old hens when the new-laying poults came in. So Dad had brought home these chickens a few days before. Now hens, especially young hens, have a tendency to want to roost in the trees. You can put them in the henhouse, but when it comes sundown, they'll fly up into the trees to roost.

So my mother and I went out and started reaching up and pulling those chickens down. We had a wire hook we'd perfected — everybody made them. You take some # 9 wire that you've shaped into the form of a hook, and you can grab the hens around the leg as they set in the tree and pull them down. I can hear those chickens yet, squawking like everything. One of us would pull chickens down and the other one would hold them, until we had three or four in each hand, and then we'd take them into the chicken house and close the door. We worked for a long time, getting those chickens down, and of course they wouldn't all be on the lowest branch, or the second branch, where you could reach them easily from the ground. It was a difficult job.

Dad said, "While you do that, I'm going to the back side of the farm and get the horses. I know they are all back there." After the crops have been pretty well harvested, you turn your cattle and horses out when the days are good, and they eat the downed cornstalks, or maybe some ears of corn that are left. When a storm comes, they will always migrate back into a fence corner. We had, I believe, nine horses at that time. Dad said, "I'll follow the fence row." There was a good solid half-mile of woven-wire fence heading north from our farm, all the way back to Bill Baker's land. Sure enough, the horses were there. He took the first horse and led it back, and all the others followed.

But when he got back home, he only had eight horses. He said, "I've got to go back and get Old Jack, the blind horse." Old Jack was a good horse, even though he was blind. Dad said, "I know he's back there in the corner, and he's blind. I've got to get him or he will perish." I remember those words so clearly: "Old Jack will perish."

So Dad made another trip on foot, back along the fence line, and eventually, he came back home with the horse. He had rescued Old Jack, while my mother and I had managed to rescue many, many new young laying hens.

This blizzard lasted for three days. We had so much snow, so much freezing cold, that all we could do was hunker down and just try to survive.

After three days, we went out to the barnyard and found three roosters that had survived. They were on the underside of the old farm manure spreader, sitting on that moving slat belt which would be used to push the manure out against the beaters. Those roosters had crawled in there, where they had protection from the top and the bottom, but the wind came through the sides. Their combs and their feet were frozen, and when we found them, they could hardly make a noise. We took those roosters in, as we would often take little baby animals into the house, and put them behind the kitchen stove, where the warmth is, and eventually they started to perk up, and they began to crow. We fattened those roosters up and they became good eating later on.

We survived the storm, but many people didn't. It was November, and duck hunting season had just opened. Thirty-two duck hunters froze to death along the Mississippi River, all the way from St. Paul down to LaCrosse, especially around Red Wing, Lake City, Wabasha and Winona — wherever there was marsh land along the river bottoms, that's where the duck hunters died. They were caught unprepared, and many of them were frozen to death. Several other people also died — the newspapers reported a total of forty-two deaths in Minnesota as a result of that storm.

In those winters of the late 1930s and early 1940s, when many county and township roads had not yet been graded-up to heights that would make them easy to clear after a storm, our roads and others in the area could become blocked for days at a time with six foot snow drifts. I've often seen the time when Dad would drive the eight miles to Stewartville with a team of horses and a sled to get a supply of groceries, chicken feed, coal — and the mail, when good old Rural Route 2 of the Stewartville Post Office became blocked south and east of Pleasant Grove. Our mailman for many years was Ed Sullivan. He could only go so far in deep snow, delivering the mail and the Post-Bulletin, which was already a day late when we got it in the rural areas.

So after the storm ended, about Wednesday or Thursday, Dad went to town to pick up our mail and also the mail for four other farms near our school. I proudly put those mail packets, all tied with twine and labeled with a name on each, into my shoulder book-bag, and set out on my pony. I stopped first to leave mail for Fred and Lena Baker as I went past their farm. Then I gave the mail for the other three families — Walter Engel, Bill Baker and Henry Oldenberg — to their kids who were attending the school. Gosh, I felt proud, helping to keep America informed! But I tried not to let the other kids see my pride.

Those blizzards carried winds that compacted the snow banks to huge depths, almost like a concrete wall. If a blizzard hit us on a Sunday or Monday, we could expect to see that big snow plow from Chatfield by late Wednesday night or Thursday. The schools stayed open, because kids walked to school, but cars couldn't move. It took the snow plow a long time to travel the nine miles west from Chatfield. It was exciting to see that behemoth of a snow plow, with its many colored lights and that big V-shaped blade in front to break the drifts. It also had a big wing blade on its right side that often pushed the mailboxes off their posts beside the farm driveways. The residents had to shovel out the blocked driveway after the plow went through, as they still do today, but they used hand shovels, not little motorized snow blowers.

Farmers' milk cans were often overflowing because the milk truck could not get through to its farm customers. Sometimes Dad would load three or four ten-gallon milk cans on the sled and go out to meet the truck a mile or two away. He would often bring back an extra empty can, just in case another storm might be brewing.

Hog High Finance

In the spring of 1941, my Dad wanted to encourage my sister and me to make money and start a savings account at the bank. Mind you, I already had a small world globe bank that Aunt Ila Flathers had given me at Christmas. In summer I mowed that big lawn with a hand push mower for ten cents a week. Sometimes there would be another contribution to the bank, like a nickel when I trapped a striped gopher or a dime for a pocket gopher. I'd count the money daily. The key that locked the bank was held to the base of the globe by a rubber band. It wasn't the most secure arrangement, but I don't recall ever experiencing a robbery.

During the late 1930s and early 1940s, Dad had developed a fine line of Spotted Poland China hogs, selling boars and bred gilts to repeat customers over the years. Sixty years later, I can still remember the names of some of those buyers — Henry Schumann of Stewartville, Logan Petit of Plainview, Lincoln and Burton Henry of Dover, and Lincoln Schroeder of Rochester. Those boars and gilts would be selling for $40 to $50 each, a good bit higher than the market price at that time.

So that spring of 1941, Dad encouraged Elaine and me to each select a young barrow or gilt for our own. The only stipulation was that we conalmost a full day that time. Lambert paid me $1.50, and his wife Amy fed me two good meals.

Well, that was pretty good. Then Jake Ellis came and said, "Can Harley work?"

But this time, my Dad said, "We've got to have him at home."

Well, Jake Ellis went and got Harlan Baker to work instead of me. Harlan worked a day or two, and he was paid $4.25. I only made $3.50, because I had to work at home, for no pay. I wasn't too happy about that!

Today, when I see Ernie Klomps, who is now turning 90, I say, "Ernie, I've still got that first two dollars you paid me, back in 1943."

I don't remember what I did with all that money. I know that somewhere around that time, I bought a BB gun at Stewartville for $1.95, including 500 BBs. I used it to shoot at starlings, and sometimes at the cattle, although that really wasn't such a good idea. If you hit them on the flank, it would just sting a little, and they would move away, but if you happened to hit them in the eye you could blind them, or even kill them if the pellet went up into the brain. Fortunately, I never did anything like that. Eventually, I sold that BB gun to Edward Doten, who went to our church and was a couple of years younger than I. He gave me $3.00 for it. I thought that was a pretty good deal!

A Pony Named King

Christmas of 1937, when I was six and Elaine was eleven, was the most exciting ever. In the early morning, before breakfast, somehow our dad encouraged one or both of us to go to the back door, open it and look out. And there was a "king-size" surprise, a little black and white Shetland pony, tied to the back fence gate post. For two weeks Dad had kept that Christmas present hidden in the old 20-by-20-foot hen house with its sagging roof — the building that a year later would be rebuilt into a hog barn. My parents sure knew how to hide gifts at Christmas time!

Dad had learned that a pony was for sale over near Racine, Minnesota, about ten miles away. At that time, our car was a 1928 Chevy that could start with the turn of a crank if the battery was low, or start in forty to fifty feet when being pulled by a team of horses. The passenger seat would fold forward up to the dash, and the back seat cushion was easily removed. I had ridden with Dad several times when he took a veal bull calf to the stockyards in Stewartville, the little animal riding right there in the car with us. So it was no surprise when Dad told us he had brought King home in the old Chevy.

Little King stood about six or seven hands high. He loved to "teach" his rider to hang on. More than once one of us kids would be left sitting in mid-air when King jumped suddenly to the left or right side without giving us any advance warning. Once he learned that we would just get right back on again, he accepted us, and we got along together just fine.

King was a friend to us, to the neighbor kids, to our dog, a big old St. Bernard named Jack, and to various cats who liked to sleep on the warm back of a horse or pony in the barn during the winter. That was an early "share the warmth" plan that only animals can work out.

Those winters of the late 1930s and early 1940s were very cold, with a lot of blizzards. On those cold, windy mornings, when the snow was blowing but not yet severe enough to call off school, Elaine would get on a big gray work horse named Gerry, I would mount King, and off to school we'd go. When we got there, we'd aim these equine creatures in a westerly direction, hook up the reins, and slap them on their butts, and King and Gerry would race those 200 rods home. If only we could have trained them to come back and get us again when school was over at 4 pm! Instead, Dad would usually arrive with a team of horses pulling a bobsled to bring us home. I think Gerry was probably one of those horses, along with his mother, Snip. Snip was a faithful old horse who raised four colts — two sons and two daughters — and did a lot of field work for us. We felt she could almost talk to us sometimes.

Shooting the Civet Cat

In the winter when we would clean barns, we would have to throw the manure on a bobsled, because in the winter manure spreaders would freeze up. You pitched it on, and then you went out in the field and you pitched it off. And after pitching the first forkful, you soon learned which way the wind was blowing. You only tossed it in the wrong direction once.

When we came back from the field, we would bring in a corn shock. This was before we started picking corn with a picker. Many farmers were still picking corn by hand in those days. It was a regular thing. You picked corn by hand, a row at a time, or two rows. There were corn picking contests. There still are, some places. It's what they call an old-time husking bee. Down around Wykoff, Minnesota, every year, they still have corn husking bees. It's a piece of farm history that is kept alive by a few of the old fellows.

Several corn shocks might be left standing in the field, if we hadn't shredded them all in the fall. By mid-winter, those corn shocks had gone through a series of rains and freezing and thawing, and rains and freezing and thawing, and the corn shocks would be frozen in. I mean, they were frozen in! You had to cut those corn shocks off at the bottom with a sharp spade. We would cut them off, throw the corn bundles on the sled, and bring them in. You'd get one shock, maybe two, each time.

And always, under the shocks, there would be a nest of mice, or once in a while, a skunk. When there was a skunk, you moved on quickly. You didn't stay around.

This one time, as we started to chop down a corn shock, we detected an odor, and I said, "Dad, it's a skunk."

Before he could answer, this animal ran out, and left us. Well, we were glad of that. Dad said, "That's a civet cat." When it comes to smelling skunks and civet cats, I couldn't tell them apart. Maybe they knew, but I didn't.

The civet cat ran, and I chased it. I didn't get too close. You never get too close to a skunk or a civet cat, because they can spray you. The civet cat crawled through the fence and went over into the neighbor's pasture. There was a big old willow tree right on the creek which went from our farm into their farm. I saw him climb up there, and I said, "Dad, I'm going to go home and get the gun, and shoot the civet cat."

I think this was in 1944, when I was twelve coming up to 13. It was early spring, starting to loosen up a little bit, although we still had snow and freezing.

My Dad continued to load the sled. I went home and got the gun, the same one that he'd used to shoot the dog that killed Polly the Sheep.

When I came back, the poor little civet cat didn't have a chance, really. You don't have to be too good of a shot with a shotgun. I stood down below him, I suppose ten feet away. I only fired once, and he fell out of the tree.

And I felt so proud of that. I remember I made an artistic display at school, called "Shooting the Civet Cat."

The Sumner Cubs

During the early 1940s, at Sumner Center Church, a number of the young men got motorcycles. They made a lot of noise, but they were good boys. They all went to church. My cousin Dale Turner had a motorcycle, and our neighbor Jimmy Caldbeck had a motorcycle in addition to his own airplane. There were others — Lyle McNamara, Loren Smith, Roger Webb. They were a good bunch of lads, but they had to go through that era of motorcycles.

Also during that era, in 1947-1948, these lads wanted to build a softball diamond. They said, "We need a place to play softball."

James Caldbeck, Sr., who lived a couple of miles from us on the way to our church, said, "I'll give you that piece of pasture, right out there along the road." He was a Scotsman, James Caldbeck; I can still hear the burr in his voice as he said that.

So the boys who were riding motorcycles and some others started going door to door, asking for money. "If we can get enough money to get lights at this ball field," they said, "we'll have a ball team." They wanted to be able to play at night, because they were farmers, and they worked during the day. "We need $500 to put up these lights," they said.

And they got it. They had about four poles put up, and a professional lighting company, McConnell Electric of Spring Valley, came out to install the lights. They had a backstop, and a few little bleachers, and a place to sell pop and popcorn. It was just a neat place to be. And of course, we in 4H got to use that softball field, too. We liked it better than Roy Finn's pasture. It was a very nice neighborhood thing.

They had some darned good softball pitching there. I remember Maury Turbenson from Spring Valley, who was a tremendous fast-pitch softball player. Another one was our neighbor Les Hinkle. Les also had his own airplane. Les and Jimmy Caldbeck both owned airplanes. They had fun playing softball, too. They played against teams from all over the area, from Rochester and other towns. People came out and enjoyed it all. This was before we had television. It was good entertainment.

The team was called the Sumner Cubs. They played on Sunday afternoon or night, and they had a regular schedule. It lasted quite a few years.

One of the people that had an interest in it also was Lyle Buchholtz. Although he couldn't run and play softball, because he'd been crippled by polio in January 1941, he was still out there doing things, running the food stand or shooting the breeze, as people are so able to do. Lyle also had a motorcycle, and he used to ride it around the base lines to entertain the fans.

The Sumner Cubs are only a memory now. You can drive by, and unless you know what happened, there's nothing there. The field is planted in corn and soybeans today. That's history for you.

Where Faith Is Nourished

Church has always played an important part in my life. In the early days, our church was the Evangelical Church. There were two Evangelical churches in the area, one at Sumner Center and one at Racine. They were seven miles apart. In 1946, the national Evangelical Church merged with the United Brethren Church, and it was then called the EUB, or Evangelical United Brethren. It remained the EUB across the country until 1968, when it merged with the Methodist Church nationwide. That merger took place in Dallas at what they called the Uniting Conference. We know the church today as the United Methodist Church.

In those early years at Sumner Center, my family was heavily involved in the church. My uncle Henry Turner, who'd threshed for us, was married to my Dad's sister, Aunt Ethel, and they lived half a mile away from the church. Aunt Ethel was the church treasurer for many years, and Uncle Henry took care of the church furnace. He'd go to the church early, perhaps even Saturday night, and get it warmed up for Sunday morning. If there was an evening service, he would climb a tall step ladder, which he kept down in the basement, and light the hanging gas lanterns, that had to be pumped up until there was enough pressure to light them. There was no electricity, no running water, no indoor plumbing.

I recall the 50th anniversary celebration at Sumner Center Church in May 1944, when I was nearing age thirteen. Many early pastors returned. There were lots of memories, musical celebrations, sermons and great food. The church at that time had two male quartets. The older quartet was made up of my dad, Homer Flathers, Earl Ellenberg, Alfred Anderson and Paul Ness. The young men's quartet had my cousin Dale Turner and the three Hagen boys, Gary, Wendell, and Keith, who were all in their 20s. The two quartets often tried to outdo each other. I had the pleasure of hearing them all sing. Usually I would hear their performance before it ever got to church, because during those years when I was growing up, everything related to church music started at my home, where they would come to rehearse. Whether it was singing or someone playing musical instruments, my mother would play the piano with them. I grew up surrounded by wonderful music.

I recall several of the pastors from that time. The first one I remember was a new pastor named Wesley Miller and his wife, Ruth. He served the churches at Racine and Sumner from 1941 till 1948. He was young, and I'm sure restless. In the winter of 1944 he had the opportunity to go on a ship to Poland, helping take a load of horses to the Poles. There was a movement on to help other countries as the war drew to an end, and he was gone for a few weeks.

Then came Leland and Irene Graben. Leland Graben served till 1950, I believe it was. He helped the congregation move the little church back from the road, raise it up, and install a basement, a kitchen, additional Sunday School rooms and even a church balcony.

John and Fran Rebstock were there from 1951 till about 1955. They were followed by a young man named Don Utzman and his wife, Ruth. Don Utzman was born shortly after his father, A.B. Utzman, had finished serving as pastor to that same pair of churches from 1924 till 1930.

During those years, there was often a series of evangelistic meetings, generally in the autumn. There would be a week when a special evangelist would come in and stay at the preacher's parsonage while the meetings went on. Then, of course, various people in the church would say to themselves, "Well, we've got to invite the preacher and his guest and their wives to dinner tonight." It was a great plan. You got to know the pastors and the evangelists, and they got to know you. Many wonderful friendships were begun — or perhaps ended — at those meetings.

In 1948, when Leland Graben was our pastor, an evangelist named Leland Trapp was there for a few days. He was a wonderful singer. When they came to our home for dinner, he told my mother, "We need to have Harley take a stand for the Lord."

Well, even though I was in high school, I wasn't ready to commit. At that age, you aren't ready to commit to anything more than just going to church and doing what you've always done. I can recall him coming out while we were doing chores. I was taking the cattle back to the pasture after evening milking had been done, and he followed me. He had on his rubber boots. As we were walking along together, he said, "I've come to ask you to take a stand for the Lord."

Well, I didn't know, really, what that meant. We kept on walking, and I didn't say anything.

Some years later, we heard that Leland Trapp and a Reverend Spong had drowned in a fishing accident in Canada, when the boat they were in overturned. It was quite a tragedy.

As I said, I had a chance to meet many of those pastors, up till around 1953, when I left the area and started my new radio broadcast career in Red Wing. I went from Sumner EUB to the First Methodist church in Red

Wing, where I sang in the choir. When I moved to Rochester in 1957, I attended Homestead Church on 13th Avenue Southeast. That's where my wife June and I were married in 1959. We joined that church in early 1961, over forty years ago.

In 1994, the Sumner Center Church leaders asked me to come back and share my memories from that 50th anniversary celebration of 1944, when my mother and dad played such a large musical role in the church. Several of those early pastors were back again for that centennial celebration.

That day, we also called up two couples who had been married in a double ring ceremony in 1942, during World War II. They had already celebrated their 50th anniversaries, but they were able to come back for the 1994 celebration. They were Joe and Hazel (Leibold) Allen, and Lyle and Lavon (Button) Wiggins. Mother had played the "Wedding March" for that double ceremony, as she did for so many weddings in the 1930s through the 1960s.

Other couples at whose weddings she played included Roger and Elaine (Ellenberg) Webb, in 1948; Lyle and Mary Ellen (Yetter) McNamara, and Ray and Phyllis (Anderson) Bartel. Mother played music again for the Bartels on their 25th anniversary in 1979. Then there were Ross and Dorothy (Fleshner) DeYoung, Dale and Adean (King) Turner, Lyle and Phyllis (Holmen) Buchholtz, Everett and Eileen (Baker) Tucker, Ellsworth and Marjorie (Baker) Huper, Earl and Bernice (King) Ellenberg, and my Aunt Ila Flathers and Fred Marlow. Both Eileen Baker and Phyllis Anderson had been former neighbors and my schoolteachers at Dogtown district 118 school in the 1940s. Mother also played music for many funerals during those years.

During my years at Homestead United Methodist Church in Rochester, I've served on various boards, committees, and as a church trustee from 1979-1985. We've seen pastors change and buildings being structurally updated. The present church dates back to 1917, when it was located on East Center Street at 8th Avenue Southeast. It was called the East Side Community Church United Brethren in Christ then. Today it is located at 400 13th Ave Southeast, and the cornerstone says the church building was constructed in 1950.

The pastors I've known who have served at Homestead Church are Vern Hilton, from 1939 till 1958, Merle and Jean Dunn, from 1958 till 1982, Dave Schneider and his wife Esther, 1982-86, Bruce Buller and his wife Greta, 1986-98, and Duane Gebhard and his wife Jennifer, 1998 through today. (I mention the pastors' wives because they were always very important in the life of the church.) It was Merle Dunn, along with young Don Utzman from our Sumner Church, who performed our marriage ceremony in September 1959. Homestead is a community and neighborhood church, and I am proud to have had a part in its work. My goal in this life is to continue "helping God's work."

Old-Style Baptisms

About a year after Dick Rogers died when struck by lightning in 1941, two other Rogers kids, Bob and Marjorie, and their parents invited my family to come witness their baptism at the Pleasant Grove Church of Christ, where Dick's funeral had been held. I'd never seen baptism by total immersion before. At Sumner Church, I was accustomed only to the sprinkling of water on the child's head by the pastor. The Pleasant Grove Church of Christ had a good-sized baptismal tank built into the floor up behind the pulpit, so that their members could be baptized in true Biblical tradition.

I recall sitting down in the pews and seeing my two friends walk across the floor and go down into the tank. Their pastor, Harvey Smith, then pushed their heads below the water with a quiet splash. Later we talked with the kids briefly as they were drying their heads and bodies with towels they had brought from home.

John the Baptist baptized Jesus in that manner, and I guess many churches follow that tradition, but not any of the churches I've attended regularly. In recent weeks, I got to thinking about this, and wondered if that little church, which later burned down, might have been a Baptist church for a time. I called my old friend Ernest Klomps, my old district 118 school neighbor, who is really a walking book of memories. He was a long-time member of that Pleasant Grove church, and he assured me that it was always the Church of Christ (not the Christian Church, which is a different denomination). It was built in the mid-1850s, around the time that Pleasant Grove was being platted in 1855. He couldn't say if the church building that burned in February 1948 was the original structure, but it very well could have been. It's believed that a furnace fan failed and the furnace became overheated, starting the fire. Ernie told me that the reason it spread so quickly that morning, when it was 36 degrees below zero without a whisper of a breeze, was that it found its way into the space between the main floor and an added inclined floor below the pulpit.

Ernie also told me that the baptismal tank was set in place when the floor of the second level was built. He said he was sure of that, because when he and Edith Toogood were baptized in 1937, they had to go to the south fork of the Root River, across the highway and southeast of Fugle's Mill. It was a popular swimming hole, with clean water, and it was summer when Pastor Harold Buckles "dunked" them there. Even after the tank was installed in the church, people preferred to be baptized in the summer, because there was no heater for the water in the church tank.

Ernie was born in 1912 in Harmony, Minnesota. His family later moved to the farm on which he lived a great share of his life, a quarter section right on the Fillmore/Olmsted county line about three miles southeast of Pleasant Grove and two miles northeast of my old brick country school. At the time of his baptism, he had been married for a year to Maxine Carothers.

When I told my cousin Lois Flathers Nelson, now 92 and a resident of Rochester, about Ernie and Edith being baptized in the river, she told me that she had watched her mother, Bertha, being baptized in a very muddy river in 1916, when Lois was about six years old. Bertha was wearing a woolen skirt that just would not go down into the water. Lois said, "I watched my mom trying to push that skirt down with her, but it wouldn't go. I was sure she'd drown. And when she came up, she was covered with mud." Neither Lois nor I think that baptismal site was the same one where Ernie and Edith were baptized in 1937. Bertha lived to be 112 1/2 years old, and died on November 21, 1997.

Ernie Klomps says that there were four boys, all born in 1912, who grew up together as members of the Pleasant Grove Producers 4-H Club — himself, Basil Bernard, Boyd Flathers (Lois's brother and my cousin) and Myron Clark. They were all still living in late 2003, approaching 91 years of age. Ernie's wife Maxine died on April 23, 1997. She and Ernie had six children, twenty-two grandchildren and twenty-two great-grandchildren.

Shiver My Timbers — It's A Shivaree

If you haven't attended a good old-fashioned shivaree, you're missing a lot. A shivaree is a surprise celebration given newlyweds a few days after their wedding. According to the dictionary, it's a mock serenade to the couple, performed late in the evening with tin cans, pots and pans, washtubs, empty milk cans — anything that makes noise. Shivarees probably originated in France between 1400 and 1600 AD, and are sometimes spelled 'chivaree' or 'charivari.' The shivaree may be dying out, at least in its original form, replaced these days by a beer blast featuring an open keg or two.

I recall a couple of shivarees from my younger days, one held in 1941 and another in 1950. I was ten years old in November 1941, when my cousin Boyd Flathers (who lived on a farm a couple of miles east of Pleasant Grove) stopped by our place one evening about 9 pm. He and his wife, Leora, told us that some friends were getting ready to shivaree newlyweds Will and Clara Anderson, whose farm was on highway 74 a couple of miles east of the Old Stone Church.

Will and Clara were no spring chickens. They were a middle-aged couple, probably in their late 60s, who had both been married before and lost their spouses. Clara had been married to Arthur Zincke, who lived a couple miles to the north of our farm and a good mile southwest of Boyd Flathers. Both Arthur and the first Mrs. Anderson had died within a short time of each other.

We agreed to join the party. Boyd and Leora, along with their friends Howard and Edna Welch, met with the others at the Old Stone Church, about three miles southeast of our farm, and led us all to the Anderson place.

The lights were out. The house and yard were dark as the entourage of ten to twelve cars approached the farm. Horns began to honk, and people got out of their cars ringing cowbells and sleighbells, beating washtubs, making noise on anything they could. Dad and Boyd went to Will's front door and knocked until finally a light came on, and there stood Will in his nightshirt, looking bewildered by all the noise. Dad and Boyd explained that their friends were throwing Will and Clara a party.

"Well," Will said, "I guess we'd better go into Pleasant Grove and get some 'goodies.'"

Dad and Boyd drove Will to Wamsgan's Grocery Store, seven or eight miles away. They awakened Ed Wamsgan, whose wife Emily was Clara's sister. I don't know if Ed gave them a brother-in-law price break or not, but Dad and Will cleaned out all the store's Snickers, Mars Bars, Milky Ways, O. Henrys and Baby Ruths, as well as boxes of cigars. They brought the candy back to the farm, where the revelers were waiting for their treats. We emptied those boxes of candy quickly, eating it all outside, with no beer or anything like that to wash it down. There were a lot of laughs that night at an unexpected party honoring a wonderful couple.

In the late autumn of 1950, I attended another shivaree at the home of newlyweds Lauren and Jean Smith. Young Lauren was the son of Newell and Minnie Smith, whom we knew well as part of the Sumner Center Church congregation. He married Jean Hanson of Rochester, and they settled for a time on a farm belonging to Merwin Leibold, located one mile east of the church. This party had a little more advanced planning; we knew about it a few days beforehand. It was an orderly event, with candy bars and ice cream. I'm not sure if there were cigars or beer. That shivaree must have been a good luck charm, because the Lauren Smiths went on to raise nine children, and they have been married for over fifty years.

Local War Heroes

As I grew up, I remember hearing my mother say, "Your Uncle Ted paid the supreme sacrifice in the first World War." When I was a little boy,

I didn't really know what that meant, but as I got a little older, and World War II arrived, I did. Uncle Ted, one of my mother's three brothers, died just a little over a month before the armistice was signed ending the first World War, between Germany and the United States and its allies. I have a copy of the certificate that the army of the United States of America sent to his family. It arrived about nine months after Uncle Ted died in the Argonne Forest of Belgium, and it reads:

> *This is to certify that Theodore E. Raabe, private, Co. D, 18th Infantry, died with honor in the service of his country on the 4th day of October, 1918. This is given at Washington, D.C., Office of the Adjutant General of the Army, the 17th day of July, 1919.*

Mother said that one of Ted's buddies, who had been with him during those years, came to visit them later, as buddies often do. He told them that Uncle Ted, who was 23 years old at the time, had said to him in the morning of that day in October 1918, "I'm afraid today I'm going to get mine."

And he did.

It was a sad story. The family coped with it, as many families do who lose a son in the war. In 1920, the Veterans of Foreign Wars (VFW) organized the Hanson/Raabe Post, #4114, to honor Uncle Ted and George Melvin Hanson, two of Spring Valley's soldiers who died in World War I. The post headquarters remains in downtown Spring Valley to this day. Recently, my sister and I bought a paver with Uncle Ted's name on it to be placed at the Soldiers Field Veterans' Memorial in Rochester.

Mary and Harry Yetter, who lived a mile straight south of our farm, had to cope with the loss of their son, Harry, Jr., near the end of World War II. Harry was just 20 years old. He had gone into the navy in 1943 and died in the bay off Okinawa in the spring of 1945. I remember Roy Finn, who was a neighbor of the Yetters, coming to school and telling us, "Junior Yetter just died in the war."

I was thirteen then, in the eighth grade, and the news of Harry's death was a shock. We still didn't understand what war was about, even though we'd been reading about the war, buying defense stamps, saving things, rationing gas, and using ration tickets for sugar, tires, butter and meat. Rationing was all over the place in those days. But it was difficult to understand that lives were being lost, too.

Young Harry Yetter was on board the destroyer USS McDermott when it was hit by shells from the USS Missouri in the bay nearby. Historians call it "friendly fire," when people are killed by weapons fired from their own side. A similar episode occurred when the plane carrying band leader Glenn Miller went down in 1944 while flying over the English Channel. In recent years, it has come to light that Miller's plane was shot down in poor flying conditions by Allied planes in the area.

The battle was hot and heavy over Okinawa during those weeks in 1945, and thousands of servicemen on both sides were killed. According to the Yetters' other son, James (who died on December 19, 2001, aged 74), Harry was badly wounded when the McDermott was hit, and was transferred to the USS Wisconsin. He died shortly thereafter and was buried at sea. James also served in the navy. He had joined in 1944, just a year after Harry. I had gone to school with both those lads. Harry was always so kind to me when he was in the eighth grade and I was in the first. James was about four years older than I, and their sister Mary Ellen graduated from Chatfield High in 1946, three years before I did.

Harry Prescher, the Sovereign Fuel man from Stewartville, lost his son, Harold, in the war. I recall Harry driving his tank truck filled with gasoline through our neighborhood in those days. He was always a smiling person. He would keep a box of candy bars in the front seat, because he often would be giving somebody a ride home from school. It was very difficult for him when Harold died, but still Harry Prescher kept smiling as best he could.

We used to buy US Savings Bond defense stamps at school. On Friday morning, the teacher would say, "Who has brought a dime for a stamp today?" You could buy one stamp for a dime, which was a lot of money for a youngster in the early 1940s. The stamps were pasted into a book with your name on it.

When you'd bought $18.75 worth of stamps, you could convert your book of stamps into a "war bond" at the bank. I bought one of those bonds in 1944, and I redeemed it in 1964, when our first son Edward was born. The bond had matured to $25.00 in ten years.

Kueker Illustration "Armistice Day Blizzard"

Kueker Illustration "Blocked Roads/ Man walking . . . also dog"

Harley & Elaine Flathers with Shetland Pony "King" & dog "Jack", 1940.

Kueker Illustration . . . Sumner Ball Diamond on James Caldbeck farm in late 1940s and 1950s.

Sumner Center United Methodist Church (with sign) 100th Anniversary 9/11/94. Photo: Elaine Flathers.

At right, Sumner Center Church (interior). Harley in pulpit as MC with 1942 Double Wedding Party. L-R: Joe & Hazel (Leibold) Allen, and Lavon (Button) Wiggins and husband Lyle. And Pastor Wesley Miller, who performed ceremony in '42. Photo: Elaine Flathers

Harley visits with Aunt Bertha Flathers on 3/30/95 . . . her 110th birthday. She lived to be 112½ until Nov. 21, 1997.

Newlyweds, Adean (King) Turner and husband Dale, leaving Sumner Center church in mid June 1953. My mom, Vivian Flathers, played for these weddings and many others during nearly 40 years at this church.

Moment 7

Radio: How and Why

Somebody asked me recently, "How did you get into radio?"

I said, "Well, there were a number of reasons. But I would say that the good Lord guided me after I'd had polio."

I guess, really, we don't always know what we're preparing for throughout life. I do know that all those years when I was growing up, radio was fascinating to me. I couldn't get enough of radio on the farm.

When I was a young lad, about seven years old, my Dad came up to Montgomery Ward's in Rochester and bought this beautiful Airline Radio. It was a console-type radio, meaning it stood upright on the floor. It was a nice piece of furniture. We did not have electricity. Instead, we had a battery that we bought with the radio. It was like a car battery, but larger, about one and a half times as big as a regular car battery. Dad had to string the antenna wire up through a window, out through the lilac bush and across to another tree — that was the antenna for this Montgomery Ward radio, for which he paid $86 back in 1938.

But oh, what a joy it was, to have that radio, and all those programs! I recall coming home from school in the afternoon, and I had to do some chores before I could start listening to radio, because the children's programs came on at 5:30. So I would get out and do a certain number of things, like pumping water into the tank for the cows to drink, and then I'd get back into the house to listen to "Jimmy Allen and His Flying Machine." It was a super program that kids loved. I didn't listen to "Captain Midnight," but a lot of people did.

There were other programs that we just lived by in the 1930s and 1940s. Families were glued to the radio. They planned their evenings, they planned lunch around radio. What made it so exciting was you used your imagination. They say radio is theater of the mind. We could imagine being there, whether it was a thrill show of some sort, a circus, or a soap opera. We could put ourselves into it.

I loved radio. I loved Red Skelton. I loved Bob Hope. Oh, I could go on and on with a list of super half-hour or hour programs. In later years, there was "Our Miss Brooks," starring Eve Arden. There was Jack Benny, with "Rochester!" and Dennis Day. In later years, I would interview Jack Benny and Red Skelton.

I especially loved "Fibber McGee and Molly" on Tuesday nights. Jim and Marian Jordan starred as Fibber McGee and Molly. They started out singing together in a church choir in Peoria, Illinois. And what a creative thing they did, getting together with comedy. Their show hit America at the right time. It went solidly from April 16, 1935, until June 30, 1953. Every Tuesday night from 8:30 till 9 was "Fibber McGee and Molly." I wouldn't miss it. I loved Fibber's closet, and all of that. When they would sign off in the spring, at the end of June, they'd say, "Well, now, we're going on summer vacation. We'll be back and see you on the last Tuesday in September." I thought it was such a long wait!

Mother had her regular programs that she listened to faithfully every day. Then, at 12:30, here came Cedric Adams with his Noontime News from WCCO radio in Minneapolis, "brought to you by Crisco and Spry." All of Minnesota remembers Cedric Adams, the premium newscaster from WCCO. The Noontime News went on for a half hour, and then at night he would do the 10 o'clock news. People wouldn't go to bed until they'd listened to Cedric Adams and the Nighttime News, brought to you Monday through Friday by "Tastee Bread for tasty toast, baked while you sleep," and on Saturday and Sunday night by "Coca Cola, the pause that refreshes." On Christmas Eve, he would have his three sons reading the news with him. It was all part of our growing up. Cedric Adams went on for a lot of years, and a lot of tears were shed when he died in 1961. I recall him from

1938 on, when he was going strong, doing the news. He was the personality of the upper Midwest in radio. Cedric was in great demand. He would go out to various functions, a graduation or a grand opening or a celebration — it was something when you got Cedric Adams there.

I grew up listening a lot to WCCO radio out of the Twin Cities, even though we were only 20 miles away from Rochester, where KROC was going strong from 1935 on. As a kid, wherever I could get "Fibber McGee and Molly," that's what I listened to. We could get it on KROC, an NBC outlet, during the day, but at night, when they had to cut power, we would pick it up on WHO 1040, Des Moines, Iowa, 50,000 watts. I didn't know why power had to be cut at night, didn't know why all the stations sort of jumbled up together after the sun went down, but that's the way it still is for AM radio.

Sunday night was a special time in those days of the late 1930s and early 1940s, when I was always asking to hear "Just one more program! Please, Mom?" Jack Benny was on at 6, Fred Allen and Allen's Alley at 6:30. Then at 7, it was time for Edgar Bergen, the ventriloquist, with his "children," Charlie McCarthy and Mortimer Snerd. Charlie was a wisecracking smart-aleck and Mortimer was really dumb. Edgar asked Mortimer once, "How can you be so stupid?" and Mortimer replied, in a very deep, silly-sounding voice, "Oh, when I was born, my brain was buckin' a headwind." And the audience roared. Effie Clinker was another of Bergen's characters. Bergen's daughter, well-known TV and film actress Candace Bergen, was born during those years when her father was a household word.

Later Sunday evening, from 9 to 10 pm, we listened to a very uplifting radio show that only those who are 65 or older will remember: "The Old-Fashioned Revival Hour," with the Rev. Charles E. Fuller. I recall hearing it on ABC, the American Broadcasting Company, which had formerly been part of NBC. (NBC originally had two networks, the Red and the Blue. They sold off the Blue network, which became ABC.) The "Old-Fashioned Revival Hour" had superb music. Rudy Atwood played the piano with all the frills a person could get out of those 88 keys. They had a choir that opened each program by singing "Jesus Saves," and a male quartet that sang old-time gospel music, followed by the Rev. Fuller's powerful sermons.

In the early part of the program, the Rev. Fuller would introduce his wife, and ask her to read some of the many letters that came in weekly. "Go right ahead, Honey," he'd say. She would read letters from soldiers in foxholes, who were fighting in the war against Japan in those tragic island battles on Luzon, Leyte, Iwo Jima and Guadalcanal. Or she might read a letter from a worker who had left his home in the U.S. to work on the Alcan Highway, which the army was building as a military supply route leading from the northwest corner of the U.S. through Canada into Alaska. (The Canadian portion of this 1523-mile-long highway from Dawson Creek, B.C., to Fairbanks, Alaska, was turned over to the Canadian government on April 1, 1946.) Those letters were a touching portion of the program.

Then the Rev. Fuller would preach. Near the end of the hour, as his voice became weaker and somewhat hoarse, he urged listeners to "write to us at the Old Fashioned Revival Hour, Post Office Box 1-2-3, Los Angeles 5-3, California." Then, very solemnly, he would say, "With every eye closed and every head bowed, continue in prayer...as we leave the air."

This program lasted well into the 1950s. My dad's cousin, Mae Flathers, who had been a missionary to China in her earlier years, knew the Rev. Fuller personally. On a visit to our home in 1950, she spoke very highly of his evangelistic work.

A Radio Without Electricity

Now, you've got to have power to make this radio business work. That rechargeable battery we bought with it would last quite a while. When the battery went dead, Dad would take it out of the back of the radio and into the garage, where he had put a wind charger on the roof. The wind charger stood on a six foot "tripod" stand, and had a great big propeller that looked like an airplane propeller. He'd bought all this equipment from Montgomery Ward at the same time, so he could recharge that battery. It worked fine when we had wind, and we always had wind in the winter in the 1930s and 1940s. Oh! Cold! Minnesota winters were so much worse then than they are today in terms of extreme temperatures and snow. It would take about three days to charge up that battery if we had good wind. I can hear that big propeller purring yet, and see the little ammeter, the needle showing the amount of electric current in amperes, swinging. And Dad would say, "Oh! Listen to that! Oh, it's taking juice now, it's charging!"

While the radio battery was out there charging for three days, he'd take the battery out of the car and put it in the house, so we didn't have to lose any radio. Sometimes, as luck would have it — maybe the wind failed and the battery wasn't getting charged — the car battery remained in the house for more than three days. Then when it came time for him to go to town on Friday, the car battery would be so low it wouldn't start the car. I can see him yet, putting the battery into the car, hitching up a team of horses, putting them up in front of the old 1928 Chevrolet, giving it a pull, and it would be started. It didn't take much to start those old cars; they didn't have an automatic transmission. Then he'd drive to town, get the battery recharged or get another battery — they'd often loan you a full battery while you were getting yours charged up — to keep everything going.

That was just part of life without electricity. We carried lanterns. We had kerosene lamps. We had a wood stove in the kitchen. I can see Mother yet on Friday baking bread. My goodness! She made eight loaves and fifty-four biscuits. I'd come home from school, and those buns would be hot. Wow! I couldn't get past those buns before I'd go out and do chores. I can remember helping my Dad cut logs with a crosscut saw. We didn't have a fireplace; we cut up logs or old fence posts for the kitchen range. It did everything you needed, that good old kitchen range, whether it was baking or canning or heating water for washing. Mother had a washing machine — as I recall, it was a Speed Queen with a gas motor — and every Monday she did the wash. That was a big operation!

They were great providers, my Dad and Mother. They were great with the garden. The garden was so vital. I'd come home from school, and I'd see the neighbors in the field, and I'd say, "Dad, don't you think you ought to be out in the field planting corn and oats?"

He'd say, "We're going to plant the garden now. If we don't plant the garden today, we're not going to have food to eat next winter." And he was always right.

He took time to do it right. He was a good gardener — I think he would probably compare to a master gardener today. He loved gardening. He loved flowers. He had certain ways of doing things, certain times and places — when to plant potatoes, when to harvest.

I can see them yet, my Mother and Dad, putting down a hundred quarts of apples in applesauce that they picked either from our trees or neighbors' trees. Mother canned a lot of tomatoes, maybe seventy-five to a hundred quarts in glass jars. We canned pork. We canned carrots and sweet corn — lots of it. When winter came, a big part of the basement was full of potatoes that we had dug in the fall. They put cabbage down in sauerkraut. My goodness! I can see them doing it yet, putting down sauerkraut in a five gallon or ten gallon crock jar and letting it ferment. It was the same thing with pork; they put the pork in brine after butchering and put it into a crock jar.

So we lived without electricity, and we didn't miss it because we hadn't had it. At the start of the war, when the Rural Electrification Administration was finalized through President Franklin Roosevelt, the lines started coming through the country and farmers had a chance to sign up and hook up. Many farms had electric light plants then. We wanted to sign up, but we were eight light poles away from where the power ended — just from the schoolhouse to our farm, about 200 rods. It was late 1941, and the power company would not extend it. They said, "It's wartime, we can't go any farther."

Dad said, "Well, if we haven't had the electricity, I guess we'll get along without it. I'll keep carrying a lantern." Finally in 1947, a couple of years after the war had ended, the Tri-County Electric Co-op from Rushford, Minnesota, was ready to string more lines, and they brought it down to our place. A man named Roland, or "Rol," Warren, from Spring Valley, and his man did the electrifying of our place. They wired our old house. They wired our barn. We had a yard light. I couldn't get over it; I was so excited! We converted the radio to electric power. We converted the washing machine. It was just fabulous! You could use as much electricity as you wanted, and there it was. We even put a radio in the barn.

All this time, I was still loving radio: 1946, 1947, 1948, 1949. In 1948, I listened to the Minneapolis Lakers professional basketball team, and heard the great name of George Mikan. The old Minneapolis Lakers were a fabulous team, and everything worked around George Mikan, who stood six foot ten. He was voted in the spring of 1950 to be the greatest basketball player of the past fifty years. In April 2001, fifty-one years later, they unveiled a nine-foot sculpture at Target Center in Minneapolis, honoring George Mikan. He's now 76, and he's lost one leg due to diabetes, but he was there to accept that honor. The Minneapolis Lakers moved to Los Angeles in the 1960s; today they're the Los Angeles Lakers. But I loved listening to the Minneapolis Lakers on radio in those early post-war years.

In 1949, when I took sick with polio, I went to Minneapolis for almost a year. There, at Sister Kenny Institute, from July 13, 1949 through May 10, 1950, I learned a lot about life — a lot of it through TV, which was brand new. The first channels that came on in the Twin Cities were in 1948: Channel 4, WCCO-TV, and Channel 5, KSTP-TV. And shortly thereafter, there were more channels.

I got a chance to see the Minneapolis Lakers play on television. It was a fabulous thing to see, and I got to appreciate sports a lot more. I became a sports fan by watching TV while flat on my back in bed. I think a lot of young men who were suffering from polio did the same thing. We were a captive audience. There was the old Minneapolis Millers baseball team, and the St. Paul Saints. Those teams were in the American Association. The Minnesota Twins came into being about a decade later. By 1961 there were no more Minneapolis Millers or St. Paul Saints — they just became the Minnesota Twins.

Radio and TV were a wonderful comfort all those years, and still are, for me. During my time in the hospital, as I watched those games being played, the great sportscaster, the voice of the Minneapolis Lakers, was Dick Enroth. He had been with radio WLOL, but soon WCCO snapped him up.

Listening To Mom's Soap Operas

It was May 1950, spring planting time, when I got home from the hospital. I was still too weak to drive a tractor.

Dad said to Mother, "Well, what do you want to do? Do you want me to try to go and hire a man ?"

"Well," she said, "if we hire a man you're going to pay him and I've got to feed him." And she said, "Maybe I could go ahead and learn to drive the tractor." So, in her mid-50s, she learned to drive a tractor, that little Ford Ferguson, and a two-bottom plow. She went out there and plowed and did field work.

And she said, "Now, if I'm going to do this, I want you, Harley, to listen to my radio programs for me."

I laughed. I said, "Oh, Ma!"

I'd always made fun of her listening to these soap operas, but you know, that was some of the greatest preparation for me in my radio career later on, though I didn't realize it at the time. I look back at this and say, "Wow! I've been guided in so many areas." All the years when I was listening before I took sick, I couldn't get enough radio, and here was another chance to listen carefully. Today I can still rattle off the names of the characters, the times of day they came on and what happened to them.

Mom had seven different quarter-hour programs that she listened to in the forenoon. First, at 10.45 am, there would be Rosemary, then Wendy Warren and the news at 11. Aunt Jenny came on at 11:15, followed by Helen Trent, Our Gal Sunday, Big Sister and then, finally, Ma Perkins. Ma Perkins sort of wrapped up the mid-morning through the forenoon of special "soaps." They called them soap operas because they were generally sponsored by a soap of some sort: "Presenting Ma Perkins, brought to you by Oxydol." I can remember that just as plain as yesterday. Ma Perkins was going strong in the era of World War II and after. Ma Perkins was sort of the grandmother and mother to everyone. She'd lost a son in the war, and the son's widow was there, and she had another son, Willie, helping her in the lumber yard. It was all so very believable.

When Willie, who was making $35 per week, wanted her to raise his salary to $40, Ma would say, "Well, I've got to talk with Shuffle." Now Shuffle was Shuffle Shober. He was her right hand man, and Ma Perkins wouldn't do anything without consulting with Shuffle, because he really ran the lumber yard.

I would listen to all of them and make notes, so when Mom came back in for lunch, I could bring her right up to date. And that's how I learned about soap operas.

Still, I couldn't wait to get out on the tractor myself. I had two Kenny crutches. For those of you who may remember the Kenny crutch, it's not an underarm crutch, it's a crutch with a piece of leather around the elbow. You learn to walk with it. They called it the Kenny method. They hoped that you would put weight on your legs and use the crutch as a guide and standing support. So for several years I used the Kenny crutch, with the leather around the elbow. In 1957, I started using two wooden walking canes.

When I first got home, my dad was putting in a bathroom, because we didn't have one in the old home. We had electricity by then, but a lot of things on the farm were still kind of old-fashioned. They weren't what we would call barrier-free. We had six steps to get up into the house, and if I wanted to go upstairs to the bathroom, it was up a long, narrow stairway. Things were very difficult. But I still had those good arms, and they made it possible for me to get around on my Kenny crutches. I've always been very thankful for those good arms. That's really what brought me through that time.

So with the help of my Kenny crutches, I would get out there on that tractor, that John Deere B, for which we had waited three years in the 1940s. I got up there and started cultivating corn and doing all the things a young man on a tractor does. I had difficulty hooking up an implement, of course. I'd say to my dad in the morning, "Dad, just come and help me put gas in the tractor, and hook up this disk. Then you open the gate, and I'm out of here. I'll go out there to the field and I'll work."

And I did. I really worked a lot. I probably did more than I should, but you can't tell an 18-year-old boy who loves farming not to do it.

Agriculture and the farm were my life. Because they knew that, I think it hurt the folks even more when I took sick. But I accepted it quite readily. This was the way life was going to be.

Following the corn and soybean cultivating, I was there to help with the harvest. Finally I could use the combine, which Dad had used the past year while I was sick. I'd waited so long for the fun of getting started on a combine. I wanted to pull that rope to start that 20-horsepower Wisconsin motor, and see that combine go. I wanted to get on that John Deere tractor and actually run it. To me, it was just everything I could ever hope for. I pulled the corn picker, that old single-row Wood Brothers corn picker, with a load behind it, and brought the corn in. I would go out there alone, in the darnedest weather. I had no business being alone, but I did it. We had a little cab on the tractor. Dad sent away to someplace in the Farmer magazine (which farmers lived by) and here came this cab in the mail. It was a $175 cab, and it really was pretty nice. It gave you protection. Nowadays, most tractors have cabs.

Well, I did this kind of thing in 1950, 1951 and 1952. But I discovered that when winter came, all I could do was sit by the fire. There were no ifs, ands, buts or maybes. I could not walk in the snow, to the barn or anywhere else.

I spent some time making leather belts, billfolds and purses, because we learned that at Sister Kenny Institute. My Dad would take a billfold to town, and say, "Hey, look what my son has done. Isn't that neat? Wouldn't you like one like that?" And he'd come home with another order. He was my best salesman. We had a man in Stewartville who ran the Our Own Hardware Store, Don Pitt, a fine person. He set up a little display in one of his counters with several of my purses and billfolds, and a sign: "Help Harley Recuperate." And some people would order a billfold or a purse. I'd hammer out beautiful designs. On some of those billfolds for the farmers I might put an Angus steer. I put a Hawaiian dancing girl on one for my cousin Dale Turner, who wanted something unique. It was interesting, but I knew that it wasn't going to be the kind of thing I could make a livelihood out of. I still have the tools, but I haven't done leatherwork for fifty years.

I Discover Radio School

Finally, in the summer of 1952, after I had done three years of farming and knew that I couldn't do it full time, the Good Lord guided me again. I was invited by some long-time family friends of ours, John Oliphant and his brother Don, to go to the KROC studios in Rochester. Their father, the Rev. John Thomas Oliphant, a retired pastor who was getting along in years, was a wonderful singer. He used to preach in Spring Valley, where my mother had been the church pianist during the upper teens and early 1920s. They knew his voice might not last much longer, so they wanted to do a recording.

We went to the old KROC studios in the 100 First Avenue building. It was the 20th of July 1952. While we were there, I saw a young man in the next studio, going in and out and running the radio programs. I didn't know anything more about it than that, but one of the Oliphant boys said, "You know, that's something you could do, Harley."

And I said, "You know, maybe I could."

I went in and talked with Don Eggerstrom, this young announcer who had been there for just a couple of years. He told me, "Oh, yeah, there's a radio school. I'll tell you where to go." He gave me the address of some people to call in Minneapolis. At that time it was called the American Institute of the Air. It was founded in 1946 by a couple named R.C. and Helen Brown, who were both polio survivors, and its name was later changed to the Brown Institute. (The Browns were efficient people, and very successful. They had no immediate family. Years later, in the late 1990s, they died together of asphyxiation, getting into their car in the garage after starting the motor.)

That summer of 1952, after talking with Don, I immediately called the institute and set up an appointment to go up and interview. First, they test your voice: "Read this for us. Oh, yes, you'll do fine. Oh, wonderful!" It was a 27-week course and cost $33 a week. At that time, in 1952, a number of men were just coming out of the service who had served in the second World War or the Korean War. These veterans were looking around to start training for something new. There were lots of new courses being set up for them, and it was very convenient for young people like me.

I made the decision that this would be my new venture in the fall of 1952. I picked the last load of corn on Saturday morning, the 18th day of October. I said, "Dad, I want to help you a little more, get one more load of corn in for you." I picked that load of corn, brought it up into the barnyard, and got in the car. And Dad and Mother drove me off to a new career.

Several weeks before my first day at radio school, which was October 20, 1952, I had arranged to live at a fine little home owned my Mabel Paschal at 3105 35th Avenue South. It was a full eight blocks away from the school, which was at 3123 East Lake Street. Fortunately, I had a ride almost every morning with another fellow from close by who was also going to the school. In the afternoon — school was from 8 till 1 — I would usually walk home. And of course in the winter — oh, man! I took some falls! It was a difficult time. I had to learn how to get on and off the streetcar when I wanted to go downtown to catch the bus to go places.

About the first of April 1953, the people at the radio station in Red Wing called me. I had been down to see them earlier. Before you finish radio announcing school, you start going out to visit stations, and I went to Red Wing and Mankato. You like to go and get acquainted, let them know who you are. Usually, they say, "Well, that's fine, good luck, we'll call you if we need you." Soon, the folks in Red Wing called to ask me to come and fill in for a couple of weeks while their man of the morning went off looking for another job. The station in Red Wing, KAAA 1250 on the dial, had started on January 5, 1949. It was a daytimer, which meant that they signed on at 6 in the morning and signed off at sundown. There was nothing else; that was it.

But it was a wonderful experience. I had two weeks there, in the middle of April 1953. I hadn't yet finished my schooling. I did those two weeks, then went back to finish the last two weeks of school.

When I graduated — they gave me a certificate — my teacher at that time, Dean Montgomery, an outstanding announcer with WCCO for many years, said, "Hey, Harley, you're okay. You can go anywhere." That was very reassuring.

So I graduated and went home. It was a Friday, about the first weekend in May. On Tuesday, Red Wing called me again. Peter Lyman, the man with whom I would work for two and a half years, called and said, "Harley, can you come back and work three more days? John Williams is going off again for a job interview in Texas. Can you come in over Thursday-Friday-Saturday?"

I said, "Yep! I'll be there."

Dad let me borrow the car. I drove to Red Wing and stayed there at the Tee Pee Tonka Hotel for three nights. When I finished those three days of work at 5 o'clock on Saturday afternoon, I went to tell the boss lady, Maxine Jacobs, goodbye. But she came out of her office and said, "Harley, John Williams just called from Texas. He's got that job. Can you come back Monday and work for us regularly?"

I said, "I think I can."

You talk about divine guidance through my life! Everything I've needed has been there. I went back to work, and was there for four and a half years.

I didn't have a car. I got to Red Wing on that little shuttle bus that ran from Rochester to Lake City, then took another bus up highway 61 to Red Wing. My Dad said, "I wish I could give you a car, but I can't. But I'll be there to help you when you're ready to buy one."

It wasn't long before I found a good used car on May 25, 1953. It was a 1951 Ford with automatic transmission from Olson Motors in Lake City. And my Dad was there with a $500 down payment.

He said, "Here it is. Don't bother paying me back. You worked a long time on the farm." That was the kind of support he and my mother gave me.

One of the things I've enjoyed being able to do, helping me to remain independent during this last half-century following polio, is to drive a car. When you can still drive a car and be independent, you're a different person.

I had to learn to drive a car all over again after I got out of the hospital. I started learning to drive my dad's 1936 Chevy in the summer of 1950, shortly after I got home. I had no use of my legs. I would lift my legs with my hands, put one on the brake and one on the clutch, and manipulate them with my hands. I taught myself to drive with a straight stick on the hills of Preston, Minnesota, because Preston was the Fillmore county seat, where I had to go to pass my driver's test, and Preston is made up entirely of hills. I wouldn't be stopped; I had to do it. I passed the test, even on the hills of Preston, moving my legs with my hands, looking over my shoulder. I even learned to do parallel parking on the hill.

In 1951, Dad purchased a 1950 Ford from the Ford dealer in Spring Valley, and it had an automatic transmission. It was almost a new car, with just a few thousand miles on it. And that was nice. It made life a lot easier, because I only had to lift one foot then. Nowadays I wouldn't even think of driving a vehicle in my condition without hand controls. But for over thirty years I drove ordinary cars, almost always with automatic transmission, from the time I started working at Red Wing until I started getting hand controls in the early 1980s. There were a lot of years that I drove lifting my foot with my hand, through places like Chicago and New York, sometimes with a car full of kids. I didn't think anything of it. It was a way of life.

Wheels, Wheels, Wheels

Every young man worth his salt always remembers his first set of "wheels" — I'm talking of powered wheels, now; in other words, that first car. I bought my first car a couple of weeks after I started at KAAA in Red Wing, in mid-May 1953. My boss, Peter Lyman, told me that he'd purchased his new Ford from Olson Motors in Lake City. He called Chuck Olson, who said, "Sure, I'll bring up a car for Harley to try out."

It was perfect. I'd told him I needed a late-model car, with automatic transmission and power steering. He brought a black 1951 four-door Ford. It had been previously owned by Dr. Bernard "Doc" Flesche, a well-known Lake City physician who had served his community for many years until his death on February 12, 1959, at the age of 54. According to his daughter Pernille, now Mrs. Robert Pope of Lake City, he went into medicine in 1935 following the deaths of both his parents from tuberculosis at Walnut

Grove, Minnesota. He served at an army reserve hospital in El Paso, Texas, and then in a rehabilitation hospital in England before settling in Lake City after World War II. Lake City's VFW Post 8729 is named the Dr. Bernard A. Flesche Post in his honor. Pernille, who is one of five children, told me that they traded in the 1951 Ford that I purchased in 1953 for a new aqua blue station wagon, which they drove that year to the western states. In 1954, Pernille (then about 8 years old) came to KAAA with a bunch of other little girls to get George Mikan's autograph, on the day that I interviewed him. I told her that I got his signature that day, too.

On January 20, 1958, I traded the Ford in on a classy-looking red and black two-door Ford Fairlane club sedan, 1956 model, which I drove for another 4 years. Then came the 1962 Chevy Impala convertible.

Now this is the only one of the thirteen cars I've owned over the past half century that I really want to brag about. It was only about six months old when I saw the ad for it in the newspaper in the spring of 1962. I went down to West-Town Motors, a small used car lot at 1510 2nd Street Southwest in Rochester, on May 20, 1962. That business, located behind where Kentucky Fried Chicken is today, wasn't a large outfit — in fact, if you blinked, you missed it — and of course it's now history. But the owner, Robert McDonough, and his salesman Robert Nordholm were happy to close the deal with us as we traded in the '56 Ford on this powerhouse vehicle.

The convertible was blue, with a white top, and it had only 7660 miles on it — just nicely broken in. It had power steering, automatic transmission, a radio (naturally) and eight cylinders providing the power of 300 horses under the hood. That white top went up and down many times over the next thirteen years, and I didn't want anybody beating me away from the stop light. I'd tromp that pedal to the floor, and the front wheels would almost lift off the ground.

At the time we bought it, I had been playing a recording by orchestra leader Billy Vaughn called "Wheels." It wasn't big in the charts, but it was a real "waker-upper," and I played it at some time nearly every morning between 6 and 9 am on my air show. One morning, I told the listeners that

I was going to play it four times between 7 and 8 am, and I did that without receiving any flak from management or complaining letters from listeners. I was spinning a lot of tunes in that era, songs by Steve Lawrence and Eydie Gorme, Nat King Cole, Rosie Clooney, Frank Sinatra and Bing Crosby, to name just a few. That song, "Wheels," seemed to go well with my new Chevy.

I've always kept a "car log" listing the make, model, year purchased, amount paid, point of purchase and whether or not an earlier car was traded in on each transaction. Over the years, we've driven a series of vehicles from sedans to wagons to minis to vans, the more recent ones adapted with hand controls. But for thirteen years, that 1962 Chevy was my pride and joy.

"I Got my Start at Brown Institute"

George Mikan Photo . . . he autographed for me in the KAAA radio studios in Red Wing, 1954.

First Car . . . 1951 Ford at Home on Farm . . . Winter 1956.

Second Car . . . 1956 Ford, red with black top in summer of 1958.

Moment 8

Starting Out in Red Wing

I started working at KAAA in Red Wing on April 10, 1953. Rock and roll was just a faint cloud on the horizon then. We were playing Nat King Cole, Frank Sinatra, Doris Day, Perry Como, Rosemary Clooney, Johnny Cash, Jimmy Rodgers. Bing was still doing his thing. Marty Robbins' "White Sport Coat and a Pink Carnation" would soon be a big hit, along with Harry Belafonte's "Jamaica Farewell." This was just before the folk music craze hit, with the Kingston Trio, the Smothers Brothers and the Christy Minstrels.

The big movies were "From Here to Eternity," "The King and I," "The Robe," and Cecil B. DeMille's "Ten Commandments." "The Music Man" and "My Fair Lady" were still to come, but we played hit songs from Rogers and Hammerstein's "Oklahoma," starring Gordon McRae and Shirley Jones. On TV, we watched "Robert Montgomery Presents." "Mr. Peepers," starring Wally Cox, came on every Sunday evening at 6:30 on KSTP-TV Channel 5. Channel 5 also carried "Your Show of Shows," with Sid Caesar and Imogene Coca, on Saturday evenings at 7. Over on Channel 4, WCCO-TV, we watched Ed Sullivan's "Toast of the Town" on Sundays at 7 pm.

Bob Ryan read the TV-5 news every evening at 6, and at 10 pm they ran "Today's Headlines" with Bill Ingram. At 10:15, following P.J. Hawf's weather report, there was Jack Horner's "Corner on Sports." Later, Channel 5 had Johnny Morris doing weather, and the exuberant Dick

Nesbit on sports. On Channel 4, they had Cedric Adams doing the news for a short while, along with Bud Kraehling on weather and Rollie Johnson on TV sports.

In 1954, rock really started hitting the air waves. WDGY in Minneapolis was the rock leader, "stirring up the listening pot" with great programs run by on-air personalities like Herb Oscar Anderson (6 to 9 am) and daytime announcers Bill Bennett and Stanley Mack on three to four-hour shifts. WDGY started giving away cash, tons of cash, to lure in the listeners. They would give clues on the air, and the only way you would know how to answer the questions was by listening to the station. Immediately WCCO radio 830 also began giving away cash — big "hunks" of cash from personalities Howard Viken and Bob White. (I remembered listening to Bob White when he was still Bob Montgomery, broadcasting in the evenings from Faribault's KDHL.) The competition between these broadcasting giants was the talk of Twin City radio. Once-faithful KAAA listeners in Red Wing began listening to those Twin City stations. It got so hot that 'CCO and WDGY began giving out each other's "clues" during their programs — "as a service to our faithful listeners!" In other words, you didn't need to change your dial to win the cash. It was a real war of the dollars to get listeners.

Rock music burst onto the scene like the fireball from a bolt of lightning. Bill Haley and the Comets released "Rock Around the Clock" in 1955, and rock was off and rolling. A former gospel singer from Memphis, Tennessee, named Elvis Presley took the nation by storm. I remember when Elvis Presley first came out in 1956, he was gyrating so much that the television cameras on the "Ed Sullivan Show" were not allowed to focus on him from the waist down.

I never really cared very much about wild rock and roll. It just wasn't my bag. I still loved good old-time music; we played a lot of that at KAAA, and a little country western. I played Kay Starr's "Rock and Roll Waltz," a neat song, but hardly in the category of rock music.

I remember the day that WDGY fired rock announcer Stanley Mack on the air. Listeners "went ballistic." In a few days, management and Mack came to terms, and he returned to the air. It was a very effective WDGY radio promotion.

This was my first radio job and there were many exciting things about it. There were only two announcers on the radio station then. I was the morning man. I would sign on anywhere from 5 to 5:30 to 6 am, depending on the time of the year, whenever the sun rose. I would take a short break from 10 am until noon, then come back and do an afternoon shift. The other man, Peter Lyman, who was the boss, took the other shifts. During his shift he would read books on the air, play records and compose radio commercials.

Every morning, Monday through Friday, from 10:30 to 10:45 am, he would read from a book. Nowadays, we wouldn't hear of anybody doing that, except maybe on public radio. But it was a popular thing at that particular station at that time. An ad in the Daily Republican Eagle on February 27, 1954, shows a picture of Peter Lyman with a book in his hand in front of the "mike" there in our studio, with the grand piano in the background. The ad says, "KAAA presents Peter Lyman's one-man drama... 'The Robe,' by Lloyd C. Douglas, Monday through Friday, 2:45 to 3 pm. A great book...a great story...a great motion picture. 1250 on your dial." He read it very dramatically, taking all the parts in various voices.

Memorable KAAA Radio Programs from the '50s

Coke Time Every Saturday, from 1 to 1:15 pm, was "Coke Time," highlights of the week's basketball or football games. The ad placed in the *Daily Republican Eagle* by one of our commercial managers, Hal Corey or Jim Bailey, read, "Win a year's supply of Coke. Tune your radio dial to 1250 every Saturday and hear Pete Petrick, Red Wing's 'Mr. Basketball,' who brings you Big Nine Conference games highlights, sponsored by your Coca-Cola dealer, Coca-Cola Bottling Company, Red Wing."

I was the young announcer who discussed the game with Pete during the basketball season. During football season, we talked with coach Russ Fechtor or his assistant, good old Ed Murphy. During those years, Red Wing High School put out some great sports teams.

Christmas Shopping Bag In December, as we neared Christmas, you heard the Christmas Shopping Bag broadcast on KAAA Monday through Saturday from 8:30 to 9 am. Presented by the Farmer's Store in Red Wing, it gave out gift ideas.

Santa Claus Advises An ad in the *Eagle* said, "and listen to Wilson's Hardware Santa Claus Show on KAAA Monday through Saturday, 4:15 to 4:30 pm, starting November 30." Usually Peter Lyman provided the Santa Claus voice, reading kids' letters to Santa, surrounded by H.W. Wilson Hardware commercials. Occasionally I had to play Santa on the air, with a "Ho-ho-ho" voice that would actually exhaust me by the time we signed off the air at 4:30 pm.

Weber's Waxworks On Saturdays from 1:30 to 2 pm, I conducted a half-hour show with four high school students from nearby schools, who "rated" the new tunes of the day. This was sponsored by the Weber Music Company in downtown Red Wing, owned by Mr. and Mrs. Jack Acaster. All the tunes featured on the show were available at Weber's Music.

During that era, their son-in-law, Bob Nelson, who also worked in the Weber Music store and who was a fine professional clarinet player, died in a tragic car crash between Red Wing and Hastings. His death was a real blow to the community. His style was like that of Ziggy Elman of the Benny Goodman orchestra, and I used to refer to him as "Ziggy" when he and I talked in person.

Record Review Because of FCC regulations, we had to close down at sundown, and December was the month with the shortest amount of daylight, so sundown came early then. As the number of days of sunlight increased, and those terribly short air-time months of November through February passed, the station's sign-off moved from 4:30 to 4:45 to 5 to 6 and so on. At 4:30, engineer Don "Speck" Wille played new record releases back to back until 5 pm, with no talk or chatter. We called it "Record Review."

Peter had recorded an "open" and "close" for the final half-hour, which Speck played at the proper times. We had no News on the Hour — KAAA had no network affiliation. Our last newscast of the day was from 4 till

4:10 pm, read by Peter. Then I followed with a "high-powered" sportscast consisting of items from the UP (United Press) wire copy and whatever I could glean locally. Sometimes I even took important sports information from the *Daily Republican Eagle* — I didn't read their stories on the air, but used information about game schedules, etc. Other wire services used by various stations included AP (Associated Press) and INS (International News Service).

From 4:15 to 4:30, except in the Christmas season, we played the Steamboat Jamboree, on the World Transcription disc, complete with script and starring Captain Lanny Ross. Then came Record Review, and finally Candlelight and Silver.

Caldlelight and Silver This ran from 5 to 6 pm daily, "for your early evening listening and dining pleasure," as Peter Lyman put it. He taped an opening and closing, and instructed the engineer which new RCA Red Seal recordings he was to play.

These were the old 12-inch wide extended play records — first on 78 rpms and then long-play 33 1/3 record albums. It wasn't long before we had high-fidelity monaural long-play recordings, or monos. And then came stereos. You could play monaural records on a stereophonic machine, but the quality wasn't as good as it was when a stereo machine had been used for the recording.

Then came the 45s, the small plastic discs with the big hole in the center. Records were identified by the number of revolutions they made per minute — rpm. In the early days, most of the records had been 78s. Now we had 33s and 45s, and even a few 16s. The 45s, which came on the scene in the mid-1950s, were used for single songs, and were bought up in large quantities by teenagers. I remember that in 1954, the Song of the Year (according to *Billboard* magazine, the radio broadcasting Bible for music and entertainment) was "The Wayward Wind," by Gogi Grant. It came out on 45s, and we played it quite a lot.

Another record that came out on 45 at that time was made by Ken Nordine, a radio voice from Chicago, who recited a piece called "The Shifting, Whispering Sands," with the Billy Vaughn Orchestra and Choir in the background. It described an old miner in the West who returns to his former haunts to find that most of the memories he had were buried by the "shifting, whispering sands." This was a lengthy piece, over seven minutes long, and it took up both sides of the record. Announcers had to stop at the end of Side 1 and quickly turn the record over for the finale. Some lucky stations had two copies of the record, and could have the second side ready on a second turntable, so they had no pause between sides. In order to keep from losing time between the two segments, we used what we called the "flying table." You cued up the song, backtracked it a quarter-turn, held it between your fingertips while the turntable was already turning, and then quickly released it. This took real skill — real "studio production."

If you accidentally played a record at the wrong speed, it could be very embarrassing. A 33 or 45 rpm record played at 78 rpm resulted in what we called a "Donald Duck" — a rapid, high-pitched quacking sound. And if you played a 78 rpm at 33, you got a low-pitched, slow wallowing sound that we called a "troll." Playing the records at the wrong speed was something that could earn you a strong tongue-lashing from the boss.

Today, you would be lucky to find a studio with even one working turntable, since most radio broadcast equipment now uses computers and CDs (compact discs).

Studio Broadcast Terminology (or What's That Again?)

The 1950s brought some dramatic changes in the way music was delivered — recordings, transcriptions, reel-to-reel tapes — and with it came new terminology. For example:

"Point Cue" — a signal to the engineer to start a tape or record. It means that you've finished talking for that moment as an announcer.

"The Cough Switch" — Say you as the announcer feel a cough or sneeze coming on. You panic, because you don't want that sound to go out over the air. You wave your hand in an upward rotating motion to get the engineer's attention, and then quickly run your hand under your chin in a throat-cutting gesture. This means, "Cut the mike for a few seconds while I cough or sneeze." When you are ready to talk again, you give him a "point cue" to turn the mike back on again. In Red Wing, each microphone had a "cough button." We announcers actually controlled this with an on-and-off switch.

"ET" or "Electrical Transcription" — This was a disc in various widths and speeds that might contain short weather and news jingles, sound effects or commercial messages prepared by an advertising agency. All these services are still available today, but the station usually must buy a whole "library" containing many CDs with different lengths of music backgrounds or "music beds" where the announcer can read a commercial message over the music and then record the result as a finished commercial.

"Open end interview" — An example of this would be when a public relations agency has prepared an interview with an entertainer, sports hero, physician or scientist, which they have recorded on a disc. The announcer in the studio reads the questions from a script, and the answers and commentary are on the disc, which plays non-stop through the feature. When you received one of these in the mail, you really had to rehearse it ahead of time, because if you did it well, nobody would say a word, but if you goofed up your timing, you really looked bad.

Today, the P.R. firms fax or e-mail information about their subject, and the announcer picks up a phone and interviews the subject "live," or the interview is recorded for immediate broadcast.

"Tape-recorded programs" — We would do these both in the studio and elsewhere. We had special tape recording machines made by such firms as Magnecord, Ampex, Berlant and Webcor, that we could take out to record community functions. They were somewhat portable, though nothing like the small, lightweight cassette machines you buy today.

I remember when Peter Lyman went out to do March of Dimes interviews in January 1954 and 1955, visiting patients at St. Mary's Hospital in Rochester, or the Sister Kenny Institute and the Swedish Hospital in Minneapolis. He tape-recorded interviews with polio patients from the Red Wing and Zumbrota area. There was a 1954 visit with 26-year-old

Alvera Lohmann, a Zumbrota resident at Rochester's St. Mary's Hospital polio ward; she was in a "rocking bed," a contraption that helped her to breathe. Previously she had spent sixteen months in an iron lung, since the onset of the disease in September 1952. Peter also visited Zumbrota's Howard Woodward, 17, who was in a wheel chair after suffering a second attack of polio. We broadcast these interviews on KAAA on Sunday afternoons in January, which was the official March of Dimes fund-drive month in Goodhue County. Peter was accompanied on those visits by engineer "Speck" Wille and Goodhue County March of Dimes chairman Lynn Beeman, owner of Beeman's Hardware store on Red Wing's Main Street.

"Carts" — At the end of the 1950s, the old reel-taped commercials were being replaced by "carts," or cartridges — little plastic boxes an inch thick, four inches wide and six inches long. The cart contained various lengths of endless magnetic recording tape that played for 40, 70, or 100 seconds, or 2.5, 3.5, 5.5 and 10.5 minutes. You chose the size cart you needed, depending on the length of your ad and the number of ads in the rotation. Each time you recorded another ad on the cart, your recording cartridge put an automatic "stop" tone or cue at the beginning of the ad. This made the "stop" for the next ad ready when the program log called for the commercial to be played. You slid the cart into the cart machine, pushed a button and played your commercial. It was important to make sure that the old cart was "wiped," or erased with the tape eraser, before you started to record a new ad. Otherwise, you had "warbles" of previous ads playing behind the one you had just recorded.

"Spot" — a short ad or commercial, also called a spot announcement.

"Remote" — a remote broadcast, occurring away from the studio.

"Drop a Loop" — This was a term used when a remote program was scheduled. In those days before cellular phones, the radio station engineer had to call the telephone company and tell them we needed to "drop a loop," or a broadcast line, to be at the site of the broadcast. These loops were used for speeches in auditoriums, for example, or when a president spoke to crowds from the platform of his train car during a whistle stop, to carry the sound back to the studio so we could broadcast it. Many loops were dropped at sporting events. I remember when we did the opening of the new Burdick Grain Elevator on Red Wing's waterfront, and Peter Lyman and "Speck" Wille were there, while I introduced Peter from the studio. Our other engineer, Bob Cooper, handled facilities hook-up procedures from the studio.

The costs for those remote broadcast "loops" could add up, unless you installed a "permanent" line, as we did at Donaldson's Department Store on the Miracle Mile in Rochester when I broadcast from there for several years for KROC. The fees were less for annual use. Nowadays, of course, we can call in to the studio from any place at almost any time via cell phone, and give a report of the happenings without relying on a "loop."

"Riding the Net" — In those earlier years, a considerable amount of network programming was carried by the local affiliate. When network programs were on, the announcer learned to "ride the net." He had to be in the studio, ready to fade out the network programming at pre-arranged intervals and insert local commercials from the station's sales department. If it was a :60 break, you filled in with two half-minute (30 second) or one minute (60 second) ad. Occasionally, you got a two-minute break. The station might be affiliated with NBC, CBS, ABC or MBS. Each net had its distinctive cue for local announcers to start local news programs. NBC, for example, had the NBC chimes that played after the announcer said, "This is the National Broadcasting Company." In the mid-1940s, CBS changed its net identification from "This is the Columbia Broadcasting System" to "This is the CBS Radio Network." ABC said, "This is the American Broadcasting Company." MBS said either "This is the Mutual Broadcasting System" or "This is Mutual, the world's oldest network."

Sporting events on the net — At KAAA in Red Wing in those early 1950s, we carried the University of Wisconsin Badgers Big Ten football games "live" from Camp Randall Stadium in Madison. Somehow we had obtained permission to pick up the signal from the FM station in Colfax, Wisconsin. When a game was about to begin, one of our engineers (either "Speck" Wille or Bob Cooper) would climb the outside stepladder to the studio roof there on highway 58, known as "radio hill," and adjust a receiving antenna or "dish" to pick up the signal. Meanwhile, inside the studio, I read any local sponsor commercials whenever the game announcers said, "Now...a time out," or "This brief time-out for our network stations to identify themselves." I would say something like, "This is K-A-A-A, Red Wing, 1250 on your dial...the Voice of the Hiawatha Valley. It's 51 degrees. Now back to the game."

Time Signals — These generally were ads that you read at special times, like at the top of the hour. You gave the time, and the sponsor. "It's 11 am — the time is presented by the Red Wing Bottling Company, bottlers of Squirt — where there's never an aftertaste." Or Nesbitt's Orange, or one of their other soft drinks. "It's 2 pm — time to take your shoes to Elmer Betterly's Shoe Repair, located right across from the Red Wing Shoe Company." "It's Coke Time, starring Eddie Fisher — presented by delicious, ice-cold Coca-Cola, the Pause that Refreshes." And then Eddie Fisher, who was at the peak of his singing career in those days, would sing for fifteen minutes — some of his big hits like "Any Time" and "Oh, Mein Papa."

1250 on Your Dial

I was in Red Wing for four and a half years. And some wonderful things happened there. I got involved in a lot of community activities. They always get the guy on the radio. They say, "He'll emcee for you; he'll judge for you." And I would say yes. Sometimes you say yes, and then you later say, "I wish I hadn't said that." But almost always I have been glad, because I met a lot of people, opened up a lot of opportunities and learned a lot along the way.

I got involved in so many things — you name it, FFA, 4H, beauty pageants. The county agent, Dick Kunau, asked me to judge 4H contests. Somebody would say, "Well, who can we get to do this?" And somebody else would say, "Oh, hey, I heard this new young fellow on the radio. I'm sure he'll do it." Well, they'd call, and I'd say yes. I didn't know a lot about what I was getting into, but it was a learning process, and really enjoyable. When it came time for the Jaycees of Red Wing to cut the ribbon for their spring home show in the Red Wing armory, I was there with a microphone, broadcasting. It was exciting to me, because you could communicate. We were the only station in Red Wing, but we had competition all over the area, mainly from the Twin Cities and KDHL in Faribault.

I loved Red Wing, there on the Mississippi. I loved everything about it. As a young man getting started, I was paid a dollar an hour for up to 48 hours, and after that I could make time and a half — $1.50 an hour — up to 55 hours. I didn't get rich, but I was so thankful I had a job. And it kept getting a little better as I went along.

Nearly three years after I joined the station, KAAA was sold to Vic and Nick Tedesco, two St. Paul businessmen who had a radio station called WCOW in South St. Paul. (That's "W- Cow," or "Woof 'n Cow," as we called it.) They were innovative, and they were starting to expand. I think they had a station in Sparta, Wisconsin, and then they bought the station in Red Wing. They changed its name from KAAA to KCUE — "K-cue, your cue for better listening." (It's still there, KCUE. I went back on the station's 50th anniversary in 1999. They sent me an invitation to be part of the 50th anniversary of KAAA. When I went back, there was one man in the crowd that remembered me. He said, "Oh, I remember you, yes." He worked in an appliance store, Primus Appliance, that had been one of our sponsors. But everybody else was so young. And they were doing a beautiful job. They now operate KCUE-AM and KWNG-FM.)

The changeover from KAAA to KCUE took effect January 1, 1956, and suddenly we had all new people. I was the only announcer left. The engineers, Don "Speck" Wille and Bob Cooper, remained there for a short period, but they soon moved on. Our new engineer was Alan Kennedy. He was a heck of a guy, newly married, with a little baby, and we became great friends. He was a good announcer and a fine radio first-class engineer. There were some others who came and went, but Alan and I stayed on the longest, and we were the ones who really were putting things together, under the direction of our new boss, Gene Elston.

Gene Elston was a big fellow, with a great voice, but I didn't often agree with him. He was very domineering, and I do not submit to people who are domineering, especially when they are above me. And he knew it.

I did a morning show, but instead of going from 5 till 9 am, it was 5 till 6:30, and then back again from 9 till something else — it was all split up. Elston wanted more announcers on the air for shorter times. But he and I stayed together a year and eight months, which was pretty good.

While I was at Red Wing, I had the joy of interviewing George Mikan, the great basketball player, and Johnny Kundla, his coach. We interviewed many folks traveling through the area. They would come and make presentations, getting their story out, telling what they were doing. Because of the proximity of the Twin Cities — we were not that far away, about 55 miles from St. Paul and Minneapolis — we got a lot of people looking for interviews.

We did shows on the levee front, water shows, broadcasting events with the water skis — sort of like the Tommy Bartlett show, but not quite as grandiose as that. And I was there. When it happened in Red Wing, I was there, from April 1953 through the end of August 1957.

Live Parade Broadcasts

We had some good things happening during my years in Red Wing. In 1956, a number of area towns were observing their centennials, even though this was two years before the Minnesota state centennial. Minnesota officially became the thirty-second state in May 1858, but a lot of those river towns were founded before that time. So we started planning the centennial broadcasts. I told the boss, "I'll try to go and sell this Sunday parade broadcast." I would find out what it was going to take, and we usually figured that $60 would cover it.

I went out during the week, after my regular morning show with its split broadcast, to the celebrating town, found a spot to originate the broadcast, and lined up a sponsor. Then on Sunday I went back and did the broadcast. Sometimes they had a parade chairman who gave me the parade lineup in advance, sometimes not, but I would always be there, doing a two-hour live broadcast. The station charged $60, and for all my work, I got $10. Well, that was pretty good back then.

The first parade that summer of 1956 was held in Red Wing. I did a live KCUE centennial parade broadcast from the portico of the St. James Hotel, sitting right up above the main entrance on the balcony. One of the parade entries that I remember well was the Kilties from Decorah, Iowa. They performed then, and they are still going strong today. Later, I did a live broadcast of a beautiful water show down at Levee Park, beside the Mississippi. It was a great experience broadcasting these events, all part of that centennial celebration.

In Elgin, my sponsor was Scheuneman Hardware, owned by Ed Scheuneman. Ed let me climb the inside stairway of his hardware store and work my way through to the front, where I could lean out the window to do the broadcast on the parade passing by below.

After Elgin, we went to Plainview. I believe I had two $30 sponsors that time. I spent a good share of the day getting these two sponsors lined up. Taylor Chevrolet was one, and People's State Bank was the other. On Sunday, I sat on the steps of the old library, right downtown, and described the parade in Plainview for our radio listeners. That library eventually was torn down and a new city library has been built.

In Zumbrota, I sat on a truck bed at Main Street level to do my broadcast. We had one sponsor there, A.E. Collinge and Son. They sold feed and seed, serving as a farm supply store. Alfred E. Collinge III had been a longtime businessman in Zumbrota, and served several terms as mayor in the 1960s. On the Friday night before the parade, I was featured on a stage program playing my musical saw. I'd called my mother, and she came up from the farm to play the piano accompaniment for me.

In Kenyon, our sponsor was Mahlman Pontiac. I had not met any of these folks ahead of time. Quentin Mahlman, who recently died at age 80, put up the whole $60 for me to do that parade. It was a lovely Sunday afternoon in late August — sweet corn time. My parents were there — sometimes they made it to these parades. After the centennial parade ended, Quentin Mahlman and his wife invited my parents and me to their house for potato salad and ham sandwiches, which just pleased me greatly. I mean, if I can have potato salad and ham sandwiches, I'll just carry on all day.

In Lake City that summer, also on a Sunday afternoon, I broadcast a Wabasha County Dairy Days street parade from upstairs in a building on Main Street. Again I was leaning out a second story window, broadcasting all of this on KCUE radio.

Then in Plum City, Wisconsin, across the river, I broadcast another parade, although I can't recall what the celebration was. All these parades were within a few weeks of each other that summer of 1956. As a young man just starting out in the broadcast field, these were all exciting events for me.

I remember one other parade, at Hastings, Minnesota, on a Sunday afternoon in 1957. It was broadcast from the grounds of the sponsor, Bahl Implement, the local International Harvester dealer. We had a young man with us that day who was working part time, a very nice fellow just out of high school named Bernie Aaker. He loved radio. He was a clothing salesman part time at Josephson's Clothing in downtown Red Wing, but he went on to stay in radio for awhile. We also had Alan Kennedy, the engineer, with us that day.

It was such a hot afternoon. When we finished the broadcast, I was so thirsty, and Bernie said to me, "Here. Have a beer."

Well, I'd never drunk any beer in my life, because I was the perfect young man, you know, brought up not to drink, smoke or gamble — but that beer was so good! That was my introduction to beer.

I Join the Red Wing Jaycees

The Red Wing Jaycees got me involved quite early as a member of their organization, which in 1954 was only for young men aged 21 to 36. I didn't do a lot with them from month to month, but I was always available when they asked me to emcee an event. As the months went by, these events seemed to mount up in number. I did several Miss Red Wing coronations and Jaycee Spring Sport Shows.

On January 10, 1956, I was emcee for a program called Bosses' Night. Among the prominent figures present that night were Mayor Harry Rardin and Red Wing Jaycee President Fred Wichlaz of the Reidell Shoe Company. The speaker was former Jaycee National Director Roland Wilsey, and the invocation was given by the Rev. Monroe Bailie of the local Episcopal Church.

In early 1957, the Red Wing Jaycees presented their Distinguished Service Award to Jack Frederich, 34, President of the Red Wing City Council and a community leader. He was one of five nominees for the award. I emceed that event.

The first Miss Red Wing banquet that I emceed was held on April 4, 1956, at the Red Wing High School cafeteria. There were eighteen lovely contestants hoping to win the crown. The winner was eighteen-year-old Barbara Richardson. After the banquet, we all went to the Skyline Ballroom, about four miles south of Red Wing on Highway 58, where the Henry Burton Orchestra was playing dance music. The actual announcement and crowning of the queen took place at the Skyline Ballroom at 10:15 pm. I guess the judges needed some time after the banquet to work out their decision. The judges that year were Dr. Max DeBolt of Winona, Fred Leighton, a reporter and photographer for the St. Paul *Pioneer Press*, and Mrs. Gretchen Lamberton, author of "The Casual Observer," a column in the St. Paul *Pioneer Press*. Both Leighton and Mrs. Lamberton were also residents of Winona. It was a great night. I was proud to be a part of it, and proud of the support that the Jaycees and the community provided for the event.

The following year, the Miss Red Wing banquet was again held at the high school cafeteria on May 1, 1957. The retiring queen, Barbara Richardson, was on hand to crown her successor, Ramona Johnson, who was chosen from a field of twelve contestants. The judges were Miss Marlene Mumford, society editor of the *Daily Republican Eagle*, Howard Bailey, manager of Northern States Power Co. in Zumbrota, and Mrs. W.

P. Iwen, president of the Cannon Valley Girl Scout Council, who with her husband owned the Iwen Box Manufacturing Company in Pine Island. This time, the invocation was given by the Rev. Warren A. Nyberg, pastor of the First Methodist Church in Red Wing, which I had been attending. The coronation dance began at the Skyline ballroom at 9 pm. Music was provided by the Midwest Caravan Orchestra from Iowa.

I remember one year the Jaycees had a very unusual membership drive stunt. Someone borrowed a goose from a nearby farm, and the idea was that when you were given the goose, you had to keep it until you recruited a new member. One day Bud, owner of Bud's Tydol Service Station on West Main Street, gave me the goose. I didn't want to carry that goose around in the back seat of my car! I had to keep it overnight, so I tethered it to the porch pillar of the house where I was living at 107 West 5th Street, owned by Lydia Thumann. The goose stayed (outside) at our KCUE radio station for a short time only, because I found a new member darn quick, you can be sure of that! I don't remember who it was, but I got him signed up and then passed the goose on to another member and heaved a sigh of relief. You really don't want to keep a goose very long in the back seat of your car!

I Speak for Toastmasters

I've always been a "pack-rat." While rummaging through a book filled with Red Wing memorabilia recently, I discovered a program from the Red Wing Toastmaster's Club's "Ladies' Night" on April 25, 1957, at 7:15 pm at Nybo's Cafe and Bowling Lanes.

A couple of years earlier, Red Wing Chamber of Commerce President Jack Adams had invited me to join the Toastmaster's Club. I knew little then about speaking before a live audience. I was more comfortable in the studio behind a microphone. I always felt less than adequate participating as an "off-the-cuff" speaker. But as I practiced, I began to develop some confidence. Today I feel a lot more comfortable speaking in public, but it's nearly 50 years later!

At that 1957 meeting, the program lists me as Master Evaluator — wow! In the column labeled "officers-elect, 1957-58," I am listed as educational vice president. The president that year was Royal Hayden and the Toastmaster Emcee for the night was Darwin Stephan. Jack Adams was the table topic master, and Sid Wilgus of the Rochester Club inducted the new officers.

Somehow I got involved in these events. Later that spring, Toastmasters held a contest, with the winner headed for the district meet. My topic was "Are personalities influenced by environment or heredity?" That little speech sent me to Rochester for the finals at the Kahler Hotel's Hemisphere Room. I came to the event alone, and faced two speakers from Rochester, Richard Dison of Dison Cleaners and Laurel Pennock, longtime elementary school principal. An old master when it came to public speaking, Pennock won the top prize "hands down."

In later years, I would serve with Mr. Pennock on the Salvation Army board of directors. He was a joy to be around, always so positive and humorous, and always having a message for those in attendance at meetings. Laurel Pennock spent forty years in education. He died on February 13, 1989, at the age of 80.

When I moved to Rochester, I did not actively continue with either the Jaycees or the Toastmaster's Club, although I acted as emcee for five Miss Rochester beauty pageants in the 1960s and did ten years of emcee work (1977-1986) for the DSA (Distinguished Service Award) banquets conducted by the Jaycees. But I certainly have pleasant memories of both organizations from my days in Red Wing.

Good Times at the Oriola Cafe

In downtown Red Wing, across from Stan and Ken's Shell Station and next to the big building known as City Hall, there was a neat little restaurant called the Oriola Cafe. Its owner, Orlen Cordes, combined his first name with that of his wife, Viola, to come up with the cafe's name. It was not large — smaller than an old railroad dining car — but it was neat, light and usually crowded. The breakfasts were good and fast. It was a great place for coffee breaks for people in the area, and you could usually find the police officers, city clerk Norma Seely, or Bert and Ernie (nicknamed "Skinny") Klitzke, owners of the Klitzke Brothers Body Shop a block away, in there off and on during the day. Other frequent visitors were Dan Metzler of Metzler Plumbing and Heating, across the street, and Dwight and Don Gustafson, owners of a TV sales and repair shop called the Red Wing Service Company.

It was a good place to sit around and talk about things like the new Milwaukee Braves baseball team, which started in 1953. I'd generally get there once or twice a day. When you're a single person and don't have a kitchenette, this kind of eating establishment is like an answer to a prayer. Millie Kuhl was the cook there for several years, and I knew her and her husband well, because her husband Elmer had been at the Sister Kenny Hospital in Minneapolis with me for several months in 1949-1950. The Kuhls were originally from Goodhue.

The Oriola Cafe was also a sponsor of our 3 pm daily news show on KAAA.

Orlen and Vi Cordes sold the cafe a year or so after I got there to Mr. and Mrs. Rufus Bee. A couple of years later, the Bees sold it to Pete and Alice Betcher.

Pete was the cook back in the little kitchen. When he and Alice took over the cafe, with their two little daughters, Barb and Sandy (Barb was then a brand-new baby), the fun really began. It was like "Laugh-In" all the time. They really liked playing practical jokes.

One day when I went back to my car after lunch, there in the back seat was a porcelain toilet, complete with attached seat and tank. When I went back into the cafe to ask about it, naturally absolutely nobody seemed to know anything about it. I had to carry that "Thunder Mug," as they called it, around with me for several days. A number of folks came out to my car to look at this thing I was complaining about. I was the "butt" of a good deal of good-natured heckling. After a few days, I was served with a "summons" and an "arrest warrant," brought by Metzler Plumbing and Heating, where the "Mug" apparently came from. City Clerk Norma Seely drummed up another document on February 8, 1956, asking me to appear in court. She even got judge Gilbert Terwilliger to sign it. "Bail" was set at $1.00.

It was good for a lot of laughs. I had to do a lot of begging over a couple of weeks before Danny Metzler finally removed the "Thunder Mug" from the back seat of my car. And it all started in the Oriola Cafe in Red Wing. Those were good days. Oh, for just a meal or two again, surrounded by those old friends of mine from those years in the early 1950s! The Oriola Cafe is long gone, but the wonderful memories remain.

The Training School Runaways

Just a few weeks after I began my career at KAAA in Red Wing, I was assigned a split shift, signing on at 6 am through 10 am and returning to the studio again from noon till 4 pm. That meant I had a break from 10 am till noon, so I usually took a morning rest and had lunch before returning to work.

On October 20, 1954, I left the studios in my black 1951 four-door Ford, and I had gone about one mile down highway 58 when I saw two young lads walking along the side of the road, heading toward town. They "thumbed" a ride.

I stopped and asked, "Where you going?"

Without answering, they both jumped in. The little fellow got into the front seat, and the larger kid got in the back. Then the big lad leaned over the back of my seat, clenched his fist beside my head, and said, "Take us to St. Paul."

I was pretty scared. That clenched fist beside my temple loomed as large as the Empire State Building. The smaller boy in the front seat seemed to be as scared as I was, for he didn't utter a sound.

I was not aware that I was giving a ride to a couple of runaways from the Red Wing Training School for delinquents. Apparently it was a common thing. The boys were on a sort of honor system, which for the most part was working, but now and then one or two of them would defect. I wasn't into the coverage of news yet in my new job, and simply was not aware of the risk involved in picking up hitchhikers in the Red Wing area.

I told the boys that I didn't have enough gas to get all the way to St. Paul. It was the truth.

The boy said, "Keep driving. We'll go till we run out."

When I got to the bottom of the hill, where the highway becomes Bush Street, I quickly pulled into the Pure Oil station in the "Dutchtown" neighborhood, a mile south of downtown Red Wing.

The big kid asked, "Where ya goin'?"

I replied, "I've got to go to the bathroom, right now."

The boys both jumped out the right side of the car and started running.

I didn't know anyone at the gas station, but I hollered to one of the attendants, "Help me! These kids are forcing me to drive to St. Paul, and I don't want to go." I was scared, standing there leaning on my crutches, shaking like a leaf.

The men gave chase. Soon the police were involved, and the two boys were apprehended without any further incident a few blocks away at the Berlin Service Station on Main Street. They were eventually sent to the St. Cloud Reformatory for further jail time. The boys were aged fourteen and fifteen. I later learned that the big kid was originally convicted of armed robbery at a St. Paul grocery store.

Later that day, my program director, Peter Lyman, read a story about the incident on the KAAA 4 pm radio news. It said something to the effect that, "Good Samaritan deed goes awry. Harley Flathers, KAAA employee, picked up two boys from the Red Wing Training School this morning, not knowing that they were runaways," etc.

Needless to say, this experience ended my kindness toward hitchhikers. It put me on the defensive. Early one very cold winter morning a couple of years later, about 5 to 5:30 am, I saw a young man running by the roadside a few miles out of town where highway 58 joins a road leading to Belvidere. He wore no hat, no coat, in 10-degree temperatures. I called the sheriff at once, and the kid was picked up. This time, it was a boy listed as a "dangerous" escapee. Instead of offering to help a stray kid, I was now working for the law.

Following this second incident, Pete Betcher of the Oriola Cafe told me, "The poor criminals don't have a chance any more when you're watching them!"

Socializing with the Goodhue County Rural Youth

While I was working in Red Wing, I met Dewey Baringer and his parents, Mr. and Mrs. Ray Baringer, local farmers who lived near the KAAA station. Dewey invited me to join an organization called the Rural Youth of Goodhue County. Rural Youth had been organized in 1936 by Goodhue County extension agent G.J. "Dick" Kunau and home demonstration agent Evelyn Snell. Its purpose was to keep in touch with boys and girls who had outgrown 4-H, from the ages of 18 to 30, or until they married. Educational trips, scavenger hunts, dances and hayrides were among the activities the group organized for these young people. There were several marriages among members, such as Avis Berg and Lloyd Cordes, residents of the Wanamingo area, both longtime members of the Goodhue County Fair board. The name of the group was changed in 1955 from Rural Youth to Young Men and Women, and its activities continued until 1966.

When the group was founded, I would have been about five years old, but now it was 1954, and I was 23 — just the right age for membership. I liked the group. We all had farm backgrounds. I recall one time inviting the group to meet in the big studio at KAAA radio. Another time, we had a scavenger hunt at Hay Creek campgrounds. There was a dance at the Zumbrota VFW Hall.

After I left Red Wing in 1957, I no longer participated in the group's activities, but in 1995, Lucille Lohmann of Zumbrota remembered me when they were planning a Rural Youth reunion at Nybo's Cafe on February 1. She asked me to come and be the emcee for the event. Sixty people came, including eight of the 29 charter members. It was a day of heavy memories and a few tears. I was likely the youngest one there. I sat at the microphone, inviting people to share their remembrances with the group, and later played my musical saw. Among those attending were the first president of Rural Youth, Phillip Nerison, who held that office in 1936-37. When I was involved, the presidents were David Lohman (1954), Lloyd Cordes (1955), Marvin Strusz (1956) and Owen Knutson (1957).

We held another reunion on April 18, 1996, at the Sawyer Inn in Goodhue, to celebrate the group's 60th anniversary. This time, ten of the original 29 charter members were among the forty attendees. I'm afraid that age may be catching up with me these days, but if there's another reunion soon, I'll show up with my musical saw, if Byron Pearson of Red Wing will bring his concertina.

Cedric Adams and the 4-H Talent Search

I'd listened to Cedric Adams, the great WCCO radio personality, for many years, as he broadcast the news at 12:30 pm and again at 10 pm. Cedric was in great demand for nighttime personal appearances, and he did many in both Minnesota and Wisconsin. I finally met and shook hands with him at the 6th Annual 4-H Club Search for Talent, held in the High School Auditorium in Goodhue, Minnesota, on Wednesday night, June 15, 1955.

This was the first show of the 1955 "Search for Talent" series, sponsored by Cargill, Incorporated, of Minneapolis and the University of Minnesota's Extension Service. Talent shows were popular in those days in many local communities, states and the nation. The goal of the 4-H Talent Search was to provide an incentive and recognize the development of talent in young men and women in Minnesota. Cash prizes of $100, $75 and $50 went to the top three winners' 4-H clubs, paid by Cargill, Inc.

Cedric Adams was the master of ceremonies that night, and Osgood Magnuson, State 4-H Club assistant leader, introduced the program. I was one of three judges, along with Mrs. Henry Swanson and Reynold Christensen, both of Red Wing. I had begun judging a number of events for the 4-H in my capacity as an announcer at KAAA. Reynold

Christensen was the longtime band conductor at Red Wing High School, and Mrs. Swanson was from the family of A. Swanson & Sons Furniture of Red Wing.

That night, Cedric Adams' 10 pm news program originated live from the Goodhue High School auditorium. When it was over, I presented to him the judges' decisions from the talent show. The seventeen acts that night had included acrobatic, vocal, tap dance, cornet, saxophone and twin accordion performances, and no less than seven piano solos. The winners were little Connie Scripture of Dodge Center, with her amazing acrobatic act, Glee Houghton of Elgin, who wowed the audience with her cornet rendition of the "Bugler's Holiday," and in first place, Lorraine Herman of Zumbro Falls, who played "Cat and Mouse" on the piano. Cedric Adams announced the winners, and R. C. Woodworth, vice president of Cargill, presented the prizes.

Zumbrota - The Hub of Goodhue County

Good neighbor to Red Wing is Zumbrota, Minnesota, just twenty-two miles away. I drove through Zumbrota many times on my way back and forth to Red Wing in the early 1950s, when highway 52 was only two lanes all the way from Dubuque, Iowa, to Minneapolis, serving every car and tractor-trailer truck on a path that was barely twenty feet wide.

I recall one neat little gas station that stood on the end of Zumbrota's Main Street, where it joined highway 52. It was owned by a man named Ed Tilton, and was called Tilly's Shell. (I had to call Charlie Buck, Zumbrota's 74-year-old walking historian, to help me remember the station operator's name. All I could bring up from my memory was "Ed.") Tilly's Shell was a very small building with two gas pumps out front — regular and ethyl. Ed was an interesting man who told a lot of stories. He kept working up into his 80's, knowing that when they built a new highway, it would eventually take the land where his station stood.

On Thursday afternoons, from 1:30 to 2 pm, we usually had a series of Zumbrota merchants as our sponsors on the air while we played old-time music from 78 rpm records. I particularly remember Cresthaven Ice Cream. I loved the sound of that name: Cresthaven Ice Cream. I vividly remember how, at the end of their ad, I would say, "Cresthaven Ice Cream, made in Zumbrota, the Hub of Goodhue County — the only Zumbrota in the world."

I didn't know Charlie Buck in those days, but he tells me that he came up to Red Wing for the first anniversary celebration of KAAA in early 1950, and sang on the air in a special broadcast that originated downtown from Nybo's Cafe. Charlie was a drummer and a charter member of the band "Art Fitch and the Polka Dots." (Art Fitch owned and operated a Skelly Service station in downtown Zumbrota.) I remember occasionally playing their music on KAAA.

While I was working in Red Wing, I crossed paths many times with Howard Bailey, who was the manager of Northern States Power (NSP) in Zumbrota. I interviewed him occasionally on the air, and served at some public functions with him. Howard loved his Zumbrota. He was a great promoter, although he didn't please everyone. One item on his legacy list was the restoration of the Zumbrota covered bridge. He clashed with many over its final location. Today, that covered bridge is a "key" of their park, and the focal point of their annual Covered Bridge Music Festival in mid-June.

I remember reading commercials every morning about 7 am for several years for Nerhaugen Chevrolet in Zumbrota, which today is Grover Auto. And in the early 1950s, before the Zumbrota Livestock Auction opened for business out near the fairgrounds, we attended the Goodhue County fair and did broadcasts from it on the air, mostly by tape recordings that we would play back later at the studio during fair week.

The Lake City Hour

I have vivid memories of one program I listened to on KAAA Red Wing when I was just newly-graduated from radio's KAIA (American Institute of the Air) on Lake Street in Minneapolis. Daily Monday through

Friday from 11:30 to noon, Peter Lyman, the program director and senior announcer, conducted the show while engineer Bob Cooper played the transcriptions. I can hear Peter yet: after a short opening, a fanfare would begin, and Peter, wearing headphones, would talk over the music, saying, "With music by transcription, it's the Lake City Hour." Then the engineer would raise the volume of the fanfare to its conclusion, after which Peter would give the Lake City sponsors credit: "The Lake City Hour is brought to you by these Lake City merchants...Jewel Nurseries...Lyon Avenue Grocery...Gillette and Eaton....Conway Jewelers...Hassler and Herman Implement...and the Hollywood Theater...And we open the show with the band playing..."

Those were the days when radio stations usually subscribed to "World" or "Thesaurus" music libraries. You paid monthly rent for the library and any number of records — possibly some stations actually purchased them. Complete scripts came with the library for a variety in programming choices. These were great for the holidays, because a considerable amount of research had gone into the planning before it arrived at any station. You got a 16-inch wide plastic-type disc with several "cuts," or selections. The engineer also had a copy of the script, so that he could play the proper "cut" when Peter asked for it, as he stood in the booth looking through the window and giving those popular hand signals, or cues, for the engineer to play the song.

I sat and listened, drinking in every word and song. At the close of the half-hour, after reading everyone's commercial once during the show, Peter gave a closing credit to sponsors and the next program started, following his station break: "You're listening to the Voice of the Hiawatha Valley, 1250 on your dial, K-A-A-A, Red Wing."

We did a number of programs regarding Lake City while I was working at KAAA. One was the "Story Lady," Lucia Simons, who broadcast on Saturday mornings from 9:30 to 10. She came up to our studios to read stories to the kids on the air. The mother of two children (Joe and Barbara), Lucia combined housework with radio broadcasting, and did it well.

The Wabasha Hour

Down the mighty Mississippi about thirty miles from Red Wing lies the beautiful city of Wabasha. At KAAA radio, we did a daily half-hour show Monday through Friday at 1 pm sponsored by Wabasha merchants in conjunction with the town's newspaper, *The Wabasha County Herald.* We played music and read ads and stories from Wabasha. This was long before Wabasha became famous as the site of the "Grumpy Old Men" movies, with Jack Lemmon and Walter Matthau.

I'm looking now at a large print ad in my scrap book dated June 24, 1954, labeled "Industrial Wabasha." There's an aerial view of the city, with the headline: "Big Jo Mill Manager Stresses Cooperation to Reach a Worthwhile Goal." And there's a picture of the manager, W.A. (Woody) Palmen. In visiting recently with his sons, Dr. Michael Palmen of Rochester and John Palmen of Wabasha, I learned that Woody served as manager of that mill, with its towering six silos, for 28 years, from 1950 to 1978. He was a community servant, always striving to bring new industry to Wabasha.

The caption under Woody's picture in that 1954 issue of the *Herald* quotes him as saying, "We have a splendid city, and have attracted visitors when they see the real fine neighbors. Others can be attracted when we sell the real enthusiasm which is a part of Wabasha. No one organization, not just a few individuals, can achieve a desirable growth of a community. It is a job of everyone." The ad goes on to encourage people to listen to KAAA for daily Wabasha news on Monday through Friday at 1 pm, and for the Saturday program from noon to 12:15 called "Progress of Wabasha Industry."

Longtime Wabasha County agent Matt Metz told me recently that he worked alongside Woody on many county endeavors. Matt did a weekly taped program on Wednesday mornings from 6:15 to 6:30 on KAAA, and I was the one on duty to introduce him: "This morning's radio feature is Wabasha County agent Matt Metz."

I was on duty to introduce those daily programs — all based on that week's edition of the *Herald*. Among the print ad sponsors on that particular page from June 1954 were the First State Bank of Wabasha, the Idle Hour Game Farm (great steaks and seafood — pheasant and mallard by reservation), Wabasha Cleaning Works (for cleaning and storing your furs and woolens in a vault), Hotel Anderson (famous for foods; dressings and preserves manufactured in Grandma Anderson's Preserving Kitchens), and Northern States Power Company (with ample power for one or a thousand industries). There was also Inskeep Motors (bring your Ford back home; for service dial 5-4450, your Ford dealer in Wabasha), McDonald's Locker Plant (ask for Louie's home-made sausages; try 'em and you'll buy 'em), Big Jo Flour Mills (the home of Big Jo Flour, the secret of better baking, a division of International Milling), Botsford Lumber Company (we build Wabasha) and E.B. Wise Furniture (floor coverings, lamps, mirrors — everything for the home). That was the outreach to build "Industrial Wabasha."

During those years when our call letters were still KAAA, when I was on staff from 1953 through 1955, it was the custom for Peter Lyman to do a 30-minute live radio interview from 2:30 to 3 pm just days before the county fairs began. He did it for Goodhue County with G.J. (Dick) Kunau, veteran county agent, with H.G. "Sey" Seyforth, the county agent from across the river in Pierce County, Wisconsin (based in Ellsworth, about twenty miles away from Red Wing), and also with four Wabasha County community leaders at fair time.

I remember those programs so vividly, and so does Matt Metz, who remembers being one of the four men crowded into that tiny booth-type studio. Peter talked about the upcoming Wabasha County fair with Matt, Woody Palmen, Walt Passe (a Wabasha County Fair Board member) and city mayor Paul Ayotte, manager of the beautiful Pem Theater in Wabasha. (I told Matt I remembered that theater very well — I'd gone "girling" there a few times.) Matt and I agreed that Big Jo Flour Mills must have paid for that program, since Woody Palmen was such a promoter of his town.

Matt Metz was county agent in Wabasha for 31 years, from 1953 through 1984, and then spent a couple more years in agricultural programs at the University of Minnesota and in farm crisis mediation during the mid-1980s. He recalled his old office in Wabasha, at the base of the old wooden bridge that spanned the Mississippi. The 18-wheel grain-loaded tractor-trailers would occasionally get "hung-up" trying to make that sharp turn at the start of the approach to the bridge. The road inclined sharply beside the big concrete silos, then made another sharp right-hand turn to cross the water. Those bridges at Wabasha, Winona, Red Wing and Hastings were all replaced between the 1950s and 1970s. The Hastings bridge had a real spiral on the way up to the "river span," and crossing it was quite an experience.

Most of the grain or wheat ground at the Big Jo Flour Mills came in by rail on tracks that took the trains through Wabasha along the river's edge. Today those old silos are gone, destroyed by implosion to make way for new residential or commercial structures. Matt Metz is pushing 79 today, and Woody Palmen died recently at age 90.

Those Sargents Keep Following Me (And I'm Glad)

During my years in Red Wing, I sang beside Maxwell Sargent in the Methodist Church choir. One Sunday, he and his wife invited me to Sunday dinner at their home in nearby Burnside, Minnesota. After the meal, I invited their two sons, Forrest (age 12) and Roger (age 10) to come along with me to the Hiawatha Speedway stock car race track, where I was doing the announcing as those wild drivers circled the track in many heats and feature races. The track was up behind Burnside, just off highway 61 toward the Twin Cities. I brought the lads right up into the viewing stand, where the judges and announcers sat.

This was in 1956, thirty years after Maxwell Sargent's father had started Sargent's Nursery in Red Wing. Maxwell took over the business in 1948, and it continues to flourish today under his two daughters, Marge and Julie, and their husbands.

Then, over three decades ago, Forrest Sargent came to Rochester and opened a nursery and landscape business on 18th Avenue Northwest, and then another, Sargent's on Second at 1811 2nd Street Southwest. I certainly never thought when I took those Sargent boys to the stock car races that one of them would eventually follow me to Rochester and become one of our longtime radio commercial sponsors here. It's heart-warming to combine memories, business and friends all in the same "moment."

A Towboat Journey and A Trail Ride

The year 1956, which had brought me both a new boss and new station call letters, had two real highlights — my first towboat ride in March, and my first trail ride in May.

The towboat was the *W.S. Rhea*, which had just made its first trip of the year north on the Mississippi from St. Louis, after the Coast Guard cutter *Woodrush* had broken the ice on the river. This was in late March, about the time of the spring equinox, as the temperatures started to rise. My boss, Gene Elston, asked me if I'd like to take a ride on a towboat, and of course, I said yes.

Gene drove me to St. Paul, where I boarded the boat about mid-morning. The Rhea had brought eight barges of coal upriver and would take back a load of grain and corn. They had a crew of about twelve to keep things in order. The skipper was a humorous little man who told me he'd been a boyhood friend of Elvis Presley, and had sung with "The King" back in Memphis and Nashville. He had his guitar, which he occasionally played over the boat's loud-speaker system, entertaining both the crew and folks on both sides of the channel with his "mellow notes." People on shore are always watching and waving at passing water craft.

I had my tape recorder along, and recorded some of the singing and the stories told by the skipper and the boat's owner, Big John Ritchie, who had come along that day for the ride. After a great noon-time meal prepared in the boat's galley, I even took a turn at the wheel, with the skipper standing by within arm's reach to make sure I stayed on course. We arrived back at Levee Park in Red Wing about 8:30 that evening. What an experience for that young announcer!

Then, in May, Gene told me that a trail riding group from Minneapolis would be coming down to spend the weekend riding through the hills and valleys just south of Red Wing. It was called the Governor's Annual Trail Ride, and they hoped to have Minnesota Governor Orville Freeman there, although I'm not sure whether he actually made it.

We all met at Mike Nelson's cabin. Mike Nelson was apparently a very successful insurance man, judging from the size of his cabin and the surrounding playgrounds. Fifty or sixty men had come down from the Twin Cities with their horses in huge horse trailers, to ride, eat, and spend time together from Friday night through Sunday. I met Charlie Saunders, owner of Charlie's Cafe Exceptionale in Minneapolis, an exclusive restaurant that everyone looked forward to visiting when they were in the Cities.

Although I didn't ride, I played my musical saw for the group and enjoyed a steak and baked potato meal prepared by three cooks whom Charlie had brought along from his restaurant. And I kept my tape machine running. I was there on Saturday, but didn't stay the night. Then I was invited back on Sunday morning for breakfast and an outdoor church service led by one of the riders, who was a preacher and singer.

Those were two great "rides" that left me with many fine memories.

The Day I Became a "Leftover"

If only we could extend the "truth from the mouths of babes" to adulthood, I'm sure the world would indeed be a better place.

This episode took place on May 1, 1956, in River Falls, Wisconsin. Our Red Wing station, which had just acquired those new call letters, KCUE, had also opened a studio in River Falls, some thirty miles north of Red Wing on the Wisconsin side of the Mississippi. The man hired by my boss, Gene Elston, to manage the new studio and sell radio advertising to local River Falls merchants was named Ed Footit. I only met Ed once, and never really got to know him well. He conducted a daily radio show on-air from 9:30 to 10 am, doing interviews with local folks and sharing River Falls news.

During the early weeks of 1956, Ed put together a project that, had the weather cooperated, would have been a real eye-opener to the world, or at least to counties along the upper reaches of the mighty Mississippi. It was called "May Day the USA Way," and was set to bring in thousands of people to hear speeches by dignitaries and music from high school bands, choirs and kids. It was intended to show the world how we in this country expressed our freedoms on May 1, in contrast to the May Day parades held in Russia. (Remember, this was five years before the Berlin Wall went up, and only a decade after V-E Day in 1945. The Cold War was in full force.)

Well, the event was all ready. Promotion had been heavy via print and electronic media. It was to have been a full-day affair, with programs and speeches beginning at 10 am and continuing until 4 pm. But, alas, one of those late winter/spring snowfalls arrived during the night of April 30, and it was heavy. The sun came out the next day, and by mid-morning the snow had started to melt away, but that snowfall just killed the crowds. I don't have a record of the attendance figures, but they were very small.

I went up to River Falls in the early afternoon with two friends from Red Wing, Dick and Carol Key, who occasionally rode with me to events and helped carry my tape recording equipment. When we arrived, we saw this huge outdoor stage, built from red cedar lumber, set in a downtown park, where speakers could stand in front of microphones and bands could play. No crowd was left — if there had ever been one. Snow was melting around the edge of the stage.

With Dick's help, I managed to climb up onto the stage, and stood there wondering how it might feel to bow to the applause of thousands, even though I was not a scheduled participant.

Suddenly, a little girl of about 7 or 8 years of age came up to me and asked me for my autograph.

I said, "You don't want my autograph. I wasn't on the program. I'm no celebrity."

She looked up at me with longing eyes, as I stood there on my Kenny crutches, and she said, "Yes, but you're the only one left."

I felt like a leftover, but what could I do? I gave her my autograph.

KAAA Radio Studio & 216 foot tower . . . Highway 58, 1000 watts daytime. Built in 1948. On air first time Jan 29, 1949. This is 5th anniversary photo courtesy Red Wing Chamber Newsletter 1954.

Harley full of vim & vigor during those early years. He and Peter Lyman were the announcing staff. English instructor Ed Powderly from the Red Wing High School was the Sunday voice.

1955 Peter Lyman, Program Director, News Director and veteran actor. He read books on the air mornings at 10:30 am and again at 2:45 pm, taking various voices to tell the story

As we were in 1954 . . . front desk, Hal Corey, promotion manager & Jim Bailey, commercial manager. Middle desk, Peter Lyman, program director. Far desk seated, Dorothy Nelson, secretary & commercial writing. Standing is owner Maxine Jacobs.

Big Studio at KAAA where many "live" shows were conducted, such as 4-H, religious broadcasts and concerts. The Old Time Westerners, Ronnie Owens, Leo Dressen & Genevieve Hovde all performed here.

Moment 9

Moving On To Rochester
Twenty Years at KROC

I left Red Wing on August 31, 1957, after 4½ years, still a single man. The boss at KCUE was rather surprised that I was leaving. But the time had come for me to make the move. I had applied at KROC in Rochester and also at KSUM in Fairmont, and they were both ready to accept me. I felt good about that. I opted for KROC, because it was closer to home, and I thought perhaps there was a better chance of establishing my roots in broadcasting here. I'd always wanted to broadcast in Rochester. I'd grown up hearing KROC and Bernie Lusk a good share of the time, because Rochester was only twenty miles away from our farm. I liked the idea of it.

Cal Smith, a longtime broadcaster, was the man who hired me. Cal Smith had just completed 21 years on KROC, beginning in 1936 at the Owatonna studios, and later coming over to the Rochester studios. He was program director at KROC and a fine newscaster, who also did a little television work on KROC-TV during its early years. Six weeks after he hired me, Cal left to take a position as executive director of the Mayo Civic Auditorium, and he worked there another 24 years before he retired. He has since become very active in service clubs and at the Senior Citizens Center. Cal is now in his mid-80s. He has always been a good friend to me, and to all of Rochester. He had such a great radio voice. I can still hear him closing up the noontime news, that ran from 12:45 to 1 pm on

KROC, saying, "This is Cal Smith speaking for M.C. Lawler's Clothing. This is the southern Minnesota broadcasting company."

Only a few radio stations did "around-the-clock" broadcasting in those days. I started out working an evening shift, from 5:30 pm till midnight, Monday through Friday, and alternate Saturdays and/or Sundays, riding the control board for the NBC programs, interspersed with music until it was time for the station to sign off for the night. At midnight, I would say, "This concludes our broadcasting on KROC for today. KROC operates on an assigned frequency of 1340 kilocycles and 250 watts [later it would be 1000 watts] of power, as authorized by the Federal Communication Commission. Transmitter and tower are located just off highway 52 in Northwest Rochester. KROC is owned and operated by the Southern Minnesota Broadcasting Company. This is your announcer, Harley Flathers, wishing you all a good night." Then we would play the "Star-Spangled Banner," tip a switch and turn off the transmitter. Then, the following morning, Donovan Edwards would sign on the air and do everything from 6 am till noon.

When I started, we still had an engineer at the transmitter to sign on and off, but later we announcers had to take an additional course to obtain a 3rd class engineer's license so that we could legally tip that remote switch ourselves.

Apparently the word began to circulate among young people from 13 to 16 years of age that this new evening disc jockey was happy to talk with them, on the phone or even occasionally in person. One young lad of 15 (I'll withhold his name because he may still be around) really got into radio. For a brief period from mid-October through the following February, this individual came down to the station several times. He was always eager to put records away for me or clear the AP wire for incoming news. We visited frequently, and he always seemed very positive.

But every so often, he would say loudly, "Disgusting!" He was referring to our new competitor, KWEB, which had started broadcasting on September 30, 1957 — just two weeks after I started at KROC. I didn't think too much about it. He was a clean-cut young man, a sophomore, and in our conversations I didn't detect any real hatred for KWEB.

Then in early April, I learned that he and three of his school buddies had gone to the KWEB tower with a set of wire cutters. They cut a couple of cables, and the tower came down.

I don't recall what the law authorities did with those lads — whether they paid a fine or served jail time. I wasn't into clipping news stories at that time. I do know that malicious mischief toward radio stations is a serious business, and the Federal Communications Commission (FCC) can and will administer strong penalties for this kind of act.

The damage was only temporary, though. It was only a few days before KWEB was back on the air.

KROC was affiliated with NBC, and so they carried network sports. I remember the network broadcast the Rose Bowl game from Pasadena, with Curt Dowdy, Braven Drier and the late Chick Hearn (who died in the summer of 2002 at 85). These were exciting times. Folks really listened to the radio for these games. Although television also had games, in the late 1950s many families still had no TV sets. They relied on us in radio to keep them informed about what was happening in the world.

We had a good time on those radio shows. For a time in 1957 and 1958 — possibly even into 1959 — I used to lead up to the close of the broadcast day by saying, "Statistics show that in Rochester there are sixteen women for every man...and I want to take this opportunity to tell my sixteen, 'Good night.'" Occasionally I played "Good Night, Ladies." In late autumn, winter and spring, when I was broadcasting the "HF Road Show" from 3 to 6 pm, I would remind motorists, "Okay...lights on for safety. Sure, you can see where you're going, but others can't see you!" I hope it helped save some lives.

After I'd spent three years on the evening shift, the boss, David Gentling, called me in one day and said, "Harley, how would you like to start going on the air doing mornings?" I'd filled in a couple of days for Don Edwards, the morning man, and I guess they figured that he was putting them to sleep and that I could wake them up. So from that day forward, I was always a morning person. I'd done mornings in Red Wing for four and a half years, so it was nothing new to me.

When I started doing mornings at KROC in 1961, I missed my evening shifts, but I really adored the morning show. I loved signing on and affecting people's lives in those early hours. We gave them the weather report and kept them informed about things that they needed to know before starting their day. When stormy weather caused school closings, I would remind the kids, "Just listen for your school closing, please...I'm reading 'em every ten minutes on the air. I'm not giving them out on the phone when you call."

On my morning show, I regularly played an early morning band number and a hymn between 6 and 7 am. There were a lot of early morning jokes, too. Pine Island dairy farmer Tom Millering, gas-station owner Scott Fritz and the late Hank Priebe, who used to be part of our silo-filling ring when I was growing up, always reminded me of this one whenever we met. "It's so cold this morning," I would say, "that when I opened the barn door, Old Bessie, our favorite milk cow, looked around at me and said, 'Oh, no...here comes old icy-fingers again!'"

I loved morning radio, because I knew people depended on it. Whether it was the simple things like the weather, the news, the sports, or the lost dogs, they depended on it. Oh, those lost dogs! People would call in, and they had a lost dog, or a lost cat. We always put it on the air. Never knew whether they were found or not, but we got the word out. That was part of it.

I did mornings at KROC in Rochester from 1961 through 1968, a seven year period. That really was my heyday in radio in Rochester. In 1957, when I came, KROC was Rochester's only AM station. Then two weeks later, KWEB went on the air, and it became Rochester's rock station. In 1963 KOLM came on the air. So then there were three AM stations in Rochester.

Then the Federal Communications Commission lifted the ban on single station ownership in a market. They said, "The FCC will now grant you an FM license if you'd like, so if you want an FM, snap it up." Suddenly every AM owner also had an FM station. In just a short time, there were seven radio stations in Rochester. Today there are fifteen, including a couple of Minnesota Public Radio stations. Station owners have been able to expand into multiple ownership — two, three, four, even six or seven stations in some markets. As long as you can prove to the Federal Communications Commission in Washington, D.C., that you can do what you said you would in the interest of the public, you can obtain an FCC permit to broadcast.

In those early years of morning radio, I always wanted to be there at work, and I managed just about always to make it. A couple of times during the winters, I had to call the police, because the snow was so deep I couldn't get through. I had about a block to travel that might not have been plowed yet on a winter morning, and so I would call the police, and Ray Wagoner and Ray Spears, two great police friends, would park their car a block away and walk through the snow drifts to help me get out. We walked arm in arm, because I couldn't fight through those drifts on my own with my legs the way they were. They'd get me through. Their police car was always equipped with snow chains, and was always able to get through those deep drifts of the early 1960s.

And when I got in to the station, I sat down and started my broadcast. People told me later, "Well, we'd listen to the radio. We knew if Harley made it to work, then any of us could make it to work." That's what drove me during those years. Ray Wagner is gone now, but he was a close friend for many years. I was always grateful to them for helping me through the snow.

Once again, I was getting involved in community activities. People would call and say, "Can you come emcee this? Can you do that? Can you sit in on this? Can you cover this?" and I kept saying yes, yes, yes. It wasn't always the smartest thing to do, because I was probably wearing myself out a little, but I was younger then. The more I said yes, the more I got into. It pulled me into a lot of speaking engagements, a lot of judging, a lot of boards, a lot of committees and fund-raising things. For a time in 1971-72, I was chairman of the local NAACP chapter. Rochester's African-American community was very tiny at that time, but we wanted to let people know that we were interested in preserving everybody's civil rights. These things were all learning experiences.

I did hundreds of remote broadcasts. The engineer, Bill Witte, would take a pair of turntables out with us, a whole unit, and hook it up. I'd take the music, sit down and broadcast for two hours, playing the music right on site. People would come and visit with you, and you'd try to get them into the store. I did that for years at Donaldson's in the Miracle Mile, in the building now occupied by Carson Pirie Scott. Every Thursday evening from 7 until 9, and every Saturday afternoon from 2 until 5, I would be there, broadcasting Donaldson's' specials of the week. Families would come in, and I got to know a lot of people. The Donaldson store operated at that location for 35 years, from 1952 to 1987.

I did that for most of the 1960s, until about 1968. Then I left KROC for a couple of years and went over to KNXR, a new FM station. I wanted to see what it was like at an FM station. I was there for two and a half years, and then came back to KROC in early 1971, and stayed there until 1980. All those years, with a few bumps, were very good.

Some Favorite KROC Jingles

Chimes — "It's 6 pm, and time to open an account at Union National Bank in Rochester." This one ran during the early 1950s in Rochester. By the middle 1950s, the bank had been purchased by the big Northwestern National Bank, headquartered in Minneapolis and St. Paul.

Weather Jingle — On top of the hour we had the famous Northwestern National Bank Weather Ball Weather. The announcer on duty needed to know what the weather was at that hour. There was a big white ball on top of the Northwestern National Bank building at 2nd Street Southwest, and it changed color according to the weather conditions. Then, at :30 before 5 pm, the announcer might say, "The Northwestern National Bank Weather Ball is red," and then he would play the proper cut on the disc that had been recorded to go with various weather conditions. When it was red, the jingle said "Warmer weather is ahead." If it was green, the jingle said "No change foreseen." White was "Colder weather is in sight." For rain, snow, or anything other than sunshine, there were cuts that went with flashing red, flashing green or flashing white, and the announcer tied in brief weather condition reports to match the singing jingle. It happened occasionally that we played the wrong jingle — say it was sunny outside and we played the flashing white rainy jingle. That was not good. We usually heard back from the boss when that happened.

RS & L Chimes — The Union National Bank used to be on the corner of South Broadway and 3rd Street Southwest in Rochester. Soon after Union National Bank became Northwestern National Bank in 1957, Rochester Savings and Loan took over that location. Promotion/advertising man Walt Bruzek gave us a new jingle with special chimes to play with the RS & L commercial on the air. The chimes were similar to the famous NBC chimes. At the end of the "spot," our closing line was, "RS & L, on the corner and on the square since 1875." Today Wong's Cafe is in that building. Wong's started out in 1952 a half block further west and moved to its present location in 1983. Wong's recently observed their fiftieth anniversary in Rochester on historic 3rd Street Southwest.

Moving On Again to KWEB

After twenty years at KROC, suddenly — on October the 20th, 1980 — I was fired. Apparently, there were two young managers who didn't like my broadcast style, and I was gone. (One of them, Norm Aldred, was fired in early November, three weeks after he fired me.)

My dismissal brought in a lot of letters to the editor, more than they'd ever seen, according to the *Post-Bulletin*. Something like 65 letters came to the editor, and 24 of them were printed, all saying how much they wanted me to go on broadcasting for KROC. But I had been let go, and that was that.

Twenty years at KROC had come to an end. Well, any time a person is fired, he takes a new look at himself, and at life, and says, "Okay, a lot of people get fired. I'll just do something else."

Fortunately, the very next day, Steve Moravec, one of the owners of radio KWEB, and his program director Ed Ripley contacted me. Steve said, "Harley, I don't know what you want to do, but if you ever want to get back into radio, come see us." Well, that was the best kind of statement I could ever have heard. On January 5, 1981, I began working at KWEB, and I'm still employed there today. There probably aren't too many people in one town who can say that they've worked twenty years at one station and twenty at another, and still love what they're doing.

One of the people who had been on the board of the March of Dimes with me was Eugene M. Oreck, the part-owner and manager of Viking Oldsmobile. Gene and Shirley Oreck were a wonderful pair. After I got back into radio at KWEB, I'm sure he said, "Let's get Harley to work. Come out to my place every Saturday morning from 10 until noon and do a two-hour live radio broadcast on KWEB." I did that for ten months. It really was a great push. While he was working with me at monthly board meetings for the March of Dimes, I was there trying to sell cars. I was getting back into the full swing of radio broadcasting, and it turned into radio sales, which was what I wanted to do. Gene Oreck died on Sunday, May 23, 1982, of an unexpected heart attack at age 55. He was one of those super people that were with you all the way, and you don't forget them.

Steve Moravec set me up to do a live five-minute program from my home, which I did from May 1, 1981 until January 9, 1999. Guests, including mayors, doctors, nurses, lawyers and neighbors, would often come to "Harley's House" for a short visit on the air between 7:30 and 8 am. Years earlier, I'd heard the late Cedric Adams do programs from his home overlooking what he called "Spit Lake" on WCCO radio, and I loved that. I never thought about doing it myself, but when someone else suggested it, I did it. Nowadays, with the cell phone, you can broadcast from any place at any time.

Over the years, I've gone from solid straight announcing to total radio sales with KWEB-AM 1270 sports. KWEB had been our competitor all those years at KROC, and now I was happy to say I was there. The owners of KWEB later added a station called KRCH-FM (referred to as Laser 101), and on March 12, 1993, they added another one called KMFX (Fox Country 102.5). In recent years they have added an Austin station, which we operate from Rochester, KNFX at 970 on the AM dial (KNFX-AM 970 The Fan Sports). Those are the four stations for which I now sell, and I'm very pleased to do it. I do most of my work by telephone, and add a little broadcasting on special events whenever I can.

A Little KWEB Trivial Pursuit

1. Do you remember the annual KWEB Treasure Hunt from the mid-1960s to the early 1970s? Clues were given on the air daily, and the prize was $1,000 in cash. Kids used to try to sneak a portable radio into school just to listen for the clues.

2. Do you remember when local beef farmer Joe Poire and Richard H. Plunkett of Rochester State Bank (and others) purchased KWEB from Northland Radio Corporation? That was on May 1, 1964.

3. Do you know what those four towers are that are located south of Rochester between highways 63 and Olmsted County route 1? In 1968, the Federal Communications Commission granted a construction permit to increase daytime power from 500 to 5,000 watts, to add 1,000 watts night-time operation, and to install a dual pattern directional antenna array. Those towers belong to KWEB.

4. Do you remember when you could hear Ken Soderberg, longtime voice in Austin, regularly on KWEB radio? In 1970, Ken was general manager and noon newscaster, following the Paul Harvey broadcast. The studios relocated to 1107 7th Street Northwest in Rochester, and Al Axelson became the daytime announcer. Al was with us for many years, and then returned to his hometown of Red Wing.

5. How many times in earlier years did Paul Harvey come to Rochester? Twice. The first time was in 1980, when he was the guest of the Optimist Club. He came again May 7, 1981 at the invitation of KWEB's owner, Steve Moravec.

6. Do you remember the classy wedding shows conducted by KWEB radio in the early 1980s, always in January? I wore a tuxedo (we all did) when we hosted this event in the Kahler Hotel.

7. Do you remember "Farm Free Forty" in the spring of 1984? John Dahl, the morning man, and I conducted this contest under the guidance of KWEB manager Jim Giebel. Farmers registered to win enough gas, seed, fertilizer and fuel to plant 40 acres. Area agri-businesses participated, providing the products, and the winner was young dairy farmer Ed Gathje of rural St. Charles, 18 miles straight east of Rochester on County 9.

8. Do you remember KWEB's 25th anniversary in the autumn of 1982? We had a big celebration with a live band at the Mayo Civic Auditorium.

All of this technical station data comes from the FCC station profile for 1957-1982.

Photo of Northwestern National Bank with Weatherball downtown Rochester on 2nd Street SW. The building today is called Brackenridge Square, an office building. Photo courtesy of Olmsted County History Center.

Looking north on broadway and 4th Street intersection. Mid 1950s. Note: angle parking. Photo courtesy of Olmsted County History Center.

Cal Smith, veteran announcer & program director at KROC radio with Harley at his 70th birthday party Aug. 27, 2001.

Harley on Sales Phone at KWEB, about 1989, setting up live broadcasts and interviews.

Harley at Donaldson's on the Miracle Mile . . . May 1963. Hundreds of KROC remotes originated here Thursdays 7-9pm and Saturday afternoons 2-5. This lasted several years.

Moment 10

My Favorite "Brit"
How Harley Met June

I've been blessed with a wonderful wife, June Jury Flathers. A number of people during the years have asked me, how did you meet your wife? Every once in a while, someone writes in to Ann Landers' column, saying, "Here's another story on 'How I Met My Mate,'" and they're always kind of unusual. Well, I think our story is rather unique.

June was born in England, and she came to this country in the summer of 1958. At that time, there was an exchange plan between various countries to send nurses back and forth, to give them the opportunity to work two years here, and two years there. I remember that we were getting a heavy influx of Filipinos then. Many Filipino nurses came over in 1957 and 1958 under that program. They would stay for a couple of years and go home — unless they got married.

June decided to come over from London with a couple of her friends. The last thing that her father told her as she got on the ship, the *New Amsterdam*, was, "Now, remember, don't go marrying a Yank."

And she replied, "Don't worry, Dad, I won't."

End of that particular conversation.

In the summer of 1958, when June arrived, I was working at KROC radio, doing an afternoon and late evening split shift. I'd play music from 3 pm till 6, then someone else would fill in from 6 till 9, and then I'd come back and wrap it up from 9 till midnight. So I had this three-hour break.

We were married less than a year later, on September 19, 1959, in the Homestead United Methodist Church on 13th Avenue Southeast in Rochester. Because June's parents weren't able to make the long trip from England to attend the ceremony, Dr. Ralph Spiekerman escorted her down the aisle. In September 2003, we celebrated our 44th anniversary.

We'll let June tell her story in her own words.

June's Story

My spiritual home is centered on the muddy south bank of the meandering River Thames in London, England. It was here in May of 1933 that I was born, and this is the area to which I returned during my next 25 years. It was here that I went to school, my character formed, and the world events of the Great Depression and World War Two helped shape my life, and it is to here, I believe, my spirit will return after my death.

My father was definitely a Londoner! No one could mistake his accent. He sounded like a Cockney — he dropped his H's and he put in an H when it should have been omitted. Alfred John Harold Jury was named for two Saxon kings, Alfred and Harold, and one Plantagenet, or French and Saxon, king, John. His name showed his parents' pride in their nation. He had two sisters, Margaret and Maud. He came from a long line of south-central Londoners from the areas of Battersea, Lambeth, Vauxhall, Wandsworth and even Chelsea, north across the River Thames from Battersea where Dad was born. His father is recorded on a daughter's birth certificate as being a military drum maker. He also led a small dance band. Dad had to dispose of the instruments when he and Mother moved to Kent. Dad's grandfathers are recorded as a prison warder and a paper stainer. One of Dad's great-grandfathers is listed as a sugar baker and another as a shoemaker on a marriage certificate dated 1872 at St. Peter's Church in Vauxhall. Other forebears are listed as journeyman carpenters or joiners. Women in general at that time stayed home after they married, and I have no record of any that did work outside the home. My father was a sheet metal worker, but when I was born in 1933, he was unemployed. It was the middle of the Depression in England, and there was no work for him at that time.

My mother was from Liverpool, a port city in the Midlands of England on the west coast (and the future home of the musical group, The Beatles). She was one of ten children born to William Green Bingham, who managed a flour mill and had originally come over to Liverpool from County Down in Northern Ireland. Of the six boys in the family, the two eldest were killed in World War One. The oldest, Robert James Bingham, died leaving his wife, Annie Letitia Bingham, a son with his name and a daughter, Jessie Phoebe Bingham. The other son killed was William Bingham. The other four boys, George Reginald Bingham, Samuel Green Bingham, Walter Newall Bingham and Albert Radcliffe Bingham, all married and had two children each. They were prison warders or Post Office workers. There were also four daughters. Two died in infancy. My mother, Edith Eileen Bingham, was the older of the two remaining girls. Aunt Elsie Norah Bingham, the youngest child, is still living in Liverpool near the street where she was born.

My grandmother died at the age of forty-eight from pneumonia. Mother was twelve when her mother died. My mother finished school at fourteen, which was the time of completion of compulsory education at that time. After that, she kept house for her father and her brothers and sister. She never worked outside the home. She met my father during a holiday in Somerset, a county in the west of England.

Dad was a great cyclist, participating in long rides with his pals. On Sunday, March 25th, 1928, the Kentish Wheelers, the group of which he was a member, put on a Novices' Scratch Time Trial. The winner's time was one hour, eight minutes and eight seconds. Dad came in with one hour, eighteen minutes and thirteen seconds! There were over 100 riders in the 25-mile race, and he came in with the middle third of the riders. Two years later, when he wanted to ask my grandfather for his daughter's hand, he cycled the whole way from London to Liverpool over a weekend. It was over 200 miles — each way!

I think that my father was much more impressed with my mother than she with him. When he walked into the house after that long ride, my mother said, "What have you come for?" Her brothers were very angry with her and came to the defense of the weary suitor. However, she accepted his proposal, and she and Dad were married June 8th of 1930 in London. She was 20 and Dad was 23.

They lived at the house at 143 Battersea Bridge Road, London SW 11, where Dad had lived with his grandmother until her death in April of 1930. Dad's father had died in 1924, and his mother died of cancer in 1926. His maternal grandparents, John and Eliza Anderson, died in 1927 and 1930 respectively. My parents rented out rooms to supplement Dad's pay as a sheet metal worker. I was born May 26th, 1933, at the newly-built Battersea Maternity Hospital in Bolingbroke Grove, Battersea, London. A newspaper clipping which my parents saved for me reported that Mrs. Baldwin, the wife of Stanley Baldwin, a former Prime Minister of the United Kingdom, visited the hospital a couple of days after I was born. She asked my mother what my name was, and when told it was June Sylvia, she said, "Oh! It should be May Sylvia!"

It was the depths of the Depression in England, as well as most of the industrialized world, and Dad was unemployed. Mother's father up in Liverpool died on January 13th, 1934. It was then, after so many deaths and turmoil, that my parents decided to start a new life in Kent. With the inheritance from my mother's father's estate and a small inheritance Dad had from his grandmother Eliza Anderson, they put the money down on a house in Sidcup, Kent, just on the south-east edge of London. The business title of the builders is a somewhat prophetic one as far as I was concerned: "New Ideal Homesteads, Ltd.!" It was not what Americans might think of as "homesteading" — street lights, indoor toilets and electricity were all laid on! My family moved into their lifelong home at 71 Brooklands Avenue, Sidcup, Kent, on September 29th, 1934.

Number 71 was built on the clay of the Thames Valley. Gardening was very tough and the drainage poor. Dad built a greenhouse in which he grew tomatoes. He also grew potatoes, marrows, runner beans, beets and lettuces, while mother grew the roses, primroses and lupines — which could be spectacular.

One of the first things that I remember is a visit from my Aunt Elsie and her husband Len McCormick, who came down from Liverpool with their two daughters. I can remember that I was rather unkind to cousin Sylvia because I didn't want to share my toys, particularly my tricycle. I pushed her into the side of the house, which was covered with pebble dash and caused some minor scrapes on Sylvia's skin. I was well chastised for that!

Another day that stands out in my memory is the day that World War Two broke out for the British people. I was then six years old, and my sister Irene three. It was the morning of Sunday, September 1, 1939. My mother was bathing my sister and me, as was her routine, in the large porcelain kitchen sink, which was more convenient than the large bathtub upstairs. She would bathe us one at a time and shampoo our hair. Before the hair was dry, she would curl our hair around her fingers in long ringlets which would remain curled for all of one day. This particular Sunday the sirens sounded and my mother started to cry. She knew what was going on. It would be announced over the radio later in the day that war had broken out. I am convinced that the general public had visions of German planes coming over that very day. My father was away at Territorial Army Camp at that time. Some neighbors, Mr. and Mrs. Jones, invited us over. They lived four houses down the street. We stayed there for a few hours, and when no Germans came, we went home!

Eventually the iron chains which graced the posts on top of the brick walls of our front garden (yard) were removed and collected, along with other scrap metal items, to make weapons. Soon we had an Anderson Air Raid Shelter installed right in the middle of our back garden lawn. It was made of corrugated metal which dove-tailed together like an upside down letter U approximately eight feet across. This was placed in a large hole, with the dirt from the hole heaped on top of the metal roof. The ends of the shelter were built of vertical corrugated metal, with a small door towards the house. We rarely used this shelter during air raids. The earthen floor was damp, making the shelter very uncomfortable. I think my mother preferred to take her chances under the stairs rather than spend miserable nights going outside to that place! (This is what we eventually had to do.) Of course, we had to observe the "Blackout," and took our gas masks wherever we went.

My father was in the Territorial Army (similar to the American National Guard). He had joined the Armoured Brigade of the Royal Artillery Territorial Army in April of 1925, and went to camp for continuous training every year. In fact, he spent the years of annual preparedness camps from 1925 until 1935 at Watchet, Somerset. My mother had relatives in Somerset, and this must have been how my parents met. In 1938, Dad was called up during the Munich Crisis for a month, but he was not fully mobilized until August 24th of 1939. From then on, he and his unit continually picked up guns and transported them to wherever "the powers" said they should be. He rose to the rank of bombardier. His war diary, that he kept until he was discharged, is a list of sites to which guns were transported. One entry tells of the road to Winchester being snowy and ice-covered. In London, the guns were taken mainly to parks like Hyde Park, Finsbury Park and Hampstead Heath.

His unit would eventually see action in North Africa, but Dad was invalided out in June 1940, because of a "weak heart." I never found out what the problem was, but he had a murmur and took large spherical "heart pills." He had had tonsillitis in the Netley Hospital in Southampton in September 1939, and then was in the Poplar Hospital, London, in April 1940 with auricular fibrillation. He was honorably discharged on June 11th, 1940, and received the War Medal after the end of the war. After his discharge, he was sent to the north of England to do "war work."

Schooling had to be continued during the war, but there were many days when we had to go to the air raid shelters, which were across the blacktop playground. The boys and girls had separate playgrounds, with a dividing brick wall which had a wrought iron door in it close to the shelters. Lessons did not continue in the shelters. The air raid alerts were of short duration, but we were given black slate boards and chalk to keep our hands and heads occupied. I remember always drawing (never my talent) pictures of ladies in pretty dresses.

Central London, as well as other strategic locations, was a target of most of the bombing. Sidcup, Kent, was in the direct line of flight to London from Europe, so often there were some unintentional bombings in our community. The times that our primary school was damaged, we had home schooling at my friend Brenda Chapman's house. The Thomas and "Tillie" Chapman family had a huge inside shelter made of thick steel that looked like a table. It was the best kind, as you could go to sleep under the shelter at night and still be warm and cozy. It also had a "blast wall" built outside the house to give extra protection. This was a foot thick and it curved around the bow window of their living room. If there had been damage to the school, we would go to Brenda's house for lessons. There were Brian Bates, Iris Eaton, Brenda and Shirley Chapman, all living along the street, who would meet at the Chapmans' together with my sister Irene and me. Miss Wainwright was our teacher.

Another memory of my childhood is sleeping in a bed with my sister in the front room (drawing room) downstairs in case of air raids. It was Christmas Eve. Irene and I had hung our socks by the fireplace. I awoke from sleep and stretched out my toes and I heard the delicious crackle of paper. Father Christmas had come! We both woke up, put on the light and were soon busy reaching into the socks for the apple, the pennies and the sixpenny pieces that were always in the socks along with sweets. We found the usual dolls which my mother always bought for us every Christmas and which always got broken. (They were made of pottery.) Suddenly my mother walked in. "Father Christmas must have just come. It is midnight. Go back to sleep at once!" she said. We had to go back to sleep!

The war was always present with us. We carried our gas masks everywhere we went and left them as we hung up our coats. I remember putting mine on (the one and only time) when they were first issued. What a nasty rubbery smell it had!

We were usually at home or at school. We also went shopping with mother. Most of our food was purchased at the "Top." This was a small parade of shops. On the first corner was the News Agent, where a paper could be bought along with magazines, sweets and cigarettes, which

Mother smoked quite heavily until she had her first stroke. It was where "dolly mixtures" could be bought — tiny sweets with all kinds of flavours. If you found a strawberry — that was a find! The store was full of large glass containers of sweets. Tantalizing for children, but we seldom had sweets. They were reserved for birthdays and Christmas.

The next shop was a green-grocer. Shopping was a two or three times a week chore. We would line up, or "queue," and take our turn very naturally. Nobody elbowed themselves in front in a rude way in those days. Everybody was in the same boat! We would buy potatoes, cabbages, carrots, beets and apples. It was not until after the War was over that we could buy oranges, bananas and many other foods. Our food was very simple but sufficient. Mother would have bags into which her purchases were placed. When we were with her, we could help carry everything home.

Next was the butcher shop, with its marble slab in the front window and a few pieces of meat on view. It was not until after the war that I saw my first chickens and turkeys hanging up in the window. Every Christmas that I remember we had a pork roast.

The next shop was a grocery store which my mother did not patronize. (There was another that she preferred.) Then there was a small shop which was converted into a cafe at some time. We never went in there. On the next corner was the ironmongers. Here you could buy nails, a hammer and many other useful tools, but we seldom went into this shop either.

Across the road were the grounds of quite a large house and some smaller houses. Several years after the war, this property was bought by a brewery for a "Pub," to the consternation of the neighbors. Here the local doctor lived in a large house along the street.

Then came another group of shops. Here was the Chemist, where the doctors' prescriptions could be filled. I was fascinated by the looks of the man who worked in there. His eyes were piercing and his skin was very sallow. Next door was "Mrs. Lundy's." It was a shop where you could buy wool and patterns to knit jumpers (sweaters) and every other article of clothing. Also, as I was to learn later, it was the place to buy sanitary napkins. We would never go into the Chemist's to ask the man with the piercing eyes for those!

On the next corner was a small post office where along with stamps one could purchase cards, paper, string and posting supplies. It was here that I remember buying my first Christmas present for my mother. It was a calendar. It was small and very delicate and it cost sixpence. It was a picture of a lady in a crinoline dress, and the skirt of the dress was made of real lace which stood out from the cardboard figure. At the bottom was the small (about two inches by four inches) tear-off calendar. I thought that it was lovely and was so proud to give it to her, and she showed her delight, too.

Across the road from the post office on the opposite corner was the bakery. I don't recall the good smells that one associates with a bakery, so it probably was only a place of distribution. The fancy pastries did not come along until after the war.

At the end of this row of shops was "Essex's," which was the grocery store that mother liked. There were counters all around the shop. On the left were the staple foods. Mother would buy a pound of flour, a quarter of a pound of tea, half a pound of sugar, and as other needs came up, those commodities would be purchased in the same small amounts. Homes did not have refrigerators in those days. The temperatures were rarely hot enough to cause most things to go bad, and shopping was done two to three times a week. The only coffee that I saw growing up was a gooey, sweet syrup called "Camp" coffee that had to be diluted in hot water. We drank tea or water only. We never drank pop. If we were thirsty, we drank tap water.

Across the shop from this counter was another counter with the more perishable items: cold meats to be sliced by a shop assistant, eggs, butter, cheese, which would all be cut up and wrapped individually by the assistant. Mother would give our ration books for the coupons to be stamped as the food was portioned out. Foods that were rationed were eggs, meat, butter, cheese, tea and sugar. Even when I started nursing school in September of 1951, we had to hand in our ration cards to the administration so the hospital could provide certain foods that were still rationed. All other foods could be bought if they were available. Apparently there was a black market in London, about twenty minutes away on the electric train from our house, but I did not hear about it until many years after the War.

It was on January 17th, 1941, in the midst of the "London Blitz," that we were first bombed out. Dad was not with us. He was stationed in the north of England in Ranskill, a little village near Worksop, in Nottinghamshire, and later at Bishopton, near Stockton-on-Tees, doing "war work," although we never knew what kind of work he did.

We had heard the sirens indicating an air raid was in progress this night and our mother hustled Irene and me to the "under the stairs" cupboard in the dining room. I can remember a smell of what must have been sulphur, a lot of noise, and then a silence. We tried to get out of the front door, but it was jammed. Then we tried to get out of the kitchen door. That was jammed! Then the french doors would not open from the dining room. My mother must have been terrified, as the incendiary bombs that had fallen caused the gas street light outside the house to be a sheet of flame, and the wooden fence that separated our small concrete patio from the neighbors' house at the back also was on fire. She broke a pane of glass in the french doors with her hands to enable us to get out of the house. The cut it made was the only physical injury that we received.

Once outside, we walked around the side of the house, where we saw air raid wardens coming to assist us. We had unknowingly walked by a 200-pound bomb that had landed by the side door. I never knew what happened to that bomb, except that the foundations of the house were supposedly destroyed, so that the entire house and that of our next door neighbor were razed and both had to be rebuilt at the end of the war.

A dear neighbor, Mrs. Barker, to whom we were forever grateful and whom we regarded highly all of her life, took us in for a while. I am sure that she plied my mother with tea and biscuits (cookies)! We probably spent the first night there, although I don't remember it. I was nearly eight years old and my sister five. Then another neighbor, Mrs. Smith, in Harland Avenue, had us for a few days, but she had all boys. That was

NOT going to work out! We were finally settled in a requisitioned house (appropriated by the authorities) whose owners were in India. We had to share it with neighbors from across the street who had been bombed out the same night as we were. Brooklands Avenue got it that night! Our street was to get it again later in the war when a "doodle-bug" — a V-2 rocket — hit the house next to Brian Bates' parents. The Fuewins, who lived there, had the sailor boyfriend of their daughter Betty as a guest, and he was killed.

We then settled into 33 Little Birches, the requisitioned house. Mr. and Mrs. Hartley, who had been bombed out the same night as us, took the upstairs. There were two large bedrooms and a small one. They had no children. We shared the upstairs bathroom. Downstairs our family (Mother, Irene and I) had the front living room for our shared bedroom and the dining room at the back of the house as our living room. The kitchen was shared with the Hartleys. Neither family had a car. There was a shed for garden tools. It must have been when Dad came home from the war work in the north of England that the Hartleys left and we had the whole house. The Hartleys had gone when we were next bombed out!

On January 28th, 1943, in the middle of the night, a V-2 rocket hit a house in Longlands Road at the back of our house. The blast blew out every window of our house, and damage was such that we lived in one room for six months. The night the bomb exploded, my sister and I were sleeping in the back bedroom, sharing a double bed. When we awakened to that ominous quiet that follows an explosion, we both climbed out of bed and padded in our bare feet to where my parents had been sleeping in the large front bedroom. My mother immediately said, "Get your slippers on at once!" There were slivers of glass all over the house. Not one window and hardly any china was left intact. I remember later drinking tea out of a King George VI coronation milk pitcher. All the furniture was scarred by the force of blown glass fragments. I remember my father cursing "those bloody Jerries!" We "made do" as best we could. It was at this time that I remember my mother getting a couple of quilts that came from America. I had never seen a patchwork quilt before!

The War was soon to be over. I still visited my friend Brenda from Brooklands Avenue, and I was there on D-Day, June 6, 1944, the day that the Allies landed in Normandy. How we cheered when we heard the news on the BBC Home Service!

As the war finished, gradually life became more settled and our house was rebuilt. My parents had only been in their "homesteaded" house for five years when the war had come. We moved back into the new and improved house on August 29th, 1947. (My parents had wanted a bigger kitchen.)

Our street was called Brooklands because there was a small stream flowing at one end of the road north through a tunnel under the Electric Railway toward the Thames River. This was the source of many fantastical adventures. We went on voyages of discovery and gave names to obstacles that we overcame. There were jungles of brambles that we fought through. We collected frog spawn and tiddlers (tadpoles). Once I was walking along the stream bed in rope-soled canvas sandals and I walked right onto a broken glass bottle. There was a trail of blood all the way home — no stitches, but I still have the little scar. To us it was a magic place. Then one day the entrance was locked and a notice placed telling us to "keep out!"

A place where we went riding our bikes was Kemnal Walk. This was a non-maintained road that was lined with old oak trees. It was close to a wooded area where we went bluebell picking. We had a freedom that would not be given to children today. I well remember riding my bike home from school in the worst smog I have ever seen. It was probably about three in the afternoon, but it was as if it was nighttime. It was after this that efforts were made to make all heating in London clean fuel burning. We had always had coal fires, but the fireplaces were converted to gas or electric fires. Central heating and refrigerators were still a luxury for the wealthy.

I attended the Sidcup Technical School for Girls and then Coopers Technical School for Girls in Chiselhurst, Kent. I did not make the infamous 11-plus cut. This was a test taken at the age of eleven years, when a decision was made whether a child went to Grammar School and possibly University, or whether that child went to a school from which the shop and factory workers were taken. Another test could be taken at age thirteen, when it could be assessed if a girl might be a seamstress or a typist. These were the days when the sexes were separated at the age of eleven. I was motivated to study and I did well at school. My name is on the Honor Roll at Coopers. I received my Oxford University School Leaving Certificate in July of 1950.

I finished school at seventeen, and because I was to enter nursing school after my eighteenth birthday, I worked for a year at a Lloyd's Insurance Broker's, Bevington, Vaizey and Foster. I think it amusing that I walked daily to work in the "City," which is the financial and business center of London, over the London Bridge — the bridge that is now at Lake Havasu in Arizona. For a year I worked as a lowly filing clerk for two pounds ten shillings a week. They knew I wasn't going to stay! Another coincidence in my life is that I worked in the "American department." We insured the Chicago Burlington railways, among many others, and I filed those policies many times and searched for many that were misfiled! Doreen Vandersteen from the East End of London, the young cockney girl who worked there with me, was quite expert in knowing where to look for those policies. She knew the habits of the brokers!

I don't know how Mother got up the courage to come with me to my interview for nursing school. She was not used to travel, and in fact, she loathed going up to London. We had to take the train to Charing Cross Station in Central London, and then take a number 75 bus to St. George's Hospital at Hyde Park Corner. When we arrived, there were kindly porters who guarded the entrance and directed people to where they needed to go. Matron Powell, the Director of Nurses who interviewed me, was well regarded in the nursing community and was eventually made a Dame of the British Empire for her services to the country.

The hospital is no longer at Hyde Park Corner. The St. George's building is now a luxury hotel called the Lanesborough, but the name of the hospital remains carved in the stone of the pediment over the grand entrance of St. George's, which overlooks the gardens of Buckingham Palace as it always did. Her Majesty the Queen used to send over left-over sandwiches from her garden parties for the nurses' teatime.

Our nursing instruction was given on the "block" system, meaning that there were periods set aside just for study and exams. When not doing a block, we worked 96-hour fortnights (two-week periods). I was glad for my days off, and usually took the electric train down to our home in Kent.

In my early years, I had had dreams of becoming a concert pianist. Eileen Joyce, a pianist who played with the BBC Symphony and the London Philharmonic Orchestra, was my idol. However, during my teen years, my goals became more realistic and I decided to go into nursing, out of a mixture of common sense and a desire to help people. The value of this desire to help people was brought home to me from time to time when I would be walking from one of the nurses' residences to or from St. George's, wearing my green overcoat and beret over my nurse's uniform. An occasional man would doff his hat to me (this was when men still wore hats!), and his respectful gesture gave me a wonderful sense of accomplishment and peace. I thought, "Yes, he has been helped by a nurse!"

My three years of training at all the St. George's allied hospitals at Hyde Park Corner, Wimbledon and Tooting were years of both hardship and joys, as with most young people. Some of the fun times were when we went rowing on the Serpentine, a large lake in Hyde Park, particularly after night duty. Lettie was an ex-Wren (Women's Royal Naval Service). She happened to be on night duty at the same time as myself, and along with a couple of other student nurses, we would go boating during the early mornings on the Serpentine with Lettie — who else! — as our Admiral. Those were golden mornings!

Another fun time was the annual Christmas Ball at the Grosvenor Hotel, Park Lane. I had a particular escort from a Guard Regiment stationed in the nearby Victoria Barracks, who arrived to pick us up in full dress uniform AND spurs! No dancing with him! The Chelsea Arts Ball was another occasion where all-night revelry and returning to the dormitory in time to go on duty the next day did not cause exhaustion!

While stationed at Possil House in Wimbledon (the nurses' residence), I went to the Wimbledon tennis matches for the first and only time. I saw Rod Laver play in a doubles match. When stationed at St. George's, one of my favorite places to go was (and still is) the Victoria and Albert Museum on the Brompton Road, just a short walk from the former St. George's Hospital. In fact, Hyde Park Corner was a wonderful place from which to explore London. The hospital was perfectly located at the center of London, and therefore the British Commonwealth.

It seems that parades and extravagant shows were as much a part of the life of 20th century Britain as in the 16th century of Elizabeth I. When Elizabeth II was crowned Queen on June 2, 1953, there was the traditional parade of the new monarch throughout the capital city. All the buildings along the route had stands built for viewing the colorful procession. Of course, St. George's was on the route! I was then working night duty on a small male medical floor called Hope Ward. We had the newly-developed television (usually afternoons only) for complete viewing of the service inside Westminster Abbey. The TV personality Richard Dimbleby was the commentator. He was to become "an institution" for describing the momentous happenings of the British Isles. His hushed voice described the anointing of the Queen with oil, as all other previous monarchs had been anointed and "set apart." The Archbishop of Canterbury presented her with the state sceptre, with its cross (denoting equity and mercy) and orb (denoting kingly power and justice). When the thunderous organ rang out with a specially composed Voluntary, we saw her slowly walk through the Abbey to her coach for the triumphant ride back to the palace.

Quickly we found our assigned seats on the St. George's viewing stands to watch her go past. Being London, of course it rained! The Queen was radiant in her gilt carriage and she did not get wet. However, the Queen of Tonga, a Polynesian constitutional monarch who was the only other monarch in the British Commonwealth, was adored by the crowd when she insisted on leaving the roof of her carriage down so that the people could see her. She held up her own umbrella! There were also units from the armed forces and governmental representatives of many nations who rode in carriages and cars. It was a wonderful day in our young lives, and we never minded having so little sleep.

After completing my year as a staff nurse, I started midwifery training at London Hospital, Whitechapel. After Part One (the first six months), I went on my first excursion abroad to work at the Maison de Sante Protestante de Bordeaux in June 1956. It was a mixed experience. My French was poor, but gradually the patients and staff realized that I knew what I was doing. I knew I had made it when they let me "faire le garde." In the Midi area of France, everybody that can takes a siesta after the noon meal. And while most of the staff took time off for the siesta, there had to be a nurse available on the floors. They called it "faire le garde," or keeping watch, and this was what I was finally permitted to do! I returned to England a little before the end of my term, as I was "homesick," but I had made a couple of French friends with whom I corresponded for years.

Returning to the UK, I worked at the local hospital, Queen Mary's Hospital in Sidcup, and then completed the second part of my midwifery training at the Parson's Green Maternity Hospital in Fulham, London. I performed the required amount of deliveries in the hospital and then was assigned to a midwife for four months. My midwife had the King's Road, Chelsea, area, just across the Thames River from Battersea, where I was born. (Life is indeed full of cycles!) I rode my bicycle through the traffic, with cars and buses on either side and my little black bag of necessary items on the rack behind me, to my patients' homes. Most cases (but not first pregnancies, multiple births or multiparous women — women who had had more than three deliveries) were delivered in their homes. It is the way of life in the UK that most babies are born at home and delivered by a midwife.

In September of 1957 I received my midwifery certificate to practice, and I was placed on the Roll of Midwives. My next job was as a "Junior Sister" at the Royal Hospital, Richmond, Surrey. A "Sister" is a nursing supervisor.

My next big move was to America! My friend Colleen McFaul, with whom I had worked on my midwifery certificate, had taken a job as an exchange nurse in Rochester, Minnesota. She wrote to me and said that she liked it there, and invited me to join her. I liked Colleen. She was fun, always laughing. I immediately set about getting the necessary visas and borrowing the fare from my father. I sailed on the SS Nieuw Amsterdam in July 1958. My father, as we were saying our goodbyes, said to me, "Now don't go marrying a Yank!" And I said, "Don't worry, Dad, I won't!" Of course, I did.

I had become part of the "brain drain," the phenomenon which occurred in Britain following World War Two. Great Britain was exhausted from fighting in two world wars. The costs of holding the scattered peoples of the Empire throughout the world together was too great. The British people had a glorious past, but what about the future? The Empire had become the Commonwealth, and any British subject throughout the world was welcomed to the small islands that comprise Great Britain. Jobs were low paying. Money was needed to rebuild homes and businesses. The universities and other institutions were putting out trained doctors, nurses, engineers, scientists and teachers who found that the living conditions and high salaries in the United States were hard to resist. The post-World War II years saw many highly-trained, valuable people leave Britain and not come back.

We found that the Sisters of St. Francis at St. Mary's Hospital in Rochester were very kind, and very soon we were settled into our new jobs. One of the most difficult parts of the job for me was understanding all the funny accents on the telephone. Face to face, people were much easier to understand.

I liked Rochester from the first day I arrived. It reminded me very much of Lourdes, the Roman Catholic shrine near Pau, south of Bordeaux in France, which I had visited during my stay there. The Miraculous Grotto, or Cave, of Lourdes is where a peasant girl, later to become Saint Bernadette, had a vision of the Virgin Mary. The grotto is hung with thousands of crutches and canes left by faithful pilgrims who claim to have been healed at the Shrine. Many people come to Rochester with the same faith and hopes. I also liked Rochester's wooden houses, which to me looked so Scandinavian. The town was so clean, but oh, all that snow! I did not ski or skate, but still I liked Rochester!

How did my family fare after I left?

In March/April 1971, Harley and I hosted a wonderful trip to Spain and Portugal. I was uneasy about my father's health. He had been sick most of the winter with bronchitis. I took a week to be with my parents after the trip. I knew Dad would probably not last too much longer when I shook hands with him for the last time — his hands were icy. He died October 10th, 1971. I was working at St. Mary's Hospital when I received the call from Irene that evening, and immediately made arrangements to go to his funeral. I spent most of three weeks with my mother, helping her get the house and her affairs in order.

Mother died in 1986, at the age of 76 years. She had had several strokes. Both she and Dad were cremated and their ashes scattered in a rose garden. It was their wish.

In 1955 my sister Irene, who had trained as a typist and secretary at school, had started training as a nurse at the Charing Cross Hospital. She married Dr. William Ashton in late 1955. They had a son, David Ashton, who later married an Italian girl, Angela. David and Angela live in Milan with their children, Samantha and Sebastian. Irene later divorced Bill, and she is now happily married to Douglas Tomlinson.

I frequently traveled to the United Kingdom through the years. My children became familiar with their British relatives and adore them. My sister in turn has come to the States with her husband Doug, and we remain in touch by phone, as I do with our children, who are scattered throughout the United States.

Harley and I were blessed with four children: Edward, born in April 1964, Jeffrey, born in February 1966, and twins Jane and Emily, born in September 1967. Harley's quip was that we had four under four on the floor! The early years were very busy years indeed! Harley on one of his early shows announced that he had just that morning mistakenly used Diaperine instead of toothpaste on his toothbrush! All the children live far away from us now, but we keep in touch by phone and e-mail. There used to be letters flying to and fro across the United States and I have kept a few of the precious letters that they wrote before e-mails finished off letter writing.

Edward John, the oldest (the responsible one, the detail person — he gets that from Harley), graduated from Gustavus Adolphus College with a BA in history and business and received an MA degree in arts management from the University of Wisconsin. Ed followed his dad in selecting his life's work. After his first few jobs, he became assistant to Geraldine Laybourne, the president (and founder) of Nickelodeon TV. Nickelodeon is now owned by Disney, but Ed is still with Geri and her associates, who have started a new TV channel called Oxygen Media. Ed has an opportunity to use the PR skills he inherited from his dad with the many people he meets, both business and show biz people. He enjoys living in New York and frequent traveling.

Jeffrey Alan graduated from Carleton College with a BA in Spanish. He is our linguist and scientist, traits he inherited from me and my father, who never stopped being curious and wanting to know what was around the next corner. Jeff received a master's degree in international management from the American College of Business (Thunderbird College) in Glendale, Arizona. Unable to find a job that he liked after graduation, he taught English in Osaka, Japan, picking up Japanese along the way. Returning to the U.S., he worked a few months as a waiter and then joined the army. Following basic training, he was sent to Fort Lewis, Washington, and then to the Presidio in Monterey, California, where he learned Mandarin Chinese and graduated at the top of his class. He also married his Chinese teacher, Chaoying Sun, and they have a beautiful daughter, Kristina. Jeff recently left the army and is teaching fourth and fifth graders in an elementary school in Seaside, California. He is very good with children, and has found his *metier*, I believe.

Jane Elizabeth (the oldest twin by eight minutes) is our "animal lover," taking after her grandfather Homer Flathers and her grandmother Edith Eileen Bingham Jury. Jane was the one who held our beloved dog Fleck when he had to be "put to sleep." She also enjoyed her horse, Cricket. She graduated from the University of Minnesota as a doctor of veterinary medicine and married Gary Nie, another veterinarian, who specializes in equine reproduction. While he started the Equine Reproduction Department at Auburn University in Alabama, Jane worked as a veterinarian in Columbus, Georgia and Phoenix City, Alabama. They have a three-year-old son, Ethan Mitchell. They later moved to Lexington, Kentucky, where Gary worked in a large horse hospital. In 2003, they resettled back here in Rochester.

Emily Suzanne is our "composer/musician." Emily is talented in both piano and violin. She inherits her musical ability from Harley's mother, Vivian Jenny Raabe Flathers who graduated from, and taught at the McPhail School of Music in Minneapolis. She and Emily share the gift of "perfect pitch". Emily graduated from Luther College in Decorah, Iowa, with a degree in piano performance and worked on her master's degree in piano performance at Arizona State University. She has enjoyed working as the Music Director and Accompanyist of the Mystery Mansions Dinner Theatre of Phoenix, using her skill at composing incidental music as well as accompanying, and using all the keys on the piano to produce the required atmosphere. She has been teaching elementary music in the Phoenix School District for 3 years and is acquiring additional choral conducting skills. She has obtained her master's degree in Music Education from Arizona State University.

I worked at the Mayo Clinic, Rochester, Minnesota, as a Registered Nurse firstly in the Clinical Research Center, then the Patient Education Center and finally the Diabetes Consulting Service deriving much satisfaction and pleasure from my work starting 1976 until my retirement in December of 1994. I became a US citizen on January 19, 1999, after a surprisingly long and arduous process that began in January 1997 with my first letter requesting an application form!

Now back to Harley.

Christmas 1958 when Harley met June. L-R: June Jury, John Twomey, a patient, Nora Freeman and Merriul Beneldini (holding the mistletoe).

Christmas 1958 . . . "Harley Flappers" as these girls called themselves. L-R: Mary Mackey, Nora Freeman, Merriul Beneldini, Harley, June Jury (seated on floor), Margaret Howard & Barbara Burroughs (far right).

June Jury, 2nd place winner in a "hat-making" contest aboard the Nieuw Amsterdam on the way to the U.S., July 1958.

Flathers 4 kiddies at home on front steps. Easter 1971. L-R: Emily 4, Jeffrey 5, Jane 4, and Edward 7. Photo by Elaine Flathers.

They All Grew Up. June 1984 at Mayo Civic Auditorium. Jeff's Mayo High School graduation. June, Emily 16, Jeff 18, Edward 20, Jane 16, and Harley.

Off To College. A stop in Waseca as Jeff and Harley are taking Ed to Gustavus Adolphus College in St. Peter. Two weeks later Harley took Jeff to Carleton College in Northfield for his first year. Photo by Elaine Flathers, Autumn 1984.

Left, Marriage of Alfred John Harold Jury and Edith Eileen Bingham, June 8, 1930.

Above, John Jury displaying his Territorial Army Medal at Camp before his medical discharge, approx. 1940.

Right, Number 71 Brooklands Ave, the "Homestead" house of John and Eileen Jury, approx. 1934.

Eileen Jury looking elegant behind the new house with little June by her side, approx. 1935.

Above, June and Irene Jury in the back yard of #71, approx. 1937

Below, Irene and June with parents at Girl Guide Camp on visiting Day, approx. 1949.

A bit of cheesecake from Irene, approx. 1950.

A small family reunion, approx. 1950. Top Row, June Jury, Samuel Bingham, Alfred John Jury, Walter Bingham and daughter Joyce. Middle Row, Millie Bingham, Eileen Jury and May Bingham. Bottom Row, Stella Bingham, Irene Bingham and Irene Jury.

Taken the day we started at the Preliminary Training School of St. Georges Hospital, Hyde Park Corner, London, SW1. September 1951. L to R, Brenda Loughborough, June Jury and Jill Lewis. NB. The uniforms were new and note the white starched aprons. The PTS was located in Cumberland Terrace, a mile or so away from the hospital.

Picture taken at the time of my engagement to Harley, 1959.

Moment 11

Special Programs and Remote Broadcasts
Those Live Saturday Programs

When I started in Red Wing, at KAAA, we occasionally did live programs on a Saturday in our big studio, complete with grand piano. I conducted the 4-H essay speakers, or the queen candidates, while the judging went on. The candidates would come to our studio, and oftentimes the winners, for an interview. Sometimes we might tape them and play the recording back later.

Occasionally talented 4-H kids did a musical half-hour. Lorraine Herman was a spunky 4-H member who came to our studios on a Saturday afternoon in 1955 to perform "Cat and Mouse" on the piano. A 1955 graduate of Rochester High School (three years before it was replaced by John Marshall High School), she lived with her family on the Wabasha/Olmsted county line south of Zumbro Falls, just off highway 63 not far from South Troy Church. She had been a talent show winner in her 4-H club, first in Wabasha County and then at the Dresser Valley Club in Olmsted County. Her next stop was the Minnesota State Fair, where she won fourth place in the talent division and received a suitcase for her participation. She also went to the State Fair as a 4-H Health Queen. Lorraine, who is now Mrs. Tom Deedrick of Rochester, recalls speaking many times for the Youth Temperance Commission (YTC) — "Teens Against Booze."

On Saturday mornings, from 11:05 to 11:30, Ronnie Owens performed live on the air. He was a fine young lad who lived at Goodhue, Minnesota, and would come in with his guitar to play and sing in 1954 and 1955.

Another local music maker, from right down the road at Hay Creek, five miles from the studio, was Leo Dressen. Leo was a country western singer. He could sing glad songs and sad songs, and he and Ronnie Owens sometimes entertained together on a Saturday night at the Skyline Ballroom, just south of our studio on highway 58. (The Skyline eventually went up in smoke, as many of those ballrooms did.) I have an ad from March 4, 1954, that reads, "Starting Saturday, March 6th, Leo Dressen and his Western guitar — Western music as you like it. Tune to KAAA every Saturday 1:15 - 1:30 pm. Sponsored by E.J. Klampe Company, awning manufacturers, Rochester, Minnesota." Leo sold awnings during the week for Everett Klampe, and then sang on Saturdays while he and I "talked" about our sponsor's product.

E.J. Klampe was one of our early sponsors. I met Everett Klampe in the early 1950s when he sponsored Leo Dressen on the air. Then later, when I got to Rochester, the Klampes became great friends of ours. Everett and Betty Klampe have now retired, and their children have grown, but they are still great promoters of their city. I worked with Everett on many things, and I want to say hats off to people like the Klampes, who did a lot of good positive promotions for their business and for their community.

Genevieve Hovde was a lovely singer whom I also met at that time. Genevieve is a dear friend of ours to this day. She started out as a little girl, nine years old, singing on the Grand Old Opry. She'd sung first in Chicago, then in Nashville. Somehow her parents were able to get her there, back in the early 1940s. When she grew up, she kept on singing. She had a sweet voice and a smiling personality. She became part of the Sunset Valley Barn Dance on KSTP television, Channel 5, in the Twin Cities, when that show went on the air in 1948. She had sung on KSTP radio earlier, and so it was a natural for her to go on to television.

Genevieve traveled a lot and got to know some of the great names in country western music. She became a great friend of Rex Allen, Roy Rogers, Jim Reeves and Porter Wagoner. Genevieve Hovde was right there, in the middle of that business. She has thousands of memories and four albums of songs that she has recorded. I was there at River Falls, Wisconsin, in 1993 when her friends put on a celebration of her 50th anniversary in show business. But during my early years at Red Wing, she was there singing live on the radio as well.

On Saturday afternoon, from 3:30 till 4, we really had a super time with a live band, Don Safe and the Westerners, on a program that I named "Anything Goes." Don played the big bass. I can see him slapping that bass yet, and singing and grinning. He was a farm boy who lived about half a dozen miles away from Red Wing. Jule Ness, from Wanamingo, played the banjo, guitar and accordion. Arvin Iverson, a farmer from Wanamingo, also played the accordion, and Bill Strusz from Red Wing often joined the group on the guitar. Occasionally Dale Smith, of Racine, Minnesota, was there with his guitar. They were good. They could do great country music, always a half hour program. I was seated nearby, emceeing the show. I told some gosh-awful jokes, probably not as bad as I think they were today.

Ronnie Owens died in the early 1980s. Leo Dressen is gone, too, and probably some of the others. But the memories of those live Saturday afternoon broadcasts in the early days at KAAA in Red Wing live on.

Featured Programs on KROC

Here in Rochester, on KROC radio, I remember every Saturday evening, at 6 o'clock, we would come on the air with a man named M.M. Hargraves. Dr. Malcolm Hargraves was one of the physicians on staff here at the Mayo Clinic, and he was a great outdoorsman. He would do a fifteen-minute program, either live in the studio or by a tape recording. He and his wife would often go to their cabin near Mikana in upper Wisconsin, near Rice Lake, and they would mail the tape back to his daughter, who would bring it into the studio in time for the broadcast. Sometimes he would have to repeat a program. Many times during the late 1950s, at six o'clock, I would say, "It's time for 'You and the Out-of-Doors,' featuring M.M. Hargraves, in conjunction with the Izaak Walton League. Now, Dr. Hargraves."

And he'd start out, "Good evening, ladies and gentlemen." Then he would start talking in a very comfortable, friendly way about various things in nature, the squirrel, or the groundhog, or the pheasant, and tell you about things to be looking for. It was enlightening and comforting. He was a top toxicologist, and an expert on mushrooms. His radio program started in 1944 and ran for twenty-eight years, ending on Saturday, April 15, 1972.

When he died, his wife Mildred asked me to come and say a few words at his memorial service, which took place at Christ United Methodist Church here in Rochester on April 4, 1981. I felt honored indeed.

Immediately after M.M. Hargraves, we went to the weather. The weather station at that time was located at Lobb Field, the old airport, where Meadow Park is now located, just east of the great ear of corn. I would say, "And now, here is your weather. Meteorologist in charge, Mr. Claude Holmes." Claude Holmes was a folksy speaker, much like Dr. M.M. Hargraves. These programs had been set up consecutively by our program director, Cal Smith, and it was lovely to hear those two men speak, one after the other. Claude Holmes talked about weather, but he also got in a lot about gardening. The musical theme that we used for his show was "The Roller Coaster." It's a tremendous theme, and that's what started the weather program Saturday evening, which was a composite of the weather of the past week and the things that were ahead. Claude didn't spend as much time on the weather as he did on some of the other things, but he had a lot of folks listening.

Some other weathermen on duty and reporting daily on KROC included Jim and Kelly Anderson, John Sloan, Glenn Trapp and Blaine "Ben" Amann, who spent 38 years here with the National Weather Service, from 1956 to 1994 — the last 22 years as chief meteorologist.

Another special program that I remember when I was with KROC in the late 1950s was a religious broadcast each morning from 8:45 till 9, featuring the pastor of the First Baptist Church. I was on the control board starting in January 1961, and I would introduce this program every morning. The preacher was Kenneth A. Muck. He had a droll sense of humor, and we used to kid one another. I recall once, just before he came on, I said, "Reverend Muck, would those parishioners of yours who live on the south end of Rochester be called 'Southern Baptists?'" And he laughed. Reverend Muck served the First Baptist Church here from 1955 to 1962. At that time, the church was located on the corner of 2nd Street and 4th Avenue Southwest. Do you remember their big sign, "Jesus Saves," that rose high above the steeple? Today, Mayo Clinic's Baldwin Building occupies that site, and the First Baptist Church is at 415 16th Street Southwest.

In 1964, our man from the First Baptist Church was Robert Featherstone. He came from New York City, and he was here in Rochester until the mid-70s. He was a terrific individual.

I remember these programs especially because in 1964 we downsized them. A fifteen-minute religious program in the morning on AM radio was getting out of the picture, because management wanted this time to sell commercials. So manager Bob Fick worked with the Reverend Featherstone and myself, and instead of a fifteen-minute program, we reduced it to a two-minute program called "Think About It," that was heard every day at 4:58 pm on my program, the H.F. Roadshow, from 3 to 6 pm.

I would introduce the program, saying, "It's time for 'Think About It,' featuring Bob Featherstone, and brought to you by Perkins Cake and Steak, two locations in Rochester, 432 16th Avenue Northwest and 1647 South Broadway. Now, Mr. Featherstone." And he would do a two-minute sermon. It was always so good. When he finished, he always said, "And, well...think about it." Then I would do the same closing.

We did that for a number of years. After a while, he and I talked about whether we could merchandise this program, syndicate it. I offered to help him, and for quite a while, he and I would tape those sermons at KROC studios while he was on the air, and he sent the tapes on to other stations. "Think About It" aired for 37 years on a large number of US stations. Robert Featherstone later worked for the Billy Graham Crusade. Following his retirement, he lived in North Carolina. He died on August 26, 2002, at an Ashville, North Carolina, hospital at age 79.

broadcast on the building's west side. There was a nice sloping lawn terrace, where we sat on that late Sunday afternoon. We had some notable people there, some senators and representatives, as well as local people. The program, which included songs by the Rochester Male Chorus, ran from 1:45 to 3:45 pm on KROC. The keynote speaker was Senator Walter Judd, who had been a missionary in China for many years.

Another kind of remote broadcasts we were doing in the 1960s and 1970s was grand openings of brand-new gas stations. Gas stations were springing up like dandelions in the spring during those years. There are two intersections in Rochester where at one time there was a gas station on each of the four corners. I did broadcasts in one place both in 1962 and 1966, for the same owner — Dick Kruckerberg, now in business at Blooming Prairie, Minnesota. It was a Phillips 66 station, and it stood on the site now occupied by Blockbuster Video on the corner of Civic Center Drive and 11th Avenue Northwest. Right across Civic Center Drive, where Home Federal Bank was located, was a little Apco service station. On the northeast corner of that intersection, where now Pearle Vision is located, was a Texaco station. I did a couple of broadcasts there, and I remember one day it was so hot that my 33 1/3 rpm album was starting to melt on the turntable. Then on the southeast corner of the intersection, where the parking lot is for the new Home Federal Bank corporate headquarters building, there was a Mobil station, and we did a couple of broadcasts there.

Today, alas, there's no sign of any gas stations on any of those corners. West of the intersection on Civic Center Drive at one time was the old Rochester circus grounds. It was rather low ground, and there were no highways going through there then. Later, at the time when those gas stations were on the corners, Johnson Pontiac occupied that site. That business was destroyed by a fire in the early 1970s, in which the owner, Mr. Dee Johnson, lost his life. Now it's the Barlow Plaza Shopping Center.

South of that area a few blocks, and west, where 2nd Street Southwest passes over busy highway 52, there were also four gas stations on the four corners. West Side Texaco, owned by Steve Freese, was located on the northeast corner, where Hardee's big drive-in stood for several years. I did more than one broadcast there. Across the highway, where the Jiffy Lube was located, Duane Madsen had his Standard Oil station, and I did a broadcast there.

On the southwest corner, where Wendy's Drive-In stood until the fall of 2001, was Scott's West Side 66 Gas, owned and operated by Scott Fritz. (Earlier, it had been a Phillips 66 station, owned by Mayo Priebe.) Scott had the pull and the money behind him that he could actually start a gas war, and he often did. He used to chuckle about it, and he chuckles about it to this day. We did more than one gas station broadcast there.

The fourth gas station was across the street on the southeast corner, where the Brandin' Iron Drive-In once stood. First it was a Mobil station, then later it became the West Side DX. A Super 8 Motel was located on that site for many years.

Now the buildings on all four corners have been demolished for construction of a new Highway 52 interchange. So that shows how well I did. All those gas stations whose grand openings I broadcast have gone out of business, and even the new businesses that took their place are today just memories.

To top that, I once did a live radio broadcast at Bud Streiff's Conoco station at 2nd Avenue and 4th Street Southwest. In 1977, my boss, David Gentling, the owner of KROC, purchased the land and built his new radio station there, where the gas station had been.

In 1961, a man named Ed Houck started a Skelly gas station on 19th Street Northwest. He had a good location, right on the frontage road of 19th Street Northwest, and I did a grand opening broadcast there in 1961. In 1986 I went back and did another broadcast with him on his 25th anniversary. Well, it wasn't long after that he sold it, said it was time for him to move on. It stood empty for short time, was rebuilt as a PDQ food store, then served as an AM-PM Store. Today all those buildings are gone for new highway construction. Ed Houck died on July 3, 2003.

Another thing that was happening in the decade before 1962 was that shopping centers were opening on the edges of town. When Miracle Mile opened in 1952, people said, "Ah! This will never make it! It was just a cornfield. What? All these stores? It'll never happen." Miracle Mile opened, and they did make it, and it's still going strong, fifty years later.

Shortly thereafter, in 1959, Silver Lake was opened, and I did the first broadcast for a number of stores there. There had been a supermarket there called Roth's Foodtown, but little by little, more buildings were put up — Hunt's Silver Lake Drug, Silver Lake Hardware, and more and more fell into place. I remember reading the first commercial for John Hunt's drug store in 1959, and then in 1999 I read a commercial again on their 40th anniversary. John Hunt voiced it with memories of the store and how it grew during the years. We also included comments from its new owner, Dave Kohler.

I remember a promotion that we did with Frito Lay for several months between 1962 and 1965. Frito Lay wanted to get their story out. Their big competitor then was Old Dutch potato chips. So Frito Lay worked out a deal with our station. The station sales representative at that time who handled the Frito Lay account was Joe St. George, and Joe could sell anything to anybody. He was a heck of a radio salesman. You could hardly keep up with all the things he would do. Bob Balance was another one. I used to see Bob every once in a while on a Monday at the Rochester Quarterbacks Club's lunch at Michael's Restaurant. Bob and Joe were part of the old radio sales crew at KROC in the late 1950s and early 1960s, good boys to work with. They have both died now.

This was the idea that Joe St. George and Frito Lay came up with. Every Thursday afternoon they would set up for one hour at a different grocery store. 'And Harley would be there to play music and invite folks in to have their Frito Lay potato chips. From 4 until 5 pm, I would leave my 3-to-6 afternoon shift and go do this promotion. (I went back again and finished up my shift as soon as I could get there until 6 o'clock. I was working a split shift then, 6 to 9 am and 3 to 6 pm.) I did that for several months, at every small and large supermarket in town. There were many supermarkets that carried Frito Lay, and I would invite people to come out there. Come in, enjoy the music, meet Harley and shake hands. I wish I had the long list of them. Many of them have gone by the wayside. However, the

Just-Rite Grocery on 6th Avenue Southwest just off 2nd Street, built in 1947 and owned today by Pat Schulte, is still going strong. And I was there in the mid-1960s, broadcasting for Frito Lay on KROC.

I did a lot of broadcasts in the 1960s from Piggly Wiggly stores — Piggly Wiggly was big back then. I was there for the grand opening of the brand-new Northgate Piggly Wiggly in 1962. Roy Tipka was the manager. I broadcast there a number of times. It was a huge store. Now that space in Northgate Shopping Center is occupied by the Northgate Health Club. Later I went to another Piggly Wiggly at the Crossroads Shopping Center, owned and operated by Dick Prochaska. He was very helpful to us in the March of Dimes. There was a third little Piggly Wiggly at 204 4th Street Southwest with Dick Bluhm as manager, and a fourth at 12 North Broadway, in the building now occupied by the Goodyear Tire Store. I was in there broadcasting several times on a Saturday afternoon. It was a regular routine — Piggly Wiggly, different place, every Saturday, between 1 and 2 pm, or maybe 1 and 3 pm, myself or Larry Roberts. Larry was another one of our broadcasters, another comical guy.

I broadcast the grand opening of the Methodist Hospital in autumn 1966. Of course, it was much smaller than it is today. The Methodist Hospital site was formerly occupied by the old Methodist church. In 1954 the Methodist church people had sold the land to build a Methodist hospital in downtown Rochester. They also acquired two small hospitals nearby, the Colonial and the Worrall, that had belonged to the Kahler Corporation, and operated them while they were building their own hospital, which was completed in 1966. That was before it became affiliated with the Mayo Clinic, although they were all using each others' services, St. Mary's Hospital in the west, Mayo Clinic in the heart of downtown, and Methodist Hospital right beside it. In 1986 they all merged together, including Charter House, a retirement living facility.

During those years, we also did special events broadcasts out-of-doors. I recall in the mid-1960s, there was a big arts festival on behalf of the Rochester Art Center, and there was a parade. Virginia Firnschild and I broadcast the parade on KROC on June 7, 1965. The parade, with

Avenue Southwest, long-time business Nelson TV and Appliance, where I had done many "remote" broadcasts over the years, was also severely flooded. All the area in and around the Mayo Civic Auditorium, along that branch of the Zumbro River, took a severe "bath."

Relief areas were set up at the Salvation Army building, the Homestead Church and other places that offered accessibility. Hundreds of homes were seriously damaged, some totally destroyed.

During the day, sports director Bernie Lusk, who had broadcast from a boat in the 1951 floods, was back at it again. About midday, he and Mayor Alex Smetka came to my location and talked about the city's condition. I played a tape that Bernie had made while in his boat near the Mayo Civic Auditorium.

When at last the power returned in the city at 3:30 pm, I finished broadcasting and went home, completely exhausted, my voice totally hoarse. What a day that was!

Mrs. America from Ohio & Harley at a Kruse Lumber Open House . . . in newly - developing Meadow Park in southeast Rochester. Starting in the early 60s in the space once called the Rochester Airport.

Dr. M.M. Hargraves . . . ending his 28-year radio series . . . "You & the Out of Doors" 4/15/72. Harley introduced him many times in the late 50s at 6pm on KROC, and assisted in taping many of his programs in the 60s & early 70s. (Post Bulletin photo)

5 KROC announcers in 1961 . . . L-R: Peter Viking, Harley Flathers, Bernie Lusk. Seated L-R: Gene Thompson and Larry Roberts. Studios were on 2nd floor of 100 First Avenue Building. Today Eastwood Bank occupies this space.

Bernie Lusk for Hamms Beer. Early 1950s on both KROC Radio & KROC-TV Channel 10.

The South Broadway at 6th Street Co-op Oil Station built in 1940. Later years it would become Greenway. It remained there until 1977 and razed for Burger King construction. (Photo - Olm. Co. History Center)

Lobb Field, The original city airport was built by Mayo in southeast Rochester in 1928. One of the finest privately owned fields of its day, it was used until the present airport opened 8 miles south in 1961. At left the famous ear of corn built in 1930 at Ried & Murdoch Canning factory. Looking northwesterly, the Mayo Plummer Building tower and at right the airport hanger with windsock & planes. Today the space is filled with hundreds of Meadow Park homes. Photo: Mayo Clinic Archives.

In the mid 1940s after World War II was over, these Quonset homes were built in Graham addition southwest Rochester providing housing for Mayo physicians & families. In the early 1960s these were replaced by new homes and present Crossroads & Hy-Vee Shopping Centers. (Photo: Mayo Archives)

Clint Kueker Illustration . . . "Remember When" KSTP Barn Dance March 30, 1947 at the Stewartville High School Auditorium with Genevieve Hovde.

Moment 12

Today's Guest Is . . . Presidents and Other Celebrities

Over the years, I've met a lot of interesting people through my profession. I mentioned earlier that I talked in 1954 with one of my favorite people at that time, George Mikan, the great Minneapolis Laker basketball player. That same year, his coach, Johnny Kundla came down to KAAA in Red Wing, and I interviewed him. I particularly remember Johnny Kundla's deep, resonant voice.

Not all of the famous people I've talked with were radio interviews. On October 18, 1960, after I had come to Rochester to work at KROC, I went back to Red Wing to attend the celebration when President Dwight D. Eisenhower came to speak at the 10 am dedication of the new $3 million bridge over the Mississippi. Today, that would be pretty cheap, but at the time, it was quite a big project. They had just announced that it would be built as I was leaving Red Wing in the summer of 1957. Like so many bridges across the Mississippi in those days, the one at Red Wing was a winding bridge that curved ninety degrees in the middle and was very unsafe. So a new bridge was put up between Red Wing and Wisconsin.

After President Eisenhower finished speaking, I went up to him and said, "Mr. President!" He turned around and we shook hands. Then I said, "We would like to invite you to Rochester."

He asked, "On what occasion?"

I pointed to the station letters on my blazer, saying, "It's our 25th anniversary at KROC radio."

He smiled. Then he got into the car with Minnesota's Governor Orville Freeman, and they soon left.

I shook hands with another president in 1962, when I was coming home from a trip to the west with my wife June and her father, John Jury, who was visiting from England. It was Friday, August 17, and we were driving back from the Black Hills, where we had spent our last night. We heard on the radio that President John F. Kennedy would arrive that day in Pierre, South Dakota, for the dedication of the big Oahe Dam over the Missouri River. It had been raining heavily that morning. We were driving easterly on highway 90, and when we got to the turnoff to go to Pierre, I said to my wife, "Well, let's go up there. The map says it's only 50 miles from highway 90."

The plane was due to come in somewhere in the neighborhood of 9:30 to 10 am. We got there well before 10, and found the airport at Pierre, which was not that big. A bunch of cars were lined up along the road leading to the airport, backed down into the ditch at an angle, so that when the procession went by on its way to the program location, they would all be in line.

As the presidential entourage started coming from the airport heading toward the site of the dedication ceremony, suddenly there was a lull. Nothing was happening. About six or seven cars had gone by. I looked over, didn't see any cars coming, so I just gunned the motor. We got up out of the ditch and right into the procession. When we reached the speaker's place, I pulled right up behind President Kennedy's Lincoln Continental convertible, which had its top down. Here I was with my 1962 blue Chevrolet convertible, with its white top, all very muddy.

President Kennedy got out of the car and went up to the speaker's platform. We could hear the speakers from where we sat. Next to the president was Korczak Ziolkowski, the sculptor who had been working since the 1940s on the Crazy Horse Monument. He was a real hero in South Dakota because of that statue of Crazy Horse. He was carving the monument out of a mountain. It was a family project; his sons were helping him. They'd blasted away hundreds of tons of mountainside since he started in 1949, and it was still incomplete when he died in the 1980s, but the work goes on.

John Kennedy spoke, dedicating the dam. I don't remember a thing he said, because I was so excited about being right behind his car. I got out of my car, and June and her father got out. I stood there, talking with a couple of the Secret Service men who were asking me questions. I guess they could see that this fellow standing on crutches did not pose any threat to the safety of the President of the United States.

Suddenly, here came the President. His speech was over. He was about to get in the car, and there I was, standing right behind the driver's door, where he had to see me.

I said, "Mr. President!"

He turned and put his hand out, and I shook his hand. Of course, my wife did not have the camera handy. Nobody had any camera handy, it happened so quickly. It was one of those memorable moments, when I shook hands with greatness, but we have no photographic record of it.

Fifteen months later, in November of 1963, John F. Kennedy would die by an assassin's bullet in Dallas, Texas, shot while riding in a Lincoln convertible just like the one he had there in South Dakota.

One of the great people I've interviewed on radio was Jack Benny, who was here at the Kahler Hotel on February 7, 1962. He had been invited by the Rochester Civic Music Program to perform as a guest artist. At that time the Rochester Civic Music was getting guest artists, notables, to come in and conduct or play with the local orchestra. The Mayo Clinic had also scheduled an appointment for his annual checkup that week.

At that time, I was on KROC in the mornings. Walt Bruzek, who was a great promoter here for many good community things, came up to the studio and said, "Harley, we're going to go up and visit with Jack Benny at the Kahler. Want to come along?"

I said, "Sure." I must have just finished my morning shift, because it was around 10 o'clock, and I finished the shift at 9. So a bunch of us, including Judy Opfer, the 1961 Miss Rochester, went up to welcome Jack

Benny to Rochester. As we came to the Kahler Hotel's Skyline Suite, where he was staying, one of us knocked on the door, and we could hear a violin playing inside. He was playing "Love in Bloom," his trademark exercise that he always used to play during the years when you'd hear him on radio, the tune that meant he was practicing.

He came to the door, and we introduced ourselves. "Come on in," he said. He did not know about this visit ahead of time. I had brought my tape recorder along. We got it all set up, and I had a nice interview with him.

Near the end of the interview I said, "Well, Jack, you're going to have a birthday soon, aren't you?" His birthday was February 14th.

He replied, "Well, I...I guess I am."

I said, "How'd it be, folks, if we sing him a Happy Birthday?"

Walt Bruzek said, "Yeah! Let's get Miss Rochester to help."

So we all sang "Happy Birthday."

When we finished, Walt Bruzek said, "Well, it wasn't too good and it wasn't too loud."

Jack Benny replied, "And it wasn't too young." That was Jack Benny.

I even have his autograph from that visit.

In 1964, I had the privilege of introducing Louis Armstrong just before a concert at Mayo Civic Center. Ben Sternberg, a long time promoter of Golden Gloves boxing and other events here in Rochester, had an agreement with the Mayo Civic Center to bring in a number of different programs, and of course, they were always notables. I remember he brought in Les Brown and the Band of Renown. Bernie Lusk introduced them.

I introduced Louis Armstrong. We had done a pre-concert interview in the dressing room. It was July 20, 1964. We had a nice visit. He was such a gracious person. He told me all about his background growing up, and how he used to be in Joe "King" Oliver's little boys' band back in New Orleans. When we were all done, I said, "Louie, thanks so much for the good visit." He said, "Okay, Pops. Me and you." That was Satchmo's way of talking.

On December 17th of that same year, 1964, Ben Sternberg brought Duke Ellington and his band to Mayo Civic Auditorium. That was a top notch program. They held it in the theater section. What a fine concert! Duke Ellington was a beautiful person, just a gentleman! He dressed immaculately. I interviewed him, and he told me about some of his earlier years.

When I finished, he closed the interview by saying, "And thank you, and tell your friends we love them madly."

I played all of these taped interviews back on KROC as soon as I could, because we in radio always wanted to be known as the one that got the interview and played it first. There's a little ego in radio people, as you can see.

In the late 1960s or early 1970s, I met Fred Waring, and had a very brief interview with him on radio. He was here to do a concert — Fred Waring and the Glee Club.

Johnny Weismuller, who played the role of Tarzan for so many years on the screen, came to Rochester in 1965. He was invited to the Joe Weis home in Northern Heights. Joe Weis and his brother Gene Weis were builders. (Gene has since died.) We did a live broadcast on KROC radio on Sunday afternoon, June 20, around Joe Weis's new backyard swimming pool. It was a Johnny Weismuller pool, so they had Johnny Weismuller there to talk with people, sign autographs, and dive in the pool. It was an advertising promotion.

We did a three-hour broadcast, from 1 until 4. I was sitting there beside the pool, playing the music. Engineer Bill Witte had brought out the two portable turntables, set them up on their legs, and draped the curtain saying KROC around the front of it. He hooked it up with what we called the Marti Broadcast Unit, a little transmitter box that we plugged in, that would shoot the signal back to the station. I would interview people all along between records.

But when I'd try to talk with Johnny Weismuller, he would just say, "Oomgawah."

I remembered hearing him say "Oomgawah!" in the movies. You'd hear the elephants going "OOO-arrr!" and Johnny would say, "Oomgawah!"

So finally, near the end, I said, “Well, thanks, everybody, for being here. Thank you, Johnny Weismuller, it’s been great having you here. Will you tell me before we go, what does ‘Oomgawah’ mean?”

He said, “It means, let’s get the hell out of here!”

On September 1, 1971, I had the pleasure of talking with Jack Paar. That was when Roger O’Day and I were interviewing together from 9 till 1 daily on KROC.

Jack told us, ”My, oh, my, I’ve been going through the Mayo Clinic. I certainly wish I had the enema concession!”

In the late 1950s and early 1960s, folk music was sweeping the country. Groups of anywhere from one to four to eight members would appear in concerts or on television. Some of the best known were the Kingston Trio, the Chad Mitchell Trio, the New Christy Minstrels and the Serendipity Singers (both of these last had eight members in their group). They all did concerts here, and I introduced them all, quite often for promoter Ben Sternberg or the IBM Club, when Bill Hudson was in charge of incoming entertainment.

When the Kingston Trio came to Rochester in the mid-1960s, I’d been working closely with a young man who wrote on entertainment for the Rochester Post-Bulletin, Chuck Glazer. He often covered the same events that I was covering for KROC. We agreed to drive our cars to the airport and bring the Kingston Trio — three very nice young men — into town. I took Nick Reynolds and John Stewart in my 1962 blue Chevrolet convertible, and Chuck brought Bob Shane with him. I don’t recall getting them into the studio for a live visit, and I don’t remember whether I introduced them at their concert at the Mayo Civic Auditorium, although it’s quite likely that I did if Benny Sternberg was promoting the event.

During the 1960s and 1970s, I interviewed a number of famous orchestra leaders who were visiting Rochester. I talked with Arthur Fiedler, longtime conductor of the Boston Pops Orchestra, on March 12, 1970. He had come to perform as guest conductor with the Rochester Symphony Orchestra. I was at KNXR-FM downtown in the Sheraton Hotel (which today is the Holiday Inn Downtown). When Arthur Fiedler arrived at the studios early on Saturday afternoon for the interview, Dave Frogner and I "ganged up" on him. He'd been walking around town a lot and was tired. I asked him if he was the "Fiedler on the Roof," and he replied, "No, I'm the Fiedler on the hoof...and my feet are killing me!"

On October 10, 1970, I visited with Doc Severinson, orchestra director of "The Tonight Show With Johnny Carson." Doc Severinson was also in Rochester as a guest conductor for the Rochester Symphony Orchestra. He was a real gentleman, and a fun guy.

I interviewed Stan Kenton, the great jazz band leader, on October 19, 1971, when he was here to do a concert at the Mayo Civic Theatre. Another time, I did a phone interview with Myron Floren of the Lawrence Welk Show. I visited with George Shearing over the phone on October 31, 1971.

I talked with Guy Lombardo at least three times, both pre-taped interviews and live in the studio. The first time was on April 18, 1969, while I was at KNXR. Then, in 1971, Guy and his songstress, Leslie Stewart, both visited me on KROC prior to their evening concert at the Mayo Civic Auditorium on November 5.

The third time was in 1979, when he was here again for a concert. I had asked him to come to the studios early on the morning after the concert. Guy told me that he was staying at the Kahler Hotel, and would be flying out pretty early. I said that I would pick him up at the Kahler shortly before 6 am, bring him to the studios for a brief visit, and then see that he got to the airport in time to catch his plane. We did the interview at 6:45 am, after which I called a Yellow Cab to take him to the airport.

Guy Lombardo was a very kind and gracious person. His orchestra, the Royal Canadians, including his brothers Carmen, Victor and Liebert, his nephew Kenny Gardner and Bill Flanagan, had been entertaining for over four decades. In the 1971 interview, Guy told me that his brother Carmen had died the year before.

The well-known newscaster and personality Jack Perkins was here in 1979 to speak before the Chamber of Commerce annual dinner meeting at the Kahler. I picked him up at the Kahler early the next morning and took him back to the studio for a radio interview before 7 o'clock, just as I'd done with Guy Lombardo.

I interviewed Al Hirt on tape and introduced him a couple of times, twice in 1964 and again on August 19, 1982, when Ben Sternberg brought Al Hirt and Pete Fountain back for a concert. They were a great pair, Al Hirt and Pete Fountain — Al with the trumpet, Pete Fountain with the clarinet. Al Hirt died a few years ago.

In 1964, I met another real gentleman, Henry Mancini. He was a fine person, and I interviewed him in our studios on May 6. We were playing a lot of his music in those years. Capitol Records, with whom he recorded, would send us the records. They would find out who the music director was at the station, and send the records directly to him. I was the music director at KROC, which meant that when the records came in, they would bring them to me. I'd take a look at them, maybe put a number on them, and get them played. There were several nice albums by Mancini, who was a super guy.

I even set up a reception for him at the Kahler Hotel. His manager called from Hollywood, and asked if I would line it up with the Kahler. I did, and then I called all the people from the other radio stations and invited them. And they enjoyed it, too, because there was food and they got to meet Henry Mancini, whose name was big then.

Another great musical gentleman, so talented, was the composer Leroy Anderson. His name was almost synonymous with American music for many years. He was the musical arranger for Arthur Fiedler and the Boston Pops Orchestra for a long while. From the upper 1940s to the 1970s, you heard his name all over the place in great orchestral music of a pops nature. One of the very early ones that I especially enjoyed was his famous "Sleigh Ride." And then he did what he called the Christmas festival, consisting of several well-known carols. We in radio loved that one, because it lasted seven minutes and forty seconds, and when you put that on, you could get a lot of things accomplished while it played — like a quick sandwich or a bathroom break.

Leroy Anderson was invited to come to Rochester on May 5, 1974, to be a guest conductor with the Rochester Symphony Orchestra. Often, with these programs, someone in the community who worked closely with the music board would say, "I want to invite the guest and his people to come to my home afterwards." My dear friend Mary Elizabeth "Puck" Love and her husband, Dr. J. Grafton Love, invited us to their home, along with many others in the community, for a reception after the concert for Leroy Anderson. It was an enjoyable time. At parties like these, the performers can just let their hair down. They've been under tension doing their concert, and now it's over. They enjoy meeting people, they talk back and forth, and get to know you a little bit. Of course, when it's over, you never see them again. The Loves and Leroy Anderson have all since died.

Between 1957 and 2000, I did so many radio interviews. I interviewed author Corrie tenBoom, from Holland, in 1971. She was promoting her book, "The Hiding Place," about her experiences with the Nazis during World War II.

Maria Anne Hirschmann, the evangelist who uses the nickname of "Hansi," also gave me an interview around that time. She later wrote to me, asking my advice about radio broadcasting.

Another time, I did an interview with Dr. Oswald Hoffman of the Lutheran Hour series, a Sunday program that we carried on KROC.

In 1982, the West Rochester Kiwanis put on a series with celebrity speakers. They brought in three speakers at different times that year: Sir Harold Wilson, the former British Prime Minister, F. Lee Bailey, the noted trial attorney, and journalist and author William F. Buckley, Jr. The first one that I interviewed was Harold Wilson. The Kiwanis committee had lined up a limo, so that I could ride in from the airport with him, and we interviewed on tape all the way along. Later in the evening, my wife and I sat at his table at dinner, and then we went to the auditorium, where he gave an address. I don't know whether it was a scintillating speech or not, because Sir Harold Wilson was not necessarily a scintillating person. But he was a notable. I believe F. Lee Bailey came next, in mid-summer, and then the last one was William F. Buckley. I interviewed all three on KWEB.

In the mid-1970s, I had the opportunity to interview the former football coach of the Ohio State Buckeyes and the Minnesota Gophers, Wes Fesler.

When I lay in the hospital in the autumn of 1949, Ohio State under Wes Fesler was a powerhouse, and that year the Gophers beat Ohio State 27-0. We Minnesotans were happy about that. The Gophers went 7 and 2 that year. Some years later, when I interviewed him, Wes Fesler had become coach of the University of Minnesota Gophers, a job he held for a year or two.

I also had the opportunity to talk briefly with Gopher coach Lou Holtz when he was here in the mid-1980s. I was at KWEB at that time. The University of Minnesota people came down here, as they still do, for the Williams Golf Tourney at the Rochester Golf and Country Club. It's a fund raiser. Paul Giel, the athletic director, and Lou Holtz, the coach, both came to Rochester for the tournament. I've interviewed Paul Giel many times. He was a Winona boy, and a heck of a nice guy. Paul Giel died on May 22, 2002, at age 69.

On December 3, 1966, I had the fun of doing a live visit with Minnesota's Senator Walter Mondale. Walter Mondale served in the U.S. Senate from 1964 to 1967, and was Vice President from 1977 to 1981, under President Jimmy Carter. In 1966, he had come to Rochester to speak at the Rochester Dairy Co-operative's annual meeting. Each year, for a number of years, the Rochester Dairy (prior to becoming AMPI) would have its annual meeting in the Mayo Civic Auditorium, usually in early December. They would invite all their patrons to come in for the day. There would be food, a program and a speaker. The members would get their annual dividend checks. They had a woman's program with recipes and prizes. There would be singers. It was an eventful day. They had me come down and emcee the program, and we would broadcast an hour, from noon until 1, on KROC radio.

I had met Senator Mondale earlier that year, when we did a car wash over on 7th Street Northwest, a property which then was also owned by the Gentlings, who owned KROC. We did a remote broadcast there, and Eleanor Mondale, Walter's wife, was there, too, promoting her new book. It's interesting to see where people will turn up. Great names often turn up where there's a microphone.

On December 16, 1972, Senator Mondale came to Rochester again to do a television program. That's when KROC owned both radio and television studios on the corner of 6th Street and 1st Avenue Southwest. I was doing a mid-day radio program, and a lovely lady named Virginia Firnschild was doing television. Virginia had been Mrs. Minnesota in 1962. She was from Rochester, and her husband, Ted, worked at IBM. They were very popular in theater; they danced and sang. She did a television program every noon hour for KROC-TV. It would start out with the noon news and weather, and then she would have maybe ten minutes with guests and public service announcements, on the lighter side. On this particular day, her guest was Walter Mondale. He'd been in the studio, helping her on television, and they had done something together, like making peanut butter crunchy cookies. After her show, she would often bring the guest up to me, on the second floor, and that day she brought me Walter Mondale. We sat down, Walter and I, and had a nice visit.

We gave Skip Humphrey — Hubert H. Humphrey II — a ride on our golf cart at the Olmsted county fair about three times in the 1980s and 1990s. In 1986, I had suggested to KWEB manager Jim Giebel that we purchase a golf cart and fix it up with the Marti unit so that I could do live interviews at the fair. We purchased Lyman Green's 1973 Pargo golf cart, painted it bright red, and Darlene Charland volunteered to drive it around the fairgrounds for me as I broadcast various events. I interviewed thousands of people with it at the fair over the years.

It was a Friday afternoon when Skip Humphrey landed at the fairgrounds in his helicopter. The politicians always came on Friday afternoon, between 5 and 6 o'clock, because they knew that if they could do it right, they would get there in time to get on camera for the live 6 o'clock TV news. So we knew it was going to happen, and when we saw the helicopter, I said to Darlene, "Would you just follow that helicopter? We'll go over there. He's got to set down just inside the fair grounds, right next to highway 63, on South Broadway."

And so we were there when he got off the helicopter.

I called out, "Hey! Here we are!"

He said, "I haven't got time. I've got a television show."

I said, "Get on the cart. I will take you to the TV cameras." So he did, and while we were driving along, I did a live interview on KWEB right there on the golf cart. He was standing on the back bumper, leaning over as I held the microphone to him, and we talked. He was a very humorous individual.

We did that a couple of times in the 1980s. Then the last time he ran, in 1998, against Norm Coleman and the latecomer, Jesse Ventura (who I was sure would not make it, so I did not use his interview), we had Skip Humphrey back again, and I gave him another ride, from DFL Headquarters in one of the buildings up to Graham Arena West, which was the big Humphrey booth. I took him all the way in. I had a little bulb horn, and as we went along, I was honking this bulb horn, beep-beep, and pointing, saying, "Next Gov! Next Gov!" It was good for a lot of laughs, and he enjoyed it.

I reminded him that in 1970, I'd had the pleasure of introducing his father, Hubert Humphrey, *the* Hubert Humphrey, who was a great name in Minnesota. Hubert Humphrey came down after being invited by the Hiawatha chapter of the National Paraplegia Foundation to speak at a Sunday morning breakfast at the Kahler Hotel, in connection with a relay or a run, a benefit to raise funds for a young man named Brian Kelly. Brian Kelly was a great young swimmer and runner who had broken his neck in a diving accident, and remained paralyzed. So the Paraplegia Foundation put on this program with former runners, who were all fine speakers. Hubert Humphrey was asked to speak because he had been a runner. He loved getting out and running. (We had Jesse Owens there in 1971, the former Olympic champion who had won a gold medal at the 1936 Olympic games in Germany.)

I emceed the program, and when I introduced Hubert Humphrey, I said, "Now, Mr. Humphrey, I have to confess to you, we are Republicans. I grew up a Republican, and you're a Democrat."

So when he came to the microphone, he said, "Well, thank you, Mr. Flathers. We accept converts."

Meredith Willson, "The Music Man" himself, came to Rochester in 1965 at the invitation of the Rochester Art Center for their Festival of the Arts, a two-day event held on June 25-26. Virginia Firnschild and I described the festival's parade on KROC as it passed our vantage point on North Broadway. We were in front of the Rochester Public Utilities power plant, just north of the railroad tracks. Meredith Willson led the parade as Grand Marshall, heading in a southerly direction.

Later that evening, he was guest conductor for the Rochester Symphony Band at the Mayo Civic Auditorium. The headline of Pauline Walle's review in her Family-Fare column the next morning read "Meredith Willson Provides Rousing Festival Beginning." An audience of over 3,000, including Minnesota Governor Karl Rolvaag and his wife, gave Willson warm applause and a standing ovation at the evening's conclusion. There was a lot of humor among those toe-tapping marches that he played. From his opening number, "Impressions of 'The Music Man,'" until the conclusion, "May the Good Lord Bless and Keep You," the program was mostly his own compositions.

One of the pieces played was "Here's Love." My wife and I met him backstage after the concert. When we introduced ourselves, he wrote on our copy of the evening's program beside his printed name, "'Here's Love' to Harley and June, (signed) Meredith Willson, Rochester 6/25/65."

Meredith Willson came to Chatfield briefly in 1982, when the Chatfield Brass Band invited him to be grand marshal of their parade. I broadcast that Chatfield Western Days parade, assisted by Ed Ripley, who actually stepped out to Willson's parade car with a microphone and greeted him on the KWEB airwaves.

I shook hands with Liberace, when he put on a concert here.

In 1966, Ed Sullivan of Sunday night TV fame came to Rochester as the key person for the arts festival. I can see him yet, doing some of the emcee work on the stage of the Mayo Civic Auditorium theater section. I shook hands with him, too.

I met Roger Williams, a world-famous pianist, when he put on a concert here in 1964. At the time, my wife was pregnant with our first child.

I introduced myself and June to him, and told him that we were just waiting, that in a few days, we would be having a new little one. I recall him saying, "Well, Harley, we hope there's another little Harley in there, that you'll be happy."

Another person we talked with just briefly, June and I, when we were coming back from one of our trips, was Roy Rogers. He was having a cup of coffee at the concession stand out at the Rochester airport, and we just sat down, introduced ourselves and visited with him. He was a real gentleman.

One very interesting, and to me very memorable, guest was on my show in the summer of 1973. Her name was Babette Bardot. She was Brigitte's cousin. Babette Bardot was a stripper, or I should say, an exotic dancer. Virginia Firnschild brought her up to be on my KROC radio program after she'd finished her television visit at noontime. She not only came up that time, she came up a second time a week or so later. She was here dancing at a place known as the Lantern Inn on South Broadway, next to C.J.'s Lounge. It was owned by Bob Traverse, who in earlier years had owned the Town House Restaurant, which had burned down. Now he had the Lantern Inn, and he was a promoter. He brought Babette to Rochester.

She was a lovely person. We visited, and she had a delightful French accent. I had her doing the weather, and some of the farm market reports. I remember talking about the weather across the state, something about St. Cloud, and she called it "Saint Clue," which was cute. I have her interview entirely on tape, and I have a lovely autographed picture of her, too.

The new Rochester Mayo Civic Center opened up in late 1986. Now we could get some really big names in there. I recall meeting Roy Clark and Mel T-t-t-tillis. They put on a super show, but I did not introduce them. I was just in the audience that time.

Then there was Red Skelton. What a person! He was here to do a show with all his memories and gosh-awful goofaws. That was June 13, 1990. I had a nice little interview with Red Skelton after his show. He told me that he would get up at 5 o'clock every morning and write seven songs. And when he was on the road all those years, he would write a letter every day to his wife. He was a very warm person. He sent me a Christmas card that December on which he had drawn a clown's face, and then his signature. I remember growing up enjoying listening to his show, and now he is gone.

Another famous person that I interviewed on radio was Tiny Tim. Tiny Tim came to entertain in 1991, and I was invited, along with my wife June, to come to Wong's Cafe on December 3, 1991, for songs and conversation and dinner. Tiny Tim was a warm and humorous human being. He would start to eat, and then he'd pick up his ukulele and sing. He had an unusually beautiful falsetto voice. He also had great memories, dating back to the year when he and Miss Vickie were married on the Johnny Carson "Tonight Show." He talked a little about that show, although he and Miss Vickie had already parted by the time he came here. Tiny Tim has since died.

There were many others. George Burns, when he was 98 years old, said, "Had I known I was going to live this long, I would have taken better care of myself." Had I known I was going to be in the radio business this long, I would have kept a diary.

Whoops!
The Beatles and The Mustangs

In early 1962, when I was music director at KROC, we received a packet of 45's (45 rpm records) from a new group of singers, a wild and shaggy-looking bunch called The Beatles. I listened to them briefly, and knew immediately that we didn't want them on our station. We played very little Beatles music on KROC during those years, because I was sure that "this group will never make it."

I gave the records away to a little teenager, a girl of thirteen or fourteen named Mary Beth Hanson. She was in the station that day visiting her mom, Betty Hanson, who was director of traffic for many years on radio and later on KROC-TV. Traffic directors create that all-important daily program log, consisting of the various sponsors, commercials, news, games, and so on that fill the air for each day.

Mary Beth was thrilled to have those records. She was really in the right place at the right time. In fact, she told me so many years later, laughing through her tears at her mother's funeral. "Do you remember," she asked me, "when you gave me that Beatles record — and you said they wouldn't make it?"

Around that same time, in 1963, four young lads from John Marshall High School in Rochester came very close to stardom as a rock band called The Mustangs. It was an easy name to remember, because Rochester had long had a hockey team by that name.

The four — Terry Klampe, Gordon Scudamore, Mark Enblom and John Bach — under the guidance of the boys' families, recorded two songs at the Tom Jones Recording Studios: "Jack the Ripper" and "You Gotta Be A Playboy." I think I still have that record.

The Mustangs entertained locally at every festival and Miracle Mile Crazy Daze. I played their songs many times, in the studio and out on remote. Terry Klampe (now a Rochester dentist) described their music as "mainly simple songs with a simple beat — yet something which is catchy."

The boys' musical career lasted only about three and a half years, but left a very pleasant memory. They joined together again, with other local groups, for a Summer of Love Classic Jam on August 17, 2002, at Mayo Civic Auditorium.

Paul Harvey Visits KWEB

Just days after I joined KWEB radio in early 1981, our owner Steve Moravec announced that he and several Paul Harvey news sponsors were bringing Paul Harvey to Rochester. KWEB radio, as an ABC network affiliate, had been broadcasting the popular news commentator since 1959, only two years after the station first hit the airwaves on September 30, 1957.

"An Evening With Paul Harvey" was scheduled for Thursday, May 7, 1981, at 7:30 pm. Steve asked me to emcee the evening at the Mayo Civic Auditorium. Mayor Chuck Hazama offered greetings on behalf of the city of Rochester, and Steve Moravec introduced Mr. Harvey, who said he was "raised in radio newsrooms."

Paul Harvey began his radio career in his hometown of Tulsa, Oklahoma, on KVOO while he was still in high school. He initiated his coast-to-coast news and commentary program on the ABC radio network in 1951 and continues to this day. In my remarks opening that evening program at the Mayo Civic Auditorium, I noted that, "Paul Harvey has taught us to be listeners. If you don't concentrate on his newscasts, you may miss not only the 'bumper snicker' he uses, you might miss the whole 'bumper.'"

He was indeed a gracious speaker. Earlier in the evening, he had attended a reception in his honor at the Kahler Hotel, where local radio sponsors of his newscasts had their pictures taken with him. They included the late Vince Majerus of Kentucky Fried Chicken, Lyle Fryer of Thein Well Company, Carl Scibetta of J.C. Penney, Tom Kadlec of Tom's Pontiac-Honda, Robert Willmarth of Mutual Service Insurance, and a representative of Mills Fleet Farm whose name doesn't appear in my notes.

Paul Harvey describes his shorter stories as "three parts news and one part entertainment." *Post-Bulletin* writer Steve Webb did two follow-up stories the next day, Friday, May 8, 1981. The first was headlined, "Harvey, Master of Maxims, Touts Freedom." Later, in his weekly "That's Entertainment" column, Webb observed, "Part News, Part Show, Paul Harvey Comes on Like Revivalist Preacher." An estimated 1,000 people heard Harvey's sixty-minute speech that night.

Paul Harvey's show had been the climax of a week overflowing with KWEB radio events. In a memo to our staff the following day, General Manager Moravec commented, "It's been quite a week. Somehow we have managed to cover a tornado, launch 'Harley's House,' become significantly involved in the Rochester State Hospital issue, initiate 'live' programming on KRCH and stage a superb day of activities surrounding Paul Harvey's visit. And we even succeeded in having Ed Ripley jailed."

Let me break Steve's statement down for you. A tornado had hit several farms over the Pine Island area a few days before. I had called Paul Munnis, a private pilot who had his own four-seat plane. Having worked with Paul in the 1980 Aviation Day air show the year before, I was sure he'd oblige my request to fly me over the damaged farms and describe the scene over my mobile phone from the plane to the KWEB studio. This we accomplished.

The Rochester State Hospital was about to close, due to action taken by the Minnesota Legislature. Our stations asked listeners to call in and add their names to a petition protesting the closing. Phone calls poured in. We even had one from a caller "protesting" our call-in program. Written petitions were turned in by a cook at the State Hospital, a nurse from Mayo Clinic and a man who solicited passers-by in downtown Rochester. A photo by Post-Bulletin photographer Jim Welch appeared in the paper's May 5, 1981, edition over the caption, "Lengthy Protest." It showed Steve Moravec and Ed Ripley, the radio station's operations manager and KWEB morning voice, holding up a 39-foot mailgram that was sent to State Senator Nancy Brataas of Rochester. It contained more than 4,000 names. Moravec hand-delivered the list of names to Western Union in St. Paul the following Saturday morning.

"Harley's House" was a series of five-minute morning programs originating live at my home. It began that first week in May and lasted almost 18 years, ending in January 1999.

As for the jailing of Ed Ripley, that was an event staged by the American Heart Association as part of its fund-raising promotion. Ed was "jailed" in a cell at Apache Mall, and needed to call friends asking for funds to "bail him out." That event was held on Saturday, May 2. My show went on the air the following Monday, I flew over the site of the tornado on Tuesday, and Paul Harvey came to town on Thursday.

It was indeed a full week!

Rochester's Terrific Mayors

I'd like to spend just a moment talking about the mayors in Rochester with whom I've worked quite closely during my 46 years here. They were all very special men, actively promoting their city. Through the years, these mayors have been great ambassadors for the city of Rochester. I got to know them very well, interviewing them often.

The first year or two after I came to Rochester, I wasn't into city events, so I didn't know those mayors as well. When I came here in the autumn of 1957, a man named Claude McQuillan was in office. He served from 1954 through 1957. He was followed for a year by Adolph Bach, who served until 1958.

Then came Alex Smekta. He served two different terms. His first term lasted eleven years, from 1958 through 1969. Then Dewey Day came in for four years, from 1969 till 1973, and Alex Smekta came back to serve a second term that lasted six years, from 1973 till 1979.

In 1970, when he was between terms as mayor, Alex and I were both attending the Salvation Army's annual meeting. I was working for KNXR then, and I had grown a mustache. Because the Salvation Army was a little bit short of its goal that year, I announced that if the crowd would come up with $40, I would shave off my moustache. Alex Smekta grabbed a tambourine and went from table to table, soliciting money, and he collected $46. Immediately,

Assistant Police Chief Harry Stai went out and got a razor, and they lathered me up for the shave. But Alex said he couldn't bring himself to cut off such a fine mustache, so he only cut off 46 hairs. They ran a story about it in the Post-Bulletin, with a photograph of him standing over me, razor in hand.

Alex Smekta also did a lot of work with Toastmasters, not only locally and statewide, but nationwide and internationally. And he was always speaking of Rochester wherever he went. He died on Thursday, June 10, 1993, of a heart attack at age 87.

From 1979 through 1995, Rochester's mayor was the very colorful, effervescent Chuck Hazama. Born in Maui, Hawaii, Chuck came to Rochester in 1967 from the Cedar Falls/Waterloo area in Iowa, where he had served fifteen years as YMCA physical director. The "Fitness Guru of Iowa" was hired as physical educator for the Rochester YMCA in 1972, and became full-time executive director from 1972 to 1979. In the late

1960s and early 1970s, we would see him working out on Channel 10 KROC-TV during Virginia Firnschild's noon-hour show. When he was first elected mayor in 1979, he served part-time with the "Y" and part-time as mayor. That lasted until 1981, and then from 1982 until 1995 he was a full-time mayor.

Chuck Hazama, with the help of city council members Darrell Strain and Pete Solinger and the federal government, turned the city around following the big flood of July 6, 1978. The Corps of Engineers did an extensive survey of the area, and between 1988 and 1995 seven dams, seven reservoirs, were constructed around the city, so Rochester would never suffer from a flood again. It was a $115 million project. Rochester's share of the cost was $34 million, paid for by a city sales tax. They widened the existing streams and rip-rapped the banks, so we can get heavy rain now and there's not a sudden gush of water through the town.

Flooding had been a long-time problem, because Rochester is set in a basin. You only realize this as you drive out of Rochester, especially when you go east or south and have to drive up a steep hill. You don't notice it so much coming in from the north or the west. Nonetheless, downtown Rochester is in a basin.

So through his sixteen years in office, Chuck Hazama oversaw the flood control project. He also oversaw the construction boom downtown that began in 1987. There was a tremendous growth at that period. At one time, I can recall looking up and seeing twelve big construction cranes looming over the city. They were building the Galleria Centerplace, the Radisson, the First Bank (now called US Bank), and the new Marriott Hotel, where the old Zumbro Hotel had been located — a tremendous growth all at once in downtown Rochester during the upper 1980s and the early 1990s. This also included the new City-County Government Center and the Rochester Public Library.

Chuck Hazama finished his final term in 1995. He remains in the area today, spending six months here and six months in Hawaii. He does a lot of traveling, and takes people on tours back to Hawaii with him. Chuck and his wife Almira (Aly) were to be honorary co-chairs of the 20th Annual

Rochesterfest in June 2002. Sadly, Aly Hazama died on January 26, 2002, in Hawaii.

Chuck Hazama was followed by another Chuck, Chuck Canfield. He served as mayor from 1996 through 2002. Ardell Brede, an employee of the Mayo Clinic for more than forty years, was elected mayor in the autumn of 2002.

Chuck Canfield and I go back well over forty years. I first met him when I was doing a broadcast at the Oldsmobile dealer's at 705 South Broadway. At that time, the Oldsmobile building occupied the space just east of the YMCA. It started out as Marti Nash, then later it became Marti Oldsmobile. When Marti sold it to Mike Stone, it became Stone Olds. Mike Stone's motto was "The car to own is an Olds from Stone."

In 1960 I was there doing a two-hour live broadcast on KROC radio. We were announcing the introduction of the new 1961 Oldsmobiles, and here was Chuck Canfield, a young man who was then division manager for Oldsmobile. I believe he was based near Chicago. I met Chuck then and had a nice visit with him on KROC radio. Oldsmobile was really putting on a celebration. They were inviting everybody to come to the store that day, and also to come to the Mayo Civic Auditorium that night, when Harold Loeffelmacher and the Six Fat Dutchmen, from New Ulm, Minnesota, would be there to play music, and you'd get a chance to see the unveiling of all the new 1961 Oldsmobiles. That was the way it was done in those days.

I didn't meet Chuck again for a number of years, until suddenly he was here, opening up Shakey's Pizza in 1967. He became a second ward city council member, and then in 1996 the mayor. He was always a pleasant person, and is a great promoter for the city of Rochester.

There were two city clerks I got to know well during my early years, and I worked closely with them as well. Elfreda Reiter was clerk from 1956 till about 1973. Working in her office was a young lady named Carole Grimm, who served as the city clerk from 1973 till 1996. Carole grew up at Frontenac, which is just eight miles south of Red Wing, and when she was a young girl, she used to come to Red Wing with her mother to watch the wrestling matches in the armory. And there I was, covering the wrestling matches for the Junior Chamber of Commerce. Carole and I often sat beside each other, and we talk about that occasionally. She was just a young lady then, in her teens, sitting with her mother, and I was ten years older, doing my work for the Jaycees, announcing the start of the show on the PA. Incidentally, her mom always sat between us!

Carole Grimm retired in 1996. Today the city clerk is Judy Scherr.

I've Made a Political Friend or Two

In the summer of 1982, I got well-acquainted with two men who've been "front and center" in local politics for two decades. I'm speaking of former First District Congressman Tim Penny and his successor, Gil Gutknecht.

I had long followed the activities of our First Congressional District. August H. Andresen of Red Wing was Congressman for 24 years, from 1934 to 1958. I never interviewed Mr. Andresen, but I had many occasions to visit with the men who followed him in that post — Al Quie from Dennison, near Northfield, Arlen Erdahl from Blue Earth, Tim Penny and Gil Gutknecht.

Tim Penny announced his plans to run for Congress one summer afternoon in 1982 in Central Park, Rochester. I was there, with a small cassette machine in hand, and ran the tape on KWEB radio news the following Monday. Tim was elected that autumn on the DFL ticket.

That same year, young Gil Gutknecht, a former school supplies salesman and auctioneer, tossed his hat in the ring as a candidate for Minnesota State Representative for north Rochester. Gil won the seat, and served in that state office for twelve years — the same twelve years that Tim Penny was in Washington, D.C. I helped Gil a number of times in the KWEB studios, recording commercials for both his auction business and his political campaigns.

During the Olmsted County Fair in August 1994, I ran into Gil on the fairgrounds, and hollered, "Gil, did you hear? Tim Penny has just announced he's not running again for Congress. Why don't you go after that seat?"

Gil replied, "I'm thinking about it." Then he got on the golf cart with me for a picture, taken beside the Olmsted County ADA malt wagon. (That picture somehow made it into a Washington, D.C., congressional publication — and no, I did not send it to them.)

The following Monday, Gil filed for the seat, and he has successfully represented the First Congressional District in Washington, D.C., ever since.

Meanwhile, Tim Penny retired. He now writes books and is in demand as a speaker. He also teaches government at the college level. In the summer of 2002, he became a candidate for Minnesota Governor on the Independence Party ballot.

I've had the opportunity to introduce both men as keynote speakers at local programs, and in Gil's case as the auctioneer for the Salvation Army Chef's Night fund raiser at the Kahler Hotel's Heritage Hall.

For the most part, the First Congressional District has had a Republican in Washington, even though Minnesota leans toward the Democrats, especially in presidential years. But all four of the First District Congressmen I have known, at county fairs or in the studios, have always been pleasant and kind men.

Harley extends a handshake to Minnesota Governor Orville Freeman following President Eisenhower's Red Wing dedication speech for the new 3 million dollar bridge over the Mississippi River. Moments earlier Harley had shaken hands with the President . . . Seated at right. Oct. 18, 1960. (Photo: Phil Revoir Studios, Red Wing)

KWEB welcomes Paul Harvey . . . as MC Harley introduces program at Mayo Civic Auditorium, Thursday, May 7, 1981.

Post Bulletin Ad . . . "See Paul Harvey"

Senator Walter Mondale, center is main speaker at the Rochester Dairy Annual meeting Dec. 3, 1966. I visited with him on the noon broadcast. At left is George Daley of Lewiston, then president of the Dairy board of Directors. (Photo A.D. Ass'n)

George Grim, noted journalist and broadcaster as main speaker at Rochester Dairy Noon broadcast . . . annual meeting Dec. 1965. Photo: American Dairy Association)

Tiny Tim at Wong's Cafe . . . before concert with Harley & June Flathers. Dec. 3, 1991.

Hubert "Skip" Humphrey, golf cart at Olm. Co. Fair, DFL booth. L-R, Harley, driver Darlene Charland & Mr. Humphrey. 1998 in preparation for Gubernatorial race.

Mayor Chuck Hazama's retirement party Mayo Civic Auditorium as Harley does a final KWEB interview, Nov. 2, 1995.

Red Skelton and Harley back stage after his Mayo Civic Comedy concert, June 3, 1990 . . . also his Christmas Card Signature in 1991.

Mayor Chuck Canfield reading my 70th birthday proclamation at party with 250 in attendance. Aug. 27, 2001.

Rochester's Mayor Ardell F. Brede.. He was elected in Nov. 2002 and was sworn in early Jan 2003. Long active in rochester's health profession, Rochester Quarterbacks Club, The Arts and dozens of other organizations. Ardell joins an outstanding group of city mayors—always selling Rochester

Alex Smekta shaves Harley as part of a Salvation Army fundraiser, Feb. 10, 1970. Post Bulletin photo.

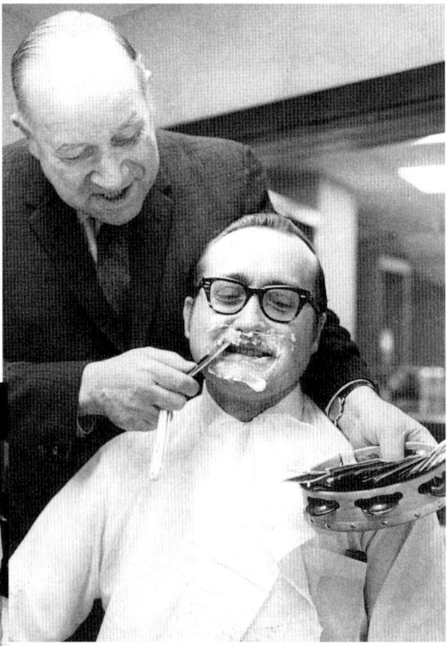

Below, Harley & Gil Gutknecht, about to announce his first Congressional, District candidacy. Olmsted County Fair, 1994.

Rochester Mustangs Rock Group, 1964. L-R, John Bach, Mark Enblom, Terry Klampe & Gordie Scudamore. The boys recorded 2 songs: "You Gotta Be a Playboy" & "Jack the Ripper". They played 3½ years while at John Marshall High School. I played their songs many times on KROC.

Moment 13

Memorable Radio Events
The KROC Sandwich Book

I got into many interesting projects during the years. One of them was putting together the KROC sandwich books.

In 1966 and 1967, the DuPont Company made available a $50 savings bond, which they sent to KROC radio. They said, "You figure out a promotion, and we'll give you the bond to give away."

I didn't set any of that up, but we did run a sandwich contest both years. The first year, 1966, it was a small event, with only fifteen entries, and we had a home economist judging the prizes down at Peoples Natural Gas. We put the winning recipes into a small booklet.

The next year, we had such a heavy return of sandwich recipes, that after the winner was announced, I said, "I'm going to take those recipes, and I'm going to make a bigger sandwich book."

We called it "1967 KROC Family Favorites." It contained fifty prize sandwich recipes. I did all the work, except the art work. For that, we had a man named Alton Page, an artist who worked at IBM. It was my idea to take these fifty sandwiches, line 'em up, and ask for fifty pictures of families of six children or more. Some of the families had taken part in the sandwich contest, but many of them had not. The idea was to have pictures of large families, who might be expected to eat a lot of sandwiches. We'd make a 50-page book and sell it for 50 cents. Everything was 50-50. (This was in 1967, the first year of the Minnesota two-cent sales tax, so we sold the book for 50 cents, but then we had to collect two cents more for sales tax!)

It was my project, with the blessing of the station. I coordinated the whole thing. I sold additional print advertising in the book, a quarter page for $25, half page for $50. I really worked. I don't know how I managed to get it all done, but it turned out to be quite a successful book. We asked for 2400 copies. Custom Printing had an overrun of 85 extra copies, and they all sold. I have just one left.

In doing that project, I got to meet a lot of local community and area people. I personally went out with my old 1947 Polaroid Land camera and took black-and-white photos of these families whenever I could get them together. At least half of the families sent us their own pictures. We had some great local names in that book, some well-known families that were business folks here during the years, who had large numbers of kids. There were the Walter Griffin, John Gadient, Earl Tieman, James Caulfield, Wes Anderson and Loren Smith families, to name a few. We put a family index in the book. The families had anywhere from six to fifteen children; the final family in the book had 22 children. They were a family from Waseca, Minnesota, the Alvin Miller, Sr., family. When the sandwich book was published, we sent a complimentary copy to every family, and some of them wanted to buy more.

Today, thirty-five years later, we are still running into these families. The children have grown up, many have moved on. Parents have died. The kids that were in those pictures are grandparents now, in many instances. It was indeed quite an event, quite a project.

I've talked to some of these people recently, and they still ask, "Hey, have you got any more sandwich books?"

I say, "No, I've only got one, and I'm keeping that. But you're in there."

The Harley Giveaway

On April 1, 1993, we had a couple of guys on radio named Greg Michaels and Alan Reed. They did the morning show on KRCH, often referred to as Laser 101. And what those two couldn't think of wasn't worth repeating. They were crazy, off the wall. Alan Reed is still with us, and great in the morning on Fox Country.

I was selling radio time then for KWEB. KRCH was one of our stations, as was the brand-new KMFX, Fox Country. I knew very little about what those two had planned ahead of time. June and I were in the midst of moving from our old home, where we'd lived for 26 years, into our present one, which was about seven blocks away, so I was a bit preoccupied.

A couple of days before April 1, they'd said, "Harley, are you going to be here on April Fool's Day?"

I said, "Well, yeah, I guess so. What's up?"

"We just want to make sure you're here."

They didn't tell me any more about it. But on March 31, they started promoting their scheme on the air, and I heard it. "Be listening tomorrow morning. If you're the 101st caller, you may be the winner of a 1931 model full-dressed Harley."

Naturally, everybody had visions of a beautiful new motorcycle, fully equipped.

As John McCormick wrote in the *Post-Bulletin* the next day:

"An April Fool's Day giveaway by a Rochester radio station appears to have jammed the area's telephone system this morning. No kidding.

"KRCH's Alan Reed and Greg Michaels told listeners that the 101st caller would receive a full-dressed 1931 Harley.

"And apparently Rochester is crazy about Hogs, especially free ones, because the station was flooded with calls.

"But the Hog turned out to be Harley Flathers, an employee at the station."

When the winner called in, he learned that he had just won $101 in cash, a limo ride and lunch at Michael's Restaurant with me, Greg Michaels, Alan Reed and the owner of the Rochester Harley-Davidson business, Judy McGuire. Judy McGuire generously picked up the tab.

Earlier that week, 1900 employees had been let go at IBM, which really shook up the town. The winner was one of those IBM employees who was suddenly out of work. I'm sure he, like many others when they found out what the prize was, must have let out a big groan: "Ooooh!"

I suppose that there were some folks that were mad, but the winner was very good-natured. He was a nice lad, and later that day, we met him at Michael's Restaurant, and we enjoyed a two-hour lunch together, complete with many laughs.

But the flood of incoming calls caused problems in the telephone system for the whole Rochester area. For a short time that morning, people could not get a dial tone or make emergency calls. Our daughter Jane was home, helping us with the move, and when she tried to call out, she told us, "I can't get any phone. What's the matter?"

I had been doing a short, five-minute radio program myself that morning from my home, and I got through with my program before the line went dead. I was luckier than many people.

Between 7:40 and 7:50 am, US West Communications reported that its switching became clogged throughout its whole calling system, affecting about 40,000 to 50,000 customers. Later we heard that Winona was also out of service, which meant that an estimated 80,000 people in southeast Minnesota were without phones for a while that morning.

Michaels and Reed told the newspaper that they felt bad about being partly responsible for tying up the phone system, but they said it was impossible for them to control how many calls they got.

"If we inconvenienced anyone, or caused a problem, we are sorry for that," Michaels was quoted as saying. "We got tons of calls."

It was without a doubt one of the finest short April Fool radio promotions I've ever known. When you can get that kind of response — 80,000 phones tied up from a sudden switchboard barrage — you know you've reached a big audience.

The H.F. Burger

In the spring of 1976, a young chef named Bob Hanson opened the Alpine Super Chef, a little restaurant at 509 1st Avenue Southwest, a half-block north of the KROC studios in the TV-Radio Building at the corner of 6th Street and 1st Avenue Southwest. At that time, I was in a studio on the second floor, with a big north and east corner window. I could look northerly and see folks going in and out of the Alpine Super Chef Restaurant.

Soon I was among those who fell in love with this little place, with its homespun atmosphere and its endless good humor. The popularity of the Alpine Super Chef grew rapidly. I may have helped, since Bob Hanson was soon advertising on my morning show, courtesy of our sales rep, Jolly Joe Burnham.

Bob Hanson asked me to conduct an on-air promotion to name two ducks who were always on the grassy area next to the curb outside his business. These were nice little neighborhood ducks, wild ones like the ones who were always flying all over the city. Do you suppose they were attracted by some food scraps that might possibly have been placed just outside the Alpine Super Chef door?

Anyway, Bob said, "Harley, do a contest. Ask your listeners to name those two ducks. The winner will get a big Alpine Super Chef burger. You can help me judge the entries."

And so the promotion began. It ran for a couple of weeks, with the entries coming in to KROC. Two other judges helped me, but I can't remember their names now. When it was all done, the winning names were "Snick and Snack, the Alpine Quacks." It was good for a lot of laughs.

A few days later, when I went in for lunch, Bob Hanson said, "Harley, I've named a sandwich after you. I hope you don't mind. It's already on the menu board — 'the H.F. Burger.'"

I was honored to have this 1/3 pound of ground beef, in a big bun with lettuce, tomato and possibly cheese, named for me. It was big enough for two people. And after you ate it, you talked, and talked, and talked...

Bob expanded, opening restaurants at Northern Hills and Eastwood Golf Courses, and excelled at catering. For several years, he ran the restaurant at the Soldier's Field Club House. Smiling Bob Hanson was a generous man, one of seven brothers, with a wonderful mother who cooked and assisted him. Thanks, Pal — you're a super chef!

Air Shows Live

In 1979, a group of pilots decided to have an air show here at the Rochester Airport. I think they got that idea following earlier airlifts to benefit the March of Dimes. Pilots who owned a two-seat or maybe a four-seat plane gave of their time, somebody else gave the gas — everybody was giving for an afternoon — and we said, "Take your kids to the airport, and for a penny a pound, you can see the city and have a 20-minute ride." The money went to the March of Dimes.

Since I was the executive director of the March of Dimes at that time, I guess they knew that I was interested in flying. A man named Warren Havens came to me as I was working there at KROC, and said, "Harley, how about you coming along with me to an air show meeting tonight at the airport."

I said, "Well, okay." I did this a lot, said okay when I was asked to do something. So I sat in on a lot of meetings, as they were planning and getting started. At the second show, held on July 4, 1980, we invited the Eagles Acrobatic Flight Team, three men in experimental aircraft, to Rochester to perform for us. The team members were Tom Poberenzy of Hales Corners, Wisconsin, Charlie R. Hilliard of Fort Worth, Texas, and Gene Soucy of McKinney, Texas. They were meeting in Oshkosh yearly for the big national air show, and they came to Rochester for one day.

We did at least seven airshows in the next eleven years — my files show one for each year in 1979, 1980, 1981, 1982, 1987, 1988 and 1990. It would be a summer afternoon — usually July 4. During the day, I would be out there at the Rochester Airport. Mike Siberling from IBM was one of the pilots, and often we would fly in his plane. They'd get me into the plane, which wasn't easy at all, and we'd strap the Marti antenna on the wing. We had a battery inside, a regular car battery, and that little Marti broadcast unit was attached to it, with a line that ran through the window and plugged into the antenna that had been mounted on the wing. Then I would do live broadcasts from the plane from 11:30 till noon. I would say, "The show's soon to start, folks! The show opens at noon! Cars are coming now, come on in!" I did that each year, announcing a schedule of acts and the times they would perform.

The Rochester Area Pilots Association (RAPA) airshows at the Rochester airport included appearances by the US Air Force Thunderbirds in 1988 and again in 1990. Their great precision flying entertainment was witnessed by huge crowds.

The very first year, 1979, we did our broadcast in the early morning a couple of days before the show, taking off from the Olmsted County fairgrounds in a hot air balloon owned by George Ibach. George Ibach is still an avid ballooner. He owns Spring Green Lawn and Tree Care in Rochester, and he uses his balloon to promote his business, but he does a lot of hot air ballooning for pleasure as well. You'll see and hear about George Ibach and his balloon at every Rochesterfest.

We took off that day at 6:30 am. It was a beautiful sunny morning. I had all the equipment lined up, and was broadcasting on KROC from the balloon as we flew over the city. When we passed Zumbro Falls, about twenty miles to the northeast, the winds started coming up. Now, you can get along pretty well in a balloon when the winds are not over ten miles an hour, but if they get up around 15 miles per hour, you start to lose control. Finally George said, "We've got to bring this down. The wind is getting too strong."

George hadn't really told me what to do when they were letting a balloon come down. We started hitting the ground, and the gondola in which we were riding was bouncing on the ground, because the gondola itself is very heavy, and we were also in there, complete with battery and radio equipment, which was yet another eighty pounds. We came down in an alfalfa field. I landed on my shoulder on the grass a couple or three times. We never did quite get the grass stains out of that coat.

Later, George said to me, "You've got to hold on to the sides of the gondola when you start to come down." Well, I wish he'd told me that beforehand!

We had to walk about a quarter of a mile through long alfalfa to get to the road where his "chase" team, headed by Sam Blackburn, was waiting. They always have a "chase" team, a response team that's usually in a pickup, following you to take you home, along with the gondola and the deflated balloon. That was something, trying to walk through that alfalfa field. I walked a lot better then than I do now, but I couldn't walk very well, even with my canes, and in that tall grass, it was a real challenge. I know George had to help me.

It was quite a day. And often now when I see balloons, I think of my ride with George Ibach, kicking off the Rochester air show in 1979.

I kept two Rochester *Post-Bulletin* clippings from that July 4, 1979, event. The first, by writer Tim Cain, was headlined, "Thousands Turn Out for Aviation Day Benefit." Police and parking attendants estimated that 15,000 people were there that day. Sherm Booen, host of the WCCO-TV program "World of Aviation," was master of ceremonies, and made us acquainted with the different kinds of airplanes as well as showing the facilities at the Rochester Airport. I was quoted in the article as saying, "about $2,000 was raised for the March of Dimes from the five-cent-a-pound rides in the air lift before the show."

The second story, by writer Ken McCracken, appeared on the same page and was headlined "Air Show Relieved By 'Dear Johns'." As McCracken wrote, "The stunt pilots and skydivers got their share of applause Wednesday at the Aviation Day air show at Rochester Airport — but the unsung hero of the day was a man delivering portable toilets. Early in the afternoon, nearly 2000 people — mostly mothers with small cranky children — were waiting impatiently in twin lines for the only two portable toilets available at the air show. As the heat climbed and tempers rose, a White House Service, Inc., truck and trailer drove up carrying four more portable outhouses — two for each sex — and the startled white uniformed driver was welcomed with applause, cheers and whistles from the suffering mothers. The moms, some dads and older children rushed to help the driver unload and put the four new portable toilets in place in record time. 'I'd say his arrival was the highlight of the whole show,' said one grateful mother as she herded two children into one of the toilets."

The following day, Paul Harvey included this part of the story on his nation-wide ABC News broadcast at noon, along with some chuckles.

Needless to say, our Aviation Day Committee put toilets on the priority list for all the following shows, and made sure we had two to three dozen of them available on the grounds.

I treasure the memories of those Aviation Day shows, and thank the chairs Paul Munnis, Jerome Perry, Brian Younge, Mike Siberling, Sherm Booen, George Ibach and countless other volunteers like Walt Halloran, Wes Anderson, and the late Warren Havens and Andy Neuman for helping to make them happen.

Travels With Harley

June and I hosted some overseas trips with Ray Moore, a local travel agent and community servant. The first one went to Spain and Portugal from March 25 to April 8, 1971. Twenty-seven people went with us, flying over by Swissair. We visited Lisbon, Seville, Madrid and more.

On the morning of Sunday, April 4, we were planning to sit in on a bull fight in Madrid. You always hear about those Spanish bull fights, so we were really looking forward to it. We were all ready to get up and go, but it had been raining. Then Ray Moore came to us at breakfast time and said, "I'm sorry. There will be no bull fight today. Nobody wants to see a wet bull."

So we visited the great Spanish museum, the Prado, instead, and that was a memorable forenoon.

I look up near the ceiling of my den and view with fond memories the $20 souvenir sword that I brought home from that Spain/Portugal trip. On our final Saturday afternoon, we took a side trip to the old city of Toledo. Toledo, Spain, is surrounded by stone walls, with rivers on three sides, with bridges and moats. It looked as if it would have been impossible for those warring tribes of long ago to penetrate it. Toledo's main industry in 1971 was hand-crafted gold and silver items, made by families who have continued their crafts through the centuries.

When I told June I wanted a souvenir, she said, "Fine, go ahead." And I chose this historic-looking sword. Now there were swords in many lengths, many sizes and styles. I took this one that was around 30 inches long, with a leather sheath and a very decorative handle.

I felt guilty paying $20 for a souvenir, but I gave no thought to the fact that I might have trouble getting it home. First I thought, I'll take the sheath off and put it in the suitcase. I discovered that a sword does not get shorter when you remove the sheath. It wouldn't fit in the suitcase. What to do now? I would have to carry it separately.

There was a lot of worry at that time about people bringing weapons on airplanes, and when we reached the airport, it looked like we might have even more trouble with that sword. It had to be declared in customs, and because it was considered a dangerous weapon, I had to leave it behind at the customs desk. I had a tearful face as we boarded the plane.

However, once we were in our seats, one of our fellow travelers, Maxine Langdon, who operated the Langdon Motel with her mother, came up to me and said, "Harley, your sword is safe. It's riding up front with the captain."

From there on home, there was no further sword problem. I keep it as a reminder of that wonderful trip.

In late May and early June 1978, we hosted a trip to England and Scotland with several of the same travelers who had accompanied us in 1971, including the late Walter Burdick. (Walter was a peach of a man. I had known him since the late 1930s and early 1940s, when he would stop annually at our farm to get my Dad to renew our subscription to the Rochester Post-Bulletin for another year. After a visit, and a piece of pie from my mom, Dad would say to Walter, "Gosh, four dollars. I don't know whether we can afford this or not." But he always renewed. In later years, Walter became a state senator from the Rochester area. By 1971, he was retired.) Also on that trip were Ethel Joyce, and Virgil and Marie Elliott, owners of Osco Drug.

When we got overseas on these trips, a bus was always waiting for us, with a guide from that area who would work hand in hand with our man, Ray Moore. Those were a couple of super trips.

I'm sorry to say that many of those travelers have died since then, including Ray Moore, who died on January 8, 2001, at age 92. Ray had started the World Travel Bureau in Rochester in 1946. He and Ed Klopp were partners then. Ed Klopp would later own the Green Parrot Cafe downtown from 1947 to 1981. It was a favorite downtown meeting place for so many years. That space now is occupied by the Eagle Drug Store, owned by the Warren Williams family.

Sneaky Awards

During my years in the broadcast world, I would sometimes be given an assignment to cover an event, or give the keynote address at some occasion.

And then they sneak an award on you!

This happened on November 1, 1966, at the Kahler Hotel Heritage Hall. Bob Fick, my boss at KROC, asked me the week before if I could get away to "cover" the Rochester Exchange Club's Book of Golden Deeds Award Dinner for the station. He said that he had two tickets, but he couldn't make it, and the news staff was "all tied up" that night.

"Harley, maybe you and your wife could go," he said.

I replied, "Sure." I later found out that the Exchange Club had already contacted my wife to make sure that I would be there.

After the meal, and after the speaker, Dr. Joseph Knutson, President of Concordia College at Moorhead, Minnesota, finished his remarks, Exchange Club President Ross Browning started reading the background of the recipient for that year's Book of Golden Deeds Award. I was taking notes rapidly, as I always did. Suddenly the description started sounding awfully familiar. I wanted to slide under the table as I heard him announce that I was the winner of the 12th annual Book of Golden Deeds award for unselfish service to others.

When I went up to the podium to accept the award, I was speechless — an unusual condition for a radio announcer! I said, "I'm sure I'm too young for this. I'm only 35. And how can I report this tomorrow morning on the radio?"

Nancy Strobel, the *Post-Bulletin* writer who covered the event, wrote the next day, "and the unassuming Flathers failed to report the news himself today — but other KROC broadcasters took care of that..."

Today a desk ornament in the form of a golden book, a gift from the Exchange Club, adorns the trophy corner in my den. That was a clever approach the Exchange Club made to me that night. Club members Bob and Barbara Domaille and Wayne and Beverly Thede were "hosts" at the table with us that night. I wonder if they knew what was going to happen in advance. I certainly didn't.

On April 13, 1978, I was asked to speak before the annual Elementary School Principals' Dinner, never expecting that at the end of the evening they would bestow on me a lovely plaque, the Friends of Education Award, given each year to someone in the community. My good friend, newsman Bob Ryan, was also given this award in the early 1980s.

Another award that dumfounded me came in the autumn of 1977, and was given on the state level by the Minnesota State Council for the Handicapped. I was named Handicapped Person of the Year.

That same week, on November 2, 1977, I received the WCCO Good Neighbor Award. It was signed by Dick Chapman, long-time WCCO personality and writer, who read the background information on the air that morning about 7:55.

I've told you that I can only fly paper airplanes. Well, the Rochester Area Pilots' Association, under the direction of the late Warren Havens, named me an "honorary pilot" after the July 4, 1979 air show, in appreciation of my public relations work for that event.

Fellow newsman Joel Jensen was very active in the Jaycees in the late 1970s and early 1980s. He used to help me sing (off key) the "First Call to Lunch" at 6:50 am on KROC, after which I would read the public schools lunch menu for the day. It was wild! Joel got me working for ten straight years (from 1977 to 1986) as emcee of the Jaycees' Distinguished Service Award (DSA) night. And at the end of the evening in 1986, they handed me a beautiful plaque for "Ten Years as DSA Master of Ceremonies." Wow! Thanks, Joel.

In April 1989, the Chatfield Rotary Club invited me to attend a special night at the Chosen Valley Golf and Country Club. I'm not a Rotarian, so I was overwhelmed when one of their members, AFC Corporation

President Conrad Fingerson, made a $1,000 gift to the club in my name, to give me the honor of being a Paul Harris Fellow. This award, introduced in 1947, is one of the finest honors that Rotary (founded in 1905) bestows.

Rochester's Chamber of Commerce "stuck it to me" on September 22, 1993 during their annual meeting at the Kahler Hotel's Heritage Hall. My station manager, Bob Jung, had asked me to be there, and it wasn't hard for me to do, because I'd been attending the Chamber's annual meetings for years.

After NBC radio sports personality Don Criqui's address, "Why Winners Win," three names were called to be honored by the Chamber's ambassadors. The Athena Award went to long-time state senator Nancy Brataas. Helen Mundahl was chosen as the Jan Warfield Volunteer of the Year. And I was given the Alex P. Smetka Memorial Award. (Previously, this award had been called the George Award, but it was renamed in honor of former Mayor Alex Smetka, a strong promoter of Rochester, who had died earlier that summer.)

In March 1996, the Chamber of Commerce Agribusiness Committee presented me with its Ag Person of the Year award at its annual dinner at the Holiday Inn South. It was the last time that this award was made, and I am proud to have been selected to receive it.

And in the middle of 2003, I was highly honored by the Rochesterfest parade committee when they asked me to serve as Grand Marshal. June 20 was a glorious evening as I led the parade, with my wife June beside me, in a 1984 Oldsmobile Delta Royale Malibu blue convertible. I had asked my barber Paul Dallman to be the driver, and he kindly obliged for the 45-minute ride.

And One Very Special Honor

In July 2002, I received notice from the Pavek Museum of Broadcasting, in St. Louis Park, Minnesota, that I was to be inducted into the Museum of Broadcasting Hall of Fame. This was a totally unexpected but wonderful surprise, and put the "frosting" on a half-century of broadcasting, as far as I was concerned.

Bob Hanson—The Super Chef. Bob opened the Alpine Super Chef, Spring 1976 one block north of KROC's studios on first Ave. S.W. I could look out studio window and see "Snick and Snack" he Alpine Quacks—2 ducks on the sidewalk.

Friends of Education winners conducted annually by the Rochester Elementary principals. Standing L-R, Karen Hammill 1993, Wanda Haqquist 1982, Al & Sharon Tuntland, 1988, and Carol Carryer 1987. Seated TV Newsman Bob Ryan, recipient in 1975, and Harley Flathers 1978 at the Radisson Hotel. 6/15/93

Rochesterfest Parade June 20, 2003. Harley and June Flathers, driver Paul Dallman driving the Grand Marshal & his wife. After 20 years broadcasting the parade on KWEB, the Rochesterfest committee chose Harley for the honors.

Former Minnesota Governor Arne Carlson, as Master of Ceremonies at the Broadcasting Hall of Fame Banquet presents Harley Flathers with his award. 10/12/02 at Radisson South, Twin Cities.

Hall of Fame Evening . . . L-R: Bob Ryan, inducted into the 2001 ceremony, Flathers, and newly inducted John Gallos. Oct. 12, 2002.

Hall of Fame Evening . . . Harley presents Red Wing Station KAAA call letters to Pavek Museum to continue museum out-state memorabilia. Harley worked 50 years ago at KAAA.

Hall of Fame Evening . . .Harley & Genevieve Hovde of River Falls, Wisconsin. Genevieve sang on the Grand Old Opry during 40s and on Harley's KAAA programs in 1954-55.

Rochester Air Show . . . Poster from July 4, 1981. Using the "Goose & Goggles Button" .

Moment 14

I'm Still a Farm Boy at Heart
Dairying and Those Lovely Princesses

The dairy industry has fascinated me from the time I was a small lad. I always wondered, how can a brown cow eat green grass and give white milk?

In 1937, Minnesota started observing June as Dairy Month. In those days, dairy herds were turned out to pasture in late May or early June as the grass became lush. There was always an abundance of milk with many cows recently "fresh" from bearing calves and with pastures "on the grow."

I have many happy memories of the things that were happening in the late 1940s and early 1950s in the dairying business. For example, Myron Clark, an outstanding registered Holstein dairy man whose farm was located in Olmsted County just north of Pleasant Grove, was the State Commissioner of Agriculture for a four-year period from 1951 through 1955, when Orville Freeman was governor of Minnesota.

We saw some excellent dairying in those years at a farm two miles northwest of ours, the Walter Bigelow farm, which was owned by Dr. Frank Mann. Dr. Mann was a physiologist here at the Mayo Clinic, and he loved dairying. He bought the farm when Ed Fleshner sold it in 1940 or 1941. I never got to know Dr. Mann personally, but I know that he and another fine dairyman named Warner Johnson and Dr. Hiram Essex used to travel together to great dairy shows all over the country, studying blood lines and the importance of good dairy practices. After Dr. Mann died in 1961, his wife and daughter Ruth established the Dr. Mann Award, which the

Rochester Area Agriculture Committee presents every year to an outstanding young dairyperson in 4H who is striving for excellence in breeding and production. On my radio broadcasts, I like to call it the "coveted" Mann Award.

When the dairy industry really started promoting its own product, one of the major publicity programs was the annual selection of a dairy princess. Local county ADAs (American Dairy Association members) operated under a board of directors to promote nature's most perfect food — milk. The dairy princesses toured the state to increase awareness of the value of milk products.

Minnesota's first Princess Kay of the Milky Way was chosen in 1954. She was 17-year-old Eleanor Maley, who came from a dairy farm in rural Grand Meadow, Mower County. Ellie tells me that 1954-55 was an exciting year and a half for her reign, since the national princess program was brand new. It took dairy officials time to get their plans coordinated on the state and national level, because at that time state contestants were encouraged to compete in a nation-wide competition the following year.

Eleanor's travels as Minnesota's Princess Kay of the Milky Way took her all over Minnesota. She even went to Washington, D.C., where she was to visit President Dwight D. Eisenhower at the White House. For some scheduling reason, she didn't see the president, but was the guest of Pat Nixon, wife of then-vice president Richard Nixon. She also spent some time with Minnesota Senator Hubert H. Humphrey, Texas Senator Lyndon B. Johnson, and others during that White House visit. But the highlight of that trip was her appearance on the NBC "Today Show," hosted by Dave Garroway. She also spoke with Edward R. Murrow on the CBS TV Network news.

In late 1954, Eleanor was invited to Paris to visit Prime Minister Pierre Mendes-France. He wanted to start promoting milk in France, and offered to give her 48 bottles of champagne in exchange for 48 bottles of milk (one for each of the 48 states then in the U.S.). This happened on New Year's Eve, December 31, 1954. Somehow the champagne didn't show up, but the cameras followed her every movement, on and off the plane.

Also during Eleanor's Milky Way reign, she co-hosted with Miss Universe at the International Dairy Show in Chicago. That event was featured on the Don McNeil Breakfast Club radio show, which originated in Chicago for many years on the ABC radio network.

One of Eleanor's greatest boosters during her nearly two years as Princess Kay was Minnesota's Governor Orville Freeman. Another was Senator Ed Thye.

The ADA benefited greatly that first year through state and national (and international) publicity. It was estimated that television, radio and newsprint advertising generated a quarter of a million dollars worth of free promotion for dairy products.

After Eleanor had served from 1954 until well into 1955, she felt her life needed to slow down so that she could work to further her education. Today Eleanor is Mrs. Richard Thatcher of Rochester. She has always maintained her enthusiasm for the dairy princess program, helping many other young contestants prepare for pageants during the years. She and her husband, a long-time swimming coach at Rochester's John Marshall High School, eventually started their own business, Thatcher Pools and Spas.

Southeastern Minnesota continues a long tradition of American Dairy Association Dairy Princess winners. Following Eleanor Maley Thatcher, Ruth Marie Peterson of Austin was chosen for 1956-57. In 1959-60, Betty Jax of Adams served as Princess Kay. In more recent years, 18- year-old Amy Polikowsky of rural Byron was crowned in 1987, and Bridget Hendrickson of Preston, also 18, became the 39th young woman to hold the title in 1992. In 2001, another 18-year-old, Kelsey Olson, daughter of Les and Jo Olson who farm four miles northeast of Racine, was chosen as Minnesota's 48th Princess Kay. Sarah Olson, 19, from Hutchinson, succeeded her on August 21, 2002. Tae Vander Kool, 18, of Worthington, was crowned the 50th Princess Kay of the Milky Way at the opening of the Minnesota State Fair on August 20, 2003.

At KROC in the early 1960s, I became involved with the Rochester Dairy Co-operative. Today this is a huge business called AMPI, which stands for Associated Milk Producers, Inc. It covers a large area. Milk from southeastern Minnesota farms is tank-trucked to AMPI plants in Rochester and New Ulm. In Rochester, a good share of this milk is turned into AMPI cheese. Another large share is sent to the Marigold/Kemps plant on North Broadway, where it's turned into ice cream. Milk is also sent to other cities in Minnesota to be dried or turned into butter and other dairy products.

Art Anderson and Wayne Nygaard, promotion employees at the dairy in the 1960s, started a heavy involvement with KROC based on my broadcast efforts. This included a couple of New Year's Eve radio broadcasts, when I would play dance music from 10 pm until 3 am, sponsored by the Rochester Dairy.

For a few months in 1958, Rochester Dairy sponsored a promotion at KROC radio that asked, "When does PM come in the AM?" It was an idea for a new product name dreamed up by promotion man Walt Bruzek. Listeners were supposed to try to figure out what the slogan meant. The answer referred to a new name for Rochester Dairy — Polly Meadows, to match the new label on the milk cartons. Thus, PM came in the AM when the milkmen delivered milk to residents' homes in the morning.

My association with the Rochester Dairy Co-op expanded in 1965 following the very successful annual meeting the previous December. Art and Wayne came up with a way to use our morning KROC radio to expand awareness of the dairy industry. Field man Frank Brand started a six-month program where we would visit area dairy farms who were Co-op patrons. From mid-January until early July that year, Frank and I drove from farm to farm, where I personally taped interviews with 23 area farm families. We would usually arrive early in the afternoon, meet the farmers and go with them to the dairy barn to see their milking set-up. Following the barn visit, we'd go back to the house. The kids were usually home from school by 3 to 4 pm, and we'd all sit at the table and have ice cream that Frank always brought along. The hosts usually had cake and coffee ready. Then I'd turn on the tape machine and ask questions for about five minutes. That interview would then be played back on Saturday morning about 6:45 on a show called "Know Your Neighbor."

At the time of playback, the farmers' names were not used. We called it "this week's mystery dairy farm," and listeners were encouraged to submit cards to KROC identifying the farm. There were weekly winners, and on July 13, we held a grand prize drawing at the Rochester Dairy Co-op office of all the weekly winners. County Dairy Princess Jill Sackett did the drawing. The grand prize winner was Mrs. Stanley Eggler, of Route 4, Rochester. All of this was taped, and the Eggler family won a trip to northern Minnesota during the week of August 20-27.

During that six months, we interviewed some great families, many of whom I've run into in later years, creating new memories. I'm sad to say, time has taken its share of those family members, but it has been a deeply satisfying experience to get to know them.

Starting in late January 1965, we went to the following area farms for the taping of the "Know Your Neighbor" radio interviews:

January	Francis O'Brien, northeast of Byron
	R. Dale Jensen, rural Kasson
February	Chuck Walker, Grand Meadow
	Henry Schumann, north of Stewartville
	Harley Boettcher, west of Stewartville
	Harold Flynn, southwest of Rochester
	Darrel and Ruby Miller, just south of Pine Island
	Fritz Sprenger, rural Zumbro Falls
March	Harry Bluhm, Eyota
	Alfred Meyer, Eyota area just off County Highway 9
	Ralph Shanks, east of St. Charles on US Highway 14
	Wilford Weis, Pine Island
	Orelles Olson, Zumbrota

(The above visits carried the program through April and early May)

May	Joyce Sprenger, Zumbro Falls
	Russell Heins, Eyota area
	Burton Henry, Dover
	David Hoeft, north of Rochester on US Highway 63

June	Leighton Ernst, Viola
	William Heydman, Mazeppa
	Dave Richardson, north of Chatfield on US Highway 52
	Kenneth Hoeft, north of Rochester just off US Highway 63
July	Willis Opfer, south of Byron
	Melvin Ebner, rural Plainview

Looking back, I can say without a doubt that this experience helped to make up for my having to leave the farm at 17, cutting short my dreams for a life in open fields surrounded by grazing cows and baby calves, the hum of tractors and combines, the rhythm of the planting and harvest seasons.

After that, I was asked to broadcast the dairy's annual meeting in December from the Mayo Civic Auditorium. These programs were certainly the highlight of the Rochester Dairy Co-operative's year. From noon till 1 pm, we had entertainment, a few words from the reigning State Princess Kay, Karen Bracken, and dairy president George Daley of Lewiston, and then a speaker — noted upper Midwest newsman George Grim from WCCO radio, who also wrote a column for the *Minneapolis Morning Tribune* called "I Like It Here." His closing line on the WCCO 8:30 am news was always, "May your news be good news." The following year, 1966, the speaker was State Senator Walter "Fritz" Mondale.

All of this led up to my acting as master of ceremonies at countless county and regional Dairy Princess contests during the years from the early 1960s through 2000. Several times I was called upon to judge the beauty pageants. I always taped an interview with the winner afterward and played it back on the radio — usually the next morning.

For three years in a row, I emceed the Region Ten Dairy Princess contest. Region Ten included eight counties. I remember the first time I served as emcee for a contest on June 30, 1973, out of doors on a beautiful Saturday evening in Lanesboro's Sylvan Park. The winner, the regional dairy princess, would then go on to compete in the state Princess Kay of the Milky Way contest at the Minnesota State Fair in August. I emceed the regional contest again on June 22, 1974, at the Holiday Inn South in

Rochester, and on June 28, 1975, in Winona, in the Kryzsko Commons at Winona State College. The Region 10 princesses crowned at these events were Kathi Siewert of Lake City in Wabasha County, 1973; Karen Boyum of Peterson in Fillmore County, 1974; and Susan Tibesar of Minnieska in Winona County, 1975. As recently as 1995, I was in Adams for the Mower County Dairy Princess program when we named 18-year-old Becky Retterath of Adams, Minnesota, the new Princess.

Today, I'm concerned with the dwindling number of dairy farms in Minnesota. There was a time when the forty to fifty-cow herd was ideal for a farm family. Now the numbers must increase if the farm is to survive. Unless there's adequate help to milk the cows twice a day, seven days a week, a farmer will simply "burn out" from the never-ending labor.

...And Some Other Beauty Queens

During the 1960s, I was also very much involved in the Miss Rochester Pageant, and before that, when I was in Red Wing, with the state beauty pageants that were being held in Austin and Albert Lea. I recall taking a young lady named Ramona Johnson, who was Miss Red Wing, to Albert Lea for one of those pageants in 1957, on behalf of the Junior Chamber of Commerce in Red Wing. We drove in a 1957 Ford Thunderbird with a retractable top — you pressed the button and the front of the trunk opened to hide the roof when it came down, and then you had a convertible. The car was supplied by Tesdall Motors at 706 West Main Street in Red Wing. I remember their address clearly from having read their radio commercials so many times.

The Red Wing Jaycees had me involved in several community broadcasts and emcee work with Miss Red Wing pageants and sports shows' grand openings, even after I left Red Wing and came to Rochester in September of 1957. Apparently the Red Wing Jaycees remembered me, because they asked me to come back in mid-January 1959 to emcee a newly-named "Goodhue County Queen Contest" to be held at the St. James Hotel. Naturally, I was thrilled to be invited by a letter from Jaycee secretary Robert Rystad. Eleven young ladies competed, and the winner was Janet Thomas, who was sponsored by Kask Electric. At that time, former Spring Valley native Dave Sanford was president of the Red Wing Jaycees.

In Rochester, too, the local Jaycees got me involved in doing countless interviews with queen contestants live in our studio or pre-taped prior to the pageants. I was master of ceremonies for at least five pageants held in the theater section of the Mayo Civic Auditorium from 1965 through 1969. Winners of the Miss Rochester contest included Susan Ties in 1965 and Connie Cords in 1966 (she played an outstanding piano solo in the talent portion of the contest). In 1967, Miss Rochester was a nurse named Josephine Javier, and in 1968 it was Elizabeth Jane Van Hook, a dancer. In 1970, an acrobatic dancer named Janice Porter took the crown. I was assisted in my 1966 emcee duties by Cindy Lyn Packard, Miss Rochester of 1964. In late 1969, when Janice Porter was crowned, Miss Minnesota, Judith Mendenhall from Edina, Minnesota, assisted me. She captivated the audience with a flute solo.

After those five years, my emcee work in queen pageants slowed down in Rochester, but I was still heavily involved in Jaycee pageants in other area towns. From 1968 through 1970, Jaycees from Plainview, Pine Island, Zumbrota and St. Charles all asked me to come and emcee their pageants. The Jaycees were always kind to me, and I started developing a friendly relationship with those communities. I recall some of those memories today when I visit those towns.

On May 4, 1968, the Plainview Jaycees pageant crowned Cheryl Ferguson, 18, a vocalist from Viola, who had been the 1967 Homecoming Queen at Dover-Eyota High School. Dr. Jim Hiebert was the Plainview Jaycees' chairman for that event. The following year, the Miss Plainview pageant was held on May 3 at the high school. The *Plainview News*, dated Thursday, May 1, stated that the new Miss Plainview would face a long journey, citing the 5,000 miles and 43 appearances Cheryl Ferguson had made during her one-year reign. Crowned that night was Elizabeth Boehlke, an 18-year-old sponsored by the Peoples State Bank. She performed a modern dance to the song "Alone in the World." There were 700 spectators in attendance as Elizabeth won out over a field of seven contestants. In the audience were eighteen other "Misses" from other cities, large and small. The one who captured the crowd's attention was Miss New Hope, Lynn Kruger, who performed a Polynesian dance in Hawaiian costume.

I was called back for another Plainview Jaycee queen pageant in 1970. That was a big year for me to emcee in area towns. In addition to Plainview, the St. Charles Jaycees asked me to emcee their pageant on April 8, 1970, at the St. Charles Catholic School auditorium. The lovely Judith Mendenhall, Miss Minnesota 1969, assisted me as femcee, as she had the previous year at the Miss Rochester pageant. Again she played her flute solo, and then helped us crown the winner, 19-year-old Marlys Wegman, who was attending Winona State College, preparing for a teaching career. As her talent, Marlys presented a serious interpretation entitled "The Drunken Driver." She was sponsored by Mel Brownell of Brownell Drug. She was chosen from a field of six contestants, and was crowned by Diane Heim, who had been the 1969 Miss St. Charles.

Two days after the St. Charles pageant, I was asked by the late Harold Severson of Kenyon to emcee the "Miss Zumbrota Dream Girl" contest at the Zumbrota High School auditorium on Friday evening, April 10, at 8 pm. Thirteen young ladies were competing for the crown, but for some reason I didn't write down the winner's name in my program, as I had always done in earlier years. Sue Fossum, originally from Kenyon and herself a former Miss Rochester contestant, supplied the organ music that night. Sue later became Mrs. Ray Sands. The Sands family has contributed greatly to music during the years. Ray was with the original Polka Dots Band from Zumbrota when it was formed in 1949, and is still going strong today.

In August that summer, I went to the Pine Island High School auditorium on the night of August 8 to emcee their Jaycee pageant. I was assisted by femcee Evelyn Adler, who had been a contestant in the 1969 Miss Rochester pageant, when Janice Porter won the crown. In Pine Island that night in 1970, lovely Bonnie Jackson, 18-year-old daughter of Mr. and Mrs. Lloyd Jackson, was chosen as queen by the judges from a field of ten contestants.

table, with Henry and Clara Snow and some of their neighbors. Clara's family is helping serve chicken, mashed potatoes and gravy, and apple pie.

They had worked it out so that Adlai Stevenson wouldn't come along at the same time. So, much later, Adlai came and did his speaking, and the joke went around that he just got chicken sandwiches.

I went back again the next day, Saturday — Plowville's final day — with my neighbor Lyle Horan, and had still more fun.

The event was well covered by my friend the late Harold Severson, who worked for the *Post-Bulletin* then. He was a Kenyon native, and he wrote many articles during the years. (Harold Severson would be the Ag Person of the Year in 1990, selected by our Rochester Area Ag Committee.)

That was early September. On October 20, I started radio school at Brown Institute in Minneapolis. When the election night came, on November 4th, I happened to wake up at two in the morning, and I thought, "I'll turn on the radio, and see how this election has come out."

Well, it was just over. I was in time to hear Ike Eisenhower make his winning speech. The one, though, that I remember best was Adlai Stevenson, who gave a very short concession speech a few minutes before Ike spoke. He was so eloquent, this Senator from the state of Illinois. When they asked him how he felt, he said, in a quavering voice, "Well, I'm like the little boy who stubbed his toe in the dark. I am too big to cry, but it hurts too much to laugh."

I've never forgotten that quote from Adlai Stevenson.

The Rochester Area Agriculture Committee

When I was growing up on the farm, there was a near-by 4-H club, known as the Sumner Sunbeams (Sumner as in Sumner township). I was in that a few years, when I was in grade school — 6th, 7th, 8th grade. I didn't go on to big things through 4-H, but we had fun with the things we did, like the softball games in Roy Finn's pasture on a Sunday afternoon and the 4-H picnics.

I took a new appreciation of 4-H after I got into radio, beginning when I was in Red Wing. I was always being asked to judge 4-H events, or to help people in speaking contests. I don't know how many speaking contests I have judged — they thought I was some sort of authority. Then when I came to Rochester, and was heavily involved in morning radio, I got involved again in agriculture and dairying and 4-H, and it just never has really stopped.

I'd been speaking before 4-H clubs and doing things at the 4-H building since the early 1960s. Then in 1978 I got involved in a group known as the Rochester Area Agriculture Committee.

Until 1996, it had been the Chamber of Commerce Agribusiness Committee. Then the Chamber wanted to go a different route, to spend more time on issues, rather than events. But we volunteer Ag Committee members wanted to continue holding our special events that would help promote and encourage agriculture. Some of us were pretty perturbed about the Chamber's decision.

Then the Olmsted County Farm Bureau Federation stepped in and said, "Let us be your umbrella, the organization that can accept your donations coming in, and pay the checks needed to do your projects, the Country Breakfast on the Farm, the FFA Awards, the 4-H Blue Ribbon Auction, and the Autumn 4-H Dairy Banquet." So that's what happened. We changed the name to Rochester Area Agriculture Committee (Ag Committee for short), and this Ag Committee, which is very dear to me, is still going strong.

The Ag Committee meets every month at the Holiday Inn South in Rochester to plan these events. We're there from noon till about 1:15, and we all pay for our own lunch. The Ag Committee is made up of volunteers from the media, bankers, farmers, implement dealers — people who are just interested in doing things to benefit agriculture and the people right here in the Rochester area. We don't go lobbying at the legislature, but occasionally there'll be a report from one of our legislators on the agenda.

In 1981, while we were still part of the Chamber of Commerce, we started National Ag Day. We had a special breakfast or a luncheon, inviting farmers to come in, and there was always a speaker. It was a good thing, and brought about a lot of awareness of farm issues. Area farmers realized that there were people around who really cared about their problems.

For fifteen years, as a part of Ag Day — usually held on the first day of spring — when we had that brunch or luncheon, we would name an Ag Person of the Year. Thanks to emcee Herb Graff for his years at the head table at those laughter-filled Ag Day luncheons.

The Ag Person of the Year Award winners from 1982 through 1996 were:

1982	Wendy Lenton, manager, All American Co-op of Stewartville
1983	Dave Kjome, Olmsted County Extension Director
1984	Cliff Pagel, Eyota area dairy/beef farmer
1985	Bill Sanborn, President, Security State Bank, Pine Island
1986	Dr. Paul Zollman, Mayo Clinic Institute Hills & Animal Research
1987	Gordon Elliott, manager, Pine Island Farmers Elevator
1988	Richard E. Badger, area beef & hog producer
1989	Joe Hain, area dairy farmer
1990	Harold Severson, Rochester Post Bulletin newspaper columnist
1991	Evelyn Hunter, community servant, Olmsted County Fair board member
1992	Merle "Mike" Gordon, membership services director, People's Co-op Power Association
1993	Don, Pat, Tom, Jerry & Barb Webster, Zumbrota Livestock Auction
1994	Larry Lamberty, NorWest banker, farmer, community servant
1995	Irv Nehring, C.P.A., finance manager for 4H Blue Ribbon Auction for many years
1996	Harley Flathers, sales representative & broadcaster at KWEB, KRCH, KMFX, KNFX radio stations

Those annual Ag Day luncheons hold many pleasant memories for me. In 1994, our speaker was Minnesota News Network farm broadcaster Tom Rothman, who spoke on "Agriculture — Still Minnesota's #1 Industry." I had asked Tom to be the featured speaker that year. George Braunreiter of KWWK radio was the master of ceremonies, and Ag Committee member Evelyn Hunter introduced the Ag Person of the Year, Larry Lamberty, who had served the area well in so many ways for over forty years.

The following year, on March 14, 1995, Larry Lamberty would introduce the next Ag Person of the Year, who was Irv Nehring, a CPA by profession, who had been associated for a long time with the financial side of the 4-H Blue Ribbon Sale and served on several other city and rural boards and committees. Father Vernon Schaefer of Holy Redeemer Catholic Church in Eyota offered the invocation. Herb Graff kept the crowd rolling with his humor as emcee, and the laughs accelerated when keynote speaker Howard Mohr of Cottonwood, Minnesota, took the stage. Howard, who wrote for many years for Minnesota Public Radio's "A Prairie Home Companion," based his address on the title of one of his books, "How to Speak Minnesotan."

Then I was asked to make a special presentation to the man who served as our host at the Holiday Inn South for so many years.

Don Yngsdal, a former milk hauler from area farms to local creameries, had been employed by the Holiday Inn South for 26 years, 18 of them as general manager. The Chamber of Commerce (which at that time was still the official sponsor of the Ag Committee) presented him with a special plaque commemorating his long association with the Ag Committee.

According to Post-Bulletin writer Bob Freund, who covered these events, "Yngsdal's meat and potatoes menus have long filled plates at the Annual Agribusiness Appreciation Luncheon." During the years, many area and regional agricultural conferences and seminars had found their hours and days at the Holiday Inn South with Don and his staff to be "filled with hospitality." Don retired two weeks later on March 31, 1995.

We stopped holding Ag Day in 1996, because times change, and we felt we needed to spend more time on our other events, like Country

Breakfast on the Farm, which was always in late June, and the 4-H Blue Ribbon auction during the Olmsted County fair, the first Thursday in August. We give out the FFA Awards from the fair in August, and then we wrap up the year's activities with a special 4-H dairy banquet in the fall, honoring the 4-H kids who've been given awards locally and at the Minnesota State Fair.

The last Ag Day luncheon was held March 18, 1996. Our speaker was Minnesota Commissioner of Agriculture Gene Hugoson. And I was honored with the Ag Person of the Year Award for my forty years of broadcasting 4-H, FFA and various other agricultural events.

Our longtime emcee Herb Graff died on March 2, 2002, at the age of 78. Evelyn Hunter, who served on the committee for many years, died on May 9, 2002, at 87.

Country Breakfast on the Farm

In 1988, the Rochester Area Ag Committee developed the event called Country Breakfast on the Farm. And I'm proud to say, this has been one festive event. I play a large role in it every year, almost more than I should the last few years. Mike Gordon, of the Peoples Co-op Power Association, located the first nine farms, asking, "Would you be the host of an event this year that might draw 2,000 to 4,000 people to your farm for a day?" Over the years we have served from as few as 809 at our first breakfast in 1988 to almost 4,000 people at the Durst family dairy farm near Mantorville in the year 2000.

We want this event to be educational. It has to be a dairy farm, because we want the little kids to come out and see the cows, pet the baby calves, and see where milk comes from. It is always held the last Saturday of Rochesterfest in late June.

Country Breakfast is strictly run by donations and the income from the breakfasts that we sell. The host family opens up their farm, but the committee has a lot to do. We may have to pitch a forty-by-sixty-foot tent in order to have a place to serve food, or to provide shade. We have to check the water. We have to see to it there are ample outhouses and parking. We map it all out ahead of time, so that everybody knows where he's supposed to go the day of the event. It's like a little county fair.

People start coming at 6:30 in the morning for breakfast, and it goes on till almost noon. They serve for five hours. We have a caterer who comes in from Rolfe, Iowa — Chris Cakes, owned by Gregg and Donna White. They've done this for us for years, and they're excellent. The catering is a show in itself. They come up with four people, and they're flipping those pancakes. There are two long lines. People go right through, and they're served pancakes, sausage, syrup, butter, milk, juice, coffee and of course cheese (because this is an agricultural breakfast). We do all that for $5 for adults, $2 for kids, under 5 free. We try to get enough donations to cover all this ahead of time. We aren't interested in making a profit, we just want, when we get done for the year, to have a few hundred dollars left to start up the next year.

The father of this Country Breakfast idea is a man named Ambrose King. Some years ago, he said, "You know, I wish we could do something like they do in Wisconsin, have Dairy Day on the Farm." He told us about it, and we got the Chamber to back us. We started at the Curt and Myrna Kroening farm, in Haverhill township, eight miles northeast of Rochester, in 1988.

Ambrose King said, "I think we will probably have 500 people there."

I told him, "I don't even want to see us suit up for 500. We should be shooting for a thousand."

Well, we had 809. It went to 1190 the next year, then 2250 by 1992. For the next three years it held at around 3600, and in 2000 we had almost 4,000. We bus the people out there, give them a free bus ride, and we want them to wear their Rochesterfest buttons, because it's an official Rochesterfest event. We get publicity and we pay to be in the Rochesterfest brochures.

Year after year, people tell me, "Oh, we look forward to coming to Country Breakfast on the Farm." It has really turned out to be a positive ag event. We changed the name from Dairy Day on the Farm to Country

Breakfast, because we wanted to include the beef people and the pork people, as well as the dairy people. We began with the idea of letting people see where milk comes from, and then the others got in there, promoting pork and beef. You might have beef patties on that tray for breakfast, or pork sausages, along with your butter and cheese. People are glad to be a part of it. They all work well together.

When the Chamber dropped the Ag Committee back in 1996, the Olmsted County Farm Bureau took over as our umbrella organization, and we were able to continue running Country Breakfast on the Farm and our other events. It really has worked out well. I have a big thank-you to give to the Olmsted County Farm Bureau, the Farm Bureau Federation, and our many volunteers. There are six of us on the Ag Committee Board that are also Farm Bureau members, including myself — I have been a Farm Bureau member for forty years. There are a lot of pluses in working together.

We had planned to have the 14th Country Breakfast, in 2001, at the Robert and Jeannette Sheehan farm, ten miles southeast of Rochester, in rural Simpson. However, because of the outbreak of hoof and mouth disease in Great Britain, they asked us early — on April 17 — to cancel it. With the large numbers of people who come to this event from all over the world, there was a concern that the highly contagious disease of cows and hogs might be imported by one of the attendees. Similar agricultural events in Iowa and Wisconsin were also cancelled for 2001. The Country Breakfast was rescheduled, however, and was held again on June 22, 2002, at Daley Farms, owned by Olmsted County Commissioner Jim Daley and his four sons, Tom, Paul, Doug and Fabian. Daley Farms is located fifteen miles northwest of Rochester in Dodge County.

These are the farms where Country Breakfast on the Farm has been held:

1988	Curt & Myrna Kroening, Haverhill Township	809 attended
1989	Ralph & Steve Nigon, rural Rochester	1190 attended
1990	Barney & Dallas Strain, rural Byron	1230 attended
1991	James Sheehan, rural Simpson	1590 attended

1992	Howard & Marion Heins, rural Oronoco	2250 attended
1993	Duane & Larry Eggler, Elgin area	2810 attended
1994	Gary & Linda Allen, Gar-Lin Farms, Eyota	3285 attended
1995	Ken & Mary Schumacher, rural Elgin	3602 attended
1996	Bob & Diane Eustice, rural Byron	3676 attended
1997	Tom & Jackie Welte, west of Plainview in Wabasha County	3600 attended
1998	Jim & Elaine Teske, Karri Teske & Todd Searles, Tesk-Holm Farm, Fillmore Co.	2869 attended
1999	Don & Gail Andring, rural St. Charles	2750 attended
2000	Durst Brothers Dairy, Dodge County	3963 attended
2001	Canceled due to foot-and-mouth disease outbreak in Britain	
2002	Daley Farms, rural Pine Island in Dodge County	2770 attended
2003	Gerald, John & Kevin Connelly, near Salem Corners	2730 attended
2004	George Stoppel Farm, adjoining the Olmsted County History Center, as part of the Rochester Sesquicentennial (1854-2004)	

First Princess Kay of the Milky Way, Eleanor Maley from Grand Meadow, Minnesota in 1954. Today she is Mrs. Richard Thatcher of Rochester.

Bridget Hendrickson, Preston, Minnesota, the 39th Minnesota Princess Kay of the Milky Way. Today she is Mrs. Tim Jacobson, Roseville, Minnesota.

Kelsey Olson, rural Racine & Spring Valley, Minnesota, the 48th Minnesota Princess Kay of the Milky Way/2001-2002.

25th Annual Meeting Rochester Dairy at Mayo Civic Auditorium. L-R: Carol Kingsbury, Olmsted County and Region 10 Dairy Princess with Art Anderson and Wayne Nygaard. Promotion and marketing at the Dairy. Dec. 1966.

Harley at KROC microphone introduces the family of Dairy Princess Carol Kingsbury crowned both Olmsted Co. & Region 10 Princess earlier in 1966. L-R: Lloyd Kingsbury, son Alan, Mrs. Evelyn Kingsbury, daughter Jane and Princess Carol. Noon 25th Annual Meeting at Mayo Civic Auditorium

Presidential candidate, Dwight Eisenhower, after speaking at Plowville, Kasson, Minnesota, Sept. 6, 1952. Estimated 100,000 crowd.

Ike dines at the farm home of Henry & Clara Snow, host family of 160 acre farm between Kasson & Dodge Center. Sept. 6, 1952. Photos from 1965 Kasson Centennial booklet.

Country Breakfast on the farm at Ken & Mary Schumacher, rural Elgin, 1995. General William Westmoreland, retired, visits with Harley on KWEB broadcast as the crowds walk the grounds.

Country Breakfast on the Farm at Durst Brothers Dairy north of Mantorville. Harley talks with Hyllah Durst, mother of Ron Durst. With him, his son John, 12. Nearly 4000 came for breakfast. June 24, 2000.

1966 Miss Rochester, Connie Cords, seated with her attendants. Members of the Rochester JC's, sponsoring organization with the pageant held at Mayo Civic Auditorium Theatre section. Your MC, Harley Flathers, stands 4th from left.

Miss Amy Alberts, Pine Island, a dairy Princess earlier and radio celebrity later. She stopped by Harley's KWEB radio broadcast during the 1995 Cheese Festival parade. I did that broadcast for 10 years . . . 1986 thru 1995.

Moment 15

Radio in Southeast Minnesota, 1953-2002
My Fellow Talkers

When I started out in 1953 at Red Wing, Minnesota, I worked first, as I've said, with a veteran, Peter Lyman, who had spent several years in the 1930s and 1940s at KROC in Rochester before coming to KAAA. He was a very talented person who had been an actor and traveled in 1934 and 1935 with a road show, the Aulger Brothers Stock Company, before getting into radio. In his early years, he worked with former President Ronald Reagan, who as "Dutch" Reagan was a sports announcer on WMT radio in Waterloo, Iowa. Peter had also done radio production for the J. Walter Thompson advertising agency in Chicago. He left Red Wing early in 1956 for Bay City, Michigan. After nearly two years in radio there, he went to Clarksburg, West Virginia, and spent the next 18 years as news director of WBOY-TV. He returned to Rochester after retiring in 1975, and died June 2, 1976, at age 67.

Rochester's third ward councilman Jean McConnell worked at KAAA in Red Wing in 1950 and 1951, alongside Peter Lyman. Jean was hired as a copy writer, but in a small station, as he told me recently, he ended up doing many other tasks in the broadcasting business. He has served the third ward for the past fifteen years.

When Red Wing's station was sold in 1956, and became KCUE, I worked with Alan Kennedy, an announcer and radio engineer. There was also Virgil Kohrs, a Lake City lad. He was also a polio victim, and had difficulty walking. Virgil Kohrs took the air name Randy Cook and became a fine announcer. He went on to instruct radio classes in the Twin Cities at Brown Institute, which we'd both attended earlier when it was called the American Institute of the Air. In 1957 and 1958, he worked here at KWEB in Rochester, when the station was very new.

When I came to KROC radio in the autumn of 1957, I was hired to do what they called the evening shift, 5:30 till midnight. We were on eighteen hours a day then, from 6 am till midnight. The other announcers included a man named Donovan, or Don Edwards, who was the morning announcer, 6 am till noon. He also did the 6 pm and 10 pm television news, so he was getting well worked. Coming in from noon until 6 pm was Larry Robitschek, who took the air name of Larry Roberts. A heck of a guy, Larry Roberts. Then from 6 pm till midnight, it was myself, plus some part-time weekend and vacation help. One part-timer was attorney William F. Young. Bill loved radio and was very good at it. He filled in at KROC wherever needed, as his law practice (Hunt, Streiff, DeVinney and Young) permitted. He became a good friend, and was one of the ushers at our wedding in 1959. Bill died March 13, 2001, at age 74.

Another man at KROC radio during those early years was Bernie Lusk, a veteran sports announcer, who was at the station non-stop from 1942 until 1982. He also was an early KROC television personality. Bernie was the "key" behind the Eagles' cancer telethon for many years, broadcasting non-stop for 18 to 20 hours. He died on June 13, 1996, after an apparent heart attack at age 78.

Also in those earlier years, Gene Thompson was on the KROC staff as an announcer and newsman from 1951 to 1967. He then moved to Northfield, where he became the news director at KYMN. He died November 30, 1981, in Northfield at age 62.

In late 1957, when Cal Smith, who had hired me, left the station, we hired Tom Bachrach as program director in his place. Tom was a super sportsman from KDHL in Faribault. He was hired because KROC was taking on another level of baseball broadcasting called the 3-I League. Bernie Lusk still had his role to play in sports, but Tom Bachrach came in as program director and sportscaster. He would travel, doing these play-by-play game broadcasts, going into Iowa and Wisconsin as well as Rochester. Tom was with us from 1958 until 1961, when he left to go to Nebraska, I believe to Omaha, to do television news under the air name of Eric Adams. He died shortly thereafter, at a very young age. Meanwhile, Bernie Lusk continued to be at KROC on sports.

From late 1968 till April 17, 1971, I spent some time as announcer/stockholder at KNXR-FM 97.5. It was a brand new FM-only station built by recording engineer Tom Jones, a genius in electronics. Dave Frogner, from Harmony, Minnesota, was an early partner and voice on KNXR, as he is still today. Jerry Miller, who had worked part time at KROC after a morning stint in earlier years at KWEB, also did part time music and news at KNXR. For two and a half years, I was the voice from 6 till 10 am, six mornings a week, Monday through Saturday. I had thought it would be interesting to work in FM, which was a new thing at that time. Then I was fired, and I returned to KROC on June 1, 1971.

A few weeks later, a young man named Roger O'Day and I teamed up to do a 4-hour radio talk show on KROC called "The Rog and Harley Show," which seemed to catch on. As I look back, it was probably less interesting, less dynamic than today's talk format. As a team, though, we worked together pretty well. That lasted intermittently into 1980, as Roger was needed on the television side of the business.

In 1965, we hired Ron Gruber away from Howard Bill, who had built the third station in Rochester, KOLM, in the autumn of 1963. Ron Gruber had a great voice, and was a super announcer. My manager, Bob Fick, had said, "Go and see if you can hire him." Well, I had guts. I went right up there, into the KOLM studio, and asked him if he'd consider coming to work for us. I recall climbing the long stairway to their studio, located in a building up above Tradehome Shoes on South Broadway, beside Osco Drug (now the site of the Radisson Hotel). I actually went up and into the studio. I don't know what his boss, Howard Bill, must have thought. I think I did that twice, and eventually Ron Gruber came over to KROC, probably for $5 or $10 a week more than he was making at KOLM.

It wasn't long before Ron was on the air midday, playing records and doing news, etc. I would open the morning from 6 till 9, then Ron would come on from 9 till 3, and I'd come back again from 3 until 6. Ron was also needed on Channel 10 television's weather shows, and eventually went into management. After 37 years, Ron Gruber retired December 31, 2002.

In the 1940s and 1950s, we heard the lovely voice of Mary Miller on KROC. She was there long before my arrival. Later, she went to KWEB for a time, and then to the TV cable system as Mary B — just Mary B. She and I worked together outside the Mayo Civic Auditorium on October 29, 1970, when President Nixon came to Rochester for a two-hour whirlwind tour. We described it on cable, for what was then called Teleprompter TV. Mary retired some time ago.

Peter Viking may have started with us in the autumn of 1959, and was there for several years. He had a tremendous speaking voice. Pete had done some theater work, and a lot of singing with a guitar. In addition to having a great on-air voice, Pete was in demand on weekends for "gigs" at local bars. One of our sponsors at that time was the newly-established King Leo's Drive-In at 516 North Broadway, owned by Rochester businessman Leon Latz. (Today, Taco Bell has that location.) Peter Viking, who was a very creative individual, composed a clever radio jingle for King Leo's, which Tom Jones of KNXR recently recreated for me, complete with music and catchy rhythm (Pete used to snap his fingers as a sound effect). It went like this:

"Old King Leo is everybody's hero
When it comes to hamburger buys
For just 15 cents
All you ladies and gents
Get a taste-filled burger
That will light up your eyes."

"There may have been a second verse," Tom says, "but my memory ran out at that point."

Around 1965, in walked Curt Curtis, who had spent a few months working for Howard Bill at KOLM-AM 1520, then a Mutual Broadcasting

System affiliate. This man wrote songs, sang them and entertained locally. As I write this, I'm looking at a 45 rpm record "shuck," or paper wrapping, for which Curt asked me to write his brief story — he even wanted me to put my picture on the back of the shuck! That was in 1966, and the song was called, "Rochester, Minnesota, where the trees grow tall." On the back of the record was "Smoke along the track," by Helms and Rose. Curt Curtis and the Rochester All-Stars performed the songs on a disc cut by Ron Lynn Recording Studios of Rochester. Curt, who referred to himself as a "transplanted country boy," was feeling a strong dedication to Rochester, his new home. I played his song a few times. but for most of the years it has been "resting" in my desk drawer. Curt left, and I know nothing of his whereabouts today, but he and Peter Viking were really two "good old boys."

In 1961, David Gentling, who was then KROC's owner, hired Bill Ingram after Bill had been released from Channel 5 television news in the Twin Cities. Bill's name was big in those days. He was with us on the 6 and 10 pm TV news on Channel 10 for three or four years, then moved to Chicago and later to Duluth. He died in New Mexico in 1991.

Bob Ryan, who had also been an early newscaster with Bill Ingram at Channel 5, was let go shortly after Bill. He went to Channel 9 news for a time and then came to KROC television in 1971. He stayed till well into 1985. There is not a finer person in the business. He has traveled in many parts of the world and written countless travelogues. He's spoken a lot on behalf of the veterans. He did the 6 pm and 10 pm KROC television news from 1971 to 1979 here in Rochester, and also was on KROC radio until 1985. For a time, the KROC television news show featured Bob Ryan, news, Ron Gruber, weather, and Bernie Lusk, sports.

I did two years of mid-day television on KROC, too, from 1975 through 1977, following Virginia Firnschild's program. My show, "Take Ten at Noon," was filled with public service announcements (PSAs) and area guests from all over southern Minnesota.

Dave Carr was a man who certainly made his mark in the broadcast world. He worked first in LaCrosse, and came to Rochester in the early

1970s. He had a great voice, and he loved weathercasting. He was soon heading up the Olmsted County emergency warning system with director Pete Canellos here in Rochester. Dave had done weather on radio and on television. His is the voice that breaks in today when the emergency broadcast system kicks on, when all the radio stations say there's a tornado watch or a tornado warning on, or there may be high winds. Dave's voice kicks the trigger, and all radio and TV stations in this area get that signal simultaneously.

Another man who started at KROC television was Gideon Klein. He was in television sales for a while, then he went to KWEB radio sales, and I believe was even in management there for a time. Then he left radio and bought a business in downtown Rochester, which he called Klein's Luggage Shop. It was very successful during the years. Gid raised his children to know how to work, and they did, growing up working in the luggage shop. For a while after they grew up, Bill and Gary Klein were in radio. Bill is still involved. He was with our station, KWEB, in recent years. For a number of years before that, he was selling radio time at KNXR, and I believe he was also at KROC for a time. Today he serves Channel 6 television in local sales. Bill Klein and I sit in on the Quarterbacks Club downtown.

The story of Judd Jacobson would fill a book in itself, as radio listeners and sponsors know if they were listening in the 1950s through the 1970s. In my files, I have a Rochester Post-Bulletin story dated October 9, 1965, by staff writer Rolf Hofstad, whose headline reads "Despite Handicaps, Radio Pair Proves 'Positive Attitude' Pays." Judd came up to our KROC studios in the 100 First Avenue building to visit me while Hofstad wrote that combined story on the two of us. At the time, Judd and I were both actively involved in the Hiawatha Valley National Paraplegia Foundation, which was holding a two-day regional conference at the Kahler Hotel. A picture with the article shows us in the big studio, near the control board and turntables, a room where I spent many wonderful hours from September 14, 1957, until the studios moved on November 1, 1966.

The article tells of Judd's diving accident at age sixteen that left him paralyzed from the neck down. He spent his life in a wheel chair with limited arm and hand use, but accomplished as much in four decades as ten men might do in a whole lifetime. When the article was written, Judd was 38 and I was 34. Hofstad said we both illustrated the importance of having a positive attitude to succeed on an equal basis with the non-handicapped.

I first heard Judd broadcasting from his bed in Owatonna on KROC radio in the spring of 1952, before I went into the broadcasting profession on October 20 of that year. The late Walt Bruzek, who had helped many people, got Judd started first in magazine sales and then in radio, broadcasting from his home through the KROC studios in Owatonna. Eventually KROC closed the Owatonna studios, concentrating on Rochester and KROC television. Judd then latched onto KDHL Faribault, both as an announcer doing community events in ten-minute newscasts and as a heckuva good radio time salesman by telephone. KDHL manager Jack Hyde really landed a good one when he got Judd. At the end of his career, Judd was associated with the Waseca station, KOWO AM & FM.

Judd was known to thousands and was in demand to emcee every kind of public function, farm or city, beauty pageants and more, always from his "wheels." But, being the great entrepreneur that he was, that wasn't enough for Judd. In 1970, he founded a travel business, in partnership with his wife, Barbara, called Travel Headquarters. It also runs a nation-wide program called Disability Flying Wheels, an air and cruise travel service for those confined strictly to "wheels." Barbara Jacobson continues that business today from her home in Owatonna.

After nearly forty years in broadcasting, Judd quit in the mid-1980s to start an elevator and wheel chair business, which was very successful. His health declined in later years, until death claimed him on February 23, 1991, just four months short of his 64th birthday. Judd Jacobson was a tremendous fighter.

Todd Hale, thirty-year radio personality at KRFO AM 1390 in Owatonna, remembers the sponsor loyalty and listenership that Judd had during those years. Todd joined KRFO in 1959 and was an Owatonna “radio fixture” until 1989, as Judd was at KDHL. Todd, who was born on April 8, 1939, has slowed his radio pace and turned to cable television in Owatonna, creating a new half-hour show that plays four times daily. He also serves as a board member for the Steele County Fair, and is in charge of much of the annual entertainment.

Other announcers have come and gone in this area during the years. One was Dale Schulz from Spring Valley, whose air name was Dale Hamilton. Dale had come to visit me when I was at KAAA in Red Wing, and asked me about radio announcing. He had also suffered from polio, and walked with a limp, but without canes. I gave him the facts, and he went to Minneapolis, where he actually roomed at the same house on 35th Avenue South that I did when I was at school there in 1952 and 1953. Dale started then at Benson, Minnesota, and came to Rochester to work at the new KWEB station in the late 1950s and early 1960s. He came to KROC when I called him one day in 1963 and told him we were going to be on 24 hours a day, and we needed him for all night, from midnight until 6 am.

He and Jerry Miller both came to KROC radio for a time. Dale stayed for twenty years, but Jerry left us in the late 1960s for KNXR. Jerry was originally from Zumbrota. He just loved broadcasting. He stood six foot seven inches tall, and had a great personality. At one time, he sang with the Rochester Male Chorus, directed by Harold Cooke, and he recalls singing at the White House during President Richard Nixon’s term in office. To this day, Jerry is still going strong on radio at Y-105 in Rochester.

At one time, in the early 1960s, Jerry did a morning show on KWEB called “JM in the AM.” It originated on the third floor of the Northwestern National Bank building, on the site that is now occupied by Brackenridge Square. I was across the alley in the 100 First Avenue building, with a KROC program called “HF in the Morning.” Naturally, we each wanted to beat the other.

Even before Jerry, Joe Burnham did a morning show on KWEB called “Jolly Joe in the Morning.” Jolly Joe eventually went into radio sales, and came to KROC in 1969, for fourteen years. He and I worked together on many broadcast projects. In autumn 1982, he went to KNXR in sales, and remains there today, along with Dick Carpenter, who'd been an early announcer on evening sports for a short time on KROC.

Also still working at KNXR is Don Anderson, sales manager since 1968. Don had worked earlier at KOLM. Veteran morning man Roy Achter retired on September 27, 2002, after 29 years of broadcasting in the Rochester area, 27 of them at KNXR. In earlier years, Roy worked as an announcer at KOWO in Waseca.

You can see that, over the years, announcers and sales people tend to move back and forth, from station to station. I've moved some, but I've always wanted to stay in the same city and establish credibility. I've now been in the broadcast business for 51 years, 46 of them here in Rochester.

It takes time to get established. At one time during the mid-1960s, KROC manager Bob Fick told me, "Harley, you have a 54 share in the morning." Well, I guess that was pretty darn good. I wasn't really working for numbers, though. I never did. I just loved the thrill of morning broadcasts, and knowing that many folks depended on my being there early, through all kinds of weather. I loved working Christmas. I loved working holidays. I felt a holiday was a day when I could talk with some people who never heard radio any other time. I felt it was an honor, and I never complained about working on a holiday. Todd Hale, that veteran announcer at KRFO in Owatonna, tells me he feels the same way. It was a privilege to be the morning man on radio.

After I left KROC in October 1980 and moved over to KWEB, I became acquainted with another fine group of radio people. In the period from 1981 through about 1987, Spring Valley resident John Dahl was the morning man on KWEB. John Dahl, sports director Carl Cunningham and newsman John Harwick created a show called "The Harcundahl Express." It was an imaginary bus, complete with the sounds of air brakes and motor. It aired each morning from 7 to 9, and it was hilarious.

Carl Cunningham joined KWEB as sports director and play-by-play man from 1983 until 1993. Carl died October 24, 1999, at age 61. Eric Peterson continued with KWEB play-by-play for many years. We recently hired veteran play-by-play man Greg Henn from Zumbro Falls as a full-time sports announcer, doing play-by-play for all the high school games KWEB and KNFX (The Fan) carry. 1984 Mower County Dairy Princess Julie Merton was an afternoon announcer on KWEB in 1987 and 1988, as Julie Grabow.

Another couple of personalities on our stations were Bob Hughes and Rob Gossman, who joined us on KWEB & KNFX-AM 970 from September 1999 through early 2003, both coming from across town at rival KROC radio. Bob had been a fixture at KROC for nearly thirteen years, and Rob for about seven. On Fox Country, Alan Reed and Tracy Dixon do mornings, 5:30 till 9. Alan is now a veteran of 25 years in broadcasting. Dave Anderson recently joined us at Fox Country as operations manager. He's a fine addition in programming, with a great voice.

Another veteran on our broadcast team was Jodi Barnet, on Fox Country and Laser 101.7. She has a sweet lady's voice that will melt the hardest of hearts. She left us in early 2003 to raise her children full-time. Her father, 40-year veteran broadcaster Gordy Hinck, is a Lake City resident who spent 33 years in sports play-by-play and sales at KDHL in Faribault. He grew up listening to me when I was new in the business at KAAA in Red Wing. Possibly I influenced Gordy, I don't know. Gordy Hinck recently went back to his home town of Lake City, and now does broadcasting and radio sales for KLCH 94.9 FM, a new station owned by the broadcast group that also operates KCUE and KWNG in Red Wing. KLCH first went on the air on December 13, 2001, with 6000 watts power.

Alan Reed has told me he listened to me as a young lad in the mornings before he caught the school bus. And Steve Skogen, sports director at KROC, came and asked me about radio when he was in his early teens. I said, "Go for it!" He's been at KROC since the mid-1980s, and has spent over 25 years in the broadcast business.

Then there is Big Mark Clark, program director at Laser 101. Mark is a big fellow, full of enthusiasm, and a joy to be around.

These are some of the good people that I've had the chance to work with during the years.

It's Friendly Time

When I met Sherm Booen at our 1980 Rochester Air Show, I reminded him that I had first listened to him on the radio back in 1942, on that great three-hour, 1 to 4 pm Saturday program on KROC and WCCO called "Friendly Time." I remembered his very distinctive voice presenting the music and reading the commercials for the sponsor, Friendly Grain Belt Beer.

Sherm had been invited to Rochester to be master of ceremonies at that Air Show. He was an aviation authority in Minnesota, who had been flying his own plane for many years and emceeing countless air shows. He had put a whole life into "The World of Aviation," a weekly Sunday television program on Channel 4 WCCO from 11:30 til noon. But the radio memories were still fresh in his mind.

I don't recall how long Sherm Booen was host of "Friendly Time." It eventually moved to Saturday evening at 10:30 on WCCO, where it followed Cedric Adams' 10 pm news show, with commentary on the news by Professor E.W. Ziebarth from the University of Minnesota and Halsey Hall on sports. The new voice for "Friendly Time" was then genial Bob DeHaven, who was already a WCCO personality.

Bob DeHaven had followed in the footsteps of a man called Uncle Mac as emcee of Saturday evening's "Red River Valley Gang" from 8:30 to 9 pm on WCCO. This musical program, which lasted for some time from the late 1930s into the early 1940s, was sponsored by Robin Hood Flour, which sponsored many programs on WCCO in those days. Meanwhile, across town, KSTP radio had the "Sunset Valley Barn Dance," a group that was in great demand around the state as an entertaining fund-raiser program for various community organizations. While I was in high school, they appeared at the Chatfield High School auditorium.

Bob DeHaven was often called "Our Own Bob" after another sponsor, Our Own Hardware, for whom he traveled all over Minnesota doing a different live half-hour radio program every Saturday morning between 8:45 and 9:15. He visited Don Pitt's Hardware in Stewartville and Underleak's

Hardware in Chatfield, among others. Bob would talk with the crowds while Gus, Jim and Curly sang. In real life, Gus, Jim and Curly were Ernie and Hal Garvin and Dick Link, fine musicians who sang and played guitar and bass. Lovely Sally, a vocalist married to producer Earl Steele, often joined them.

Gus, Jim and Curly performed regularly at the WCCO studios in the early mornings from 6:45 to 6:55. Then for five minutes at 6:55 am, storyteller Clellan Card was featured, sponsored by "delicious Butter Nut Coffee." In between jokes, you would hear him slurping his cup of Butter Nut Coffee. Clellan always finished up by saying, "Birdie with a yellow bill, hopped upon my window sill, cocked his tiny eye and said..." Then he'd finish up with a funny catch-phrase good for laughs to start the day. Quite a "card" was Clellan!

Around the Dial in Southeast Minnesota

We can't talk about radio personalities in the Rochester area during the last half-century without mentioning some of the stations. The very first radio station in Rochester was KROC, at 1340 on the dial, founded by Greg Gentling on September 30, 1935. It was an NBC affiliate.

KLER-AM 970, an ABC affiliate, was on the air from December 1, 1948 until May 31, 1952. It was started by Alice Mayo, wife of Dr. C.W. "Chuck" Mayo. She had seen all the kings and queens and heads of state coming to Rochester and visiting KROC, and she wanted her own station. She started that station in lavish studios up above what is now the Iridescent House at 227 1st Avenue Southwest. They were connected with a fine network, ABC. I used to listen to their programming in my high school years, and even when I got out of the hospital in early 1950 and 1951. They had "The Lone Ranger," and Sgt. Preston and his dog, King. There was a very good ABC news network. They had Bert Parks and "Break the Bank," and various other programs during those years. Then KLER 970 "went dark," as we say in the business. They went out of business and nothing happened for a long time. The frequency was available, but it lay there unused for ten years, until in 1961 it was revived as KQAQ Austin.

KWEB-AM 1270, where I am located now, first came on the air two weeks after I started at KROC in 1957. It was our big competitor, a "big rocker" back then. It was founded by Nick and Vic Tedesco of St. Paul, for whom I had worked at KCUE in Red Wing.

KOLM, at 1520 on your dial, was founded on November 1, 1963. It was a member of the MBS, or Mutual Broadcasting System. It was started by its present owner, Howard Bill, who is now a veteran in the radio business and still going strong at nearly 80 years of age.

In the early 1960s, when the Federal Communications Commission loosened up all their regulations, immediately in addition to our three AM stations, we had four more FM stations. There was KROC FM, at 106.9. KWEB began an FM at 101.7 in the spring of 1965, under the call letters KNCV (North Central Video), and Tom Jones started KNXR FM on December 24, 1965, under the corporate umbrella of the United Audio Corporation. KWWK, the FM for KOLM AM radio, came on July 4, 1967. They called that one "KWWK (pronounced 'quick') Country."

It wasn't long before there was a community college station. Rochester Community College founded KRPR FM 89.9 in 1976 under the direction and guidance of James Kehoe. He was an instructor in journalism and psychology at the college, and he did a good job getting young folks involved in running the station. Today, he continues to teach journalism and does counselling at RCTC, although he is no longer associated with KRPR.

Christian radio started in 1981 when KFSI FM 92.9 was founded by the Reverend Ray Logan. The station's call letters stand for Faith Sound, Inc.

In 1974, Minnesota Public Radio came on at KLSE FM 91.7. About 15 years later, in 1989, MPR added a news channel, KZSE FM 90.7.

When Steve Moravec became the owner of KWEB on May 1, 1978, KNCV FM was renamed KRCH (short for Rochester). Don Seehafer, from Wausau, Wisconsin, bought the stations on January 1, 1983. He discovered that too many people were confused when it came to filling out Arbitron surveys. They didn't know what station they were listening to. Was it

KROC or was it KRCH? So in 1988, he decided to change the station's name. Manager Bob Jung came up with the name "Laser 101." Then we would say, "Laser 101 is KRCH." That word really caught on, and to this day everything is "laser, laser, laser."

In the spring of 1993, KROC radio established KYBA FM 105.3 in Stewartville, and they called it Y-105.

In late 1992, Don Seehafer sold KWEB AM 1270 and Laser 101 to Bob Ingstad Broadcasting, from North Dakota. Under Bob Ingstad, the KWEB family of stations expanded still further. He started KMFX FM 102.5, licensed to Lake City, on March 12, 1993. There was a station then in Wabasha called KWMB AM 1190. It was also purchased by Bob Ingstad and became KMFX AM. Bob Ingstad also started and owned KNFX FM 104.3 in Spring Valley. KNFX AM 970 in Austin had been KQAQ, owned by an Iowa corporation, when it took over KLER's abandoned frequency in 1961. Bob Ingstad Broadcasting acquired it in 1993, and renamed it KNFX in 1995. So in addition to KWEB and Laser 101, Bob Ingstad owned four other stations: KMFX FM in Lake City, KMFX AM in Wabasha, KNFX FM in Spring Valley and KNFX AM in Austin.

Bob Ingstad sold the KWEB family of stations in 1998 to Cumulus Broadcasting. The Spring Valley station was sold to Jeff and Mike Borgen, owners of KFIL in Preston. On October 2, 2000, all five stations — KWEB, Laser 101, KMFX FM, KMFX-AM and KNFX AM — were purchased by the current owners, Clear Channel Broadcasting, based at San Antonio, Texas. It is these stations that I sell for today. KWEB, KNFX and Wabasha 1190 (all AM stations) became KFAN Radio, a Minnesota-based sports network from KFAN 1130 in the Twin Cities, on July 29, 2002.

Another station started by Howard Bill in recent years is KLCX FM 107.7. It is broadcast here in Rochester, but it's licensed to St. Charles. They call it CD-107. It opened on April 1, 1998.

Today there are 15 radio stations in Rochester. There are also three television stations. KTTC television, Channel 10, is owned by Quincy Newspapers Inc. of Quincy, Illinois. KROC television was established in

1953 and sold to Quincy owners Tom and Dave Oakley, who renamed it KTTC, in 1977. The station opened three miles west of Rochester on highway 14, then for 35 years was located at 1st Avenue and 6th Street Southwest. It recently acquired the Warner Brothers network affiliation whose programs are shown on cable channel 18. Austin's station KAAL-TV, Channel 6, was also established 1953. KXLT, Fox 47, was founded by John Ganahl in January 1998. Its studio is on Bandel Road on Rochester's far northwest side. Shockley Broadcasting Company L.L.C., KXLT's current owner, recently worked out a cooperative agreement with KTTC to share facilities. FCC regulations prevent the sale of KXLT to KTTC, but do not exclude joint operations. Both of these television stations are now located at the Fox 47 building on Bandel Road in Rochester.

And then, of course, we can receive all the cable television network. Our local cable service, which is now Charter Communications, was named Able Cable when it started in 1958. It's gone through a number of name changes during the years, too.

A powerhouse radio station that started in 1948 in Faribault was KDHL, at 920 on the dial. The DHL stood for the three owners at the time, Palmer Dragston, Jack Hyde, and Herb Lee, from LaCrosse, Wisconsin — Dragston, Hyde and Lee, DHL. It was a great farm station, and still is. As I said earlier, Tom Bachrach came from there. Judd Jacobson worked for them for a while. Longtime farm director Dean Curtis was there. The station quickly became established as a center for sports and old time music, as well as a lot of farm programs.

A man named Obed Samuel Borgen (we called him Obie for short) made quite a mark on radio in this area. Obie died unexpectedly in St. Paul on July 26, 1999, but his sons carry on the business. Obie had been a television sales person with KROC in 1958. A short time later, he went to KWEB radio, where he was general manager from December 8, 1960 through 1964. In 1965, he left and opened up a station in Preston. We all sort of laughed at that, because who's going to go to Preston? Well, he had the idea that you didn't need a big city around you if you served an area, and he was right. His station reached out a long distance. The Borgens have done very well at that Preston station, KFIL AM 1060 on the dial. They expanded and now have an FM there, and in recent years they've purchased the Spring Valley station, which we had owned as KNFX FM 104.3. They renamed it KOOL-104, put up more transmitters, and cover more area. Obie Borgen was responsible for starting the Wabasha station, KWMB, and others. Eventually he started a station in the Twin Cities.

At the time of Obie's death, his son Greg was managing the family's stations in the Twin Cities, WMNN (News Network) AM 1330 (radio news) and WDGY AM 630 in St. Paul. In Preston, sons Mike and Jeff Borgen are in charge. They've done a good job in radio, covering a lot of southern Minnesota and northern Iowa.

It's interesting how these stations got their names. In KROC, of course, the ROC stands for Rochester. KRCH (now Laser 101) was the same thing, which is why people used to get them mixed up. Austin has KAUS — AUS for Austin. Mankato had one called KTOE and another called KYSM. In Winona, when they started KWNO, WNO was for Winona. Winona also had another station called KAGE, owned by Jerry Pappenfus, and he called it "Cagey." Sometimes they just put special monikers on these stations. Where I started, in Red Wing, KAAA ("Radio's First Call") was established in 1949 and changed to KCUE ("Your cue for better listening") in 1956. Later, in approximately 1990, they established an FM station called KWNG — the WNG standing for Wing: K-Wing. Albert Lea has KATE, called "Kate." Those were the original AMs. They've had so many FMs during the years that I can't even begin to keep up on those.

The 30th Annual Eagles Cancer Telethon in 1983 as Host Bernie Lusk presents a plaque commemorating the millionth dollar given to research to Dr. Charles Moertel of Mayo Clinic.

Curt Curtis, Rochester, Minnesota & Smoke Along the Track. This was the record shuck for those two songs by this local KROC announcer in 1966.

The Harcundahl Express Bus . . . a popular KWEB morning radio program from 7-9 am featuring the team of newsman John Harwick (Har), Sports director, Carl Cunningham (Cun) and announcer John Dahl (Dahl). It was an entertaining and hilarious two hours, complete with bus air brakes and horn. 1985-86.

KWEB *Radio*
Invites you to attend

COMMUNITY CLUB AWARDS

A CONTINENTAL BREAKFAST
AT THE
RAMADA INN
1625 SOUTH BROADWAY
ROCHESTER, MN 55902
MONDAY, NOVEMBER 23, 1987 10:00 AM

In 1987 & 1988, KWEB conducted the Community Club Awards with kick-off Continental Breakfast at the Ramada Inn

Community Club Awards Breakfast at the Ramada Inn. At right, John Dahl (with beard) and I assist in registration of the participating businesses. Nov. 23, 1987.

Preparation for the Olmsted Co. fair noon day KWEB broadcast in 1987. John Harwick adjusts Marti Unit antenna . . . then will do the noon news at picnic table where John Dahl and I are ready to do weather, sports and "live" interview with Richard Badger, Jr. of the Beef Producers.

Harley & announcer Julie Grabow on Golf cart to do more Olmsted Co. Fair broadcasts from 1 til 9 pm each day, 1987.

Harley ready to MC 1982 KWEB Wedding Show at the Kahler Heritage Hall, March 20, 1982.

January 1984 KWEB Wedding Show at the Kahler with entire Management & Sales Staff. From L-R: Craig Bomgars, Eng., Chuck Mahlman, Judy Anderson, Janet Baxter, Sue Besch, Office Mgr., Harley Flathers, Marijoyce Carpenter, James Giebel, Gen. Mgr. and Marie Hlava, Receptionist. (Back when AM Radio was "King".)

Moment 16

It's Not All Radio, Folks
Chatfield's Mighty Brass Band

Chatfield, Minnesota, has been famous for its music for a lot of years. All the years I was growing up, there used to be occasional summer parades, and it seemed there was always a home town band or two. But in October 1969, the late Jim Perkins, who was an attorney in Chatfield, started the Chatfield Brass Band. Jim Perkins was a great promoter who really loved music. He spent so much time walking and talking bands, it left a real impression on everyone. It seemed he hardly had time enough left over to do any law practice, and yet he was a good attorney.

Jim Perkins was a French horn player, and he started by inviting all the musicians who lived nearby, who simply wanted to play in a band again, to come and join him. When he started the band, he had been out of high school for about fifteen years, so he was probably between 33 and 34 years old — he graduated about five years after I did from Chatfield High, where he played in the school band.

Not only did he form the Chatfield Brass Band, but he also managed to get various grants to start the Chatfield Music Lending Library. He put letters in various periodicals, saying, "We will accept your sheet music that you no longer use." And they started receiving boxes and boxes of stored treasures — sheet music, perhaps even some old records — so much that the building that they built to store it in was overflowing, and it was a big building. But through the Green Thumb, a government-sponsored senior service organization, and various other groups volunteering, they were able to get most of it catalogued. People would call and say, "Can you send me this or this?" They had music coming and going all the time, and still do, over thirty years later.

Jim Perkins would go to conferences all over the country, sitting in with the musicians and band leaders, talking band music. During those years, he brought back many great band masters to play with the Chatfield Brass Band. There was Meredith Willson, and Merle Evans, long-time bandmaster for the Ringling Brothers Barnum and Bailey Circus. Jim Perkins died at age 54 on December 25, 1990, of a heart attack, but he left a lasting impression on Chatfield, both with the Chatfield Brass Band and with the Chatfield Music Lending Library.

I became closely associated with the Chatfield Brass Band myself in 1970, when Jim Perkins asked me to come down to Chatfield and emcee three band concerts a year. He knew I appreciated band music. We would do one in the spring, one in the summer, and a Veteran's Day program in November. We did this for several years, and he would manage to underwrite my cost of $35 with grants from People's Gas of Chatfield, or various other businesses. He had great support from the Chatfield community, and to this day, the band has extensive support by people from all over. Some of them are getting along in years, but the band program gives young folk a chance to get involved, too, and to do a series of summer band concerts.

The band plays in a lot of parades. They've acquired a beautiful band wagon, and now whenever the Chatfield Brass Band takes part in a parade anywhere in this area, they are an impressive sight. That big wagon is painted up just like a circus band wagon. It's pulled along by a tractor or a pickup, and it has become a special part of any celebration.

I have taken part in several of the Chatfield Brass Band's circus concerts. The first was on Friday, April 28, 1972. Three of us musical saw players — Bob Thompson, the Rev. Samuel Cook, and myself — performed, accompanied by Carol (Mrs. Harland) Johnson on the piano. No, we didn't play circus music on our saws, but the brass band, directed by Vernon Anderson, did.

The band has gone through a number of different conductors. Clarence Arsers, the Chatfield High School band director from 1933 until 1954, was a guest director occasionally. Clarence was well respected. You could not talk about Chatfield then without having Clarence Arsers mentioned. Finally, he and his family moved to Maryland. He had three sons who played in the Navy Band — the Navy Band — Ken, John and Sam Arsers. I went to school with Ken, who was a year older than I, and Sam was a year younger. We were all great friends during those years.

H. Leroy Lidstrom was another director of the Chatfield Brass Band for many years. Lid, as we called him, had been a band man here in Rochester at John Marshall High School, and was also well respected. He has since died.

The Chatfield Brass Band is near and dear to me, and it's still going strong. The present director, Carmen Narveson, shares her duties with Curtis Peterson.

The people of Chatfield are always ready to work and to play. They hold several Thursday night summer concerts in the Chatfield park. In 1999, the town built a new band shell. The old band shell that was built back probably in the 1920s was torn down and replaced, because it was too small. I remember doing narration in that old band shell in the park in 1970, and there was hardly room enough for me to be up there with the musicians. It was just an open shell, with a set of concrete steps and a concrete block wall around it. Still, it was better than some little city bandstands, and the new one is even finer and more spacious. Recently, they've been able to build a tourist information center, too — both within a little one-block square in Chatfield's City Park. All this has been financed by donations over the years. People give $5 or $10 or $50, or somebody dies and they put memorials toward it. It's gratifying to see what has happened in that little Chatfield City Park.

Meindert Zylstra and the Chatfield Music Lending Library

Following the death of Jim Perkins in 1990, Meindert Zylstra and his wife Wilma stepped in to carry on the massive task of sorting, indexing, shipping out and receiving complete or partial scores of band music from all over the world for the Chatfield Music Lending Library. With some assistance from Green Thumb volunteers, who are paid on a part-time basis, the library not only survived Jim Perkins' death, it flourishes. Meindert and Wilma have acquired four computers to facilitate the library's services.

If you've ever attended a Chatfield Brass Band concert, you've likely seen Meindert in the horn section. At the age of 78, he is the only remaining charter member of the band still playing today.

Meindert was born in Holland. He has two middle names: the first is "music" and the second is "work." One of his sisters immigrated to America and settled in the little village of Hamilton, Minnesota, south of Racine. After some correspondence, she convinced the rest of the family — seventeen in all — to come to America in 1952, and helped the boys to find work as hired men on area farms.

In 1953, Meindert married Wilma. They bought the Will Anderson farm, on highway 74 southwest of Chatfield in Fillmore County, in 1964. (This is the same Will Anderson who appears in the shivaree story in an earlier part of this book.) Meindert and Wilma are still active farmers to this day, in addition to the three days a week that they spend working at the Music Lending Library. Meindert says he has no plans to retire. Why should he? His father, Herman Zylstra, is 105 and still going strong down in Sheldon, Iowa.

Merle Evans, Circus Bandmaster (1891-1987)

I'd like to say a little more about Merle Evans, who was bandmaster for the Ringling Brothers Barnum & Bailey Circus for fifty years. Born in Columbus, Kansas, on December 26, 1891, he began his musical career at the age of ten, and by 13 was conducting the band for his uncle Josh Spruceby's melodramas. He played in minstrel and medicine shows before joining the circus band, and later claimed that he had done everything musically except grand opera. In 1969, he retired from Ringling Brothers, and lived in Sarasota, Florida, until his death on December 31, 1987, at the age of 96.

Chatfield Brass Band founder Jim Perkins loved circus history, and knew that the Ringling Brothers Circus had appeared in Chatfield often through the early 1900s. Jim contacted Merle, who came to Chatfield and appeared several times with the Chatfield Brass Band. At his first appearance, on May 17, 1974, I acted as emcee and "ringmaster," which required my blowing a whistle at high pitch between the various numbers. All 800 seats were filled, and another 100 people stood to hear that annual spring concert of the Chatfield Brass Band conducted by Merle Evans.

He returned on April 30, 1976, and I did an extended stage interview with him at that time. He was then 83 years old. I recently listened again to that tape, made 26 years ago, as Merle recalled some of the perils associated with circus life. He spoke of the great Hartford, Connecticut, "Big Top" fire on July 6, 1944, that claimed 169 lives and caused many injuries. The circus big top tent was destroyed, and performances for the rest of the season had to be held in ball parks. Ringling Brothers Circus was hit by $4 million in lawsuits as a result of that fire. He also talked about occasional train wrecks, and times when high winds would blow the big top down, and those high supporting tent poles would come crashing down on audience and performers alike. He praised the late, great Karl King, from Fort Dodge, Iowa, who wrote music that "all could play."

The following day, May 1, 1976, Merle Evans was on hand to help "christen" the new Chatfield Brass Band wagon, which was parked in front of the Tam-O-Shanter Inn (that we had known during the years when I went to Chatfield High as the Chatfield Hotel). Later, he conducted a concert on the stage in Potter Auditorium, where I had graduated from high school 25 years before.

His final appearance with the Chatfield Brass Band was at the American Band Conference held on April 23-25, 1987, in Chatfield. One hundred people registered for the three-day conference, and over 400 musicians played at various times during the festival. On Thursday night, April 23, Merle Evans led the band in his famous circus routine in a concert at

Apache Mall. The conference finale, a John Philip Sousa concert, was held on Saturday, April 25, at the Potter Auditorium in Chatfield. Four conductors took turns conducting: Merle Evans, Herbert Schultz, Keith House and Paul Yoder (a longtime conductor-arranger). At the end of the concert, a representative of Minnesota Governor Rudy Perpich presented several plaques. One was awarded to Jim Perkins, for his efforts in bringing the conference to Minnesota, and another to the Chatfield Brass Band for hosting the conference. Merle Evans was presented with a certificate proclaiming April 25, 1987 as Merle Evans Day in Minnesota.

Merle Evans, who was known as the Toscanini of the Big Top, conducted band clinics at schools in Chatfield and at various service clubs in Rochester. At the time of his death, he was serving on the board of directors of the Chatfield Brass Band.

When Merle Evans died, the world lost a gentleman, a humorist, an educator, a talented performer and most of all, a friend. He was a warm individual who touched the lives of millions, including mine.

Music in Rochester

Rochester Civic Music began when Harold Cooke was asked in 1919 by the Mayo brothers, Dr. Will and Dr. Charlie, to become conductor of the Rochester Park Band, and later a Rochester Symphony Orchestra. He founded the Rochester Male Chorus in 1930. Harold Cooke left Rochester in 1934 to become a member of the faculty at Stout Institute in Menominie, Wisconsin, but he returned in 1949 to resume the job of director of the Rochester Civic Music Program and continued to hold that position until 1963.

Rochester Civic Music, the Rochester Civic Theater, the Rochester Arts Center were all first supported by the Mayos. Then, as time went on, the city took over, and today our city tax dollar helps pay for all these things. They get a certain amount of funding from the city, and then depend on grants, memberships, ticket sales and donations the rest of the way.

During the 1930s and 1940s, thousands attended concerts in Rochester's Mayo Park. In addition to concerts directed by Harold Cooke, the work of prominent Rochester composer Orvis Ross was often presented. According to his obituary, which appeared in the Post-Bulletin on January 29, 1979, Ross's career in the arts brought him friendships with such famous people as Percy Grainger and author Henry Miller. I interviewed Orvis Ross on both KROC and KNXR radio during the 1960s and 1970s. He was a very warm individual, a longtime piano teacher and a composer of international reputation. In fact, it was said by some who knew him well that his music was better known in Europe than in Rochester. His opera about the life of children, "The Crescent Moon," was performed here at one of those concerts in the park.

From 1965 to 1975, Orvis Ross and Mary Ellen Malkasian performed an annual duo piano concert that was a highlight of Rochester's music year. After teaching vocal music in Rochester's public schools for eighteen years, Mrs. Malkasian continues to volunteer after school hours, still doing what she loves to do — teaching middle school children to sing. How wonderful it would be if, just once more, we could hear one of those Ross-Malkasian concerts on a Sunday evening at the Arts Center!

In 1962, Harold Cooke asked me to come and emcee the Civic Music Band's Fourth of July band concert at Silver Lake.

I said, "Well, sure." I was honored.

He said, "We will have Merle Evans as our guest conductor." So when Merle Evans came to Rochester in 1962, that was the first time I met him, and we talked a little bit. He was just a delightful person. I was working for KROC radio then, but I don't believe we broadcast that particular concert.

That was how I started emceeing concerts. It seems that Harold Cooke took a liking to me. The following summer, he contacted me again. He apparently had been listening to me on KROC in the morning. In those days, I was on the air, "full of wim and wigor," from 5 or 5:30 am until the shift ended at 9.

One morning Harold Cooke came over to the second floor studio in the 100 First Avenue building and said, "Harley, I'd like to have you start doing the commentary for the summer Sunday night band concerts in Mayo Park."

I replied, "Well, Harold, I know nothing about this. I know very little about symphonic music, or band music."

He said, "I will help you." Those were his words: "I will help you." Now, here's how he "helped" me: he gave me a little three by five card with the songs that they were going to play that Sunday night written on it — the name of the piece, what it was, whether it was a piece of an opera, or a band composition, and who it was by. And he didn't say any more than that.

So I'd take the card and go up to the library, and I would cram for a couple of hours. And, you know, that was some of the best education I could get. I would put the information together, and introduce the music. By then we had it set up that we were broadcasting these concerts on KROC.

That was in 1963. We usually did about nine concerts each summer on Sunday evenings, from the middle of June until the second Sunday in August. I liked that, because I was getting paid 25 big dollars per concert.

Harold retired as director of Rochester Civic Music in 1963. Then he said, "Before I retire, I want to announce that we're going to form a boys' choir." Now, he was already conducting the Rochester Male Chorus, which appeared maybe once during the summer concerts, and a lot of other places year-round. It has been rewarding to see, over the years, Rochester's Male Chorus become great ambassadors for Rochester, singing at the World's Fair, making international trips. Harold Cooke went with them in some of the earlier years.

But Harold said, "Now we're going to start a boys' choir, a Rochester Boy Choir, for boys from about 8 through 14 years of age." And it really took off, because they had the mothers behind it. The mothers got together and created identical vests and hats, little tams, for the boys to wear. It was a lively group, and it continues till this day. Of course, the boys that started out in 1963 have grown up now, but a number of them have moved right on into the Male Chorus. That was Harold Cooke's plan.

So even though he'd retired, Harold continued directing both the Boy Choir and the Rochester Male Chorus for several more years. He would come back frequently, too, for a guest concert appearance. The last time he did that was on July 4, 1974, and I emceed that concert, which was held as usual at Silver Lake Park. But eventually he had to slow down. Harold Cooke, Rochester's "Mr. Music," died unexpectedly of a heart attack at Methodist Hospital on October 11, 1974, at age 80.

I was still doing the Silver Lake July 4th concerts. I emceed them from 1962 until 1983, a little over twenty years. Then Jere Lantz came and started conducting, and he took over the master of ceremonies duties. I hated to give it up. It had become just a part of my life, being there July 4th to emcee the patriotic concert just before the fireworks.

After Harold Cooke retired, Gerhard Schroth was conductor from 1964 to 1966, followed by Henry Charles Smith, a dynamic person, from 1967 to 1968. From 1969 to 1974, Thomas Lewis was the conductor. He was succeeded by Ron Stoffel, from 1975 to 1976, Wolfgang Balzer, from 1977 to 1980, and Jere Lantz, from spring 1980 to the present. Wolfgang Balzer married Cynthia Fiksdal of the Fiksdal Flowers family, and they now live in Germany.

On the evening of May 6, 1964, Henry Mancini gave a concert indoors at the Mayo Civic Auditorium. There were two conductors that night: Gerhard Schroth and Henry Mancini. "Mancini Sound in Concert Success After One Rehearsal," read the headline of Bob Oudal's review the next day, May 7, in the Post-Bulletin. Oudal reported that a crowd of 3500 witnessed the impressive spectacle of this famous musical personality "deliberately submitting himself to public exposure and risking the loss of a thoroughly developed image" by directing the Rochester Symphony Orchestra in a concert with only one rehearsal. Mancini praised the performers, and spared no words in complimenting the Rochester Symphony. After all, the musicians hadn't had the opportunity to perform in the Mancini style before that rehearsal.

Bob Oudal's review went on to say that, after my opening comments as emcee, Gerhard Schroth made an immediate impact with a "virile performance" of the opening number, the prelude to Act III of "Lohengrin" by Richard Wagner. Then Mancini directed "The Baby Elephant Walk," "Moon River," music from "Breakfast At Tiffany's" and David Rose's "The

Stripper." A standing ovation closed the evening, and Oudal reported that "The whole evening was first-rate entertainment."

I recall one Sunday evening band concert held on July 23, 1967, at the Mayo Park Band Shell, an old wooden shell that had been used by many bands and conductors over the years. I introduced Dorothy Combs, a woman with a marvelous soprano voice who had recently moved to Rochester from St. Louis, Missouri, with her husband, Dr. Joe Combs, and their children. Dorothy was a graduate of Duke University, and the first female soloist to tour with the Duke Men's Glee Club. She sang three delightful songs that Sunday night, accompanied by the Rochester Symphony Band under the direction of Henry Charles Smith — the spiritual "Sweet Little Jesus Boy," Handel's "How Beautiful Upon the Mountain," and an Irish tune, "The Kerry Dance."

Dorothy quickly became involved in the Rochester music scene, and in 1969 — the 50th year of Rochester Civic Music — she came up with the idea of having a full week of musical events, a Rochester Music Week, running for six days from October 6-11. She began stirring up the community, and once the word spread, folks started volunteering to help. She never asked anyone for a penny to fund the event, although she did "comb" the car dealers for a car to give away as a door prize at the final concert, performed by Victor Borge, the "clown prince of music," at the Mayo Civic Auditorium on October 11 at 8 pm. Joe Adamson from Adamson Motors, then located across from the YMCA downtown, agreed to supply the car, a 1964 Chrysler Newport with air conditioning and power steering. Pepsi Cola created a "mini-soda" drink in small cups for spectators at the parade and concerts.

The parade, held at 10:30 am on Saturday, had 100 units marching from Soldiers Field to Silver Lake. Gene Eiden, Lourdes High School band and choral director, was the parade chairman. Unit #15 in the parade featured Dorothy Combs, chair of Music Week, riding on a rocking chair. Her float was pulled by the car that Adamson Motors had donated.

Musical performances of all sorts filled six days and nights. There were organ concerts by Bob Scoggin, a "Battle of the Bands," a teen dance at Mayo Civic Auditorium, a big street dance outside the old City Hall on 1st Avenue Southwest, and a concert at the beautiful St. Mary's Hospital Auditorium in which a congregation of choral groups all sang the finale together as a massed chorus.

There was also a contest for a special song written for Rochester. Starting April 11, I was assigned the promotion of that event, to secure song entries. Two dozen entries came in. Thomas Lewis, who had taken over as conductor of the Rochester Civic Music program that year, agreed to head up a team of judges who would select the winning song. The winner was Mrs. Bruce Anderson from Edina, Minnesota, with a song entitled "Rochester, My Home." It was sung on Tuesday of that week by the massed chorus at St. Marys Auditorium, as part of an 8 pm concert called "Sounds of Our Town," directed by Thomas Lewis. As fine as Mrs. Anderson's song was, I don't believe that it has ever been used again in local concerts.

I introduced Mrs. Anderson at Victor Borge's final concert at Mayo Civic Auditorium and presented her with her $250 prize check during the concert intermission. Alas, Victor Borge is gone now, as are so many of those fine entertainers I met and introduced at those music programs.

A Concert With A U.N. Flavor

Some may recall attending the 1961 United Nations Day program in Rochester's Mayo Civic Auditorium. The keynote speaker that night was Mrs. Franklin Delano Roosevelt. Dr. Charles (Chuck) Mayo, who had been long involved in U.N. activities, introduced her. Eleanor Roosevelt was actively involved with the U.N. from its beginnings in 1945 until her death a year after her Rochester appearance.

This was before the Rochester Civic Music program got me involved in musical presentations large and small. That night I was only a spectator. It was a Sunday evening, October 22, 1961. Harold Cooke conducted the Rochester Symphony Orchestra and several choral groups, including the Rochester Male Chorus, the Rochester Oratorio Society, and the St. Mary's and Methodist-Kahler Student Nurses' Chorus. (This was back when nurses still wore those beautiful white caps, which I still adore.) In this program, dedicated to the United Nations, Mr. Cooke led the singers through a work by William Simon called "The United Nations Charter" and "The Last Words of David" by Randall Thompson. The orchestra played Morton Gould's "Latin-American Symphonette." For the finale, the chorus and orchestra performed Howard Hanson's "Song of Democracy," a setting of a poem by Walt Whitman.

Symphony At Sundown

Back in the 1960s, long before Rochester Civic Music began its popular summer series, "Down By the Riverside," we had a period of Sunday night concerts in Mayo Park called "Symphony at Sundown." They began the year following Harold Cooke's retirement, and I believe that the name was dreamed up by the music board and its new conductor, Gerhard Schroth. The first concert was presented by the Rochester Symphony Band on July 12, 1964.

When the "Symphony At Sundown" concerts began, we were using a new sound system. Bob Oudal, writing for the Post-Bulletin, reviewed the first concert, composed of band music that leaned somewhat toward the classics — "The Bombasto March," "The Royal Fireworks Suite" by Handel, "The Ballet for Young Americans," and as a finale, "Thunder and Blazes." His headline read, "Sound System at Concert Seems Promising. More Audience Needed for Symphony at Sundown."

Bob wrote such nice words in his Post-Bulletin column on Monday, July 13, about my part of the program that I'm almost embarrassed to repeat them — but here goes: "The congenial voice of Harley Flathers was present to provide verbal continuity to the program, which for the first time was making use of a new sound system. With microphone in hand, Flathers was very much at home, and he emphasized the importance of involving the audience in making efforts to evaluate this new system."

Kal Chafoulias and the Beaux Arts Ball

We were blessed with some excellent guests on the "Rog and Harley Show" on KROC in 1971 — names like Jack Paar, Corrie TenBoom, Wes Fesler, and Frank Leahy, the former Notre Dame football coach. I actually taped a visit with him at St. Mary's Hospital.

The success we had in getting this continuous string of great guests was due in large part to a young lady named Kal Chafoulias. She really knew what was happening in our community, and who the visitors were that had name recognition. She set up numerous radio interviews for us, or else gave us a tip on whom we should call. Kal really loved her community — as the Chafoulias family has for decades. Her brother Gus Chafoulias, and his son Andy, continue literally to build our city. Gus's wife Ann was the chairperson of Rochester's 125th anniversary celebration in 1983.

Kal Chafoulias and I were involved in the planning and broadcasting of two popular fund-raising events for the Rochester Art Center in 1971 and 1972. This grandiose event was the Beaux Arts Ball, a real crowd pleaser, held at the Mayo Civic Auditorium. The 1972 event, held on Saturday evening, May 6th, had as its theme "Riverboat Ramble." Jazz and Dixieland music filled the dance floor from 9 pm until 1 am. Dancers in "riverboat" attire were entertained by two fine bands: Doc Evans, and Les Fields' Turkey River All-Stars. Doc Evans was internationally known in Dixieland and jazz circles. After graduating from high school in West Concord, Minnesota, he went on to Carleton College, receiving his degree in 1929. When he played for the Beaux Arts Ball, he was conductor of the Bloomington Symphony Orchestra. Les Fields, originally from Cresco, Iowa, was rising rapidly with the band he started in 1968 for a last-minute Christmas party. Playing with his All-Stars that night was Lowell Schreyer, a banjo player of national renown, who was at that time associated with Mankato State College as director of its news bureau and teacher of music. Lowell had been playing since 1934.

The auditorium was decorated with silver streamers to create the illusion of a starry night over a replica of a riverboat. In her review in the Post-

Bulletin on May 8, 1972, Pauline Walle said, "Walking in twos and threes from a social hour at the Art Center, 'The Saints Came Marching In' to Mayo Auditorium Arena, led by the Stars of Dixie, who climbed aboard a gigantic showboat. Reflecting several generations along the great river, dancers wore flouncy Southern belle ball gowns, poke bonnets and calico, the garb of river gamblers. But the greatest showpieces were the selections by Les Fields' Turkey River All-Stars and Doc Evans. At one time there were five banjos in the band shell, including Lowell Schreyer. The new sound belonged to Eddie Tolck with jazz vibes from St. Paul."

This dazzling evening might compare to another annual event held by the Rochester Civic Music from the early 1980s to 1988, called "The Party." The Party was held at Apache Mall, which gave volunteers a lot of room after the stores closed to decorate. Then the doors would open at 8 pm and the fun lasted until nearly midnight, with bands and combos of all sizes, including the Turkey River All-Stars and the 37th Street Gold. Guests paid good money to enjoy the evening, and the Civic Music benefited.

Oh, the fun of these great fund raisers!

The Rochester Area Council for the Arts

Tom Lewis, conductor of the Rochester Civic Music programs from 1969 to 1974, was the one who really got the Rochester Arts Council started. As I recall, he sent out a note saying, "We need a Rochester Arts Council. A bunch of us who are interested will meet Sunday afternoon at the Congregational Church."

It was a Sunday in January 1970, and I was among those who came. I was still covering all these things on the radio and doing commentary at the concerts. Even though I was at KNXR from 1968 to 1971, I was still involved in the various city music programs.

Tom said, "Here's what we need. We've got so many artistic events going on in any one given night in Rochester that we need to have a master calendar. We need to have people who'll take care of this."

So we formed the Rochester Arts Council. Founded in 1970, it was officially chartered in 1972 and continued until late 1997. It's official purpose was to coordinate and encourage cultural activities in the Rochester Area. It supported cooperative planning, research and public education programs that encouraged participation and appreciation for the arts.

A number of folks served on the board — some volunteered, some were appointed. Usually there was one person representing each organization: the Arts Center, the theater, the high school theaters, the Rochester Male Chorus, the Chatfield Brass Band, and so on. The first board of directors probably had fifteen people on it. And then, of course, we had to have a president. Each year we'd elect a new president.

I was the third president of the Rochester Area Council for the Arts (RACA), as it was called, from 1972 to 1973. And I was the last president from 1995 to 1997, before we decided to abolish the Arts Council. By that time, we had accomplished what we were formed to do — to encourage artists and artistic groups to perform, to inform the community about their existence, and to help them to build their own financial base so that they could grow.

During its early years, the Arts Council went through some real growing pains. These are things you don't forget. I became very well acquainted with what it means to get your 501-C3 designation from the State of Minnesota, meaning you are tax exempt. Fortunately we had a young man named Tom Elkins, an attorney, who was a great help. Tom and his sister Joan Elkins were good people, as were their parents, all of them very actively involved in community activities.

The presidents of RACA were:

1971	Dick Husband	1982-83	Tutti Sherlock
1972	Dr. Stan Lovestedt	1984	Carole Shulman
1973	Harley Flathers	1985	Beryl Byman
1974	John McCally	1986	Kathryn Kalahan
1975	Mrs. Mary Barnes	1987	Shirley Hill
1976	Carl Schroedel	1988-89	Dr. Joe Duffy
1977	Ardell Brede	1990	Connie Maragos

1978	Matthew McConnell	1991-92	Dr. Vivita Leonard
1979	Lynn Williamson Didier	1993	Sally Duffy
1980	David R. Slone	1994	Todd Wilkening
1981	Lynn Williamson Didier	1995-97	Harley Flathers

SEMRAC - Southeastern Minnesota Regional Arts Council

In 1973, while we were getting the Rochester Arts Council set up, the Minnesota State Arts Council, under executive director Dean Myre, moved to organize regional development commissions. In each region, there would be a series of things that needed to be addressed. One of the reasons we had such strength in Rochester was because Anne Marie Plunkett, who sat in on the Rochester Arts Council, had earlier been appointed to a seat on the state arts board. Anne Marie was the wife of Richard Plunkett, of the Rochester State Bank on the Miracle Mile, now known as Rochester Bank. Anne Marie Plunkett convinced the Minnesota Arts Board to divide the state into eleven regions, under the newly-formed Regional Development Commission. Eight southeast Minnesota counties (expanding two years later to eleven) made up Region 10. It was her dream that the arts could be developed outside the Twin Cities' metropolitan area through the use of regional councils which could receive block grants of Minnesota legislative dollars to be shared with art groups in each region's counties.

Anne Marie saw what I was doing in my endeavors for the Rochester Arts Council, really promoting it, trying to get the story out. One day in 1973, she said, "Harley, we need a person to be the executive of this regional arts council. Why don't you put in your name for it, before the board?" So I did, and they appointed me as executive director of SEMRAC, the Southeast Minnesota Regional Arts Council. And I've always been grateful to her for hand-picking me for that job.

It was a part-time paid position. I started getting very much involved, making trips to the Twin Cities and sitting in on some of the quarterly meetings of the state arts board, which I didn't really enjoy. I didn't want the politics of it. I wanted to have them say, "Just go ahead and do it," and then let me do it. I was executive director for four years, from the middle of 1973 until the autumn of 1977, and I enjoyed it very much. It was another learning experience. When I started in 1973, our SEMRAC arts budget was $25,000 annually. Today, it's $400,000, funded by the Minnesota Legislature and the McKnight Foundation.

I recall one New Year's Day, sitting in front of the TV, watching Bowl games and trying to sift out three different mailing lists — from the Civic Theater, the Civic Music program, and the Arts Center — to make a new mailing list for the Rochester Arts Council's new quarterly newsletter. Every three months, we would come out with a line-up of events taking place all over the city. Becky Meredith was the newsletter's editor the first year. After that, I wrote up the newsletter myself or assisted others.

For a number of years, from 1973 to 1976, I would get the events together, type up the schedule, go down to the Johnson Printing Company on 1st Avenue Southwest to have it printed, proofing it, and then put it into bulk mailing (we got a bulk mailing permit). I would take the flyers to the Post Office and get them mailed personally, and I didn't rest until all that was done. And as soon as one newsletter was mailed, you started on the schedule for the next three months. Little by little, other people started volunteering to help, and by 1977 we actually had a group of people that would sit down together to work on the newsletter. People would call off events that were scheduled on any given day, and I would type them in. This was before personal computers came along to make the job easier.

I was also lining up ten $50 sponsors per quarter, to pay the costs of producing the newsletter. To publish that list of events four times, I needed to find 40 businesses willing to spend $50 a year. There were many fine businesses that gave their support to the Arts Council, and we'd list them at the bottom of the sheet. We'd say, "Thanks to these people for making this page possible."

Finally, to get away from the hassle of mailing, we said, "Let's put the list in the *Post-Bulletin*." We'd fill a whole page in the Rochester *Post-Bulletin* with the upcoming events. Several times, I took that list of coming events down to the newspaper office, and they would set up the page. Then I would proof it all, and when it came out, I would heave a sigh of relief.

Pauline Walle, who covered the Arts Council for years for the *Post-Bulletin*, was very helpful. Pauline Walle was a long-time friend and supporter of the arts in Rochester. She wrote many stories on the arts, concerts, religion, exhibitions and events that were coming up, and she just did it so well. She retired on June 30, 2001, after 39 years at the *Post-Bulletin*.

SEMRAC, the South Eastern Minnesota Regional Arts Council, started out with eight counties — Goodhue, Wabasha, Dodge, Olmsted, Winona, Mower, Fillmore and Houston. In 1974-75, we added three more counties — Freeborn, Steele and Rice — for a total of eleven counties in Southeastern Minnesota. We were the nation's first regionally funded arts council.

The members of SEMRAC's first board, formed in 1973, were:

Dodge County	Nancy Agerter, rural Kasson
Fillmore County	Jim Perkins, Chatfield
Goodhue County	Marge Vogel, Red Wing
Houston County	Donn Young, Caledonia
Mower County	Ione Bell, Austin (vice chairperson)
Olmsted County	Gabor Koves, Rochester
Wabasha County	Dana Gartner, Lake City
Winona County	Jim Hanzel (chairman), Winona
At Large Members	
Mower County	Robert M. Gill, Austin
Goodhue County	Peter Leach, Dennison
Winona County	Dr. John Lucas, Winona
Advisory Panel Chairpersons	
Music	Bob Oudal, Rochester
Dance	Judy Vilter, Rochester
Theater	John McCally, Rochester
Visual	Judy Onofrio, Rochester
Legal Counsel	Tom Elkins, Rochester

State Arts Council Chairperson	Anne Marie Plunkett, Rochester
Executive Secretary	Harley Flathers, Rochester

The board met quarterly from January 1, 1973 to October 1977. I feel that we did what was needed, helping many arts groups with grant writing, publicity and moral support. We stimulated existing arts councils, fostered new ones and delivered funding to those who qualified. In fiscal years 1974 through 1976, SEMRAC received 131 grant requests, totalling $154,263. We funded 78 grant requests for a total of $65,907.63. The largest grant, for $3500, went to Lake City in 1976.

My work as executive director of SEMRAC ended in 1977. The regional development commissions were winding down, but SEMRAC continued. Today it's called SEMAC, Southeast Minnesota Arts Council. And one person here is in charge. She is Pat Alcott, who has been executive director since July 1978. It still covers the same eleven counties, and is still non-profit funded. SEMAC serves southeastern Minnesota arts even better today, with more legislative and foundation funding. I'm glad to have been a part of this arts support process during the 1970s.

Ralph "Sammy" Samuelson, The Lake Pepin Splasher

One of SEMRAC's more notable projects was a tribute to the sport of waterskiing, which began in Minnesota eighty years ago. Earlier, I had interviewed the man who made it all happen.

In the autumn of 1971, my boss, Bob Fick, asked me if I'd like to talk with Ralph Samuelson, a turkey farmer living near Pine Island. Bob told me that this might make a good interview, as "Sammy" (as he was known to his friends) was the "father of water skiing," which had started right on Lake Pepin at Lake City. So I called him, and we brought him into the studio for a series of taped interviews, which I still have.

The year was 1922, and young Ralph Samuelson was an adventurer, a kind of "barn-stormer" who had created water skis out of a couple of bent boards. They were not as streamlined as the commercial waterskis of today, but they did put him in the spotlight. First, he cut the boards into what he believed would be the right length and width. He then had to soak them for a long period of time in a tank of water to soften them up. Then he bent the skis around a wash boiler to curl the tips. Soon he had his skis ready, and was entertaining crowds along the banks of Lake Pepin in the area near the "Point." He told me he always greased the skis and the ramp before making a jump. Being towed by a motorboat with a powerful motor was best, although Sammy was even towed occasionally by an airplane. Eighty years later, Ralph Samuelson (who died in August 1977) is still remembered for his efforts in putting Lake City, Minnesota, on the map as the birthplace of water skiing.

That radio visit in 1971 took place a couple of years before SEMRAC was formed. I was executive director of SEMRAC in early autumn of 1976, when I attended the dedication of one of our funded projects in Lake City's Ohuta Park. Today, when you drive along in that park, not far from the water's edge, you can see a large bronze sculpture by Thomas Hartman, called "The Wave." It depicts a wave from Lake Pepin rising from a permanent base, and it commemorates the birth of waterskiing. This was one of our "lasting visuals," as we called them. The SEMRAC guidelines directed advisory boards to study grant requests and make decisions in the four disciplines of music, dance, theater and visual arts. From the $25,000 budget we were given by the state Arts Board, we gave this project $3500. Our own Bob Ryan, KROC television newsman, gave the keynote address at the dedication ceremony, which I was proud to attend.

Rochester's Summer Music Project

You can't talk about the Rochester arts scene without including the Summer Music Project (SMP), founded three decades ago by three young music lovers, Chuck Blattner, Lois Lenz and Henry Brommelkamp, Jr. I remember those three coming to visit me at the KNXR FM radio studios downtown in the lower level of the 16-story Sheraton Hotel (today the Holiday Inn Downtown). Excitedly, they told me of their plans, and I thought, "This is a winner!" This was in 1970, just about the time that plans were being made for the Rochester Arts Council.

Chuck Blattner was a likeable lad, full of vim and vigor and encircled with music. Born in 1950, Charles Blattner had grown up in the Rochester area. June and I had watched him as director of our Homestead Memorial Church youth choir from 1964 to 1969, and I had always thought this boy was going places. Now he felt that it would be an excellent community project to have families come together during the summer to sing.

Built on donations and family participation, the SMP brought several dozen families to sing once or twice a week at rehearsals, usually at the Congregational Church on the southwest beltline of Rochester. For eight weeks, from early June to early August, they would hold various activities, including picnics, a Twins game, a trip to Valley Fair, etc. After the final concert, everyone would go to a reception at the Congregational Church. This went on for twenty years, with the exception of 1973, when the SMP was suspended because so many young men had gone off to the Vietnam War. Chuck always asked me to emcee the final Festival Concert, usually held the second Sunday in August at the Mayo Civic Auditorium Theater, and including several choirs and a concert band. I did this for fifteen years.

I remember that on July 28, 1979, five of us played our musical saws at an SMP picnic concert on the church lawn. My mom, then aged 86, came and played the piano to lead us. In 1985 and 1986, when the Mayo Civic Center was being expanded, the final concerts were held at the Mayo High School Auditorium.

Over the years, I've interviewed Chuck Blattner many times on the radio. He directed music and choirs for about ten years in Chatfield and then returned to Rochester to lead all the choirs and orchestras at the Rochester Community and Technical College (RCTC). I've aired an hour-long Christmas concert from RCTC in recent years on December 24 and 25 on both KWEB and KNFX. Today, in addition to his college duties, Chuck conducts several choral and band concerts annually as part of Rochester Civic Music, including appearances at the summer Sunday evening Down By the Riverside Concert series.

Senior Citizens Center

The Senior Citizens Center in Rochester has been important to many of us. It has been located in the old Rochester Armory, at the corner of 2nd Street Northwest and North Broadway, since February 1979. The Senior Citizens Center was incorporated officially in 1961, and it was in other locations through the years before finally moving into its present site. Executive director Sally Gallagher has been there since 1989. She and her staff serve several hundred members annually through a variety of programs.

In 1991, Sally and her program assistant Kathy Suffrins started numerous radio programs with me, describing the happenings there. We did this on KWEB radio's "Harley's House." We would pre-tape short bits, a minute or two, about what was coming up, and we'd do a couple of these a week. We could sit down and rattle off three or four weeks' activities at a time, pre-taping them.

Later, in January 1994, we started a monthly television program on KTTC-TV Channel 10. This half-hour program for and about seniors in Rochester, northern Iowa, and western Wisconsin, continued for eight years, airing each Sunday morning at 6:30, and the following Tuesday, Wednesday and Thursday on Cable Access 10 from 6:30 to 7 pm. It officially ended on December 31, 2001.

One of the programs I did for the seniors involved a couple of hours of dance music that a friend and I had put together in 1989, called Nostalgia Productions. Ed Rucker was a former restaurant and bar owner who loved big band music. He came to me and encouraged me to invest with him on turntables, speakers, an amplifier — everything it took to set up Nostalgia Productions. We sent out flyers reading, "Nostalgia Productions proudly present Harley Flathers and his Big Band Bash for a dance." On the bottom of the flyer was the date, the time, the place and the admission, which was usually $3.

Ed loved big band music — a lot of people love big band music — but most of our audience was getting to the age where after dancing to one or two numbers, they would tire out. We made a few appearances, although I don't suppose we did over fifteen shows in the course of half a dozen years. We played several dances at the Byron American Legion and the Plainview American Legion. We provided music at the Moose Lodge New Year's Eve party one year. And we did programs at the Senior Citizens Center and Charter House. Residents of that vintage appreciate the big bands of the 1930s and the 1940s. I think we did a Valentine's Dance a couple of different times, and a Christmas Dance at the Senior Center. Now the program has gone by the wayside. It was a fun time, but it was short-lived.

The Birth of Rochesterfest

Rochesterfest began in the summer of 1983, when a group of citizens made plans for the 125th anniversary celebration of Rochester, dating back to 1858. Now, there are a couple of different theories about when Rochester actually started. History will tell you that it was 1854 when George Head came from Rochester, New York, punched a stake into South Broadway, and said, "I'll name this town Rochester." Later, in 1858, the settlement officially became a city when it was registered with the state.

Anyway, in 1983, we had a 125th anniversary celebration, and it was a terrific occasion. Many local people in different organizations participated. There was even a church night, when all the churches had activities going on. It was a week-long celebration, filled with historical events and parades.

When it was over, several people said to then-mayor Chuck Hazama, "We had so much fun. We need more of this." They decided to make it an annual event, and they called it "Rochesterfest: A Celebration of a City."

The nine to ten-day annual Rochesterfest takes place the third full week in June. It always includes a big street parade on Friday night. We've had some notable people who've served as grand marshals. In 1995, I remember, we had General William Westmoreland and a detachment of Vietnam War veterans. Another year, Jim Fowler, from the TV series "Animal Kingdom," was the grand marshal. On June 20, 2003, I was honored as the parade's grand marshal.

Everybody gets out there and gets involved. There is usually a hot-air balloon lift-off, and a lot of things for kids. Downtown, there are vendors. And on Thursday, Friday and Saturday nights, there are big street dances, where huge crowds attend and are entertained by area rock and country bands. Since 1988, we've had Country Breakfast on the Farm at a nearby dairy farm on Saturday morning from 6:30 till 11:30, and that usually attracts between 2,000 and 3,000 people.

Rochesterfest just keeps on growing. We held our 21st annual festival in 2003. Rochesterfest chairs since 1983 are:

1983	Ann Chafoulias	1993	Rick Lovett
1984	John Withers	1994	Leigh Geramanis
1985	Earl Jorgenson	1995	Bill Davis
1986	Steve Youngquist	1996	Ann & Glen Larson
1987	Joan Anderson	1997	John Wade
1988	Harry Algyer	1998	Wally Arnold
1989	Mary Lund & Tom Dyer	1999	Andy Krogstad
1990	Lora Schwartz & Steve Borchardt	2000	Ginger Holmes
		2001	Mary Kay Costello
1991	Marcia Marcoux & Steve Thompson	2002	Ann Larson & Ginger Holmes
1992	Jan Blattner & Joe Powers	2003	Greg Walters
		2004	Dennis Hanson

In 1954, while I was still at Red Wing, I would come home through Rochester on the weekend, on my way to the farm about twenty miles southeast. I remember listening to Walt Bruzek that year on the radio. Walt was a promoter, and during 1954 he was occasionally on KROC radio. He was doing the parade broadcast for the Rochester Centennial that year, and I remember thinking to myself, "Someday I'd sure like to do a Rochester parade."

During the 125th anniversary celebration, I was perched up on top of the balcony of what at that time was the Olmsted County Bank on South Broadway (later the Marquette Bank and now First Federal Bank), broadcasting the first parade for KWEB radio on August 14, 1983.

I'm happy to say that I have broadcast the description of the Rochesterfest street parades on KWEB radio every year for the past two decades. And I don't just broadcast the parade. I lay out the scripts, after the information is given to me from those who apply to be in the parade — something over 100 units. Then I contact six people who'll do the public address information along the set parade route. I arrange six public address systems, and whatever it takes to put the broadcast on the air. It gets to be a busy time for me in Rochesterfest, but it's always enjoyable working with Carole Brown, executive director of Rochesterfest, and the parade committee. I envied Walt Bruzek getting to do that Rochester centennial parade in 1954, and now 49 years later, I've broadcast about twenty parades in Rochester.

CERTIFICATE
OF
APPRECIATION

FOR AN EXCELLENT JOB EXCEEDINGLY WELL DONE.

Harley Flathers
Recipient

THANK YOU

MUSIC FESTIVAL 1969

Dorothy J. Combs
Chairman, Rochester Music Festival

Dorothy sent Harley a Certificate of Appreciation for conducting the song writing contest with Music Week.

Rochester Music Week Parade . . . Chair Dorothy Combs in her rocking chair Saturday morning . . . 7 days & 7 nights of Nonstop musical programs. October 11, 1969. (P-B photo)

Harley presents a $250 check to Mrs. Bruce Anderson while husband Bruce looks on. This occurred Saturday night just before the Victor Borge Concert at Mayo Civic Auditorium. Man with flowers ready for winner is Ed Fiksdal. Song title: "Rochester, My Home." (P-B photo)

Zippy the Clown . . . Harley in a clown suit when he was MC of the Chatfield Brass Band Circus Concert, May 17, '74 . . . Potter Auditorium. Merle Evans, Concertmaster 50 years with Barnum & Bailey Circus directed this concert. (P-B photo)

I went to many a concert as MC or as a speaker during 60s—70s—80s Beauty & Dairy Pageants . . . band and symphony concerts.

rochester arts council

THE ARTS

1974 OFFICERS AND EXECUTIVE COMMITTEE

John McCally, President
1623 - 9th Ave. N. E.
Rochester, Minn. 55901
507 - 289-2674
Mary Barnes, Vice-President
Martin Peterman, Treasurer
Faith Reilly, Secretary

Robert Scoggin
Judy Vilter
Mary McElroy Harvey
Clifford Johnson

PAST PRESIDENTS:

1. Dick Husband - 1971
2. Stan Lovestedt - 1972
3. Harley Flathers - 1973

33 MEMBER ORGANIZATIONS:

AAUW
American Guild of Organists
Barbershop Quartets
Chatfield Brass Band
Community Concerts
Friends of the Metropolitan Opera
Great Books
Heritage Associates
IBM Singers
Keyboard Club
Lourdes High School
Minnesota Orchestra
Olmsted County Historical Society
Oudal Chorale
Rochester Art Center
Rochester Art Center Music Comm.
Rochester Artists Group
Rochester Ballet Guild
Rochester Civic Theatre
Rochester Community College
Rochester Dance Arts Association
Rochester Figure Skating Club
Rochester Male Chorus
Rochester Music Board
Rochester Park & Recreation
Rochester Public Library
Rochester Public Schools
Rochester State Bank
Rochester Symphony
Rochester Symphony Guild
St. Mary's College, Winona
Sweet Adelines
(Zumbro Valley Chapter)
University of Minnesota,
(Rochester Center)

OCTOBER – NOVEMBER – DECEMBER 1973

ROCHESTER CIVIC MUSIC

PRESENTS

THE MUSIC MAN

STARRING

DON JOHNSON

LINDA JENSEN

OCTOBER 8, 9, 10, 11 and 13

8:00 PM

MAYO CIVIC AUDITORIUM THEATER

TICKETS ON SALE NOW ONLY AT MAYO CIVIC AUD. BOX OFFICE

THE SPIRIT OF 76
(Trombones, that is)

During the short five years he has headed the Rochester Civic Music program, Tom Lewis continues to stage dazzling productions, utilizing the best talent in the area, old and new. The Music Man, this early October, is now upon us. Former Chatfield resident Don Johnson is Professor Harold Hill, vigorously forming a boys' band for River City while bitten by the love bug in the town's library. Marian, the Librarian, stars the lovely Linda Jensen of Spring Valley, and current Miss Rochester. If you haven't picked up your tickets, reach for the phone and order yours now as you read this, to assure your reserved seat at the Mayo Civic Auditorium Theatre, starting October 8th.

Rochester Arts Council Newsletter combines first presidents, board members and member organizations. This quarterly letter emphasized the Music Man by Rochester Civic Music, directed by Tom Lewis. Autumn 1973.

SEMRAC

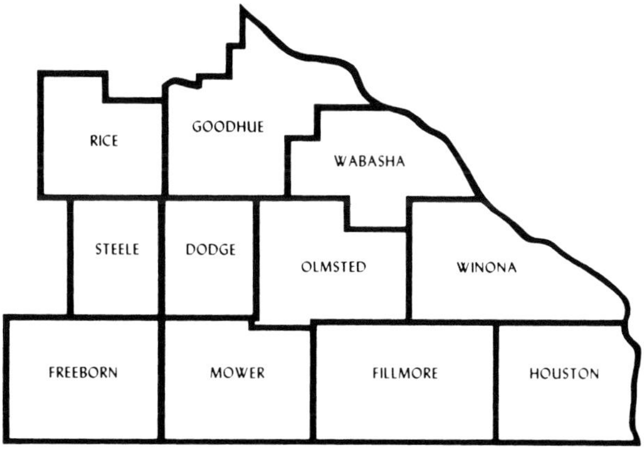

Region 10

SouthEastern Minnesota Regional Arts Council

The Nation's First Regionally Funded Arts Council

SEMRAC - Region 10. . . 11 Counties in S.E. Minn. Regional Arts Council. The Nation's first regionally funded Arts Council, Harley served as Executive Secretary during its 4½ years in existence. From Spring 1973 until Autumn 1977.

The final "Seniors in Touch" Channel 10 TV monthly show ending 8 years from January 1994 thru December 31, 2001. L-R: Standing: Bob Fenske, Geezer. com . . . Shirley Stuart, Field Operative Administrator for Geezer.com & Experience Works. Seated: Harley Flathers, Show Moderator and Pat Brown, Experience Works Staffing Service in Rochester. Photo by Wayne Brown with the Bob Fenske camera.

Moment 17

I Keep Getting Involved . . . National Paraplegia Foundation

When I first came to KROC in 1957, I did a little over three years of early evening radio, from 5:30 till midnight. That was when we had NBC programming, so occasionally there'd be programs from the network. I would play a couple of hours of music early, then there would be network news, and the last couple of hours I might play pop records, taking requests. During that time, I got to know a lot of people by telephone.

One was Jim Swenson. Jim was a young man who'd had a skiing accident at the age of 16, back in 1937. He hit a tree, broke his spine, and was a paraplegic for the rest of his life. Jim was a unique person. For many years we'd see his little ad in the paper: "Jim Swenson, Magazines." Someone had helped him get started in the magazine retail business. He lived at home, where his mother took care of him, and he developed a very fine magazine subscription service. Later, he married a beautiful wife, Luz, who was from the Philippines.

Knowing that I was a polio survivor and partially paralyzed, Jim called me one day and said, "You know, we've got something called the Hiawatha Valley National Paraplegia Foundation. You ought to come and join us."

Founded in 1948, the National Paraplegia Foundation (NPF) was a nationwide organization of people who had suffered some kind of spinal injury. Its goal was to get people together, to raise awareness, and to ask, "What can we learn, doctors? How's the research coming to mend or rebuild a spinal cord that's been damaged through accident, polio, or something else?" Although progress has been made through the years, they still haven't been able to wave a magic wand and get the spine rejuvenated.

We had a lot of fun in the NPF. We often referred to our Hiawatha Valley NPF chapter as "The Big Wheels." Many of our members were in wheelchairs or on crutches, but we were blessed with many others who were physically okay. Among them were Dr. Joe Janes and his wife Helen, two very fine people, and Jerry Cunningham, a longtime sheriff here, and his wife Gert. Jerry's deputy, Judd Reifsnider, and wife Dorothy were always there, too. And there were many more. They were available to help, to push wheelchairs, to carry casseroles of hot food and picnic supplies. We went on several picnics. It was a great social outlet, and it went on for several years, into the early 1970s.

At one time, I was president of the club. I didn't know all that much about being president, but who did? I hadn't done that kind of thing before. Once, when we were in the midst of fund-raising, a man named Bob Gilbertson, the owner of a horse arena in northeast Rochester called Meadowlane Stables, came to us and asked if he could do a horse show as a fund raiser. He figured we'd do all the publicity and he'd have some money coming in. We said yes, and we really went to work to put on that horse show. It was an outdoor arena event. I remember, I worked my buns off on that thing for a couple of years, but it was not run right. By the time we got all the awards and trophies paid for, there was nothing left for the chapter. But boy, we sure learned!

With the help of countless volunteers, we also wrote and produced several stage shows — including one old-time Gay Nineties Minstrel Show, complete with bands, comedy, end-men and interlocutor. That April 1961 show was held at the beautiful St. Mary's Hospital Auditorium, a building that is now only a memory. Marion Martin wrote and produced the show with theatrical consulting by Jim Cavanaugh, for many years the director of the Rochester Civic Theatre. The "Footlight Frolic of 1961" included eighteen acts and a cast of 80. It was supposed to be two hours long, and there is nothing in the review by Gary Sukow that appeared in the Post-

Bulletin the following Monday to indicate that it seemed too long. The house was packed, with nearly 950 in attendance. Our $1 admission price raised $900 for the NPF. The acts included the well-known group called the Notochords, a baton team from Lourdes High School, the John Marshall Pony Chorus, the Filipino Dancers (a group of nurses from both St. Mary's and Methodist hospitals), a barbershop chorus and a girls' chorus from Rochester Junior College, and little Tommy Wooner, the page-boy, who came out between acts running across the stage and shouting in a high voice, "Paging Mrs. ——." The name changed each time, and it was good for laughs, as were the six black-faced end-men who swapped stories with each other and with me. I was the interlocutor in a tux and a tall black stove-pipe hat. Dr. Bruce Douglas and Mrs. Leonard (Ann) Aaro brought down the house with their duets of the semi-classical songs "Vienna Dreams" and "Sweethearts," performed so beautifully and followed by a very off-key rendition of "April in Fairbanks." Sukow's review observed, "Perhaps the best facet of a show of this type, however, is the fun of sitting in the audience, watching a new act come onto stage and saying to your companion in a whisper, 'I didn't know he could sing.'"

The NPF did another "Footlight Frolic" in 1966 at Mayo Civic Theatre, produced and directed by Ted and Virginia Firnschild. It was entitled "A Gay Day in May," and had an outdoor picnic setting. It appeared on Sunday, May 15, and the program says that it was the "5th Annual" performance. The next day, Maxine McKnight's story in the Post-Bulletin's Family Fare section was headlined, "900 Entertained at Footlight Frolic." At the end of the story, it notes that "Harley Flathers, president of the Foundation, said the Gay Day in May should net $1000." What made this show such a hit was the way-out comedy routines of Bill Ketchum and Bob Martin. In real life, Bill Ketchum spent many years at IBM and Bob Martin was a pharmacist. Other acts included the Filipino Flirtation Dance by five Filipino dancers, a piano solo by the 1966 Miss Rochester Connie Cords, a wives' quartet from Leroy, Minnesota, called "The Better Halves," the Don Hanson Trio, the Larry Robarge Trio, the St. Mary's Triple Trio and a group from John Marshall High School called The Prophets (Jeff

Gossman, Jimmie Hightower, Bruce Qualey and Pete Erickson, with guitars, bass and vocal). Adding a lot of class to the show was dancer Linda Wooner, whom Maxine calls "as sparkling as a Fourth of July rocket...in a besequined red dance costume. Miss Wooner did a jazz step number to the music of the Larry Robarge Trio." The Red Wing High School Band, directed by Harold Cooke, played the overture and the finale was performed by the Dick Chaffee Orchestra. At one point, Brenda Bovine, a real Gurnsey cow, strolled across the stage in an act entitled "The Gurnsey Gallop." Only Ted Firnschild could have pulled off something that outrageous. There was also a hilarious "Miss NPF Contest," conducted by both Bill Ketchum and Bob Martin, who attempted to keep some order while the five male beauty queen contestants made three costume changes throughout the evening — "all of which," as Maxine wrote, "may have set beauty contests back at least half a century." The contestants were Miss Pent (Ray Ralston), Miss Chapen (David Potak), Miss Fortune (Bob Martin), Miss Bigot (Les Holtan) and Miss Yewsed (Bill Ketchum). There was no indication in Maxine's review as to a "winner," which is probably a good thing. I believe this was the final Footlight Frolic show by the NPF. The Hiawatha Valley chapter slowly dissolved over the next few years, but had lasted the better part of a decade from its founding in 1958.

All this time I was also doing my radio work, so it was natural for me to be promoting things like the NPF. That's how I got into so many of these things. The Hiawatha NPF, with its annual meetings and monthly meetings, the March of Dimes meetings, Arts Council meetings — it was a natural for me to be involved in them, because I found them interesting. You'd go to these meetings, and suddenly you were on a board, or a committee. You didn't ask for it, but when they nominated you, you'd say, "Okay, I'll try." Sometimes you ended up as president.

Jim Swenson had a very successful magazine operation for a number of years. He did a lot of radio advertising with me in the 1980s. Then in the 1990s, he said to me, "You know, I can't do this any more. I can't stay in business, because there is so much competition from other groups. The schools, for instance, they're all selling magazines as fund raisers. I can't even begin to compete. There's no sense in my even writing up orders. The subscribers, even those who've been buying from me for years, the schools give them a real deal, and they sign up with the kids. So the schools make the money instead of me." But he carried on. Jim died on April 30, 1995, at the age of 74. Jim Swenson was a great person who touched a lot of lives.

Another member of the NPF who's done very well is Jim Anderson (we called him Andy). Andy had fallen out of a tree in 1962 and broken his spine. Several of our NPF members had suffered a swimming accident, or a skiing accident, or a fall. Anyway, Andy was left a paraplegic. He and his wife, Gretchen, were very active in the NPF. They founded Anderson Wheelchair, which is located across from St. Mary's Hospital, and it has done a good business all these years. Andy and Gretchen have pretty much retired now; they have sold the business to their son and son-in-law. Andy Anderson was active for many years at promoting hockey and kids' sports, even in his wheelchair. We certainly need to honor him.

When I talk about people who have managed to make something of their lives even after suffering some degree of paralysis, I always like to mention the wives, because so many of us have wonderful wives without whom we could not have done half of what we've accomplished. We owe a great deal to those wives.

Campaigning with the Salvation Army

During my years here in Rochester, I had an opportunity to play a role in the Salvation Army's local program. I started working with them in 1963, when Capt. Raymond Sweazy, with his wife Dorothy and their three oldest children, came to Rochester from Hibbing on August 26 to take over as the corps officer. Ray Sweazy was a colorful character, and we took a real liking to the whole family.

I began by announcing the Christmas totals for the kettles on the radio. Somehow soon I was involved in the Army itself. Franklin Ruhl, a banker at First National Bank, was on the Salvation Army Board, and one day he asked me to come and speak to their annual meeting. The next thing I knew, he asked me to come on the board.

That was in 1981, and I served on the local Salvation Army Board for the next twelve years. I was the board chairman for the last three of those years, until April 11, 1994. We had a very caring board, people who were dedicated to helping the Salvation Army's work in the community. What's the saying on the calendars? "Heart to God, Hand to Man." We certainly tried to live up to that.

The Salvation Army first came to Rochester in 1896. For 41 years, from 1930 to 1971, their headquarters was downtown at 11 First Street Northwest. I still remember Ray Sweazy, standing by the red kettle on the corner by Dayton's at Broadway and 2nd Street Southwest, singing Christmas carols while Dorothy accompanied him on her accordion in the cold night air.

When the Apache Mall opened in 1969, Dayton's moved out of the downtown location where it had been for 18 years and into the mall. So did J.C. Penney and many others. During the Christmas shopping season, there was a huge KWEB-KRCH Christmas Sharing Tree in the J.C. Penney courtyard. About six weeks before Christmas, through the 1980s and into the 1990s, we broadcast a live KWEB tree-lighting ceremony each year, and Salvation Army Board member Evelyn Hunter regularly put the first gift under the tree. Dorothy Sweazy played her accordion by the Salvation Army kettles in front of the Dayton's store at the Apache Mall for many years.

In 1971 the Salvation Army moved its headquarters to the present day citadel at 20 First Avenue Northeast. I had become interested in the Salvation Army's activities, and started attending its annual meetings, usually held in late January or early February on what seemed like the coldest night of the year. It was during the February 9, 1970, annual meeting in Christ United Methodist Church that former mayor Alex Smekta "shaved" my mustache to bring in additional funds. The next day, the Post-Bulletin carried a story by Pauline Walle headlined "Spring Ground-Breaking Goal Is Planned at Salvation Army." The fund drive for the new building had at that point reached $260,258, and more pledges were still coming in.

Construction took nearly eighteen months, and it was November 7, 1971, when the new citadel was dedicated.

One of Captain Sweazy's many talents was cooking. He prepared many a meal for the needy during his four decades with the Army. During the Olmsted County Fair, he took the Salvation Army Canteen to the fairgrounds. This was a large van on wheels that had been fitted out with kitchen facilities and a long serving window on one side that opened to the public. It was also ideal for emergency runs to areas that had been struck by tornados or floods, where Capt. Sweazy would serve food to the disaster teams. One of his specialities at the fair was lasagna, although he also served the usual burgers and hot dogs. The Canteen would be parked all week long under the trees just outside the fair office building, where today you would see an emergency rescue vehicle.

There are some outstanding people involved in the Salvation Army in Rochester, and they do some great work here in the community, as they do nationwide. I was happy to help, even though I was involved with my own church. This seemed to me another way I could help God's work during those years. So in 1981, I joined the board, and all the way through the 1980s and into the early 1990s, there were endless meetings — committee meetings, monthly board meetings. And there were enjoyable fund-raisers, like the Chef's Night in early March, when chefs in the area restaurants give their food and their time, and we would go to the Kahler's Heritage Hall to eat and enjoy. People would pay $15 per ticket, and that money would go to the Salvation Army. I have great memories of the Salvation Army here, and my association with it during those years.

The Salvation Army Thrift Store has grown during the years, giving residents an opportunity to donate clothing and other items they no longer need and providing a place for shopping at great bargains. In its earlier years, the thrift store conducted business in a small outlet on 2nd Street Southwest across from St. Marys Hospital. Then for a few years it was located downtown at 227 First Avenue Southwest, across from City Hall, in the building that now houses the Iridescent House antiques and collectibles store. On December 13, 1980, it moved into the former Depot

House Restaurant building, which had once been the town's train depot. The Salvation Army also ran a boutique shop, the Emporium, at 314 South Broadway, that carried ladies' very fine second-hand apparel. Dorothy Sweazy worked there for long hours, often well into the night, sorting donated items and pricing them for sale.

Then in the mid-1980s, the Minnesota Highway Department announced that it would be constructing a new highway — today's Civic Center Drive — that would pass through the property on which the thrift shop in the old depot building was standing. Another building fund drive began to construct a new store for the thrift shop and the Emporium. As a member of the board, I was part of the team responsible for sharing the story with the public. Hal Henderson, president of Construction Collaborative Designers, the architects, estimated the cost of the new building to be $646,000. Alvin E. Benike, Inc., did the construction. The building opened for business on July 8, 1991. In a Post-Bulletin story on July 4, 1991, Pauline Walle announced that "Darlene Charland, who has been with the Salvation Army for seven years, will manage the new facility." Pauline quoted Darlene as saying, "It is a beautiful, multi-purpose building, not only offering flexibility for changing exhibits, but was earmarked for potential future uses, such as a gym, offices or chapel."

Evelyn Hunter, Stan Davis, Amy Waugh and other veterans of the Salvation Army Board, had learned that Captain Sweazy had always wanted to take a trip to Australia, so in 1985 an effort was begun to raise the money to send him and Dorothy there. We kept the project a secret from the Sweazys. Evelyn brought young Paul Kanz, a realtor, onto the board, and we met twice monthly from July to November to plan for a great night at the Kahler Hotel's Heritage Hall to honor the Sweazys. At those morning meetings held at the northwest Howard Johnson's Restaurant, we went to work on a "This Is Your Life" program, complete with photos and slides from the past, provided by their daughters, Marsha and Denise. We wanted it to be an evening that would really go down in history. About $15,000 was raised through donations for the Sweazy Appreciation Night, which was attended by over 300 people on November 21, 1985.

We had Ray and Dorothy and their four children up on stage, where everyone could see them, as the pictorial show was presented on several screens. I narrated the program, which had been created with the help of their daughters and friends, including Carl Bainter, owner of C.J.'s Midtown Lounge. Captain Sweazy often stopped for coffee and a visit with Carl during the day, and they had become close friends.

We learned that night that Dorothy Sweazy had joined the Salvation Army when she was 13 years old. She met Ray at a revival meeting in St. Louis, Missouri, in 1949. Dorothy, who was an officer at the time, was serving at the Salvation Army headquarters building. She went to the Harbor Light for a week of revival meetings, at which she was a speaker and Ray was an usher. He told his friends, "I'm going to marry that woman." When he gave her a box of candy for Valentine's Day on February 14, 1950, she got the hint. Daughter Denise said, "She knew for sure then that he liked her. She had been hoping all along."

They were married on July 7, 1950. Dorothy had to resign her commission, in accordance with Salvation Army regulations of the time, because she was an officer and Ray was not. The couple went to Minneapolis, where they worked for several years on Skid Row, ministering to alcoholics and others in similar situations. In 1960, they were both made auxiliary captains. They spent three years in Grand Rapids and seven years at Hibbing before coming to Rochester in 1963. When they retired, the Sweazys had a combined total of 90 years of service with the Salvation Army.

Captain Sweazy and his wife retired on June 26, 1989, after twenty-six years as corps officers in Rochester. They had been in on the planning for the new building, and had seen it under construction, although they spent much of their time at their summer home near Grand Rapids in northern Minnesota. They were succeeded by Captain John Mowers, a terrific man, and his wife, Nancy. The Mowers both rose to the rank of major after serving in the Salvation Army for fifteen years. They headed the corps in Rochester for four years, from 1989 to 1993, overseeing the construction of the new thrift store, which was the first building specifically constructed for the storage and sale of donated items. Today, Major Mark Welsh and his wife Sue are the local corps officers.

Capt. Ray Sweazy died on September 6, 1991, at the age of 67. Dorothy asked me to plan the funeral, since I had been very close to them in their final years here. I was honored to line up speakers and casket bearers. Dorothy suggested the hymns. Capt. John Mowers presided at the service, held at Christ United Methodist Church. I read the obituary. Fellow board members Evelyn Hunter, Stan Davis and Vern Clark spoke, and Nancy Mowers sang a solo. Major George Watt gave the message, entitled "A Christian Soldier's Farewell."

Dorothy Sweazy died on February 13, 1999, at Mercy Hospital in Coon Rapids, Minnesota, at the age of 85. She and her husband are buried at Grandview Memorial Gardens in Rochester.

The March of Dimes

When I got out of SEMRAC in 1977, it was a relief, because by then I was holding a part- time paid position with the March of Dimes, doing much the same work for the March of Dimes as I was for the Arts Council, and still doing my full-time job in radio broadcasting. I've already explained how I got involved in that. I was executive director of the March of Dimes from 1976 through 1981, following ten years (1966-1976) as a volunteer chapter director for the Olmsted County chapter.

It all worked well, because I was in the broadcast business, and I understood public relations. We were forever involved in various fund-raising projects. There was the famous Mothers' March, when volunteers would go door to door collecting for the March of Dimes. On a given night in January, volunteer nurses from St. Marys' Marian Hall would gather, and we'd have volunteer drivers take them out door to door, wherever people had their lights on to say, "Yes, come here. We'll give you a contribution for the March of Dimes."

Thanks to a great board, we managed to increase the amount of money we raised annually from $11,000 to $47,000 over the fifteen changing and challenging years that I was associated with the local chapter. Among the volunteers who gladly stayed on the board for periods of 25 years or more were Larry Lamberty, Dave Welte and Mary Kubiatowicz. Virginia Gruhlke told me recently that she served for fifteen years, beginning as one of the chairpersons for the Mothers' March in January 1967. She and her friend, the late Loma Sorenson, had been leaders together in the Cub Scouts, so organizing teams to collect from door to door was easy for them.

A couple of those March of Dimes annual meetings took place at picnics at the farms of Darrell and Ruby Miller, of rural Pine Island, or Larry and Dorothy Lamberty, on 50th Avenue Northwest, Rochester, a short distance north of Olmsted County road 4. Larry called his farm "Oleo Acres — one of the cheaper spreads." At the 1977 annual meeting, we honored Larry Lamberty for his 26 years as chapter secretary with a plaque and a Holstein heifer calf named "Oleo." The calf, donated by Darrell Miller, came complete with brass cowbell.

Board members came and went during the years. When I first joined the board in late 1966, Marcia Gray and Milt Rosenblad were around the monthly conference table with Erv and Mary Miller and Mrs. Frank Whitcomb, all of Eyota. Sharon King, Art Kistler, Mrs. Harold Mahon and Helen Vitek were also faithful attendees. Then Nancy Swenson, mother of our 1973 poster child Ty Swenson, joined us. Soon we "encouraged" Donna Bartoletti to line up nurses to go door to door on an always cold January night to collect cash during the Mothers' March. Other faithfuls were Lois Hruska, Bill Brunner, Shirley Wermager, Marian Chrysler, Darlene Coffman, Ann Hoag, Rose Kleiber, Sharon Copeman, Erlene Jahn, Karen Meisner, Mrs. Art Jordahl, Dona Fisher, Eileen Tuseth, Cy Champa, Mrs. Lowell (Jo) Linnes and Bill Beaupre.

In 1979, Bill Beaupre introduced "Sno-Ball," a fund raiser that involved playing summer softball in February, using a bright orange ball. The "field" was laid out in deep snow at the fairgrounds. The headquarters was in the 4-H building, where players could go inside to warm up over burgers and coffee. "Sno-Ball" has become an annual event for the March of Dimes.

In 1980, Bill Beaupre and his volunteers raised $3567 with their "Sno-Ball" game. Someone brought a portable TV into the 4-H building that Sunday afternoon, and we watched part of the Olympic Games at Lake Placid, New York. That was the year of the "Miracle on Ice," when the U.S. Olympic hockey team defeated both Russia and Finland to capture the gold medal. One member of that team, coached by Herb Brooks, was Eric Strobel, a graduate of Rochester's Mayo High School. Eric was a fine hockey player, as was his father, the late Art Strobel. I remembered their triumph as I watched the veterans of that 1980 team light the cauldron at the 2002 Winter Olympics in Salt Lake City. I'm sad to report that their great coach, Herb Brooks, a leader of many state, national and Olympic teams, died in a one-car accident just north of the Twin Cities on August 11, 2003. Over 2500 people attended his funeral in St. Paul five days later.

Another winter fund raiser for the March of Dimes was the annual snowmobile ride, with over 100 miles of trails mapped out around Olmsted County. Area clubs from surrounding towns participated. The real action started with Chuck and Carole Ramthun and the Byron Snow Bears, and we had great assists from Cy Kubista and Gordon Koenig. We generally had a good response in pledges, even in years like 1973 and 1980, when there wasn't enough snow on the ground on the scheduled date for the snowmobiles to travel. In 1978, when there was plenty of snow, the snowmobile ride raised $6504; in 1980, we raised $4200, even without the actual ride taking place. The event usually ended with a chili feed at Ramthun's Warehouse in Byron, where Chuck was a home builder. In 1978, Chuck secured over $1,000 in pledges, and we awarded him with a special patch from the state March of Dimes office, proclaiming him a member of the "$1000 Club."

We got the kids involved. Local high school rock bands eagerly played at the teenage dances we sponsored. In 1978, we had three dances going on the same night, February 24. The bands that played that night were Euphoria, at the Olmsted County fairgrounds 4-H building in Rochester, and Boot Hill in the Stewartville High School gym. KWEB disc jockies Karen Wong and George Creedle played records at Dover-Eyota High

School in Eyota. Those three dances brought in $736 for the March of Dimes. Later that spring, on March 17, the band Company played for a dance in Byron, and on April 21, Ascension played at another one in Pine Island.

On January 22, 1972, high school swimming coach Jerry Peirce raised $1200 at a Swim-a-thon held in the John Marshall High School pool. His swimmers completed 567,000 laps in the pool, more than 322 miles.

The following June 7, when we had our chicken-and-potato-salad annual meeting at Darrell Miller's farm, we presented Dr. Hymie Gordon of the Mayo Clinic with a check for $3500 to be used for genetic research. I had interviewed Dr. Gordon a number of times about his continuing research into the causes of birth defects.

In that year, 1972, we surpassed $12,000 in fund raising. The next year, we went over $17,000. During those years, we welcomed insurance men Darwin Olson and Hartley Barry to lead Mothers' March teams. We called 1973 "The Year of the Big Dime." My scrapbook has a picture of a smiling Jo Linnes, the Mothers' March chairman, incoming chapter chairman Bill Brunner, from Rochester State Junior College, and myself, all holding a three-foot wide "dime" at the chapter's annual meeting at Oleo Acres.

Vikings' running back Dave Osborne headed up a Bike-a-thon on May 8, 1976. It started at 9 am at Dayton's in Apache Mall and circled for thirty miles from Rochester southwest through Salem Corners, Rock Dell and back. The good-natured Osborne, then 33, greeted the riders and autographed pictures for them when they returned.

The Rochester Jaycees conducted penny-a-pound airlifts for us. I don't remember when they began, but during the late 1960s they were going strong. This was a benefit project, with all planes and services provided free of charge by local pilots and plane owners, members of Rochester Aviation and Gopher Aviation. The Post-Bulletin carried a news article in October 1968 saying that the event would be held at 6 pm on October 20 at the airport, near the weather bureau building, about a quarter mile west of the main terminal. Children and adults could ride for 7 to 10 minutes for two-cents a pound, or a donation of $1.50. An FAA operations inspector from the Minneapolis office was on hand to observe and conduct safety inspections.

The October 21, 1968, Post-Bulletin headline read "Operation Airlift Draws Nearly 300." They quoted me as saying, "The airlift was $1.50 short of $600, which will be turned over to the March of Dimes." There is a picture of Robert Harms of Rochester, with his sons Timothy, 4, and Richard, 2, scrutinizing the plane before boarding for their flight. Also in the picture was Mr. Garland Dinter, sales consultant for Rochester Aviation. Five airplanes and ten pilots took part in the donated airlift.

I put together four Skate-a-thons at Skate Country, north of town on highway 52, in the building that now houses Circus World Bingo. We selected a "no-school" day in January, or a day during spring vacation, for these events in 1977, 1978, 1979 and 1981. I begged for great prizes from merchants around town — new bikes, a TV set, a radio/cassette player and many more. On April 4, 1977, participants skated for six hours and raised $4323.88. Gosh, I'm proud of those kids! They helped to raise funds for the scholarships that we gave annually to high school seniors who planned to go into health-related fields in college. The scholarships ranged from $250 to $500. As our funds increased, we were able to give more.

When I asked Priscilla White to join the board in 1980, she volunteered to head up the Reading Olympics, held in twelve area elementary schools. Kids read like crazy during November 1980, and raised $5578 in this new event. To raise those dollars, the kids read 6,701 books. A January 14, 1981 story in the Post-Bulletin shows Priscilla handing out a Reading Olympics gold medal, on a patriotic red-white-and-blue ribbon, to Pamela Kaldenberg, a fourth grader from Pine Wood School. We went to all twelve schools and presented 473 replica medals to the winners. The topfund-raising reader was 11-year-old Katrina Schut, a fifth grader at Principal Dave Malcolmson's Harriet Bishop Country Club Manor School. Katrina read 34 books and brought in $341.27.

When we added the "Haunted House" event to our fund-raising list at Halloween in 1977, we never dreamed how much work would be needed to make a big space into a scary place. That first year, we used a vacant store in the Northbrook Shopping Center. After that, we held it a couple of times at Hillside Elementary School. (The school is gone now; today Hirman Insurors occupies that location.) Then we held it at the Olmsted County fairgrounds.

In 1980, Priscilla White and I went to see Cedric Paine, owner of Paine Furniture Store, and begged him for the use of his retired 1942 Packard hearse. I'd seen it parked in the back of his store, where it wasn't visible to regular shoppers. I asked him if we could take it to the Olmsted County fairgrounds to be part of our Haunted House. He said, "Sure, and open it up, so the kids can see inside."

Priscilla, with her friend Georgia Toogood riding along for moral support, drove the old hearse to the building we were using for the Haunted House. Just think how many times that old hearse had roamed Rochester's streets, from the church to the cemetery and back, during the 1940s and after! Needless to say, the old hearse was a big hit for those five scary October nights, raising just over $1000 for the March of Dimes.

In the spring of 1981, we announced the M.O.D. Squad Trash Catch. Kids and their parents picked up trash along the highways, bringing in another $500 for the March of Dimes. Kentucky Fried Chicken supplied snacks for the participants. The first prize for the top fund raiser was a hot air balloon ride, donated by George Ibach and his Rochester Sport Balloons. Board member Pete Viker headed up this project.

A fine team of physicians served during those years as medical advisers to the March of Dimes chapter. They included Dr. George Malkasian, Dr. Gordon DeWald, Dr. Donald Erickson, Dr. Bob Konicek, Dr. H. Jean Vine and Dr. Clayton Bennett.

I have a *Post-Bulletin* clipping from early 1973 that reads, "Chapter Honored — National Foundation Unit Here Best in Minnesota." Olmsted County's March of Dimes was cited for its overall promotional and educational activities during that year's fund drive, when we raised $16,000. The honors were presented by Arthur Gallway, vice president of the National

Foundation of the March of Dimes, at a regional program orientation meeting in St. Paul. A special citation was also presented for exemplary work done by the medical advisory committee of the chapter, headed by Dr. George Malkasian of the Mayo Clinic.

Those were busy, interesting years. In April 1981, we had a big, very successful fund-raising event for the March of Dimes — the Walk America, where people walked from Douglas to Pine Island and back, and collected pledges for doing it. The pledges totaled $10,000, which isn't much in today's pledge line-up, but was quite a lot for the time. After it was over, we collected a little over $9900. I personally got on the phone to go after the people who had asked for pledges but hadn't turned in the names of those who pledged. That was still another learning experience.

Nowadays, we have all kinds of walks going — Walk This and Walk That — but every year here in Rochester, we still have a Walk America for the March of Dimes. Whole communities get together and walk 30 kilometers (18 miles) to raise money to battle birth defects. It gets people out and builds awareness.

When that first Walk America was over, I said, "It's time I slowed down. I can't do what needs to be done for the March of Dimes." The state office wanted me to do more on the state level. Physically, it was getting impossible. You needed to go to area towns carrying projectors, showing movies, carrying boxes of materials, and I just couldn't do it. So the March of Dimes accepted my resignation in October 1981.

The March of Dimes board then gave me the Franklin Roosevelt Award for volunteer service to the March of Dimes. I was very, very pleased to receive it.

After I retired from the March of Dimes, I went back full time to the business of radio. There had been a few months, after KROC had let me go in October 1980, when I didn't know what I was going to do, but I was so busy with the March of Dimes that I didn't have much time to worry about it. It kept me going until I got back into radio at KWEB on January 5, 1981.

Their "Touch" Continues

Swenson, Diamond, Applequist, Parkin and Bardwell — it sounds like a law firm! However, those names — of individuals who have overcome serious physical challenges in their lives — have been examples to us all for decades.

Swenson is *Ty Swenson*, son of Nancy and Tuck Swenson, who was our March of Dimes poster child in, I believe, 1973. He was born with a birth defect that left him without a lower right arm. After 1955, the March of Dimes focussed on battling birth defects through research and education. Ty's mother was a strong supporter of the March of Dimes, serving for many years on its board, including a stint as chairman. Today, Ty Swenson is a vital member of the staff of the Mayo clinic, an upbeat, smiling man wearing a prosthesis on his right arm. We're proud to claim him as one of "our" boys.

Cheryl Diamond was born on April 5, 1967, with spina bifida, a separation of the spine that usually occurs in the lower back. The daughter of Meyer "Mike" Diamond and his wife Elaine, Cheryl was the Olmsted County March of Dimes poster child in 1972. During his forty years as manager of Snyder Drug on the Miracle Mile, Mike Diamond was always very supportive of our requests for help in fund raising for the March of Dimes. Cheryl has always been a spunky little gal. Today, with a limited ability to walk, she depends mostly on "wheels" and is a resident of Newbridge Apartments, a downtown facility for the physically challenged who live and work in the heart of our community.

Charlie Applequist was born on January 1, 1963. He had cerebral palsy, which gave him mega-problems right from the start. His parents, Chuck and Sharon Applequist, cared greatly for him, realizing that this little guy had a mind of his own. He was our March of Dimes poster child in 1977. In his earlier years, he was equipped with a brain pacer, which helped to coordinate his mind and body for a time. Later, his father says, it was removed.

Today "Charlie the Tuna" carries a smile with him on his four-wheel scooter, with crutches attached. He's self-sufficient, living in his own apartment, and thrives on doing volunteer work. At present, he is Minnesota secretary of ARC, the Association for Retarded Citizens, and has served as an advocate for ARC, Possibilities Unlimited and the United Way. This motivated fellow is a credit to us all.

Gene Parkin was born on July 7, 1928, and is now 75 years of age — pretty good for a spina bifida child originally given only a month to live. When he was born, the doctors told his parents, "If this baby survives at all, he will become little more than a vegetable." I first met Gene when we were together in the Hiawatha Chapter of the NPF in the early 1960s. Gene was always there, in his wheel chair. Few of us knew the battle he had won up to that point. Born in Minneapolis, Gene had been in and out of operating rooms many times, and spent two full years, between the ages of 7 and 9, at Gillette Hospital, where he underwent numerous surgeries and spent a lot of time in body casts.

They said he probably wouldn't make it in school. But "they" didn't know Gene, or his wonderful mother. Gene "wheeled" his way through high school and one year of college.

In 1963, he rolled his wheelchair sixteen miles from Pine Island to Rochester — six hours and 15 minutes on the road — to promote our NPF "Footlight Frolics" stage show. As I recall, there was a moving car ahead of him and another behind, for safety. At the end of his ride, I met him at Donaldson's Department Store on the Miracle Mile, where I was doing my Saturday afternoon 2-5 pm broadcast. He described the long ride as "exhausting."

Gene battled cancer in 1997, and won. Today he is heavily involved in volunteer work at the Mayo Clinic's Siebens Building, Rochester Civic Music and the Chamber of Commerce. He says, "Volunteering is the joy of giving back." Like Cheryl Diamond, he lives in the Newbridge Apartments in downtown Rochester.

Bob Bardwell's life story would fill many books. Bob was born on May 25, 1947. His "walking life" ended suddenly in a construction accident near Plainview in 1973. The next three years were filled with rehabilitation, combined with an increasing faith in God. Eventually, he was blessed with an idea that led to the founding of Ironwood Springs Christian Ranch west of Stewartville, Minnesota. Many organizations and individuals support the ranch. Sixty different agencies send youngsters, physically challenged and healthy alike, to this recreational project, which in 2001 served 20,000 people. Bob has introduced many summer camp activities, including horseback riding, to those who never dreamed they could do it.

Bob is in great demand as a motivational speaker. He and his wife and their four daughters, Hannah and triplets Abigail, Lydia and Elizabeth, travel regularly to his speaking engagements. He has written a book called "Marathons of Life." His goal was to take part in 100 wheelchair marathons by the end of 2002.

Those of us who have listened to Bob Bardwell speak in person or interviewed him on radio always come away inspired. As he says, "It's not what happens to you in life — it's what you do *after what happens* that counts."

And to that, I'll say, "Amen!"

Photo of the the entire Footlight Frolic Cast at St. Mary's Hospital Auditorium for the show . . . "The Gay 90s." Surrounded by End-men, I'm the Interlocutor, 3rd from right. April 21, 1961. Photo by Ted Saby.

The Olmsted County March of Dimes board presented me with the Franklin Delano Roosevelt Award upon my retirement Oct. 31, 1981 following 15 years with MOD. L-R: Harley Flathers, Bob Traub from the state office as field director, Darrell Miller, Pine Island, Nancy Swenson, Stewartville, both board members and Priscilla White incoming as executive director. (Post Bulletin photo)

The Sweazys retirement party at Salvation Army Citadel . . . June 30, 1989. L-R: Ray Sweazy, Harley, board vice chair, and Dorothy Sweazy.

Moment 18

Is It a Tool or a Musical Instrument?

When I was recuperating from polio at home, from 1950 until the autumn of 1952, I had time in the winter to look through a lot of magazines, books and newspapers. In January 1951, I was reading a *Popular Mechanics* magazine, and I saw an ad saying "Learn how to play the musical saw."

I said to my Dad, "Look here. I've always wanted to do this, since I heard the saw played on the Major Bowes Original Amateur Hour." During the 1930s and 1940s, every Thursday night we listened to the Original Amateur Hour on radio. Major Edward Bowes had been a major in the first World War. When he came back, he got into radio, and he had a very popular show. Frank Sinatra was one of many who got his start on the Major Bowes show, as was George Beverly Shea, who still sings with the Billy Graham Crusades. People would come and perform. The judging was done with a gadget they called an applause meter. It measured how loud the applause was for each act, and the one that got the biggest hand was the winner.

During those years we would hear people play music through a tire pump, by deflating an inner tube, with spoons — you name it, people made music on it. I'd heard the musical saw played many times, and it just was an eerie, hauntingly beautiful sound. I wondered how they made it happen. I hadn't ever seen it done. I'd just seen this picture.

I said, "Dad, I want to play the musical saw." But I wasn't going to spend money on something without doing some checking first. I said, "What I should do is borrow one of your saws and your violin bow, and see what I can do, based on what I'm seeing in this picture."

According to the picture, you sat and laid the saw across one knee, tucking it under the other leg and holding your knees together. Well, I couldn't hold my legs together, because of the polio, so I strapped my knees together. Then I put my dad's saw across my lap, got the violin bow, and lo and behold, I made music! Out of a regular saw!

After I'd tried this a bit, I said, "Dad, I'd like to order one of these, but I've got no money."

He said, "Well, I've got none either."

I said, "It's going to cost $15.85. And what we need to do is send a check to a place called Mussehl and Westphal at Fort Atkinson, Wisconsin."

The man who started the mail order musical saw business was named Clarence Mussehl. He started it in 1919. I learned that later, when I was corresponding with him.

I sent for the saw. When I got it, with Mother accompanying me on the piano, I began playing music immediately. Oh, I'm sure the first few days there was a lot of screeching, and the folks wondered what's this world coming to, but my folks were very understanding.

Soon I was playing music all over the place on my saw, for Farm Bureau and 4-H and the Ladies' Aid. I played for pieces of pie, coffee, ice cream, or a dinner. Eventually I got to the place where I played for the Fillmore County Farm Bureau's annual meeting. Ed Hale took me down to Harmony, Minnesota, for the event. He lined me up as an entertainer, and gave me $5 as well. I knew it wasn't going to be a big money-making thing. In fact, I had different people tell me, "Well, Mr. Flathers, it's interesting, but don't give up your day job."

Clarence Mussehl eventually died. He was in the musical saw business at Fort Atkinson, Wisconsin, for 60 years. When I wrote to mail-order a second saw, he told me in his reply, "Don't ever get rid of that first saw." It was a 31-inch saw, and it was made in England of very high temper steel.

He said, "All the others we've made since are shorter."

I had the saw with me when I went into radio school in Minneapolis in the autumn of 1952. I started school on October 20, and in early November there was a promotion in Minneapolis run by Ted Mack, who followed Major Edward Bowes as host of the Original Amateur Hour. That show was now appearing on national television, and I'd been watching it. At that time, the show was temporarily off the air, and Ted Mack was roaming the country with his orchestra to line up new talent.

There was a note in the Minneapolis paper, saying that there was going to be an audition at such-and-such a place tonight, come and try out. I don't remember for sure, but I think I did two auditions — if you pass one, they call you to come again. The preliminary audition was held at Klein's Super Market at 3119 West Lake Street. There were 200 contestants, and I was one of those chosen to go on Ted Mack's stage show at the Minneapolis Auditorium on November 21st. My picture was on the front page of the Minneapolis paper on November 14th. There I was, very seriously playing the saw — one of those who had been chosen by Ted Mack.

The Ted Mack Road Show was a real highlight. They had a fifteen-piece orchestra under the direction of Lloyd Marx. I suppose that maybe we got to rehearse once, I don't know. But there was some excellent talent present. There were singers, dancers, drummers, probably an accordionist — there always was an accordionist somewhere. I was the only musical saw player.

Ted Mack announced that three of us would be picked to go to New York to fame and fortune. I was one of the three.

They said, "Okay, we're going to call for you, maybe just after the first of the year, because we're still working, but we'll be sending for you and telling you when to come and appear."

Time went on, and on, and on. It was getting along up into April and May, and finally I wrote them. I got a letter back from Lloyd Marx, saying, "We're still working. We'll be calling you."

Well, the year passed, and nothing happened. I wrote again. And they're still working, and nothing's happening.

In another year or so, I read that Lloyd Marx had died. So I knew Lloyd Marx wasn't going to be writing letters any more. It was all just a flash in the pan, but I came very close to fame and fortune.

Over the years, I have had a lot of great joy with that musical saw. When I was in Red Wing, I entered another talent contest in 1955, sponsored by the Goodhue County Farm Bureau as part of the State of Minnesota Talent Find. Winners would go on to the American Farm Bureau Federation convention, to be held in Chicago. We began on a low key in Goodhue County. I don't know how many people entered, but I was a winner. Then we went to the state contest in St. Paul, and again I was a winner. And suddenly Harley Flathers and His Musical Saw, from Red Wing, Goodhue County, Minnesota, was going on an all-expense-paid trip to Chicago on the train, with the delegates from Minnesota, to the annual meeting of the American Farm Bureau Federation at the Sherman Hotel on December 11, 12 and 13, 1955.

Now, that was fun. We arrived at 4 pm Sunday, and the program was Sunday night. Twenty-seven of the forty-eight states had someone there with a talent of some sort. The show was over two hours long. There were 2,000 people in the Sherman ballroom, where we had a big dinner, followed by the talent show.

When I got up there on the stage, I had a tape recording with me of my mother playing the piano to accompany me. It played on a reel-to-reel Wilcox Gay recorder. I plugged it in, and I think I announced, "Well, I'm going to play this musical saw, and my mother's here on tape." They told me later that I patted the tape recorder and said, "Mother, go ahead."

I guess I wowed 'em. The man who was master of ceremonies of the show, Norman Kraft, was the farm director at WGN, that great Chicago agricultural radio station. He said, "We're going to pick ten acts out of this program tonight that'll go on my radio show. We'll record it and play it back next Thursday night." It would be played right in the heart of American Farm Bureau Federation Week.

I was one of the ten acts he chose. We left the ballroom and went down to the studios to do this taping about 2 or 2:30 in the morning. I'd never played with the man who accompanied me at the piano, but he was excellent. He was a studio piano performer. If you needed a piano player in the studio, there he was. I told them we were going to play "Whispering." "Whispering" was my theme song, and I'd played it earlier at the show. And he went right through it. I don't think we even rehearsed first. It came out, really, as about the finest performance I'd ever done. I've got it on a recording, and I'm so proud of it. It was professionally recorded. It sounded good, and I've used it many times.

There again was my close call to fame.

I came back home to Red Wing and went to work, but I kept on playing the saw through the years. I don't know how many times I've performed on the saw. You name it, they want you there for this or that, a wedding reception, a grand opening, whatever.

In the autumn of 1966, I ran into the Reverend Samuel Cook, who was then the rector of Calvary Episcopal Church in downtown Rochester. People kept telling me, "Sam plays the saw." And he was a good sawyer — that's what we call it, a sawyer.

Then we discovered Bob Thompson. Bob Thompson was a man who loved music. He owned a number of properties in downtown Rochester that he'd inherited from his father. He rented them out, and that was his job, just overseeing his real estate. I hadn't seen him for a lot of years. We first met when I was still in Red Wing. I had entered a talent show in 1954 here in Rochester, put on by the Chamber of Commerce. It was called the Family Home Fair. They held it in March, in the old Mayo Civic Auditorium, and it was a big event. I won $50, with a chance to come back the next night to win the big prize of $200. I came back, but I didn't win that big one. The winners were eleven-year-old Danny Steenblock of Rochester and Jerry Easler, an eighteen-year-old baritone vocalist from Harmony, Minnesota.

After I'd done my first afternoon presentation, when I won the $50, Bob Thompson came backstage and introduced himself. He said, "I like that saw. Where can I get a saw to play?"

I told him where to send for it, and then I didn't hear from Bob Thompson again till in the early 1970s, when I ran into him again, after I'd been in Rochester a whole decade. When we met, he said, "I've got that musical saw you got me started with."

I replied, "My gosh, I'd forgotten all about that."

The Reverend Sam Cook and Bob Thompson and I became a trio. We did quite a lot of entertaining in 1971 and 1972. We even played at a Chatfield Brass Band circus concert on April 28, 1972, where the Mayo High South Town Singers, directed by Gerald Smith, also performed.

We formed a musical saw group that at one time had about eight members locally. We would have as many as six people playing saws at one time. But most of the time Sam, Bob and I would go out alone.

I remember we played on December 13, 1975 at a Christmas party for the White Shrine, above the old Weber and Judd Drug Store. (Now, of course, that's the USBank building). Lloyd Stoddard accompanied us on the piano. We had five musical saws that year. It was a lot of fun, doing a Christmas party for the kids.

We went three times to St. Charles, once for the annual meeting of the Production Credit Association, a great farm lending group which exists no longer. Twice we had to go up a long flight of stairs at the Masonic Lodge at St. Charles to play songs. I think Sam drove, and I managed those stairs — there were 35 or 40 steps, which was difficult for me. The last time they had a chair lift, so that was helpful.

It has all been so much fun. I played the saw in Zumbrota and Pine Island many years ago. I played at many community events. It went on and on and on. There's less performing now, but I really enjoyed it for many years.

I played the musical saw every Christmas for 35 years at the Maple Manor Nursing Home. I started out there in about 1965, when they first opened. I'd met David and Dorothy Blum, the owners, and they asked me to come and play. They had seven sons, and I think three or four of them are now in the health care business. Every Christmas, Patrick Blum, the manager there at Maple Manor, invites me to come back and play the saw.

It's gotten to be quite a tradition. Sometimes it's difficult, because it's winter and there's often ice, and I'm still working, getting Christmas tapes of school choirs ready. That's the only concert that I really do any more at Christmas time.

I was sorry to learn that Dorothy Blum died on April 20, 2001. My two old friends, Sam Cook and Bob Thompson, have also died, the Reverend Sam Cook on November 22, 1999, at the age of 79, and Bob Thompson in a car accident on December 31, 1998, in Winter Haven, Florida, where he and his wife Louise were spending the winter. He was 81. Another fine musical saw player, Bob Mross, died on July 13, 2001, also at age 81. He had worked thirty-nine years at the Mayo Clinic in mechanical maintenance.

As I said, we had eight saws at one time. We called ourselves the MSSR — Musical Saw Society of Rochester. Once I found people that could play the saw, we started corresponding, and soon I had a mailing list going, people exchanging letters. That was in the early 1970s. I would add a name to the list, and we would exchange names and addresses. I corresponded with some very nice people, some of whom I'm sure are gone now.

A few years before Bob's death, I had a letter from Bob and Louise Thompson. During their winters in Florida, they had become acquainted with Nanette Fabray, the longtime actress in movies and television. Nanette Fabray is a fine saw player. I'd seen her in years past playing her musical saw on the Johnny Carson Show. Many of us old-timers remember her antics with Sid Caesar on the "Show of Shows" in the late 1950s, after Imogene Coca left to start her own TV series. In the 1990s, Nanette spent some time in and around Winter Haven, Florida, and she and the Thompsons became friends. Bob asked me if we could present Nanette with an award and honorary membership in the MSSR. Naturally, I said, "Absolutely!"

Bob came up with the following certificate, and presented it to her:

MSSR CUTTING EDGE AWARD
NANETTE FABRAY — GREAT CITIZEN

Whereas, this lady has kept America laughing with her show business antics —
Whereas, this humanitarian shows no signs of stopping —
Whereas, this outstanding individual is one of America's finest musical saw players
I do hereby bestow upon her the honorary membership in the MSSR — she's now in the "Saw of Fame."

Musical Saw Society of Rochester, Minnesota
Harley Flathers, Founder and still President
Saw Player since 1951

February 6, 1994

Through the course of the years, I've acquired eight musical saws, only two of which I've purchased. The rest have all been given to me. One day Earl and Betty Labresh called me and said, "Hey, we've found a musical saw out here in the street. It was in a bag, complete with bow. Can we bring it to you?"

I said, "Yeah." So that's one way I got another saw!

Saws are funny. You make the music by bending the saw and putting the violin bow on the smooth edge of the saw, moving it back and forth to create a vibration. You can get some very beautiful music. Saws and violins go very nicely together. I always hoped that I would get a chance to play the musical saw in some bit part with the Rochester Symphony Orchestra, but it never happened.

I want to say thanks to the many fine pianists and organists who accompanied me during the years when I performed on the musical saw. Of course, my mother was the first, and she accompanied me off and on for several years. In Red Wing, I had Eddie Dougherty, a resident of Ellsworth, Wisconsin, who was a salesman for Hammond organs. He could do anything with that machine, and was in great demand. Pianist Rita Diercks of rural Goodhue also accompanied me in Red Wing.

Coca Cola's Jim Grantman was another pianist who played for me while I was in Red Wing. Jim, his brother and his parents owned the Coca Cola Bottling Company in Red Wing. Jim was always active in his community and in the arts. He got me into the Red Wing Barbershop Chorus. When we did a big show, they would have me sitting onstage in a barber's chair, with lather on my face, "getting a shave" while the others sang. Jim accompanied me when I played the musical saw at community functions occasionally from 1954 to 1957.

When I came to Rochester, I met Jerry Tupper, a fine organist and pianist. He played on Channel 10 TV during the noon hour, along with saxophonist Frank Evangelist and guitar player John Lyman. Their trio was entertaining with Bernie Lusk as daily emcee on Friday, November 22, 1963, when the news came in that President John F. Kennedy had been assassinated. Jerry Tupper died of an unexpected heart attack on August 14, 1965, at the age of 46.

On several Eagles Cancer telethons, I was accompanied by Lloyd Stoddard, the Eagles' secretary and manager for over 35 years. He was a most congenial person, so very polite and talented. I recall him playing the piano to accompany his daughter, Jo Daigneau, who sang so beautifully on the telethon. Lloyd was a good friend. He died on May 3, 1988, at age 82.

Others who have faithfully supplied the piano accompaniment for me over the years include Judy Kereakos, who played the keyboard with the Rochester Boys Choir and the Rochester Male Chorus from 1963 to 1993. Diane Klingsporn Toogood, whom I first met in the summer of 1954 as a little girl with a large accordion in Pine Island, also played for me. Franklin Ruhl, a banker at First National Bank, accompanied me at Salvation Army functions. I credit him with getting me started on the Salvation Army Board, where I served for a dozen years. For several years, Kathryn Kalahan, the Channel 10 TV weather girl, accompanied me. She was a very talented person who sang and played the piano not only with me, but with the entire MSSR in 1976. Carlyle Horstmeier, my daughter Emily, Kathleen Norby and Shirley Wheeler from my church have also served as my accompanists. Ruby Dendler from our church was another;

she died of cancer on July 15, 2001. Several times in recent years, Dean Robinson, who has been the Mayo Clinic's Master of the Carillon in the Plummer Building since 1958, has supplied the piano for me. I have enjoyed collaborating with all of these talented people.

When Governor Al Quie and his wife, Gretchen, came to Rochester in the late 1970s, they'd often come into the KROC studio, sit down and visit. Sometimes it was just the governor, sometimes his wife. Gretchen Quie would come and visit with me on the air at "Celebrity Corner," which aired from 8:45 until 9 in the morning, about some of her projects. They were both very personable people, very available.

In autumn of 1980, they invited people from different areas of the state to come and be their guests for dinner at the governor's mansion at 1006 Summit Avenue in St. Paul. June and I were one of about ten area couples who were invited on October 7, 1980, for a memorable evening of dinner, good conversation and entertainment.

I took along my musical saw. After the meal, we sat around talking together. Nobody was trying to override anybody else's ideas. It was just like talking to your neighbors.

I got out my musical saw, and I said, "Well, now, Governor Quie, I would like to teach you to play the musical saw, so that when you go to Washington, you'll be able to cut through some red tape."

Everybody chuckled. I gave him a lesson, and after one screeching attempt at playing the saw, Governor Quie assured me, "Harley, I think it's best that I stick to governing, and you play the musical saw."

Songs I Saw

For those music fanciers who want to reach the "cutting edge" by learning to play the musical saw, I have prepared a few pointers.

First, select a hand saw (with teeth) from your hardware store. You won't know if you have a winner until you practice bending it and dragging that violin bow across the smooth edge.

Sit with the saw placed flat on top of your lap, teeth toward you. If you're right-handed, take the bow in your right hand, but *NOT* as a violin player holds it. Hold the bow in a vertical position with your thumb between the bow-stick and the horsehair. Your thumb and forefinger should be about five inches from the place where the stick and the hairs join. Move the bow with up and down strokes, dragging the bow hairs across the smooth edge of the saw.

Tuck the handle of the saw under your right thigh just far enough to cause a slight bend near the saw's handle.

With your left hand, grip the end of the saw in your fingers, making a slight curve with your thumb near the end. If the saw has a slight "S" bend, you'll have tension in the steel. You may want to wear a light cloth glove to protect the hand on the end of the saw.

Now, hold the saw as flat as possible, keeping a slight bend near the handle and the small end of the saw. You are now ready to drag the bow over the smooth edge. Low notes come from nearer the handle. Higher notes result as you bend the saw toward the floor. Move the bow toward the small end to obtain the desired notes. Your "ear" will tell you if you're on the right notes. So will the audience, if you aren't.

Start vibrating your left foot up and down. This gives the music its beautiful wailing sound.

Select songs that fit the saw's range — about 12 to 13 notes maximum, or an octave and a half. And you may play a lot of notes that could have come out of the cracks between the 88 keys on a piano.

It helps to have someone accompany you on the piano, organ or accordion. Instruct them to lead you, but do not let them "drown you out." If a five-piece ensemble is leading you, tell the drummer to sit on his sticks until the end, when the applause begins.

Slower songs are best.

Now rehearse, rehearse, rehearse!

Occasionally during your rehearsals and concerts, you may need to apply resin to the bow, just as the great violinists do. That greases the smooth edge of the bow.

Now you're ready to become the neighborhood "cut-up."

Playing the saw is like riding a bicycle; you may fall off the first time or ten, but you'll get it eventually, and become famous (or not).

Here are a few songs that you may want to try:

In the key of C — "When Irish Eyes Are Smiling," "My Wild Irish Rose," and "Whispering" (which was my favorite).

In the key of E-flat — "I Dream of Jeannie With The Light Brown Hair."

Some other goodies you can try, in whatever key works for you, are "Beautiful Dreamer," "The Londonderry Air," "The Old Refrain," "I'll Take You Home Again, Kathleen," "Blue Hawaii," "The Missouri Waltz," "I Love You Truly," "The Old Rugged Cross," "Amazing Grace," "Bless This House" and "God Bless America." Your accompanist must be able to improvise, because sometimes you have to change keys in the middle of the song.

These rules for playing the saw are entirely my own. They weren't copied from any books. I've learned them since I began playing the saw, back in 1951.

The musical saw is a novelty instrument, but we "sawyers" really think it should be considered a string instrument, since we play it with a violin or cello bow.

Good luck, and remember, stardom comes slowly, so don't give up your day job!

Harley with musical saw and 5 musicians on the channel 9 Slim Jim TV show in Minneapolis, Oct. 1955. (Photo courtesy KMSP)

Harley plays musical saw in Chicago's Sherman Hotel Ballroom, representing Minnesota in the Young Peoples' talent division. 2000 in attendance at this opening night banquet program of the American Farm Bureau Federation meeting Dec. 11, 1955. (Photo, American Farm Bureau)

Two Old Sawyers as Musical Saw Players are called. At left, The Rev. Samuel Cooke, rector at Calvary Episcopal Church in Rochester many years and Harley. Autumn 1966.

Six MSSR members. L-R: Harley Flathers, Jim Dalley, Jay Roeder, Mary Roeder, Jay's mother, Bob Mross and Bob Thompson. Pianist is Kathryn Kalahan, also well known for her work on Channel 10 TV weather programs. (Photo, Robert Akins Photography.)

A new member is inducted into the MSSR. She is Nanette Fabray, famous for TV & movies and an accomplished Saw player. L-R: Bob Thompson who presented the "Induction" scroll, unnamed Mistress of Ceremonies, and Miss Fabray. Presented Feb. 6, 1994 at Winter Haven, Florida where Bob & Louise Thompson spent the winter months.

Moment 19

Other Great Rochester Memories
Those Wonderful Old Movie Theaters

I have great memories of the few times that my father, mother, sister and I would go to the theater to see a movie. There were three different theaters we went to: the Capitol Theater in Chatfield, the Lake Theater in Stewartville, and the State Theater in Spring Valley.

I saw "The Wizard of Oz" at the State Theater in Spring Valley. It was during the period between Christmas and New Year's in 1939. Our teacher, Phyllis Anderson, and Jo Mae Engel's mother, Doris Engel, drove two car-loads of us kids to Spring Valley to see "The Wizard of Oz," with Dorothy and the Yellow Brick Road and all the rest. It was a very special occasion for all of us.

Our family went to about three movies a year, usually one during the winter months, another after the threshing was over, as sort of a celebration, and maybe one in late autumn. In the mail, we would receive the monthly calendars of "Pictures Coming." That was always exciting. I wish I'd saved one from the Capitol Theater in Chatfield, because it had the whole month listed. It told what the movie was and who was starring. I'd have that hanging on the wall, and I would forever be wanting to go to this movie or that movie.

Whenever you did go to a movie, the preview of coming attractions was just about more than you could stand. You didn't want them to end. The big feature was always Sunday-Monday-Tuesday. Then there was a lesser picture on Wednesday and Thursday. On Friday and Saturday, there would be a Western or a comedy, maybe starring Abbott and Costello. We went once to a Fibber McGee and Molly picture called "Look Who's Laughing." Or we might see an Edgar Bergen and Charlie McCarthy picture. We also saw "The Egg and I," which introduced Marjorie Main and Percy Kilbride as Ma and Pa Kettle. Some other great films I recall were "Meet Me In St. Louis," with Judy Garland and little Margaret O'Brien, "One Foot In Heaven," starring Frederic March and Martha Scott, and "Scudda Hoo-Scudda Hay," with June Allyson, Lon McAllister and Walter Brennan, all of which we saw at the Stewartville and Chatfield theaters.

About 1940, my folks and I went to a Charlie Chaplin film in Spring Valley called "The Great Dictator," a spoof of Adolf Hitler. It was shown in a building called the Porium. I suppose the name was short for "the emporium," but they just called it the Porium. Soon after that, the building was turned into a Sears & Roebuck farm store, and today it is the Spring Valley Community Center, where they hold all the major events of the community, plus meetings of their service clubs and various other groups. The Spring Valley historical association holds its annual meeting there.

There was something wonderful about those old movie theaters — the thick carpet, the usher with a flashlight, the smell of popcorn (which I always wanted, but never seemed to get).

When I worked in Red Wing in the early 1950s, I did a lot of radio ads for a man named Jim Fraser, operator of the Chief Theater and the Auditorium (today called the Sheldon Auditorium). He told me to come and see a movie any night and every night, if I wished. "Just walk in," he said. "You don't need a ticket."

Well, that was just about as fine an offer as I could have. During 1954-1955 I went to five or six movies every week. I was young, and usually alone. I guess I saw 200 or more movies that year. Later, Jim Fraser would come to Rochester and open Cinema 21 in the Northbrook Shopping Center.

Rochester had four movie theaters when I came to town, the Chateau, the Time, the Empress and the Lawler. And of course, there was the fun of the outdoor theaters. The Starlite Drive-In, a big outdoor theater, was located where the Bear Creek Post Office is today, in southeast Rochester, just off Marion Road and highway 14 east, from 1947 to 1977. Later, owner Bob Toogood opened another outdoor theater on the north side of town, on highway 63 north, called the Starlite North. It was in operation from 1971 to 1988. Those outdoor theaters have gone by the wayside now. Where that second theater once stood, the Stock Lumber Company operates today.

One Memory that Didn't Flood Away

"These are my babies," Johnny Jennison said on KROC-TV in 1954, and for several years after. Old-timers will remember Johnny standing in the TV studio, a quonset hut three miles west of Rochester on highway 14's Hennessey Hill, with a pair of new Goodyear tires that he was offering for sale. It was a straight-forward, honest pitch that ended with this line: "And folks, these babies are on special at Nelson TV and Appliance. Come in and see me tomorrow."

Yes, you could buy tires at Nelson's, along with many other things. In talking recently with John Hanlon, stepson of Nelson's original business partner, D.O. "Don" Redelings, I learned that Nelson TV and Appliance had started out as Nelson Tire Company in Winona. It was owned by Dewey Nelson. Don Redelings was an area traveling wholesale distributor for Goodyear tires, and Dewey was one of his customers. They soon struck up a partnership, and the Rochester store was opened around 1948, in good time to be well-established when television came on the air here in 1953.

According to John, Don Redelings was a real entrepreneur, something of a risk-taker. He was the first (and only) Edsel dealer in Rochester. That short-lived business was located where the Dos Amigos II Restaurant is today, in the old depot on 4th Street Southeast. Redelings had also been a salesman in the dairy bulk tank business, and a partner with Jim Barry of Barry Plumbing and Heating.

Soon after Don and Dewey opened Nelson's TV and Appliance in the 500 block of 1st Avenue Southwest, the store was filled with new TV sets, refrigerators, freezers, washers and dryers, and lawn, garden and fishing equipment by the train carload. My longtime friend Arthur Anderson of Millville was on Don's sales staff, and recalls overhearing conversations between Don and the factory in Chicago where he bought his appliances. "Well, if I take a second carload of refrigerators, can I get them for $X? What about if I take three carloads?" Art says that Don was shrewd and on-the-spot, purchasing carefully and selling immediately.

At that time, TV viewing was starting to "sizzle." Color came in during the late 1950s. John Hanlon remembers working at the store while he was in high school, before he graduated in 1959. He got a small ice cream cart, went over to Rochester Dairy for ice cream, and sold it from business to business downtown, when he wasn't working on tires in the basement of Nelson TV and Appliance.

Later, Don Redelings sold the appliance business to three employees and opened Nelson Tire Town west of Rochester. It was a recapping business, in operation from 1961 to 1970, when it went up in smoke.

Meanwhile, Curly Hrubetz and partners Rod Pagel and Paul Swanson kept on selling appliances downtown until the flood of 1978 put them out of business. I did many live in-store and outdoor tent broadcasts there during the 1960s and 1970s. Eventually the building was razed, and today the SMMPA (Southern Minnesota Municipal Power Agency) building occupies that location.

My Favorite Clip Joints

When you've lived in one place for forty years, you want to say thank you to a few barbers who've put up with you during that time. The barbershop is a place where a lot of world problems are settled.

When I first came to Rochester, in 1957, it wasn't long before I found some great barbers at the corner of 1st Street and 1st Avenue Southwest, on the corner that is now occupied by Wells Fargo Bank, near the Peace Plaza downtown. At that time, a gentleman named Lee Furnstahl was the proprietor. Ted Kettelhut also worked there. There were others, but those are the two I remember best. It was just across the street from where I worked at 100 First Avenue.

One icy day in 1958, as I was on my way to work at KROC, I fell in the middle of the street, right in front of their place. I really banged my knee. A young man named Chuck Haugen, who was in the barber chair inside, came running out to help me. Chuck was a writer for the Post-Bulletin. We met that day, and became friends. Chuck stood up with me as best man at our wedding in 1959. After he and his wife moved away from Rochester, we continued to exchange letters at Christmas. I guess that's how we make our friends. We fall down, they pick us up, and we put them to work.

Chuck Haugen was only six days older than I, and he and his wife were married about the same time as June and I were. We chatted about those days together not long ago, as I was putting together my memories for this book. A few days later, on October 5, 2001, Chuck Haugen died in a fall from a ladder at his home in Summit, New Jersey.

When that building at 1st Street and 1st Avenue Southwest was torn down in mid-1963 to make way for the bank, Lee Furnstahl moved his barbershop to Northbrook Shopping Center, and I went there for haircuts a number of years. Later, I started going to a barber shop in the basement of the old Zumbro Hotel, run by Dean Nelson, who was also a well-known taxidermist. From 1969 to 1975, I went to Joan Jereczak, a beauty operator who always worked with the Miss Rochester contestants, and in the late 1970s, it was Carol Olsen. For a decade or more in the mid-1980s until 1998, I went to Jim Urness. Today, it's Paul Dallman of Dallman Barbers, in the lower level of the Kahler, near Heritage Hall. You see Paul Dallman driving his 1967 red Pontiac Firebird with the Zagalas Car Club in the Rochesterfest and other parades.

These barbers, some of who've been there thirty or forty years, are just super people. When they cut your hair, you get to know them, they get to know you. If I missed some of you barbers, I'm sorry. I've outlived some of you, I know. I just want to say thanks, fellows and gals, for putting up with me a lot of years.

Rochester Area Builders Association

Hats off to our many great friends at the Rochester Area Builders Association (RAB), established in 1953! There are builder members and associate members, and our four Clear Channel stations belong as an associate member. I've been the KWEB radio representative since 1985, attending the monthly dinner meetings, rubbing shoulders with old friends and always making new ones. It is one fine organization, and I'm proud to belong to it.

Each year, our radio stations are involved in the Builders' Home Show, which takes place on a cold February three-day weekend, Friday, Saturday and Sunday, at the Mayo Civic Center. Each year since the Home Show started in 1980, I have done live KWEB radio broadcasts from this show, during the first two or sometimes even all three days. The first year, the event was held at Graham Arena at the fair grounds, but when it outgrew that space, it moved to the Mayo Civic Center. The show draws over 10,000 visitors in its three days, viewing new ideas in building, remodeling, and whatever the builders and exhibitors display. Kudos to Sandy Friend, the association's executive director, and her staff, for continuing to run such an excellent organization.

Chamber of Commerce

I want to mention, too, the Chamber of Commerce. It's been my pleasure to be involved in events with the Chamber for over 40 years. It was E.J. Klampe who recruited me to the Chamber. Everett Klampe was always working to get new members. My job, if I elected to be on his team, was to see how many new members we could get in any given few weeks' time. And we were always successful.

Among the Chamber's many programs is one that I really enjoy, a trade show called the Business Expo. It started in 1984, when it was called Business to Business. Members of the Chamber rent space in a booth for one full day to tell their story. Others can come and view the contents of the booths. The firm might offer the services of a computer, or anything to do with business systems, banking, insurance, tax information, or 100 other products and services in their booth displays. Business is so highly technical today, and some of these booth displays are fascinating.

The Chamber of Commerce does this show every year, and I'm proud to be a part of it. It's always held in October. I've been there each year since it started, doing broadcasts. The first year, it was held in what was then the Hoffman House, now the Best Western Apache. A lot of events still take place in that building. That's where the Rochester Area Builders have met each month in recent years. The Chamber held its Business Expo there one year, and then they were at the Kahler's Heritage Hall for a couple of years. Today the show is held at the Mayo Civic Center.

There are always 100 to 125 booths or more. I put together what we call an advertising package. Then I do live broadcasts on the air from the booths of businesses who spend money with us at KWEB. I do the same thing at the Builders' Home Show in February — I do all this, plus the festival and fair broadcasts, by cell phone from my three-wheel scooter or the golf cart.

Covering these events is always a joyful time for me, because it gives us a chance to keep radio alive. I did the same kind of thing for many years at the county fair. Getting people to spend money with you is always important. That's the sales part of my job. But I am interested not only in selling commercial time to businesses, but also in telling their story, when I can actually interview them about what it is that they do. I've always wanted to take radio to the people. That's been the joy of my side of the business.

Rochester Quarterbacks Club

Sports have always played a big role in Rochester, whether it's high school sports, Golden Gloves, or programs up at the University of Minnesota. During the many years I was involved at KROC, we carried hundreds of broadcasts of University of Minnesota football and basketball games. The football was broadcast for many years with Bernie Lusk doing the play-by-play out of doors from Memorial Stadium in Minneapolis.

Since 1953, there has been a group in Rochester called the Quarterbacks Club. It was started by the late Ben Sternberg, a local promoter. Ben and some other people who loved sports would gather every Monday noon at Michael's Restaurant and talk sports. They still do it to this day. The current president is Ed Rauen. There's a $15 membership per year. You pay for your own meal. You show up when you want to. If you're not there for several weeks, nobody comes after you.

The club is always promoting high school sports. The members are all very interested in the University of Minnesota and anything to do with Minnesota sports, but high school sports is really their special interest. They are always having local coaches come to talk about their teams and tell about what will be happening this season.

Retired banker Ken Rohde, a longtime member of the Quarterbacks Club, originated the idea of a Quarterbacks Club Hall of Fame. Ken died September 24, 2003 at the age of 83. Since 1991, a Hall of Fame committee has met to select inductees for the annual ceremony. Each year, four people are honored who have contributed notably to local sports, or who have made great strides either in playing the game or in coaching. In 1999, they honored five people, because two brothers — Peter and Dick Galuska — shared the award for their accomplishments at Lourdes High School in the 1960s.

This was a highlight of my life, because I had broadcast the event on KWEB from 1995 to 2001. Finally I was just unable physically to be there, but KWEB continues to broadcast it nonetheless. KWEB radio is a total sports station, and so we want to be a part of anything going on in the field of sports.

Here is a complete list of "Hall of Fame" honorees from 1991 through 2003:

1991

Ben Sternberg - Promoter/Sportsman/Manager

Bernie Lusk - Broadcasting

Roger Hagberg - Football

Evar Silvernagle - Swimming Coach

1992

Darrell "Shorty" Cochran - Football/Basketball/Baseball

Dick Kimball - Diving

Walt Bruzek - Baseball/Radio

Marv Hanenberger - Tennis

1993

Oliver "Hon" Nordly - Basketball/Football/Track/Softball Coach & Athletic Director

Bob Schmidt - Football/Basketball

Dr. Ed Henderson - Team Physician/Sports Medicine

John Drews - Football Coach

1994

Steve Jackman - Swimming

Dr. Joe Janes - Hockey/Team Physician

Joe Mayer - Football Coach

Eric Strobel - Hockey

1995

Mark Lutz - Track

Kent Kitzmann - Football & Track

Joe Rockenbach - Coach/Athletic Director

Lynn Esau Zimstowski - Golf

1996

Dave Nelson - Football/Basketball/Track

Maurie Daigneau - Football/Basketball/Baseball

John Philo - Wrestling

Fuad Mansour - Soccer

1997

Kathryn (Kak) Johnson - Swimming/Track & Field/Volleyball Coach

Dr. Dave Daugherty - Basketball/Tennis/Football

Sister Kathy Reichert - Golf

Kerwin Engelhart - Basketball Coach & Athletic Director

1998

Steve DeVries - Wrestling/Football & Wrestling Coach

Don Fox - Football/Baseball/Basketball & Football Coach

Jeff Latz - Swimming

Al Wold - Basketball Coach

1999

Dr. Bruce Brown - Diver

Linda Barsness Bay - Volleyball/Basketball/Track

Ken Johannson - Hockey & Hockey Coach/Administrator

Dr. Richard Galuska - Football/Baseball/Track

Pete Galuska - Football/Baseball/Track

2000

Arley Carlson - Hockey

Gene Sack - Hockey

Chuck Darley - Tennis

Gene Eiden - Lourdes Band

2001

Cy Champa - Football

Carole Shulman - Figure Skating

Mark Brandenburg - Basketball/Tennis

George Schlief - Football/Hockey

2002

Dick Thatcher - Swimming Coach

Ron Werner - Track Coach

Scott Lecy - Hockey

Christy Vitse Amaris - Track

2003

Bryce Kommerstad - Football/Basketball/Baseball

Steve Kereakos - RCTC Football Coach

Donna Gathje Mueller - Lourdes Track/Cross Country

Wally Brunsvold - Mayo Basketball Coach (21 years)

At its 50th anniversary celebration held at the Kahler Heritage Hall on April 14, 2003, the Rochester Quarterbacks Club recalled the sports personalities who served as Hall of Fame speakers from 1991 through 2003. They were:

May 31, 1991 at Holiday Inn South	Joe Garagiola, NBC Sports
May 7, 1992 at Kahler Heritage Hall	Paul Giel, former U of M Men's Athletic Director
April 19, 1993 at Kahler Heritage Hall	John Gordon, Minnesota Twins (filling in for Herb Carneal, Minnesota Twins)
April 22, 1994 at Kahler Heritage Hall	Herb Brooks, Hockey
April 24, 1995 at Kahler Heritage Hall	Lou Nanne, Hockey
April 22, 1996 at Radisson Plaza Hotel	Ray Christensen, WCCO U of M Sportscaster
May 5, 1997 at Kahler Heritage Hall	Dave Mona, WCCO Sports
April 20, 1998 at Radisson Plaza Hotel	Jim Dutcher, former U of M Gopher Basketball Coach
April 26, 1999 at Radisson Plaza Hotel	Bernie Kukar, NFL Referee
April 10, 2000 at Radisson Plaza Hotel	Dr. Mark Dienhart, former U of M Men's Athletics Director
April 23, 2001 at Radisson Plaza Hotel	Dr. Jeff Schemmel, U of M Men's Athletics Senior Associate Director
April 15, 2002 at Kahler Grand Hotel	Jerry Seeman, former NFL Referee
April 14, 2003 at Kahler Heritage Hall	David Stead, Executive Director, Minnesota State High School League

Hats off to Michael's Restaurant and the Pappas family, who have made their restaurant a sports headquarters all these years! Many great names in sports have eaten there, and Michael's has their pictures and signatures hanging on the wall. It's quite a gallery to go through. Established in

1951, Michael's Restaurant is still on South Broadway, with the same owners. They celebrated their fiftieth anniversary in 2001.

Walt Bruzek and the Bear Fax Club

There are dozens of men, in southeastern Minnesota and out of state, who over the years have become members of the "Bear Fax Club." The club, which boasts membership in 38 states and seven foreign countries, held its first annual convention at the Kahler Hotel's Heritage Hall on January 26, 1971, with 200 attending. Yes, I'm proud to say that I'm a Bear Fax Club member, and I was there. So was Walt Bruzek, the founder, his "helper" Ben Sternberg, Bernie Lusk, and everybody's friend, Joe Garagiola, who was the featured speaker.

It was the easiest club in the world to join — but you had to be asked in person by Walt Bruzek, the "old Bear." The annual dues of 25 cents seemed reasonable, and we each paid for our own meal at a banquet on an evening filled with laughter and sports stories.

The Bear Fax Club was founded by Bruzek in 1938, when he was writing a column in the Owatonna newspaper and broadcasting on KROC radio from its studios in Owatonna. In the early days, there were no dues, no meetings...of course, no paid staff...no taxes or IRS investigations. How could you beat that? How could you think of saying "no" when Walt asked you to become a Bear Fax Club member?

On March 26, 1968, a reorganization took place, involving new membership cards and a filing system, and dues began being collected. Walt put Ben Sternberg in the position of "watchdog" over the funds with treasurer Leroy Quam. Occasionally money from the fund went to a "worthwhile project." We sent $50 to buy shoes for Indians in Guatemala, and gave donations to the Halfway House at Willmar, Minnesota, and the historic old Dunnell House in Owatonna.

"Meetings take place when any two Bear Faxers meet," Walt explained. "The one thing you have in common is that you both know me, the screwball who started it all." We even had a motto. Walt put it this way: "It's an organization of people who like people, and our motto is, 'Keep your chin up — not out.'"

In February 1978, 100 vice presidents were added. Twelve members furnished the materials needed to paint, insulate and drywall a meeting room at the Olmsted County Historical Society.

Walt died four years later, on December 31, 1981. Now that he and his wife Edith are gone, the Bear Fax Club is just a memory — but it's a darn good one!

Fleck the Wonder Dog

"Mommy, can we have a dog?" said sons Jeff and Ed.

Jeffrey was nine, Edward eleven. They and June had gone to London in mid-July 1975 to visit her sister Irene and her mother, who was living yet at that time. Apparently, everywhere they went, they'd seen people with dogs. So, after their return, every time the boys saw a dog, they said, "There's a cute dog, Mom. Can we have one?"

We'd had a dog earlier. Our first little dog, Gigi, was killed by a car in the late 1960s. After that, there was a time when there was no dog in our home, and the children were growing up.

On September 27, 1975, I finished my morning shift at 9 am Saturday and went out to building number 40 at the Olmsted County fairgrounds. It was one of those Saturday mornings when people have every kind of silent auction, flea market and baked goods there. There might have been some garden products, too. It's a place that you just like to go to meet a few friends. It was "The Peoples' Market" started by a lady named Zeppy Arch.

My neighbor Julie Siem came to me as she saw me getting out of the car, and she said, "Harley, inside there's a basket of puppies." She knew of our kids' wishes, because, you see, our back lawns joined, and so our neighbors all knew that our kids wanted a dog.

I found out that they were giving the puppies away, so the price was right.

I immediately came home and told the kids. There was a mad scramble for the car. Everyone was in a high element of excitement and anticipation — finally, a puppy!

When we got there, each child immediately picked up a puppy and said, "Daddy, this is the one."

But I insisted we would take "This one!" — the one I wanted. I chose him because of his looks, his shiny coat, and his alertness. When some of the puppies may have appeared sleepy, this one was wide awake!

Immediately this little dog was loved. He was a full four weeks old when we got him home. He was a combination of Norwegian Elkhound and Dandie Dinmont Terrier, a medium-sized dog with an Elkhound curl in his tail. He was black, with brown eyebrows, and just enough gold flecks above his eyebrows and on the top of his head that he would be called Fleck.

During the upper 1970s at KROC, I signed on the radio at 6 o'clock in the morning, following the all-night man, Scott Carpenter. I'd tell Scott when I came in that I could only get to work on time with the help of Fleck, who shared my morning toast at home, fifteen minutes before air time. And that was true — he'd often eat the last piece. Scott nicknamed him "Fleck, the Wonder Dog," and the nickname stuck.

The little dog became very popular during the 1980s by barking when I was on the air for my five-minute "Harley's House" program, broadcast daily on KWEB from my den at home. Some people knew me better by my dog on the air than they would have otherwise. Perfect strangers downtown would see me on the street, and instead of saying, "Hello, Harley," they'd say, "Hey, how's Fleck, the Wonder Dog?"

On Saturday, November 3, 1983, the Rochester Art Center staged a night of impromptu paintings by Rochester notables. After the paint was dry, auctioneer John Kruesel auctioned all the finished works as "Rembrandt Rejects." According to a Post-Bulletin story the following Tuesday, those paintings raised $5000 for the Art Center. I had chosen to paint a picture of little Fleck the Wonder Dog. The portrait was purchased for $105 by Jeannie McFadden for her brother, Ron Bishop, a Hollywood screen writer, who has since died. Jeannie then lived on a ranch in Idaho, but was at the Art Center that night for the auction. The painting is hanging today in a cabin near Cody, Wyoming. I would buy it back in a moment if I could. I tried to reproduce it again the following year, but I could never do a repeat of the original portrait. It was really a good likeness of the little dog in oil, and I'm no painter.

Fleck helped clean up a lot of plates from 1975 until we eventually had to put him to sleep 16½ years later. He was like a member of the family. Most of us cried when he was put to sleep, although we knew it was the humane thing to do when an animal no longer can control life's functions due to age. That was in February 1992. By that time our children were either finished with college or nearly done. Our daughter Jane, who at that time was working toward her degree in veterinary medicine, came home from the University of Minnesota in St. Paul to be with Fleck in his final moments. She held him in her arms as Dr. Charles Guthrie at the Cascade Animal Clinic put him to sleep. The memory of that day still brings tears to my eyes. There was no replacing Fleck.

On The Cutting Edge

Let me tell you about my quarter century doing home sales of Cutco cutlery and Wearever cookware. I wanted to learn more about selling, so in 1960 I answered an ad in the Post-Bulletin from a man named Charles Heinz. He was the local Cutco/Wearever area distributor. (Charles Heinz died in mid-July 2001 at the age of 79.)

Thus began another interesting part of my life, meeting local families for 25 years, from 1960 until 1985, and displaying the world's finest cutlery, cookware, china and flatware, right in their kitchens. Oftentimes they would buy a knife or two, or maybe a whole set of knives.

Here I was, hobbling along on my crutches, trying to carry a display case. Usually somebody would come out and get it for me, and one of the kids might carry it back to the car afterwards. Many people recall my cutting a copper penny in half with the Cutco shears to demonstrate their "cutting edge."

I met so many wonderful friends and neighbors during that period. Even today, people will sometimes tell me, "Harley, I still have those knives you sold me." That part was always more meaningful to me than the income. It was just a part-time venture, but it was a lot of fun. Sales in any way, shape or form can be a highly honorable profession, and I love being in it to this day.

I Love Those Commercials!

I'm now doing radio sales for four stations. I have worked for eleven different owners in my 50 years of radio broadcasting, from the time I started in Red Wing through the present day ownership of the KWEB stations by Clear Channel Broadcasting, based in San Antonio, Texas.

My job is radio commercial sales. I can do this now simply by telephone, and I like that. But I still like to tie it in with broadcasting, even though I'm not broadcasting in the studio any more, nor from my home. The broadcasting I do will be out at Rochesterfest, or at Country Breakfast on the Farm. In the past, it's been the Olmsted County Fair and events such as the Builders' Show. Often in March, I cover the Agri-News Show from Graham Arena. I've had six or seven different projects each year, during the last two decades, that have been both sales and broadcast tied in together.

Currently, I sell commercially for "the FAN" stations KWEB AM 1270 & KNFX AM 970, with its tower and transmitter based at Austin, KRCH FM 101.7 (nicknamed Laser 101), with classic rock music, and KMFX FM 102.5, Fox Country. I sell commercially for any or all of those four stations. Keep in mind that there are fifteen radio stations in Rochester, so we know what competition is.

You build sponsor relationships, and you try to keep those relationships going. Most business people will say, "Well, we can't buy time on 15 stations."

And I'll tell them, "We know that. Let's get started on one, or maybe two of our stations." I'm working with them, building their trust.

So that is my work, and I'm very thankful that I am able to do it by telephone, because with weather the way it is, sometimes stormy conditions, there are days where I will not go out to a studio. I can do things from my cluttered den at home, by typewriter, by telephone, by fax machine. That way, I can continue doing this profession, which I really love. And I can still keep current with the radio broadcast industry.

Usually, if you're somewhat successful in sales, you'll last quite a while. That's been my plan. You can't always keep up with corporate America. I've had to take it at my speed, and the people I work for know that, and they've agreed to that.

I want to thank a couple of people that have made it possible for me to continue in recent years. One of them is sales manager Mary Ann Nonn, who joined our station at the start of 1984. After myself, with my two whole decades on the same station, she is the next in line in terms of longevity, having worked here now for nearly 20 years. Another one who's been there a long time is Dan Hovel, a peach of a guy, who was just a little boy in the crowd, three years old, when I broadcast the Zumbrota centennial parade in 1956. I kid him, saying, "Yeah, I think I remember waving at you, Dan." And now here he is, one of our fine salesmen at the station, and it's a joy to work with him. General manager Bob Fox, a long distance runner, is a super guy and a great sports fan.

There are many others who are more recent. It's been a good sales team. I work closely with the staff we have for our four local radio stations, based at the Best Western Apache here in Rochester, where all studios and sales offices are located on the second floor of the section called Midway Office Plaza.

People ask me, "How long are you going to keep working?"

I tell them, "There's no timetable. As long as I feel able to do, and the people that sign my paycheck say, 'Keep doing,' I'll do it." I've been doing it for 51 years so far, and it's still fun.

Rochesterfest 1993, downtown on 1st Ave. S.W. I'm calling the KWEB studio preparing to do a "live" broadcast with festival office volunteer, Bea Demaray.

Olmsted County Fair team Harley and volunteer cart driver Darlene Charland. We did hundreds of live broadcasts from the fair between the hours of noon & 9pm.

Harley prepares to talk with 4-H Dairy winners following judging at the livestock building, 1995.

First a weeding . . . then the Olmsted County Fair, Carrie Larsen & Mark Ostman & party head to the ADA milk wagon early Aug. 1999. This former dairy princess and entire wedding party drank a milk "toast" to their friends and the dairy industry.

L-R: Dick Carpenter, Mary Ann Nonn and Jolly Joe Burnham at Harley's 70th birthday party.

Co-MCs Alan Reed and Bob Hughes at Harley's 70th birthday party.

Five of the 49ers: the 1949 high school graduates at Chatfield. L-R: Bob Holets, Joanne Follensbee Aug, Beverly Overland Simpson, Joe Mae Engel Hess all drop in to the 70th birthday party. Those others would all have their 70th by the end of October that year of 2001.

At Harley's 70th, Genevieve Hovde sings and leads the crowd in Happy Birthday. She sang on my KAAA radio program in mid 1954-55 in Red Wing.

Les Fields and The Turkey River All Stars Dixieland band at Harley's 70th birthday party.

Moment 20

Other Rochester Area Polio Survivors: They Were Fighters!

Polio was a devastating disease. It struck without warning, and for so many of those who survived, their lives were changed forever. I'd like to take a minute to pay tribute to some of my fellow polio victims, who have learned to live with the aftereffects of polio.

Lyle Buchholtz was a neighbor from just across the field, where he and his parents, Reinhold and Hazel, lived along with his younger brother Leonard and his sister Beth. Another daughter, Donna, was born while they lived there. Lyle was stricken with a severe case of polio in early January 1941, just eight months shy of his twentieth birthday, which was on September 8. It awakened him in the middle of the night, and he fell out of bed. His lower extremities were hit hard. Although the strength came back in his left leg, his right knee would not lock. But to this day, as he said to me recently, he "was and still is stubborn." He went to Gillette Hospital in the Twin Cities for seven months, returning home at the end of October. He tried walking with a brace on his right leg. This was before the "walking brace" had been perfected, the kind that I use. Lyle said, "The brace slowed me down. I couldn't get on and off the tractor." So he took off the brace and walked by reaching down and putting his hand above his right knee to "lock" it into position. Lyle would not stop. In the later 1940s, he was instrumental in raising money for the Sumner Center ball diamond. He used to ride his 1947 Indian motorcycle around the base lines at ball games. Lyle was one of half a dozen young men in the neighborhood in the late 1940s who rode motorcycles. In 1953, he took a lovely bride, Phyllis Holmen, who had been a telephone operator at St. Mary's Hospital. Phyllis Buchholtz died in mid-June 2003. For over twenty years, Lyle was the bookkeeper for Brown Electric in Rochester. Since 1956, he's used a leg brace and two full crutches. That's his way of life. What a fighter!

My dear friend *Harvey Bernard* of Chatfield was born January 2, 1930, just a year and a half before I was. He and I were farm boys who lived about three miles apart. We were in 4-H together, used to play 4-H softball in Roy Finn's pasture on a Sunday afternoon. (We always laughed, saying we had to change the pasture because the bases got so far apart. That's an old cow pasture joke.) On October 16, 1946, Harvey was hit with polio, and he was hit hard. He was a Golden Gloves boxer — Golden Gloves was big back then — as was his brother, Nado Bernard, Jr. They were sturdy lads. All of those sons of Nado and Isabele Bernard were. The Bernards had seven sons and two daughters, and they lived just a couple of miles east of Pleasant Grove. Harvey was hit with polio shortly after boxing one night here at Mayo Civic Auditorium in the Golden Gloves competition. It really knocked him out. It hit more than just one arm and one leg. It put him in the iron lung, and it took him a long time to recuperate. He was in St. Mary's Hospital a long, long time, in and out, back and forth.

During these last 57 years, Harvey has developed a fine art of painting. He is a painter, a designer, a woodworker. He makes some beautiful silk-screened memory boards that you can hang on your wall, pictures of the old threshing scene, the Sunday morning church services, and many other rural scenes. They were in great demand, and he and his wife Doris Childs of Chatfield (with whom I went to school) had a very nice mail order business for a time, sending those boards out by mail. They still sell his art work at tractor shows every year. He calls his business "Country Art." Harvey Bernard, hats off to you! What a guy! What a fighter!

Our neighbor *Charles Hale* was twenty-four and married, with a little daughter Roberta aged 1½ , when polio hit him on August 19, 1949. He had been threshing flax on the Hale farm east of Stewartville. Dr. Alden

Risser sent him to Sister Kenny Hospital in Minneapolis, where he stayed for a short time, but because of the distance and his wife's need for child care, he soon transferred to the St. Mary's Hospital polio ward in Rochester. He was affected in both legs and the right hand. Charles soon moved back home and came to the hospital daily for therapy. With the home surroundings and daily treatment, he was soon begging to get back on that Allis Chalmers tractor, which worked for him because it had a hand clutch. This was in 1951. He was still in a wheel chair, but his uncle, Robert Hale, would help him get up on the tractor, and he would drive it. The desire to get back to your first profession — farming — is tremendous for many of us.

But as in my case, Charles found that he would have to change professions. He was living in Chatfield, and he answered an ad from the *Post-Bulletin* calling for an agent to oversee the delivery of newspapers by boys in the Chatfield area. In 1953, he shot pictures of the Chatfield Centennial and sold them to the *Post-Bulletin.* That landed him a full-time photographer's position with the *Post-Bulletin*, which he held from 1960 through 1986. During those years, he advanced from canes to crutches to a leg brace. Charles took many photos at all hours of the day and night, of highway accidents or anything else that was happening. He is now retired and living in Rochester. Charles Hale — what a fighter!

Claude Bernard, a distant cousin of Harvey Bernard, was at one time a neighbor and hired man on our farm. He was severely hit by polio in early September 1952, during the nation's worst — and last — polio epidemic. At that time, he was a young dairy farmer, living east of Eyota, and he first noticed something was wrong when he couldn't operate the milking machines as he tried to attach them to the cows. He was twenty-seven when he was taken to St. Mary's Hospital polio ward, where he remained for nine months. He recalls that on the day he entered St. Mary's, twenty-six polio patients were admitted — and half of them died. Polio affected his arms and legs, and it was two years before he started walking again. He credited the good therapists at St. Mary's with helping him to regain some strength. The Bernards moved to Elgin, where they purchased the beauty shop that his wife operated for many years until her death in 1991. Claude spent twenty-eight years with GUSA Electric in Elgin working in repair, sales, purchasing and bookkeeping. Recently, he underwent three by-pass surgeries. Claude died March 25, 2002, at the age of 76. Claude Bernard — another real fighter!

Dale Edberg, from Belle Plaine, was in the bed next to me at Sister Kenny in 1949. He was the same age as I, and he had polio in both legs, although one was worse than the other. He was a very energetic fellow. You couldn't keep him down. He loved to dance. After I went home in 1950, he came all the way down from Belle Plaine to visit me. He went back to farming after he got out of the hospital. Years later, he died accidentally while driving a farm tractor.

Mildred Hollenbeck, a first cousin of Lyle Buchholtz, came down with the polio virus within days of Lyle's illness in 1941, when she was twenty-one years old. She was also brought to Rochester for treatment at the St. Mary's Hospital polio ward. On May 5, she went to Warm Springs, Georgia, for the water treatment used by President Franklin D. Roosevelt. After two weeks, she had recovered some slight leg movement, and by May 19 the strength was also beginning to return to her arms. After five months at Warm Springs, she returned to Chatfield. Through a relative, she learned about Mesa College in Colorado, where she enrolled in secretarial and bookkeeping classes that she took while in her wheelchair. Her niece Elaine Hermanson Goetz told me later of the obstacles that Mildred faced because of the difficulty that physically challenged workers had in being accepted in the workplace. But with her tremendous smile and personality, Mildred would not be stopped. She learned to sew, and was hired by a business in Grand Junction, Colorado, to demonstrate and sell sewing machines. She also handled the office work for the business. In 1970, she married Joe Dowdy, a fine gentleman who supplied her with extra support at home and when they traveled. I corresponded with them at Christmas for many years. Mildred died in November 1998. What a fighter!

Larry Lamberty is another trooper who battled back from polio not once, but twice, in November 1950 and again in September 1952, shortly after Plowville USA national plowing competition was held that year near Kasson. He was in St. Mary's Hospital for six months in 1950, when he was thirty-five years old. His whole left side was weakened severely, but he recovered enough to go home and get back to work. Always a farmer, Larry became involved with planning the Kasson Plowville event, working with Marion Roberts, the Soil Conservation Commission's chairman for the project. Larry told me that he personally called the White House to invite President Dwight D. Eisenhower to attend the event. Eisenhower's opponent in that year's presidential election, Illinois Senator Adlai Stevenson, also came. After Plowville ended, Larry worked in a government program for veterans in agriculture until polio again brought him down later that year. He was back in the hospital then for two more months.

Larry spent twenty-five years, from 1953 to 1977, in the banking business, first at Union National Bank and then at Northwestern National Bank (now Wells Fargo), always working in agricultural loans. He retired in 1977. After years in and out of wheelchairs, often using a cane, he is now 87, and walks with a limp. He used to clerk auction sales in all weathers. He served as treasurer of the March of Dimes when I was chairman, and we used to hold meetings at Northwestern National Bank, where he was employed. Larry Lamberty, what a fighter!

Jerry Snow was the twelve-year-old son of Henry and Clara Snow, who owned the farm west of Kasson in Dodge County where Plowville USA 1952 was held. Jerry, a budding future farmer, was asked by his dad to keep the cars out of the farm yard. There had been a constant stream of "lookers" from all over the country coming early in the week to see what was going to happen, and none of them would obey Jerry's orders to keep out. "Who is this kid, telling us we can't come in?" was the response he got.

On Monday night, Jerry's whole body became racked with pain. That night was filled with nightmares. The next morning, Henry and Clara took him to St. Mary's Hospital polio ward, where a spinal tap showed positive for polio. But this story has a happy ending. Jerry suffered absolutely no paralysis or pain following that first day. By Wednesday morning he was up and running around again, which must have relieved his parents. They had enough on their minds in preparing for the thousands of people who poured into the huge plot west of their building site on Friday and Saturday.

I attended Plowville USA, and heard candidate Dwight "Ike" Eisenhower give a powerful outdoor speech at 3 pm. It was carried on KROC. I recall seeing the KROC morning announcer and farm director Jerry Boyum on stage prior to the president's speech, to introduce the radio broadcast. This interested me, because I was set to begin radio school myself six weeks later in Minneapolis.

During the day, "Ike" and later his opponent Senator Adlai Stevenson visited little Jerry Snow at St. Mary's. The newspaper later carried a picture of President Eisenhower shaking hands with Jerry. That photograph of Eisenhower and Jerry Snow was later used as a poster for the national March of Dimes Foundation.

The doctors released Jerry the day after Plowville ended. He didn't get to attend it personally, but gained notoriety because two presidential candidates visited him in the hospital.

Today at age 62, Jerry Snow still has his love for agriculture as owner of that farm and its many adjoining acres. Slowing down in active farming now, he also works part time as a rural mail carrier west of Kasson, Minnesota. His father Henry died in 1994 and Clara in 1998, leaving Jerry with many wonderful memories. He was surrounded by greatness for those few days in 1952. He has not suffered any serious aftereffects of polio to this day, for which he is amazed and thankful. He is a survivor — and a fortunate fighter.

Lorraine Litin, the wife of Mayo Clinic's noted psychiatrist Dr. E.H. Litin, was stricken with polio in the summer of 1952 and was hospitalized for an extended period, first in an iron lung and then gradually changing over to a portable chest respirator called a "cuirass." She literally spent the rest of her life on a respirator. The Mayo Clinic's physiology and rehabilitation doctors and technicians developed a "turtle-shell" respirator for her that made it possible for her to live outside the iron lung. My neighbor, Dr. Fred Helmholz, now aged 92, assisted with that project. Lorraine needed muscle transplants in her hands and wrists just to be able to write. She always maintained a very positive attitude through good times and bad. At about the same time that she became ill, her little daughter Nancy Joe, aged five, also came down with polio. Nancy Joe, who still wears a leg brace and uses two canes, is employed today by the city of St. Paul. Lorraine's son, Dr. Scott Litin, now on the Mayo Clinic staff, was a year old when his mother became ill. He told me, "My mother got her positive attitude through the love of the Sisters of St. Francis who cared for her at St. Mary's Hospital, especially sisters Mary Brigh, Generose and Lauren." Lorraine Litin wore her "turtle-shell" respirator for three decades, battling polio until she died in 1983. Nancy Joe and Lorraine Litin — what fighters!

In mid-July 1946, *Marvin Foss*, a 22-year-old farmer from Chatfield, was also stricken with polio. Marv went to the dentist that morning, and when he came home in the afternoon, he became very weak. Returning to Chatfield, he saw Dr. Harold Skaug, a Chatfield physician, who personally took him to St. Mary's Hospital that evening. Paralysis took out his legs entirely, with total weakness from the waist down, a situation similar to that of President Roosevelt and myself. Marv spent nine months at St. Mary's, and after going home returned regularly for therapy for another four months. He managed to enroll at Winona Secretarial School for a one-and-a-half-year accounting course. Following that, he wore his two full-length leg braces up and down the thirty-two steps of the Rochester Dairy business office in the Riverside Building for three years. Then from 1952 until fire destroyed the business in 1955, he was bookkeeper for Hervey Implement, the International Harvester distributor in Chatfield. In September 1957, Marv began a thirty-year career as comptroller at KROC radio and TV. He signed a lot of pay checks for me. He retired in 1987, and lives with his wife Colleen in Chatfield. He walks, but also uses "wheels" a lot of the time. Marv Foss — what a fighter!

Mary Ellen Jefferis graduated with me in early June 1949 and was married to Lewis Barth four months later. On October 16, this new farm wife could not step over the threshold from room to room in her new home. Polio hit Mary Ellen on the left side, from the hip and knee down. She told me that it began with a terrible backache, followed by a severe headache. She went to see Dr. Theodore Clifton in Chatfield, and he advised her to see Dr. Healey, a Chatfield dentist, and have a tooth removed. After suffering a very stiff neck on the weekend, she consulted Dr. J.P. Nehring, who advised her to "get to St. Mary's." She spent ten months, from October 1949 to July 1950, at St. Mary's, and continued several more months of treatment after returning home. While she was in the hospital, Dr. Joe Janes performed surgery on her ankle, called a lambernutti, which involved the removal of most of the cartilage in the ankle. Since her left leg was so weak, especially from the knee down, they had provided her with a single spike ankle brace, but the corrective surgery did away with the need for it. Mary Ellen also had a muscle transplant in her hip. She always remained very active, being involved in the V.F.W. Auxiliary and the American Legion Auxiliary and crocheting many afghans for her friends and family. Nothing stopped her, indoors or outdoors, using her cane and crutches. Now she has graduated mostly to wheels. Mary Ellen had six children, ten grandchildren and one great-grandchild. What a trooper you are, my classmate! Mary Ellen Jefferis Barth — what a fighter!

When I entered Sister Kenny Institute in July 1949, someone gave me a copy of a book that had recently been written by a polio "graduate" of EKI (as the Elizabeth Kenny Institute was often called). "My Soul More Bent" by *Rev. Allen Lee*, who came from the Rock Dell-Hayfield area, was an inspirational volume. Allen Lee, who was about 40 years old in 1949, had graduated from Stewartville High School in 1926 and received the Lord's call to evangelism. In preparation for his ministry, he spent four years at Luther College in Decorah and almost the same length of time at Luther Seminary in St. Paul. During his senior year in 1939 he was struck with polio. First he was in an iron lung, then he had long treatments to restore strength to his arms and legs. His widow Helen, who still resides in the home they shared for many years, said, "Allen was in Sister Kenny for a year or more, and had not yet become an ordained minister. I was a student nurse at Asbury Hospital in Minneapolis, which was affiliated with the Sister Kenny hospital." Sometimes as part of her studies, she was sent to the Sister Kenny Institute to read patient charts, which was how she met her future husband. The two "hit it off," and when he was ready for release, he called her and asked, "What should I do?" She replied, "Let's get married."

Allen Lee was soon ordained as a minister in the Evangelical Lutheran Church of America. For the next thirty-five years he preached the gospel, traveling by car and doing his own driving for thirty-five weeks every year. Helen said, "I'd help him into his specially-equipped car on a Monday morning as he would start out alone on a three-hundred-mile trip to northern Minnesota, with tears in my eyes at the thought of his being alone on the road with no walking capacity whatsoever. He always told me, 'Don't worry, honey, I've got the same Lord on the highway as I do here at home.' Allen's life was filled with blessings through his evangelistic teaching all those years."

The Reverend Allen Lee's book was an inspiration to me in my first months at the Sister Kenny Institute, showing me through his example that life with crippling polio was not an end but a beginning. Rev. Lee lived a full life for nearly seventy-one years, fulfilling his "faith journey" and doing the Lord's calling until his death in 1980. He had two children, a daughter Rebecca who is pastor of a church in Fargo, North Dakota, and a son James, who works in St. Paul. I never met the Rev. Allen Lee, but I feel I know him very well. Allen Lee. What a fighter!

Dale Schulz, better known by his radio moniker of Dale Hamilton, was born May 2, 1932, only nine months after I was. He grew up on a farm about a mile south of what was then called the Midway Church, three miles east of Spring Valley on highway 16. Dale was starting his senior year at Spring Valley High in the autumn of 1949 when polio suddenly put him in an iron lung. He was in and out of St. Mary's Hospital in Rochester for a year. Fortunately, he got out of the iron lung in a little over a week, but his right side was paralyzed, and while he gradually regained some strength in his limbs, he never completely recovered.

I recall Dale coming to visit me in 1954 at the KAAA studios in Red Wing with his friend Dave Sanford, a Spring Valley boy who had entered the funeral business and was at that time employed at Ferrin's Furniture and Funeral in Red Wing. I suggested to Dale that he go to the same school I had attended, Brown Institute in Minneapolis. Following his schooling, he went into radio engineering and announcing in Benson, Minnesota, from 1956 to 1958. He spent about three years at the new KWEB station in Rochester, then went to Austin television, where he did TV weather for a time. We managed to snare Dale between jobs in 1963 to start the all-night stint on KROC, and he worked there until the mid-1980s, giving him a total of nearly forty years in the broadcast industry. Life was not easy for Dale Hamilton. Polio had set him back a year in high school, but he fought, and struggled...and won. I'm glad I know him. What a fighter!

Virgil Kohrs was also a radio announcer; he called himself Randy Cook. I had the good fortune to work with him during my years at Red Wing, when we were both at KCUE. Born on June 22, 1937, at Lake City, Virgil suffered a hard bout with polio at the age of fourteen, during his first year in high school. Both his legs and one arm were severely weakened, but he didn't have to use an iron lung. He underwent numerous muscle and nerve transplants here in Rochester, and he spent some time at the Rehab Center at the old Samaritan Hospital.

It didn't stop him. After graduating from high school in Lake City in 1955, he entered Brown Institute, where he became Randy Cook. He worked for a short time at a La Crosse radio station, and then came to Red Wing, where I worked with him, Bernie Aaker, Alan Kennedy and Rip Stanchfield. Both Kennedy and Kohrs later came to KWEB when it opened up in the Northwestern National Bank building in Rochester on September 30, 1957. I had been working at KROC for a full two weeks then, and we were watching this new "rocker" station, KWEB. And they were good, right from the first day. Randy remained at KWEB radio a couple of years, and then went to the big new "rocker" on the east side of St. Paul, KDWB AM 630. He spent several years as instructor and personnel director at Brown Institute.

Finally, he and his wife, the former Vonnie Wohlers of Lake City, left Minnesota. He said he just got fed up with the ice and snow. Following a heart valve replacement in 1999, Randy Cook retired to Esper, Florida, on the southern edge of Fort Myers. He continued to do some radio work, read to the blind, and was the electronics man for their church's sound system. On November 23, 2002, he died of a stroke. Randy Cook — what a fighter!

Randy Cook's sister, Darlene Kohrs Schmidt, has vivid memories of that polio epidemic of the mid to late 1950s. After watching her brother struggle to regain a certain level of strength that made it possible for him to develop a career in radio, she became a nurse's aid at St. Mary's polio ward and rehabilitation center. Between 1957 and 1958, she cared for several polio patients, including Lorraine Litin and Dave Madden. She still remembers what tremendous individuals they were, always positive, keeping a smile throughout their ordeal. It was a great experience. Darlene Kohrs married Fred Schmidt on September 26, 1959. She and her husband are longtime land developers and home builders in the southeast area of Rochester. She remains very active in the Olmsted County Republican Party. But she still remembers those polio years!

Dave Madden was a farm boy from Eyota who spent more than a decade at St. Mary's before he died. He could only move the fingers of his left hand and turn his head as he lay in the iron lung. He was totally helpless. When Dwight D. Eisenhower visited young Jerry Snow at St. Mary's during Plowville 1952, Dave was in the same ward, and he was in the photograph that appeared in the newspaper the following day, in his iron lung. Eventually, the "turtle shell" respirator was invented to allow patients who were in an iron lung to be out of it for a time and sit up. As Dave's personal aide, Darlene Kohrs helped Dave to start a business that rented TV sets to patients while they were confined in the hospital. It turned into a big business, for that period of the early to mid 1950s when this new thing called television was really getting started.

These men and women were all just tremendous fighters, who refused to let their disabilities get in the way of living their lives. We have to salute them all.

And Finally....

It's difficult to end a book with so many stories still to tell — but as Anne, my faithful assistant, says, I have to leave some for the next book.

There are a couple of things I want to accomplish soon. First, I want to help the Olmsted County History Center construct a musical saw display for their museum, located in southwest Rochester. It won't be earthshaking, but it should be educational, with photos, actual saws, and a cassette or two of songs that I've recorded during the years. Hopefully, visitors will be able to press a button and the music will start. I promise to keep the songs "cut" short.

Second, I want you readers to be inspired by this collection of my life's happenings to start writing your own stories. One of my first interviews in broadcasting in 1954, nearly a half-century ago, was with "Little Joe," a talking rooster. The bird came to our studio with his owner, Colonel Larson, and Larson's little daughter Judy. The colonel told me what words to use, what questions to ask, and then Little Joe would answer. Some of those answers were better than the ones I got from shy people whom I've interviewed during the years! I didn't encourage Little Joe to write a book, but I am asking you to think about writing your own story.

Many interesting people — thousands of them — have sat across the microphone from me, in the studio and out on remote locations. I've asked several of them if they have started to write their life's story. Very few of them had. Usually, they would say, "Oh, I could never write!" I replied, "Do what my Dale Carnegie instructor, Bob Olson of Winona, used to tell us in class back in 1968: 'Talk for one minute on the subject you know best — yourself.'" Bob Olson was the owner of the Chevrolet dealership in Winona for many years, and he loved what he was doing, instructing, selling, telling stories. He kept us rolling with laughter.

I'm sure that some of my stories parallel your own memories and associations. You will likely remember other stories that I've overlooked. That's fine: use them. But get started today — not tomorrow. Remember, if you start a walking tour of thc planct carth, the first step will be the easiest. Then just keep walking. Happy writing!

Harley Flathers

A Lighter Moment

An Irish Prayer

During my many years as emcee of numerous programs, I occasionally closed with something called "An Irish Prayer." This is another Irish Prayer, not as serious as the more famous one, that was offered to me one day by my physician, Dr. Thomas McLeod, a young man whose Irish roots go a mile deep. (I learned long ago not to argue with your doctor — he may have "inside information!")

It goes like this:

"May those that love us, love us.
And those that don't love us,
May God turn their hearts.
And if he doesn't turn their hearts,
May he turn their ankles,
So we'll know them by their limping."

One Last Word

As I leave you, I recall a little Bible verse that always served as the dismissal of our Sunday School hour at Sumner Center Evangelical Church in the days before it merged with the United Brethren in 1946. After the children's classes ended, three or four groups of various ages would return to the church sanctuary, where the adults held their Bible study, and the Sunday School Superintendent, Harold King, or Earl Ellenberg, or somebody else would lead us in reciting Joshua 1:9: "Be strong and of good courage: be not afraid, neither be thou dismayed: for the Lord thy God is with thee, whithersoever thou goest."

"Y" Member Drive Opens . . . L-R: Dr. Jule Block, YMCA new member drive chairman and Harley Flathers, Program MC. Theme: "Be a Winner—Join the YMCA". The idea was to Zoom Off at a Fast Start. Post Bulletin photo Nov. 5, 1970.

St. Mary's Hospital annual picnic bar-b-q. Harley MC's a 4-hour talent show of employees. This picnic area is now all buildings, parking & roadway. Where event was held is now occupied by Sister Mary Brigh & Sister Generose Buildings. Aug. 19, 1964. (Post Bulletin photo)

A Tall Broadcast - Fire Prevention Week, Oct. 8, 1981.
L-R in the fire engine bucket . . . Deb Nerby, Miss Rochester, Harley broadcasting on KROC, and fireman Bill Haas. Looking westerly on 2nd Street downtown Rochester. Mayo Clinic 1928 Plummer building is behind us. (Post Bulletin photo)

And Finally . . . Down to Earth. I'm narrating the July 4th, 1976 Silver Lake Band Concert, Clayt Tiede directs the Rochester Park band. I assisted in the July 4th concerts from 1962-83. (Post Bulletin photo)

Homer & Vivian Flathers were ready to attend Centennial Parades and Celebrations in 1954. That's dog "Chum". I took this photo on the farm lawn near Dad's favorite old lilac bush

It was a fund raiser for a fun evening. Guests went as "book characters". Harley as Sherlock Holmes and June, Lady Holmes. Photo, our home 1985.

One wedding I didn't attend. My cousin Ivah Turner and Arthur Leemis, Oct. 1949 in Rochester's Methodist Church. That church was soon razed and today, Rochester Methodist Hospital has replaced it. The lady assisting the newlyweds is my Mom, Vivian Flathers, who provided nuptial music at many weddings over 40 years.

Wedding, Harvey & Doris (Childs) Bernard at St. Matthews Episcopal Church, Chatfield, Nov. 12, 1955.

Remember when by Clint Kueker . . . "Remember when the opening of the Stewartville School was temporarily postponed due to the polio outbreak, Autumn 1946.

Remember when by Clint Kueker . . . Another historical moment in "health history". "Remember when the Simpson School District 14 was closed for several weeks on Oct. 24, 1924, due to an epidemic of scarlet fever among the students. Today the building is only a memory.

Ray Aune, Olmsted County Fair Secretary comes back for a visit with old friends in 1996. Ray died Sept. 20, 1998 at age 98.

Index